Persistence of Vision

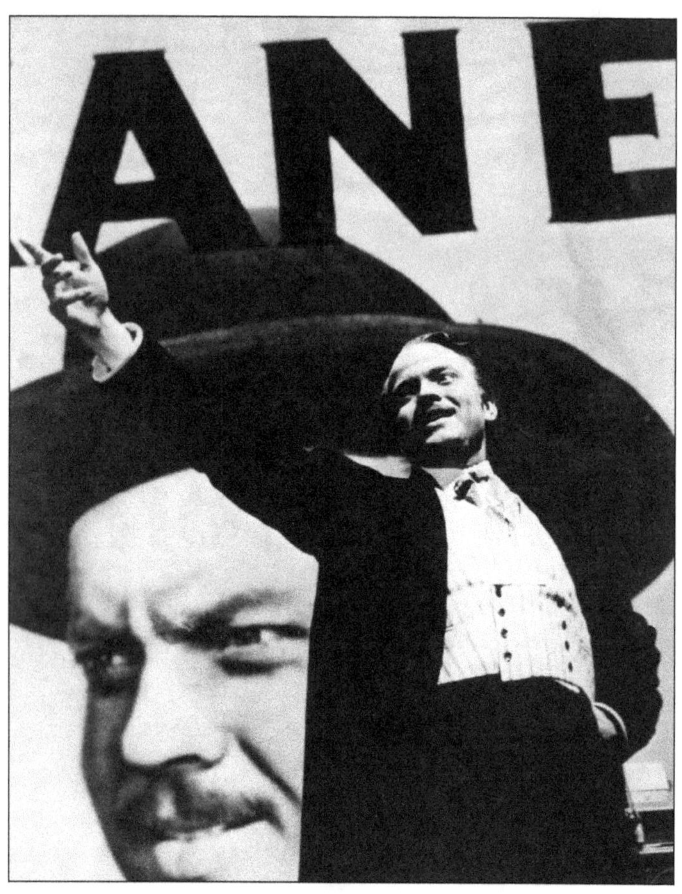

Persistence of Vision

A Collection of Film Criticism

Edited by Joseph McBride

A Wisconsin Film Society Press Book

Sticking Place Books
New York

Front cover: "The last champions of John Ford have now gathered around *7 Women* as a beacon of personal cinema"—Andrew Sarris, 1968: Anne Bancroft as Dr. Cartwright in Ford's last feature, *7 Women*, set in 1935 at an American mission in China (1966). (MGM)

Frontispiece: "The film that "consecrated a great many of us to the vocation of *cinéaste*"—François Truffaut: Orson Welles giving a political speech as Charles Foster Kane in his Hollywood filmmaking debut, *Citizen Kane* (1941). (RKO)

ISBN 979-8-89976-052-5

Also published by
The Wisconsin Film Society Press, Madison:

Studies of the Documentary (1958)
Edited by J. Quinn Brisben

Film Notes (1960)
Edited by Arthur Lennig

Classics of the Film (1965)
Edited by Arthur Lennig

Dedicated to John Ford

Contents

RECENT FILMS

CAREERS

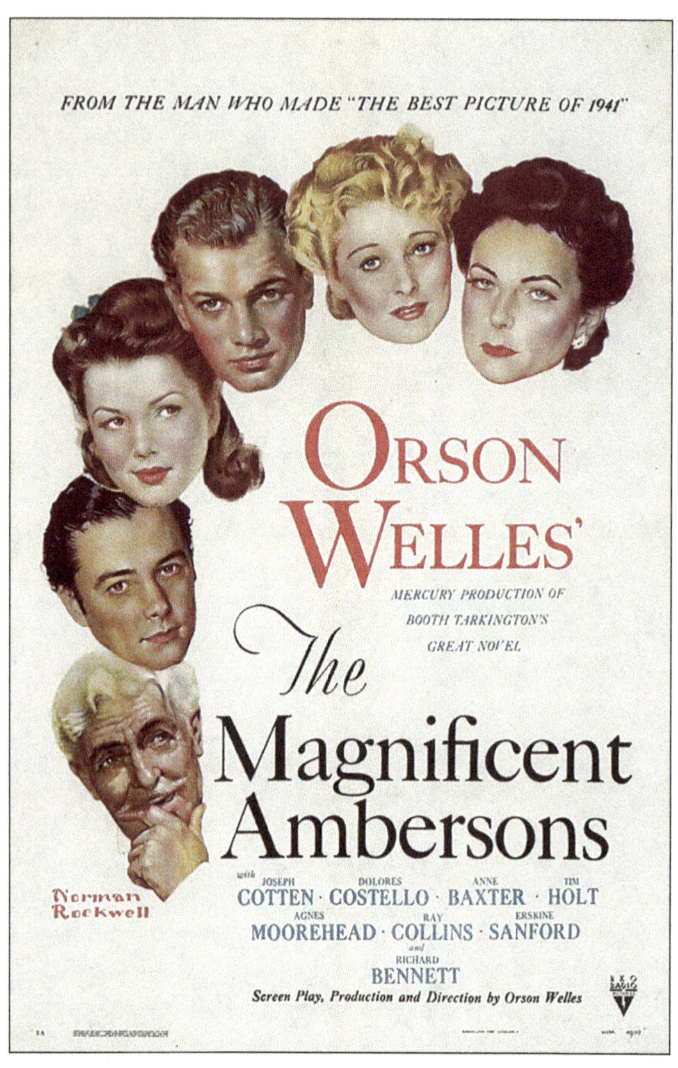

Norman Rockwell's poster for Orson Welles's second Hollywood feature, *The Magnificent Ambersons* (1942), a mutilated masterpiece based on Booth Tarkington's Pulitzer Prize–winning novel. (RKO)

Introduction to the 2026 Revised Edition
Joseph McBride

During the nascent period of film studies in the late 1960s, one of the best places to study film in the U.S. was Madison, Wisconsin. Not because the University of Wisconsin had a formal film program—that would come later, when academia fell under the spell of the theoretical, semiological, and Marxist package that came to dominate film studies—but Madison's film culture mostly flourished because we were part of the film society movement. Our campus was among the informal chain of scattered university environments where film societies set a new standard for film scholarship. A heady blend of movie fanaticism and intrepid archival digging helped revolutionize film tastes by making popular Hollywood films as acceptable as the more overtly artistic foreign cinema.

We had an amazing array of thirty-five film societies in Madison, so students could chose among several films each night, advertised with posters tacked on trees and pasted on walls. We had an extensive film and document archive at the State Historical Society of Wisconsin (now the Wisconsin Historical Society)—including the pre-1948 Warner Bros. and RKO films in 16mm—a treasure house that stimulated the founding of a respected film journal, *The Velvet Light Trap*. And our Memorial Union showed 35mm films each weekend, chosen after ferocious arguments between two warring but still friendly factions, the "Politicos" (Godardian radicals) and the "Aesthetes" (devotees of auteurism, John Ford, and John Wayne). All this disparate artistic wealth made Madison a paradise for cinephiles. The influence of what we called our

"Madison film mafia" of about twenty-five ambitious cine-philes who went on to professional careers spread far beyond our politically charged campus to make a substantial impact on the worlds of film scholarship and filmmaking.

The Wisconsin Film Society, of which I was president, was the official campus film society for many years until we antagonized the university hierarchy and the city authorities. In October 1968, we let the brilliant, iconoclastic stage director Stuart Gordon (later a prominent horror film director) put on his "Nude *Peter Pan*" play instead of a scheduled program of Buster Keaton films. After the UW and the local district attorney tried to shut down Stuart's cheekily political twist on James M. Barrie's classic—an allegory of the violent upheavals at the 1968 Chicago Democratic Convention—our members voted to turn the B-10 Commerce auditorium over to his hastily restaged production. The day after that elec-trifying and provocative protest event, we were stripped of our official status, and the DA launched an abortive attempt to put Stuart behind bars. Harassed by the university, Stuart left town to start an influential new venture in Chicago, the Organic Theater Company. But our eclectic film programs continued without a hitch into the Seventies, after I left town, even if we had an increasingly expanding plethora of compe-tition.

One of our most passionate activities, stemming from our longstanding practice of writing and distributing original film notes at screenings, was to publish book collections of criticism by our members. The books included this volume I edited, which appeared in October 1968, the same month as the Nude *Peter Pan*. This fourth book we put together was self-published at a local print shop with our screening profits. It was the first book I published, though I had already written a book on baseball slang that didn't find print until 1980, and I was busy writing my critical study *Orson Welles*, which would be published in 1972 in the British Film Institute's Cinema One series. My example in getting articles and inter-views published in such magazines as *Film Heritage, Film Quarterly,* and *Sight and Sound* from 1967 onward prompted others on our campus to follow me during a time when the new field of film studies was open to fresh young talent.

Unfortunately, I hadn't realized how impossible it was back then to get bookstores to carry a self-published book, although I tried. The stigma of the so-called "vanity press" shadowed such maverick enterprises; it would be many years later that the computer revolution and the Internet enabled self-publishing to thrive and become respectable. *Sight and Sound* declined to review *Persistence of Vision* because its typeface was too small; the amateurishness of the original printing process and layout didn't help. But *Persistence of Vision* did receive a laudatory review in what was then the leading American film journal, *Film Quarterly,* by its adventurous editor Ernest Callenbach. He praised the collection's "excellent and often iconoclastic articles and reviews, of both early and recent films… and sometimes mordant re-examination of classics." That review led to about fifty orders from university libraries. But I'm embarrassed to say that I had given up on the book by then out of frustration and didn't bother fulfilling most of the orders, which would have kept *Persistence of Vision* alive at least on more library shelves. Instead I let the remaining boxes of printed books languish in the basement of the campus Bureau of Audio-Visual Instruction, where Andrew Holmes had kindly let me watch any of the films rented for classes in every department. After I left for California, those books disappeared along with the building, and *Persistence of Vision* became a lost book, a rare volume that only occasionally pops up in used-book stores and on eBay. So this new edition, which I am grateful to Paul Cronin for publishing through his Sticking Place Books, will be fresh to most people who read film books.

What is the enduring value of *Persistence of Vision?* Re-reading it after many years pleasantly surprised me with the lively, erudite, and enjoyable nature of the eclectic collection of essays by our members and a few outsiders I roped in to gratefully acknowledge their influence on our thinking about the field of film studies we were helping to pioneer (including our intellectual guru Andrew Sarris). But some immaturity is on view here too, both in individual cases and because of the groundbreaking nature of our work. Some of these essays contain old-fashioned sexism and other cranky bygone attitudes (I've left those as they were to represent the period honestly), and a few pieces suffer from glibness and what one reviewer called "bitchy college journalism." But the diligent scholarship, boldly exploratory energy, and passionate prose of the book's essays needs no apology. It's regrettable, though, that the contributors are all male. I remember wishing at the time that we had more women in our "Madison film mafia," but there were a few, and I could have encouraged them to contribute, so it's my fault for not making this book more inclusive.

Persistence of Vision, among its other virtues, demonstrates the varying approaches of the developing state of the art of film criticism and historiography in its nascent stage. As you read these pieces, you can watch us feeling our way, mostly with success, in seeking the best methods of writing about films we either love or disdain while illuminating their artistry and social contexts. You can detect the literary influences and backgrounds of some of the critics who came from the English Department before film was a recognized discipline, which accounts for their elegant prose and a judicious, historically situated form of generalized commentary. But also evident in this collection is a vigorous and experimental engagement with the special qualities of the film medium, its visual and aural dimensions, with close textual readings. I remember being strongly influenced by Susan Sontag's comments on film criticism in her 1964 essay "Against Interpretation," including her assertion that

> cinema is the most alive, the most exciting, the most important of all art forms right now. Perhaps the way one tells how alive a particular art form is, is by the latitude it gives for making mistakes in it, dissolves considerations of content into those of form…. Equally valuable would be acts of criticism which would supply a really accurate, sharp, loving description of the appearance of a work of art. This seems even harder to do than formal analysis…. These are essays which reveal the sensuous surface of art without mucking about in it…. What is important now is to recover our senses. We must learn to *see* more, to *hear* more, to *feel* more.

The rebellious methodologies we helped develop in this collection as we broke free of previously dominant ideologies may not be fully formed here but are prescient in signaling where the field of film studies, at its best, would develop. Since Madison at the time had only three film courses (all in the English Department), we followed our own ruggedly individual paths of scholarship. Our writing did not slavishly follow the academic lines that would ossify the English language and erect snobbishly chosen cinematic canons to gratify pedantically conformist prejudices. Instead we thrived in the free-flowing essay format, an approach and style that is more intelligible, engaging, and illuminating to read, influenced by Sarris, Robin Wood, François Truffaut, and a few other pioneering critics while taking defiantly, idiosyncratically personal stands. That is the approach many critics, including me and other writers whose work is included here, would choose to follow in a parallel track (mostly outside academic rigidity) over the subsequent decades.

Some of the best essays in this collection, such as Richard Thompson's refreshing, eloquent, and witty pieces on John Ford's *7 Women* and Howard Hawks's *Red Line 7000*, cogently defend late works by major directors that were grossly misunderstood and underrated by hidebound American reviewers. Those and other essays in this volume show the intrepid excitement of discovery, unpolluted by the prevalent condescension toward our national cinema, that distinguished many younger critics who would go on to do their own influential volumes of criticism, history, and biography.

There's a certain sadness involved in looking back over this early work and realizing that although our generation championed film as "The Art Form of the Twentieth Century," it is now the Twenty-First Century. The kind of intense, dedicated cinephilia we shared in Madison and devoted our lives to pursuing is in danger of becoming a lost art. But our "film generation" rising up throughout the country in the late Sixties carried the day by revolutionizing film appreciation and setting the stage for serious study of both American and foreign cinema; foreign films were another eye-opening passion of that period that is amply recognized here. The collection surveys the full panoply of film history from the silent days up through the transformative period of the late 1960s.

Classic silent films, as well as vintage horror films, are covered by an expert in those fields, Arthur Lennig, at the time an assistant professor of art at the State University of New York at Albany. Lennig, who also contributed an iconoclastic essay on Robert Flaherty, was a former president of our film society and the editor of two of our three earlier volumes, *Film Notes* (1960) and *Classics of the Film* (1965). Lennig gave me valuable advice on this collection. My mentor at the UW, William Donnelly, while earning his PhD in English, taught me much about life and film and chose me to run the Wisconsin Film Society. Bill urged me to put together this collection, helped with the planning and editing, and contributed some characteristically provocative pieces; his wife Mary Kelley Donnelly, who collaborated on one of the amateur movies I directed in Madison, suggested the book's title. ("Persistence of vision" is the name given by Peter Mark Roget in 1824 to the optical phenomenon on which the existence of moving pictures rests; first advanced in ancient times, that theory has since been challenged by some scholars.) Bill went on to a distinguished 41-year career as an English professor at Grove City College in Pennsylvania, and after his death in 2015, his book *Fragments: A Collection of Short Stories,* was published as a memorial in 2017. Another of our former presidents, R. C. Dale, contributed a richly layered essay on *King Kong*, a film that had caused me some controversy when I shortsightedly called it "camp junk" in a film note for our members.

Among others of our "Madison film mafia" who went on to major careers was Michael Wilmington, who became a film reviewer for the Chicago *Tribune* and the Los Angeles *Times.* He is represented here in characteristically stylish and pugnacious essays on the Sidney Lumet film version of *Long Day's Journey Into Night,* Norman Jewison's *In the Heat of the Night,* and Alfred Hitchcock's *The Birds,* which first appeared in our campus newspaper, *The Daily Cardinal,* and a related publication, *The War Baby Review.* Mike and I would begin writing our critical study *John Ford* in 1969 (published in 1974 in the BFI's Cinema Two series), and he was a sounding

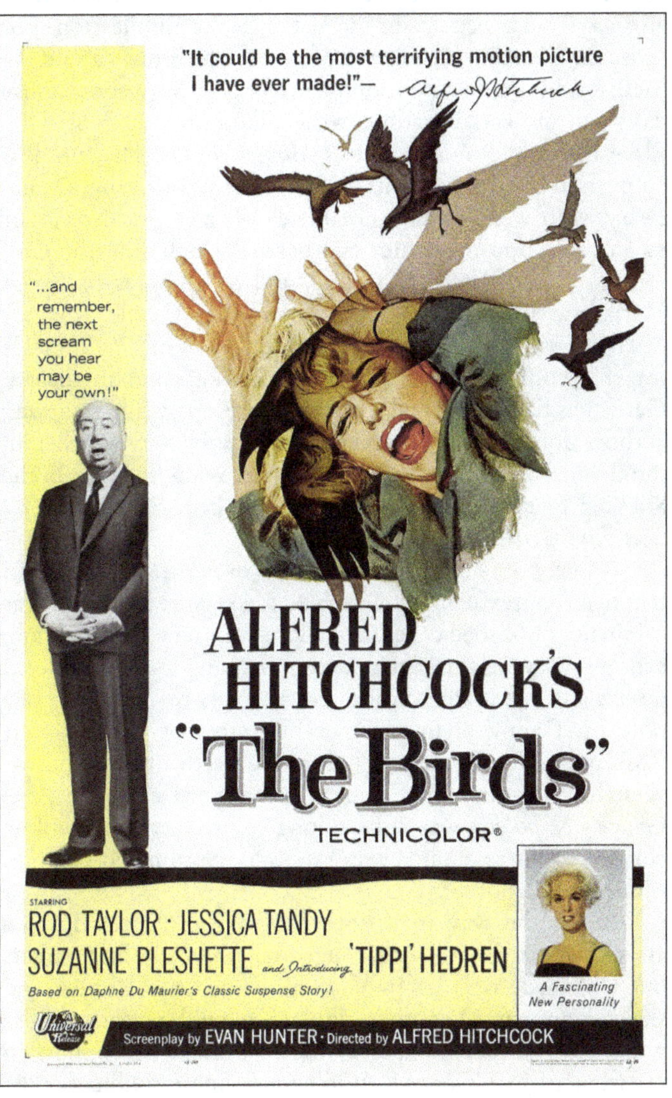

A key part of Alfred Hitchcock's success was his ability to market himself and his films, such as with his apocalyptic 1963 thriller, *The Birds*, a tour de force made without the benefit of CGI. (Universal)

board and source of ideas for *Persistence of Vision*. Mike also gave me assistance in the last stages of publication. For those interested in further and often colorful stories about the Madison film mafia, I've commented extensively about those days and my collaborations with Mike in my 2025 Sticking Place interview book, *I Loved Movies, But...* That book is comprised of conversations with another of our gang, Danny Peary, who went on to a notable career as a prolific author of valuable books on film and baseball, including the *Cult Movies* series, *Alternate Oscars,* and biographies of Roger Maris and Gil Hodges. Danny's brother Gerald, another Madison pal, contributed an insightful essay on W. C. Fields for this volume, drawing from his background in theater. Gerry has had a long and admirable career as a film reviewer, author, documentary filmmaker, and university teacher in the Boston area; he contributed an engrossing memoir in the Sticking Place series on film critics and historians, *A Reluctant Film Critic* (2025).

A few words on some other parts of *Persistence of Vision* that need contextualizing. I decided to keep the book as it was originally published other than adding this new Introduction, dropping my original introduction, making a few bracketed inserts and silent corrections, and adding a revised prefatory note on Danny Stein's memorable interview with Robert Rossen, conducted shortly before the death of that controversial writer-director. Lennig's impassioned essay on Abel Gance's *Napoléon* was written long before Kevin Brownlow completed his celebrated restoration of the film and Georges Mourier did another.

Along the way in various essays, I've let stand some assertions that could be challenged as dubious or incomplete, but I've made only a few corrections of factual errors and shaky grammar. One other indulgence will be clear to those who read Jon Zwickey's essay on the influence of opium on the films of Jean Cocteau. While programming films for the film society, I tried whenever possible to show what were then called "Underground" films, or avant-garde films, but we were limited by the high rental cost of most work in that category. Still, I wanted to touch base with that realm of esoterica by including two essays by Zwickey, including his impenetrable reflections on Cocteau (a section of a book Jon was writing) and his more accessible, eloquent piece on the Underground feature based on Kenneth H. Brown's protest play *The Brig*, directed by Jonas Mekas, Adolfas Mekas, and Judith Malina.

I had to make a decision about how to deal with my long essay on Orson Welles's *The Magnificent Ambersons.* It is in a section of this book that includes parts of my work-in-progress on Welles, also including my essay on *Citizen Kane* that elicited mockery from Pauline Kael in her infamous 1971 *New Yorker* essay on the script credit for that film. I wrote a rebuttal to Kael's claims about the scriptwriting process of *Kane* in *Film Heritage,* the same magazine that published my *Kane* essay in its Fall 1968 issue and launched my career as a film scholar (the magazine's editor, Tony Macklin, has an essay here on Luchino Visconti's film of Albert Camus's *The Stranger).* Andrew Sarris pointed out in the course of that Kael controversy that ironically, my Appendix on the *Kane* screenplay by Herman J. Mankiewicz and Welles, which appears in this book, was the first serious attempt to acknowledge and analyze Mankiewicz's contribution to the film. Kael falsely claimed Welles had little to do with writing *Kane,* but my analysis here and elsewhere argues that the joint screenplay credit, with Mankiewicz in first position, is accurate. Robert Carringer's authoritative research into the various drafts of the script has settled that issue.

My *Ambersons* essay here was the first attempt at a verbal "reconstruction" of that mutilated masterpiece. Written in August 1968, the same month I took a break to protest at the Chicago Democratic Convention with Stuart Gordon and other Madison friends, that piece has always been my favorite among my critical writing. But after including it in this collection and in my 1972 *Orson Welles,* I did a fairly extensive rewrite for my 1996 revised and expanded edition of *Orson Welles* published by Da Capo Press. The reason for the rewrite was that the shooting script originally was all I had to gauge how Welles intended the film before RKO began recutting and reshooting *Ambersons* after a disastrous preview when he was away making a documentary for the U.S. government in South America, *It's All True.* But in the interim before I published my new edition, Carringer's 1993 book on *Ambersons* reprinted and added information to the RKO cutting continuity of the 132-minute Welles version, a secretary's exact transcription of the actual dialogue and action as they existed before the film was previewed. I used that document and the thirty-six-age appendix by Peter Bogdanovich and Jonathan Rosenbaum reconstructing the missing scenes in *This Is Orson Welles* (1992) to be more precise about how the two versions of the film actually differed.

When I first met Welles in 1970, shortly before he put me into his film *The Other Side of the Wind* on the first day of shooting, I saw that he had a copy of *Persistence of Vision* on his mantelpiece. I had sent him a copy in care of his lawyer without knowing whether it had reached him. Welles expressed his gratitude for what I had written, greeting me with, "I finally meet my favorite critic." When I asked why he thought that, he said, "You're the only critic who understands what I try to do." We touched on *Ambersons* only briefly in our long conversation that day but more extensively discussed *Chimes at Midnight* (about which I had written only the brief piece included here, later augmented for my critical study) and the upcoming *Other Wind*.

Since there is no practical way of inserting enough bracketed corrections or comments in my intermediate study here of the differences between the studio cut of *Ambersons* and Welles's earlier conception, I decided to leave the piece largely intact for this edition, aside from correcting a few factual errors about the production and postproduction while inserting some information in brackets (I tended to put too much of the blame exclusively on editor Robert Wise, before I realized that the situation was more complex). I believe the essay has value in its original form not only because it represents the first attempt to "reconstruct" the film in print (Roger Ryan did a fascinating partial restoration of the film in 1993 using stills of missing scenes with actors doing the original dialogue) but also because this is the version of the piece that Welles read and appreciated. Readers who wish to learn how the long pre-release version differs drastically from the butchered RKO cut can watch my half-hour interview on the subject on the 2018 Criterion Blu-ray edition of *Ambersons*

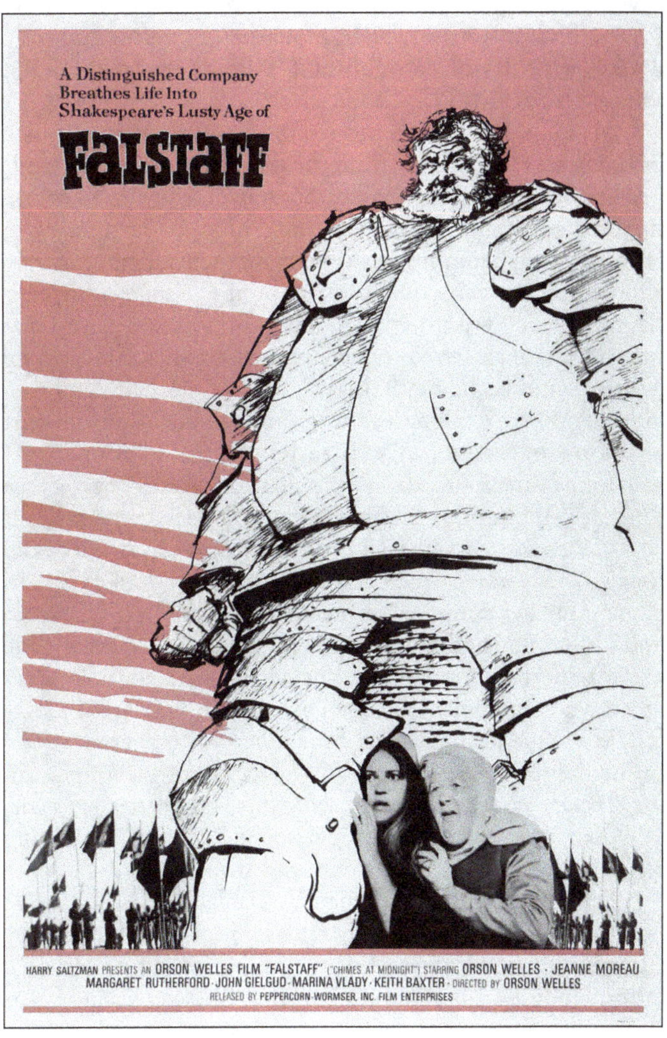

Orson Welles's *Chimes at Midnight* (1965), his adaptation of Shakespeare's saga of the lovable rogue Falstaff and his tragic relationship with Prince Hal (later Henry V), was retitled *Falstaff* for its abortive 1967 release in the U.S. (Peppercorn-Wormser)

(which, among other topics, is more precise about who shot new scenes for the film) and read my revised chapter in my 1996 edition of *Orson Welles;* though that book is currently out of print, I will be publishing a newly updated edition soon with Sticking Place Books.

An issue arose with the section on *Casablanca,* which includes an essay by Howard Koch, one of the three credited screenwriters. Koch takes too much credit for his work, slighting the team of Julius J. and Philip G. Epstein, twin brothers who shared credit with him for the Academy Award–winning script. Subsequent research on *Casablanca* made it clear that Koch was inflating his contribution, so I clarify that situation in an inserted, bracketed paragraph while keeping his contentions, however biased, intact for their historical interest. When Koch agreed to let me use his essay and part of the treatment he had written for Warner Bros. (which I had found in his papers at the State Historical Society of Wisconsin), I noticed that he had failed to say enough about how *Casablanca* was based on a play, *Everybody Comes to Rick's,* by Murray Burnett and Joan Alison. So I asked him to insert a further comment, which he did, though it tended to unfairly minimize the important contribution the play made toward the film's story and characters. Readers who wish thorough commentary on the complicated writing of *Casablanca* (which also involved four other writers) are referred to the definitive 1992 book by Aljean Harmetz, *Round Up the Usual Suspects: The Making of* Casablanca—*Bogart, Bergman, and World War II,* revised in 2002 as *The Making of* Casablanca: *Bogart, Bergman, and World War II.*

The Robert Rossen interview by Daniel Stein is a highlight of this book and deals candidly with some of the difficulties he encountered in his career. But the interview and my original introduction to it ignored the fact that Rossen became notorious as an informer to the House Committee on Un-American Activities, naming the names of sixty people in 1953 in order to get himself off the blacklist. Rossen, along with Koch, had been among the Hollywood Nineteen who were subpoenaed to appear before HUAC in 1947, although neither was called to testify then; Koch endured a period of blacklisting, as did Rossen after he partially took the Fifth Amendment

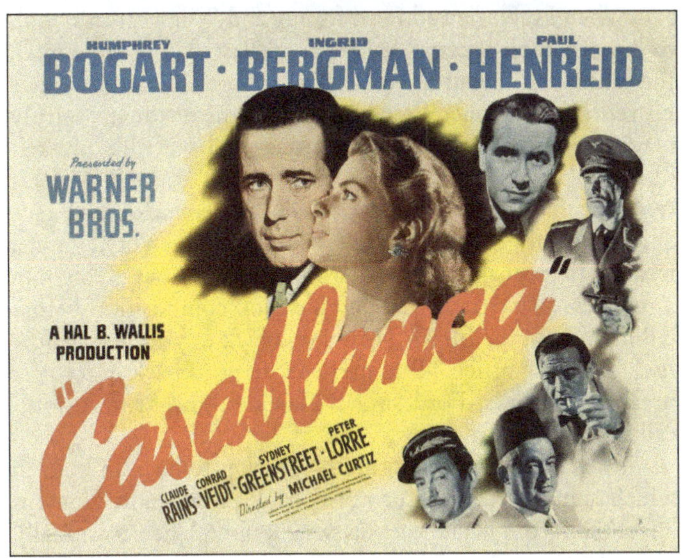

The politically charged, allegorical 1942 World War II love story
that became a favorite of idealistic 1960s youth audiences,
Casablanca. (Warner Bros.)

in his first appearance before HUAC in 1951. Failing to
mention that important history was my failing as this book's
editor. While I was in Madison, I was largely ignorant of the
history of the blacklist period, which I learned more about
after becoming a Hollywood journalist and screenwriter
and researched extensively for my 1992 biography of Frank
Capra, whom I discovered had been a secret government
informer in order to save his own skin.

Under the circumstances, I am glad that Mike Wilmington talked me out of dedicating *Persistence of Vision* to
the Hollywood Ten, correcting my somewhat distorted and
romantic perspective by pointing out that despite their perse-
cution by the government, including jailing for contempt of
Congress, they were more complicated figures than I had
realized (especially Edward Dmytryk, a director who later
turned HUAC informer). So after Mike rescued me from my
youthful naivete, I decided instead to dedicate this book to
John Ford, who had already become my favorite director.

When I interviewed Ford for my and Wilmington's book in his office on August 19, 1970, the last day of his career, the cantankerous old director took the occasion to announce his retirement. Generally he behaved in the obstinate, unruly manner Steven Spielberg captures so well with his portrait of Ford (played by director David Lynch) at the end of his semi-autobiographical 2022 film, *The Fabelmans.* Ford gave Spielberg only a couple of memorable minutes of his time, treating the teenaged filmmaker rather gruffly but giving him a priceless piece of advice on cinematic composition before telling him (in the film), "Now, good luck to you, and get the *fuck* outta my office." But after the lad pops back in to offer breathless thanks, Ford smiles, chuckles, and says sardonically, "My pleasure."

I was fortunate as a future biographer to have an hour in which to make a closer study of Ford. I learned more from his affect than from what he actually said, though he occasionally offered bits of verbal wisdom in the midst of his overall obfuscation. I was mostly put through the wringer by his gruffness but also experienced a moment at the end when he let down his guard, revealing his carefully protected softer side, the aspect of his personality that comes out in his moving, beautifully composed film work. At the end of our time together, I gave Ford a signed copy of *Persistence of Vision* and opened the book to the dedication page. Ford lifted his glasses to peer closely at the page so he could see it. Then he said, "Oh, that's sweet."

Joseph McBride
February 1, 2026

EARLY FILMS

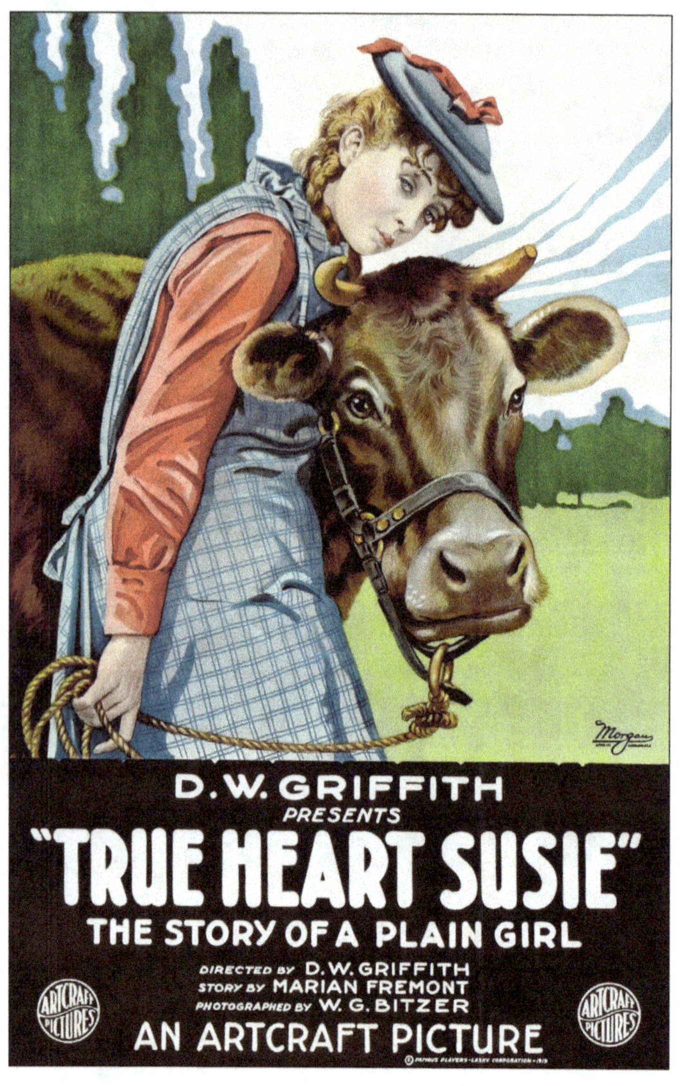

Original poster for one of D. W. Griffith's small gems,
True Heart Susie (1919). (Artcraft/Famous Players-Lasky)

True Heart Susie
Arthur Lennig

True Heart Susie is a much-neglected, though somewhat minor work of Griffith's. Made swiftly in the spring of 1919, it offers no startling advance in the medium. The film, in fact, is far less audacious, far more restrained and subdued than his more famous works. With no last-minute chase, no threatened rape, no cataclysmic social revolution, the film is not as melodramatic and mechanical. He was dealing with no civil war, no gigantic theme of intolerance, no American or French revolution. His only intent was to render faithfully the plight of a young girl, good-hearted and sincere, seeking love in the lonely paths of rural America. Unlike some of the doctrinaire theorists of the cinema, he was able to suit the style to the action, to weave a simple design upon a simple fabric.

Although Griffith hardly spent a large amount of time or money on *True Heart Susie*, he did not depart from his basic philosophy. In fact, this film, so immediate, so sentimental, so sincere, is probably a more accurate glimpse into the heart (not the mind) of Griffith than any of his other productions. Its story seems straight out of a woman's magazine of a generation or so ago. It tells the sad tale of a "plain and simple" girl (to use Griffith's words) who lacks the attractive vice of being "painted and powdered" and the ability to scheme for a husband. Long in love with a childhood sweetheart, she sees herself treated only as a sister and watches brokenhearted as her beloved marries a girl of cheaper, more flashy character. The fast wife soon proves uncongenial to her husband, but he suffers silently along with Susie. Only after the unworthy wife dies does he finally realize that Susie is the one he truly loves. Although this story can be dismissed as soap-opera—and certainly if it were a piece of literature it would be—the fact that Griffith tells it so well, with so many sensitive insights, so many accurate details of small-town Americana, redeems it from being inconsequential, merely a moving tintype from an earlier era. Admittedly, the film's story is so familiar that to many audiences it will creak and groan like an old grist mill. But there is more than corn; there is, through blurred and sentimentalized, a sincerity that overcomes its intellectual drawbacks.

A laudatory review in *The New York Times* of June 2, 1919, said that Griffith

> has brought meaningful humanity to the screen more nearly pure, less mixed with artificiality, than it has ever been in a motion picture play, except in other works of Mr. Griffith's, with the best of which, considering its pretensions, it holds its own.

Time has shown that there was a little more "artificiality" than was obvious in 1919, but the observation that it brought "meaningful humanity" to the screen remains correct.

The strength of *True Heart Susie* does not lie so much in the story as in its heartfelt sympathy and sentiment, its close and almost reverent attention to rural Americana, and its visually beautiful evocation of nature. Indeed, the shots of the countryside (like those in *The Birth of a Nation*) once again reveal that Griffith, far more than other directors, had a fine pictorial eye, a deep veneration for the loveliness of the out-of-doors. His country scenes have a kind of primal quality; they are suffused with a tone, an air, a lyricism, so that they do more than depict a setting: they seem to distill its very essence. The tree in which the young lovers carve their initials, the vine-overgrown picket fence, the way the light falls on the front porch, the smell and feel of the meadow where the cow feeds, the dust and sunshine of the country road—all seem to glow with an artist's skill. Few films made since then have created that kind of Wordsworthian awareness of the beauties of nature, that nostalgic light in which we

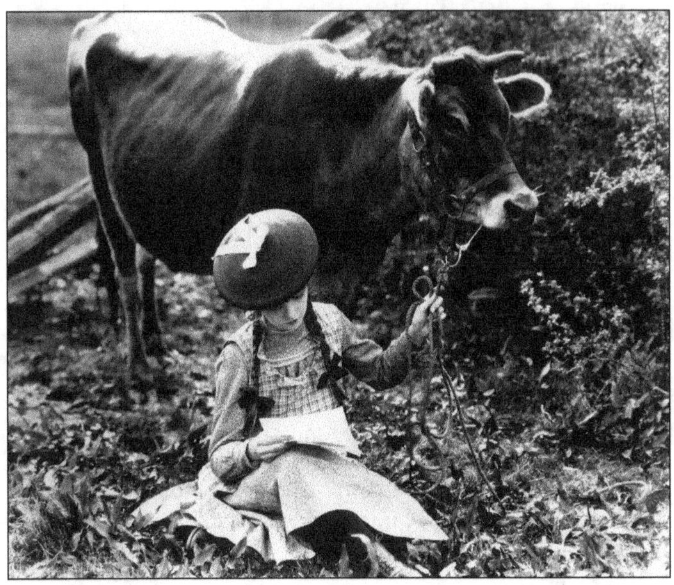

Lillian Gish gives one of her finest performances as the sensitive country girl in the comedy-drama *True Heart Susie*.
The romantically bucolic cinematography is by Griffith's frequent collaborator G. W. (Billy) Bitzer. (Artcraft/Famous Players-Lasky)

so often bathe the past. Griffith sees nature in much the same way as the poet defined in "Tintern Abbey":

> For I have learned
> To look on nature, not as in the hour
> Of thoughtless youth; but hearing oftentimes
> The still, sad music of humanity…

There is something wistful, something melancholic, perhaps even something bitter about *True Heart Susie* that lends its story and its visuals a kind of inner illumination, an illumination suffused gently by the "still, sad music of humanity." Griffith's longing for the time past, for the gentleness and simplicity of his youth, can perhaps be explained in Wordsworth's lines:

> What though the radiance which was once so bright
> Be now forever taken from my sight,
>> Though nothing can bring back the hour
> Of splendor in the grass, of glory in the flower
>> We will grieve not, rather find
>> Strength in what remains behind;
>> In the primal sympathy
>> Which having been must ever be;
>> In the soothing thoughts that spring
>> Out of human suffering;
>> In the faith that looks through death,
> In years that bring the philosophic mind.

Griffith himself never quite found the contentment of "the philosophic mind," nor did he, as did the poet, "grieve not." More sentimental than Wordsworth, he grieved plenty; he continued to long not only for his own past, but for the past of his country.

True Heart Susie represents a tendency in Griffith's work which was to doom him, but which, because he was so stubborn, so unwilling to change, does in a large measure redeem him. Griffith, like the glorious mammoth of old, refused to accommodate himself to a changing environment. He refused to follow the sun of popularity or, perhaps, even more pitifully, could not entirely perceive in what direction that sun lay, and so perished in a frozen north. Experimental in the medium he was, but his ideas about humanity, about motivation, about good and evil never changed. Some critics have intimated that he tried to pander to the low tastes of his audience. Perhaps in his later years he tried to accommodate a bit, but he was genuinely trapped by his integrity. His vision of the world, whether his audience liked it or not, could not be subdued. He could not think in the "now" fashion. Caught with a Victorian vision of women, a nostalgic love for a past that perhaps never was, a veneration for the transitory stage of being "passionately in love," and faced with the awful dichotomy of being a realist and an idealist at the same time, he could not give his audiences what they wanted. In 1914 he was not too far from public sentiment, but by 1919 a world war and a moral revolution had taken place. He tried to ignore this transformation, but his audience had been affected and was already starting to laugh at some of his creations. Soldiers returning from the war, girls reading Freud, petting in Ford cars, the beginnings of jazz, short skirts, all prompted the inevitable transformation of innocence into experience, of shyness into worldliness, of moral absolutes into relativism. The process is still going on, of course, but Griffith was starting to appear as corny to his contemporaries as he does to us. We, at a later period, have the advantage of being indulgent about his excesses, but to his contemporaries no nostalgia softened the shortcomings of his work.

Griffith had made the fatal error of lining up with the parents against the children, with the old rather than the new, unlike the diabolically clever showman Cecil B. DeMille, who, like a weathervane, always seemed to know which way the wind blew. In never anticipating a trend, but rather by advocating what was no longer in vogue, Griffith was sacrificed, not without some injustice, on the ringing altar of financial expediency.

Many of Griffith's problems stemmed from his vision of girls. To him, girls were always sugar and spice and everything nice. He was, in fact, a bit short on the spice, but long on the nice. He was in many ways a woman's director. He shows sensitivity and warmth toward his heroines, shares their idealistic dreams, their disappointments, and worships their innocent youth and their tragic vulnerability. In so doing, however, he errs, like the Victorians, in that his girls mince and coo beyond credibility. Ironically, then, this woman's director fails at what he was most sensitive. Mae Marsh, Lillian Gish, Carol Dempster—all of them are essentially the same: the little girl smiling through tears, the little girl victimized by sadistic admirers, or neglected by an indifferent world.

Since Griffith is a "warm" director, his work has been harshly interpreted by the progressively "cooler" generations since his time. Audiences are cynical about human emotions. When a Griffith girl receives good news and jumps up and down, they are more inclined to interpret the action as a Freudian kind of sexual release than a more innocent expression of happiness.

Griffith himself was aware that he was torn between the reality of his own times and the nostalgia he felt for his youth. He wisely placed the date of *True Heart Susie* back ten years to 1909 as if to signify that the small-town America he depicted was waning or perhaps had already vanished. Furthermore, he set the story in Pine Grove, Indiana, in the Middle West, which still, along with the South, resists change the most.

Although the film is sentimental, the titles are not; they provide a slightly cynical attitude which saves the film from being mawkish. It seems indeed as if Griffith is mocking his own dreams, that he knows that what he is presenting is perhaps a fantasy. In short, it was as if his heart told him one thing and his mind another. In one of the titles, he refers to the lovers as "simple idiots," but intimates knowingly that we are all idiots when in love.

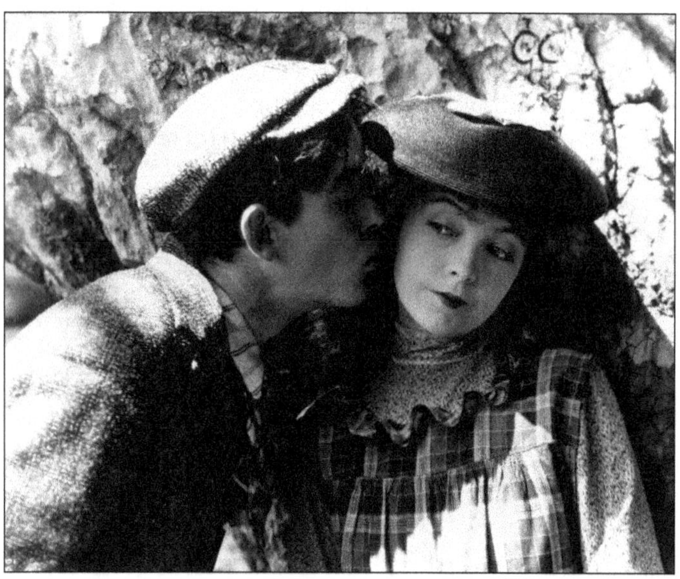

Susie and her flighty beau, William (Robert Harron), are timid about romance, but she remains constant in her affections toward him. Harron died the following year of a possibly accidental gunshot wound. (Artcraft/Famous Players-Lasky)

The film opens in a small town. Susie (Lillian Gish) and William (Robert Harron) attend a one-room school. They are moony for each other, and his hesitations as he tries to get up enough courage to kiss her are delightfully true. William's family doesn't want him to go to college, but Susie sells her cow and some other items to send him the money anonymously, although William thinks it has come from a traveling philanthropist.

Griffith's knowledge of people is perceptive and saves many scenes in this film from being merely outlandish. When William receives the letter (actually from Susie) saying that he will be given money for college, he runs over to Susie's place and wants to kiss her. He jumps up and down a few times, lunges towards her, but cannot quite get up the courage. The scene is amusing, yet is touching because it is real, because we have all been in such a situation.

Off at school he writes back occasionally and tells Susie that he has not yet met anyone in school he has liked better than those at home, a statement which she interprets as a piece of encouragement. When William finally returns, he takes her to town for a dish of ice cream. This scene, as he marches down the street, tweaking his mustache and reveling in his having grown up—Susie at the same time trying to steer him clear of all the young girls giving him the eye—is brilliantly handled.

Soon a flapper observes him. She doesn't really love him, but he's better than no husband at all. William is smitten but, lacking courage, stops by one day at Susie's and asks whether he should marry. She says "Yes." Shortly afterward he tells her, "I've taken your advice, Susie." When she finds out he is marrying someone else, she is heartbroken; a tragic moment which Lillian Gish's acting and Griffith's direction capture superbly. Soon after, when the marriage vehicle drives away, she stands along by the fence, walks a few feet, staggers, and sinks to the ground by some flowering bushes. The scene in its composition and tone resembles an old engraving.

After the honeymoon, Griffith shows William envisioning how married life should be. In soft focus we see the wife attentive, good food on the table, and lots of affection. But then in clear focus reality shows us the wife with her hair tied up in curlers, poor food on the table, and little attention. Her temper flares. "I hate this damn place," she says wrathfully. In disgust and anger he walks away. Meantime, Susie has decided to destroy her letters from him. She walks toward the fence—that symbol that Griffith so unobtrusively creates—as William approaches. "Love letters?" he says. The irony of this to Susie and of course to the audience is particularly painful. William tells Susie (seen now in an iris), "Be sure you get the right one." He is thinking of his own mess, but the audience is thinking of Susie's plight as well.

William's wife is two-timing her husband. One night she tells William she has a headache and sneaks out to have a party with her friends. She also stops along the way to get a book that William wanted. William, sad, depressed and unable to sleep, looks out his window at Susie's house. Griffith then cuts to Susie (staying up late to nurse her sick aunt) as she looks through her window at William. The sincerity of this scene of the separated lovers redeems it from being gimmicky.

That night, the wife is caught in a rainstorm, and returns home, where she discovers that she has lost her key. Desperately, she asks her neighbor, Susie, to cover for her. Susie lets her share her bed, and although she makes a fist at her sleeping rival, she soon forgives the wife and cuddles her.

As a result of the wife's running out in the rain, she catches cold and dies. The title is precise: "So she dies, as she has lived—a little unfaithful." But William thinks that she has died as a result of getting a book for him and vows never to marry but rather to uphold her memory. Susie of course wouldn't tell him the truth. As a title says, "Susie would never break his faith." And so the situation for a time remains. He sits on the front porch and she continues to pine. Fortunately, one of his wife's partying friends finally tells him the truth. He rushes over to Susie's. She is at the cottage window, surrounded by climbing rose bushes, watering a flower box. He tells her he wants to marry her. She coyly hides behind the watering can, reverting to Griffith's Victorian conception of the shy girl, but William finally kisses her.

The next shot—the last one—shows a beautiful country road with William and Susie walking arm in arm. It is a happy ending, a fairy-tale ending, and a title places the film in a peculiar perspective: "And we may believe they walk again as they did long years ago." The use of the *conditional* "may" and the word "ago" clue us as to Griffith's attitudes. They reinforce the "once-upon-a-time" quality and say too that Griffith was depicting life the way much of it was but shaped it at the end to conform with the dream of what it ought to be.

Both Griffith's *True Heart Susie* and *Way Down East* (1920) are almost documentary visions of a vanished era and its lost sensibilities. To add to them Henry King's *Tol'able David* (1921) would create a three-cornered base of early Americana. In contrast to this vision a more world-wise view would be offered only a few years later: *A Woman of the World* (1925), *Dancing Mothers* (1926), and many others. They showed a different kind of America and a different kind of heroine. She was no longer the innocent maiden, but rather a mixture of virgin and vamp: the modern girl who smokes, drinks, and makes love when she feels like it. Modernists will argue that she has moved from hypocrisy and frustration to honesty and satisfaction. This may indeed be, but she—and the males who relate to her—have lost as much as they've gained. The day of quality has gone and quantity has taken its place. The handmade object has succumbed to the pounded-out item. The differences between Lillian Gish and Jayne Mansfield are in more than bust size or make-up. Admittedly, the male of fifty years ago might grow exhausted chasing his girl around trees trying to give her a kiss, but it was certainly a more romantic exhaustion than passing out from what Eliot has described as "pneumatic bliss."

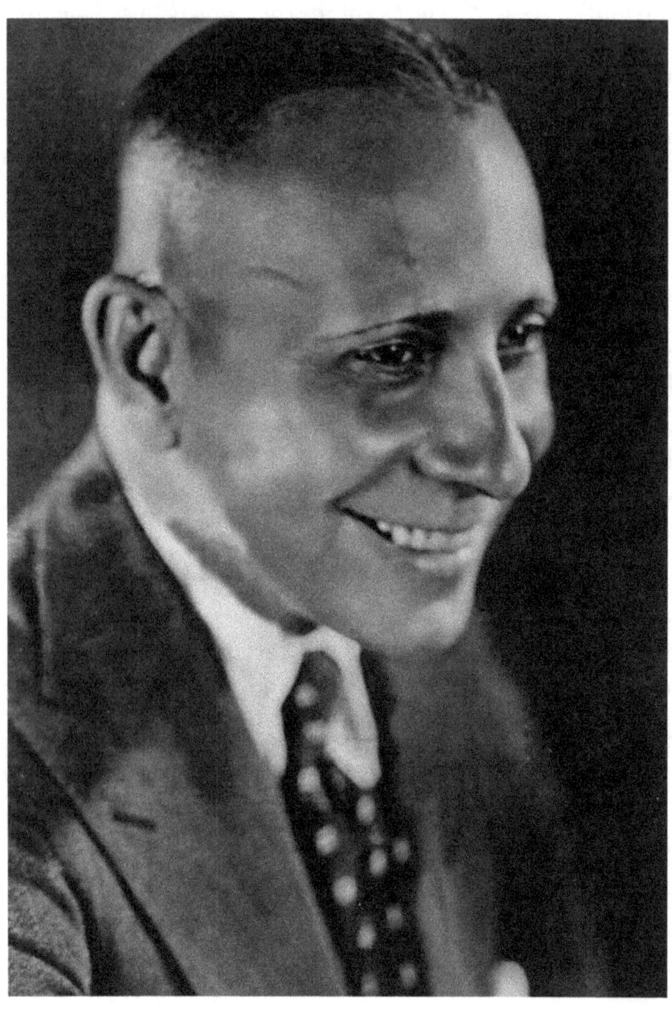

Erich von Stroheim was both popular as "The Man You Love to Hate" in screen performances and a revolutionary in advancing the sophistication of Hollywood's view of sexuality as a director. But his lavish filming led him to become the first major director fired by a studio executive (Universal's Irving Thalberg) and caused the evisceration of some of his films.

Merry-Go-Round
Arthur Lennig

The history of von Stroheim's films is a nightmare for critics, and *Merry-Go-Round* is no exception. In fact, this 1923 film is perhaps the most difficult to discuss, not because of its intellectual complexity, but because of its confused authorship. Von Stroheim's other films had been cut and mutilated by others, but at least he had done all the filming. On *Merry-Go-Round*, however, he was fired midway in the film and replaced by Rupert Julian. The new director redid much of the footage shot and made changes in the story; thus the responsibility for various scenes or even for the individual shots within them cannot always be ascertained. We have Julian's statement that he used only about six hundred feet from von Stroheim. But even if this is so, these 600 feet definitely establish the von Stroheim vision. Julian's additional footage cannot always sustain, though neither can it refute, that peculiar mordant tone, that bitter, cruel yet imaginatively honest atmosphere that pervades von Stroheim's films. To this Austrian director the human hand was skeletal fingers padded with flesh, the human soul a cluster of lustful drives and the body a conglomeration of original sin as well as sins of man's own making.

The story of *Merry-Go-Round* was written by von Stroheim and then adapted by Rupert Julian and Harvey Gates. Von Stroheim's improvers were trying to sidestep all the unpleasant insights the Austrian director hoped to impart. They were looking for quick and superficial peeks of life, peeks that would occasionally be shocking but would more often than not cater to the stereotyped romantic needs of the average audience. They succeeded; a review in *Variety* of July 4, 1923, referred to *Merry-Go-Round* as "a whale of a picture." Von Stroheim had his sentimental side, a side we all have, but he never forgot to juxtapose such feelings with material which would redeem them from being sentimental. He mocks man's pretensions not because he does not like those pretensions, but because he knows that man cannot maintain them. Like Jonathan Swift, but without his sprightliness, von Stroheim cuts through the facade to present a tragic picture of man's unworthiness, of his inability to be good and even at times to perceive what good is. But his comprehensive though somewhat soured vision of life was short-circuited by Rupert Julian so that in the midst of the devastating and even cruel panorama of life in Vienna—that peculiar juxtaposition of high life and low, of, indeed, lust and love, of practicality and the dream—picture-postcard views and romantic posturings try to cover, in an unctuous and even pandering fashion, like white satin over rotting flesh, the grim reality beneath.

As a result, the rhetoric of Julian's love scenes is completely opposed to von Stroheim's realistic tone. This is not to say that von Stroheim would not have had romantic moments in the film—he had them in some of his other works—but they were always contrasted, amidst their apple blossoms or Viennese violins or moon-bathed balustrades, with certain indications of the baser needs of men. He could see the beauties of love amidst the sordid mechanics of courtship, but he never let his romanticism take complete hold without intermixing it with more "basic" material. He depicted his male protagonists, even when they were in love, as also rejoicing in the fact that they were "racking" up another conquest on their scorecards. These dichotomies he presented with humor—not the guffaw of the groundlings or the nudge in the ribs—but rather the sneer of a man who knew too much to believe entirely in love. This film, then, with its divided authorship, provides devastating insights and then controverts them with romantic posturing, Griffith-like heroines, and love scenes unrelieved by reality. As a result, the film's *Weltanschauung* alternates between life as it is (von Stroheim's vision) and life as it ought to be (Hollywood's vision).

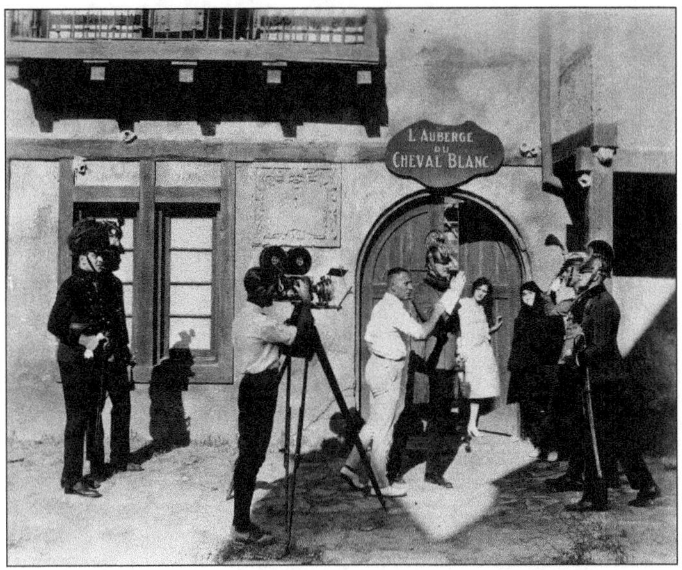

Stroheim filming *Merry-Go-Round* (1923) on a Universal set representing Vienna. The film was taken away from him and mostly reshot by another director, Rupert Julian. (Universal)

Merry-Go-Round is essentially a love story, but a rather unconventional one even with Julian's happy ending. It tells of a Count, Franz Maximillian von Hohenegg, a rake who, under the guise of being a necktie salesman, meets, falls in love with and seduces Agnes, "a girl of the people." Affectionate, attractive, and virginal, the girl is an organ grinder at the Prater, the amusement park of Vienna. She is lusted after by Schani Huber, the carnival boss, who domineers over her father (the Punch and Judy man) and torments and finally tries to rape her. She is liked also by Bartholomew, a hunchbacked but sensitive fellow who takes care of a caged ape. Schani finally is killed by the ape, the father dies during the war, the Count returns and marries Agnes, and the hunchback is left only with his ape.

The film's story is obviously not particularly impressive, but what makes it at all worthwhile is the texture of individual scenes. The film opens in the Prater, where the Count, accompanied by some girls, arrives in an open carriage, and goes to a shooting gallery; there he picks up a rifle and punctures a number of heart-shaped targets, the kind of symbolism in which von Stroheim delighted. Schani Huber, the large and unpleasant head of the carnival, torments the daughter by stepping on her foot, a bit of sadistic byplay that only von Stroheim would have thought of. When Agnes' Mother is dying, Schani prevents the father and Agnes from attending the mother's last moments—the show must go on, according to Schani, not necessarily to please the public, but to get a few more pennies. Only a providential rain shower which scatters the crowd allows the old man and the daughter to go to the deathbed. The storm swings open the shutters and a bird flies in the room. The dying mother sees the creature as some angelic and apocalyptic omen and then dies, a touch that was surely von Stroheim's, considering his usual preoccupation with religion and superstition.

Schani does not reserve his unpleasantness for his workers but plagues his wife also. During lunch he slams a knife down on her hand when she tries to take a piece of wurst. He deliberately cuts off a large slice of meat for himself and gives her a paper-thin one. Later, when displeased with her—not for what she has done but perhaps just for living—he throws a mug of beer in her face, a realistic scene which far antedates James Cagney's shoving a grapefruit in his girl's face in *The Public Enemy* (1931).

Schani is an example of von Stroheim's handling of lower-class people. Like *Greed, Merry-Go-Round* shows that people—or at least some people—are far from Hollywood's concept of "nice." Nor does von Stroheim neglect to be critical of the upper classes as well. After introducing the heart-piercing Count at the amusement park, von Stroheim then cuts to the rake's royal apartments. The Count's valet comes in to wake him up and touches his face gently. The Count feels the hand and begins patting it (a reasonably subtle indication of his usual habits of waking up with someone). A few minutes later, when the valet draws the water for the bath, the Count's dog jumps in the tub. The Count, shaving, doesn't see it and, the valet smiling to himself, he steps in the now-dirtied bath water. After the bath, the Count dons his mustache-band and telephones his fiancée, who, attended by her maids, is lying down on a couch smoking a cigar. Certainly this realistic and rather disenchanting aspect of courtship—he with his mustache-band and she with her cigar—was von Stroheim's particular province. Lubitsch was not the only director to show intimate and debunking glimpses of upper-class life.*

Von Stroheim provides more of his "continental" touch in a banquet scene, footage which Julian acknowledged he had borrowed. The Count sits between two women; when one becomes too flirtatious, the other takes a knife and tries to stab her rival. The Count coolly takes the knife from her—he's been through this jealous charade before—and nonchalantly throws it over his shoulder. A moment later a large bowl is carried in and placed on top of the table. The Count excitedly starts pouring bottles of champagne into the top of the bowl, and out of it eventually come the arms and shoulders of a beautiful wench seductively writhing. This elegant pre-world-war sensualism was actually not too uncommon among the so-called higher circles in Europe and America. Today it might seem "far-out," merely an extravagant invention of von Stroheim's, but such classical orgies had occurred, even in proper old New York.†

Meanwhile, lust seeks similar, if less beautiful forms among the amusement park people. Schani Huber spies Agnes sweeping the floor, locks the door behind him, turns off the lights, and starts after her. She tries to escape and hides among the now quiet horses of the Merry-Go-Round. Aroused as well as angry, he grabs a bridle rope from one of the horses and begins to whip her. Finally the father, hearing her screams, enters the room (by cutting through a canvas curtain) and stabs Schani. Just at this moment the police arrive and arrest the father, though Schani has not been badly hurt.

Later on, the Count meets Agnes on the street and takes her to his "love-nest." Nude statues add an inspirational

---

* One sequence missing from the print shown at the Museum of Modern Art shows the fiancée who returns from a morning ride and on entering the stables draws a groom into a dark corner, letting her affections have full reign, but strikes him with her riding crop when he would likewise express his aroused passion. (*Variety*, July 4, 1923)
† James Gibbons Hunecker recorded a fictional account of one of these New York parties in his novel *Painted Veils* (1920).

note to his dress. She holds herself back from him and he, in passion, takes a violin in his hands and starts tightening one of the strings which finally breaks and snaps his mood. She leaves the room, reconsiders, and returns.

Following shortly after is a dated, almost period-piece setting in a public park. She is seated on a bench (made up of tree branches); he stands behind it, and both are surrounded by giant trunks and a canopy of leaves.

Although the Count definitely is in love, he chooses to mention this fact to his cronies, who laugh at taking such a "girl of the people" seriously. Acting out of pragmatism, he proves himself aware of his own career and of his social standing by marrying his fiancée, the cigar-smoker. It is a loveless match.

Meantime, Schani is angry at Agnes' father for interfering with his rape, for attacking him with a knife and for leaving Schani's economic empire. The old man has a rival show next to Schani's, but the evil boss tries to cure that problem by climbing upstairs and pushing a potted tree down on the old man's head. At the hospital Agnes and the Count have been intimate. At this awkward point, the wife of the Count enters and Agnes realizes that her necktie salesman is really a married man and a Count besides.

If retribution at the moment is at abeyance for the erring principals, at least Schani gets his just deserts. One night he throws something at the ape and when the hunchback forgets to lock the cage, the ape climbs up the side of the building and apparently kills Schani, though any evidence of the murder or any mention of it later on is absent.

Retribution too seems to occur to the whole Western world, for war has broken out. The Count visits Agnes to beg forgiveness. She turns from him; after he leaves, she stands by a tree in the lovely park and cries. The war rages and the Austrians are fighting on the Italian front. Coincidentally, the Count finds Agnes' father on the battlefield, wounded. The old man curses the rake, and the Count, remorseful, hands him his gun. Agnes' father aims the gun at the Count's head but dies before he can pull the trigger. (This scene, one hopes, von Stroheim would not have included; it is a bit too extravagant and operatic to be believable.)

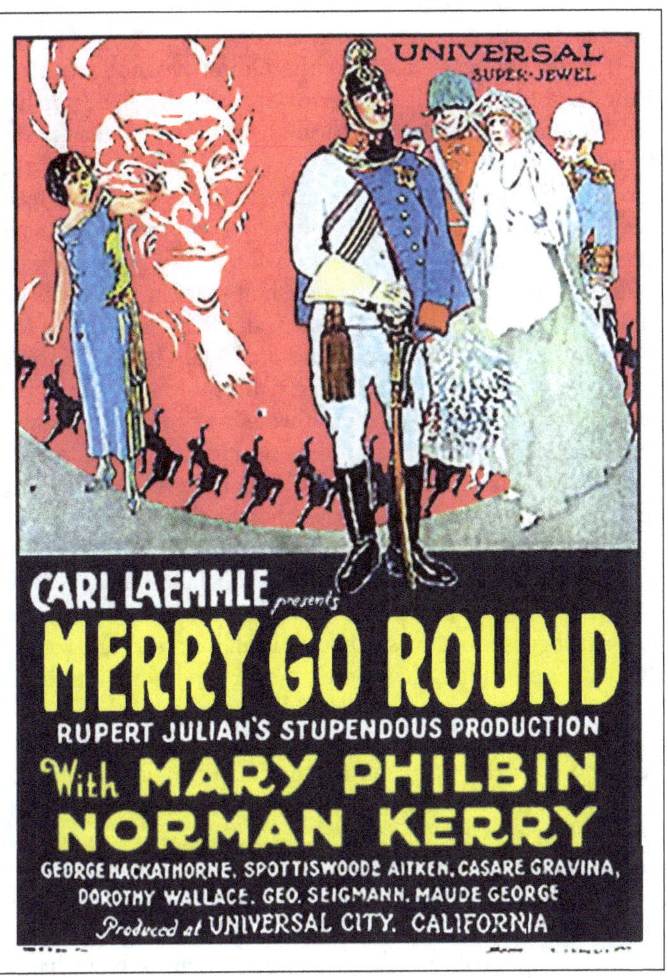

Stroheim's name is not mentioned on this
Merry-Go-Round poster. (Universal)

In the midst of the war a curious allegorical shot occurs; it shows a naked God of War spinning a merry-go-round. This type of symbolic shot stems from Griffith (recall the last scenes in *The Birth of a Nation* and *Intolerance)* and is similar to shots depicting money lust in *Greed.*

Finally the war ends, but the Count has not returned; Agnes is told that he is neither on the casualty lists, nor has been found. Loved by Bartholomew, the hunchback, she decides to marry him. But one day, while she is grinding the barrel organ outside the amusement park, she thinks she feels the presence of her lover. She looks up and yes, indeed, he is there. The Count entreats her, saying he was sorry, and asking again for her forgiveness. She tells him that she had forgiven him even before he had left for the war. He informs her of the fortuitous event—that his wife has died—and that everything can be all right and they can marry. Bartholomew leaves the ape cage and sees both of them through a broken window—symbolic of his own shattered dreams. He returns to the cage, crying, and holds the huge paw in his hand, a scene that today appears slightly comic. The last shot of the film is set in a luxuriant arbor full of bursting flowers and lush foliage in which Agnes and the Count embrace to a fade-out.

As can be seen, the title of the film is significant in many ways. It suggests, of course, that life itself is a merry-go-round, that just as one horse chases the other around a circle and gets nowhere, so does mankind. In addition, it puts Schani's lust, the Count's seductions, Bartholomew's vain hope for happiness and even the war itself on the same circular plane. Life is by no means an amusement center—the Prater is a dream, like happiness. One pays to ride the merry-go-round and the price may be more expensive than the fun to be derived. Admittedly, the happy ending tends to change this tone, but the ending is far more dependent on Julian than on von Stroheim. Unhappiness, helplessness, and disillusionment haunt the film.

Merry-Go-Round has echoes of von Stroheim's earlier works. It employs the Austrian setting of *Blind Husbands,* the fun atmosphere of Monte Carlo in *Foolish Wives,* the male rake of both these films and the personal cruelty as revealed in *Greed.* The film also hints of themes which would be more fully developed in later works: the officer who falls in love with a lowly girl being at the same time married or engaged to a royal woman (as in *The Wedding March* and *Queen Kelly*). As in all of von Stroheim's work, the background settings support the action faithfully and often comment ironically on what transpires. Unfortunately, the film lacks much of the irony and bitterness—except at certain points—which distinguish a von Stroheim film from the typical Hollywood product. But the von Stroheim visions appear often enough to make the film worth viewing and are an additional reminder that in this wild and stubborn Austrian director lay one of the cinema's major talents.

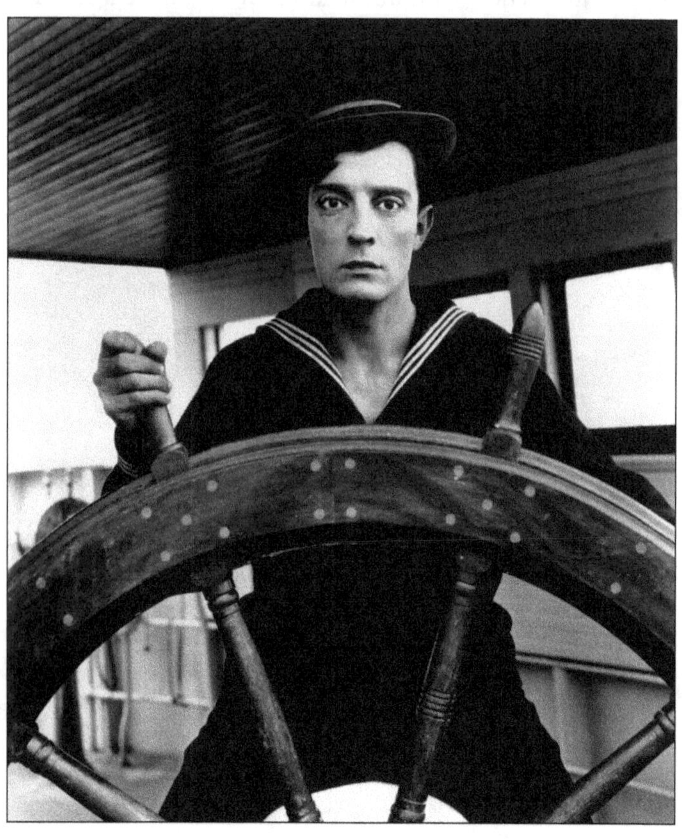

Buster Keaton at the helm of *The Navigator* (1924), one of his classic silent comedies. He plays a rich youth, Rollo Treadway, stranded on an ocean liner with only his girlfriend, Betsy O'Brien (Kathryn McGuire), while the two learn to survive and make do with their lavish surroundings. Keaton shared the directing with Donald Crisp. (Buster Keaton Productions/Metro-Goldwyn)

The Navigator
William Donnelly

BUSTER KEATON

Buster was given his nickname by Houdini, a fellow trouper in vaudeville who admired his acrobatic daring. Born in 1896, Keaton joined his parents' acrobatic act at the age of three and evaded school successfully enough to be one of vaudeville's top stars throughout his youth. His act consisted of his being beaten and tossed "brutally" around the stage. He brought his fame and his experience as a laugh provoker to Hollywood in 1917 and learned the craft of filmmaking from his friend and fellow comedian Fatty Arbuckle. Keaton was phenomenally successful as a director and comedian and the career that started in two-reelers reached its peak before the advent of sound in such features as *The General, The Navigator* and *Sherlock Jr.* Alcoholism, sound and interference by executives which undercut his judgment and authority ended his career as a director, but he remained in Hollywood as a bit player and a designer of comic sequences for other stars until his death in 1966.

KEATON'S COMIC STYLE

Silent comedians are either buffoons and butts, victims of painful psychosexual awkwardness, plagued by accidents the rest of us evade, or they fit into a more complicated category and their neurotic buffoonery is dispelled when they achieve the love of the heroine. Harry Langdon's blocked development which leaves him in a state of perpetual babyhood, Fatty Arbuckle's grotesque infantile bulk, and Laurel and Hardy's latent homosexuality make them merely the objects of our laughter. But in comedians like Keaton and Chaplin love allows the buffoon to overcome his handicaps, and the strange traits which were at first an impediment become superlative and unique virtues.

In *The Navigator*, Rollo Treadway—a name hinting at a life mechanically spent on a kind of rolling treadmill—overcomes the rigidity of an overcivilized life. He and the heroine find each other after a comic search with existential overtones and try to live in a world in which they are almost children. Finally they are frightened into spending a night together and as a result achieve a marvelous mastery of their environment in a few weeks, a mastery which stands the test of an attack by cannibals (who, like the Negro couple early in the film, may symbolize the anarchic tendencies of the id).

Such a psychoanalytic reading of the film's contents scarcely explains much of the particular appeal of Keaton's style. Keaton presents himself as more than an impassive stoic, and the kind of fool he is predicts the kind of hero he will become. The plot of *The Navigator* is pretty much borrowed from the standard Douglas Fairbanks plot: the pampered and supercilious Eastern millionaire made into a man in the egalitarian West; but Fairbanks' mollycoddle is a bit of an exhibitionist in his decadence and even more of the crowd-pleaser in his triumph. In *The Navigator*, Keaton's millionaire sees the world in terms of conventions—one goes for a long walk when disappointed, one orders steamship tickets if one plans to get married—but his emotional deadness leads him into error when he tries to behave conventionally. Nonetheless he has an admirable directness and simplicity in his attempts. He does not hesitate or consider his ego when he embarks on a task, and we pity him for his incomprehension. The directness makes him a clown in his attempts to master the world of the ship's kitchen, but it makes him a hero in coping with the leak in the boat and with the attacking cannibals. The essence of Keaton's character is directness and economy. Just as he wastes nothing on the direct expression of emotion for others to perceive, so he wastes no motion in his mastery of the ship's kitchen. This directness, inventiveness and economy is reflected in the film's style.

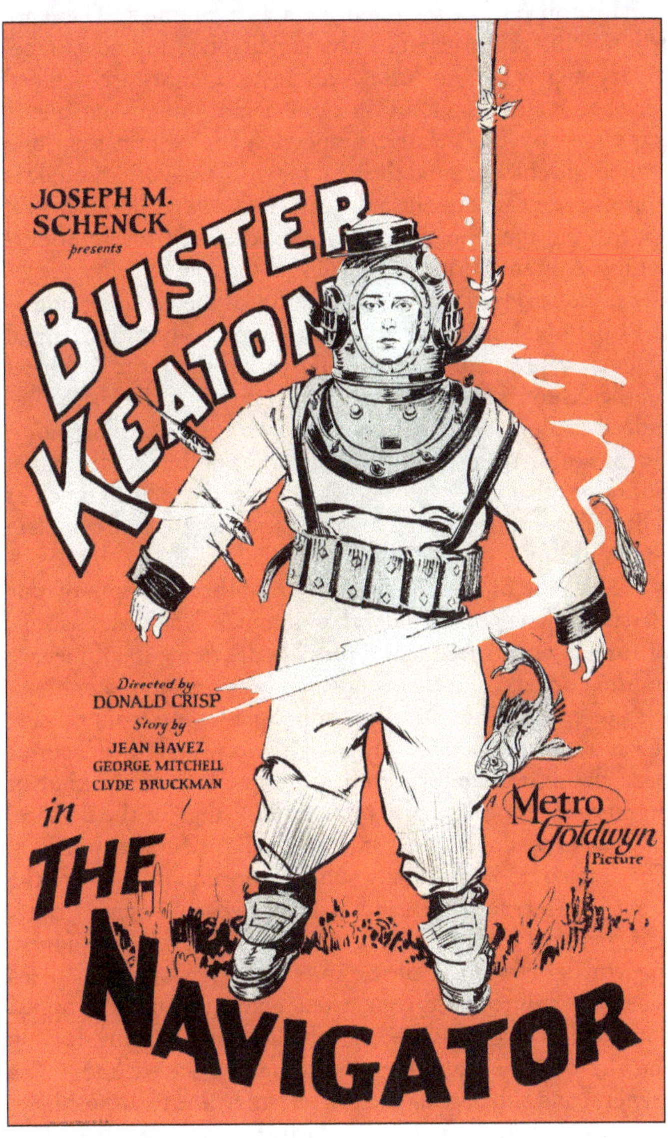

An original poster for *The Navigator*, showing Keaton in a diving suit he uses to fix a leak in the ship. (Buster Keaton Productions/ Metro-Goldwyn)

Keaton rarely uses the camera as a gimmick. There are few moving camera shots, only one dissolve, and no extraordinary angles in *The Navigator*. Instead, shots are planned for the greatest economy in camera movement, and one is impressed by their classic simplicity. The culminating long shot in the chase around the boat between the young couple is impressive I think because the camera is placed in the perfect spot to tell the whole story without the need for additional setups. A French critic has suggested that the effectiveness of the scene springs from the utilization of the receding line of the boat combined with the exploitation of both horizontal and vertical reaching a kind of flowering when the two meet on the diagonal stairway. And I will agree that the chase does indeed exploit the whole range of distances and dimensions. But it seems to me that there is no magic in the diagonals, but rather that the magic here is like the magic in so much of what Keaton does: in the restraint and elegance of complete economy.

The plot of *The Navigator* is another example of this classic tendency to simplify and minimize. The machinations of foreign agents frequently provide the elements of menace in film comedy, and this is not just because the pretentiousness of spy films invites lampoon. Spies come from outside the normal, predictable order of society, and their actions raise the clown's efforts to a grotesque and giddy kind of dignity since the fate of nations often hangs in the balance. In *The Navigator*, the spy frame is used for another purpose. The ship could just as easily slip its moorings due, say, to the inept interference of Treadway as he gets on board. I think it is included to provide a contrast between the determined, vigorous effectiveness of the spies and the state of the hero when he is introduced soon after. The spy story is dropped completely as soon as we meet the hero and heroine, leaving the film without the persistent external menace we find in *The General* and shifting the focus from story line to atmospheric and thematic development. Similarly, Keaton does not end his film on a Fairbanks-like note of jingoistic egalitarianism. We have no resolution pointing back to the bewildered ineffectuality of the rich. Instead we see the couple aboard a submarine, a kind of submersible *deus ex machina,* with a large lever in the center of the frame. When this lever is pulled the sub tilts. And watching this tilt, we suspect that only the camera is actually tilting, until the whole set turns over before our eyes. Keaton frequently used this kind of device, cozening the audience into thinking that fakery was involved, and then pulling back to reveal that no fakery was involved at all, only the simple truth.

Though Keaton eschewed the jingoism of Fairbanks and the bathos of Chaplin, it is inaccurate to say that he is merely a dummy. The scene in which he climbs down the ladder in his diving suit, head slightly tilted to one side like a figure in a religious painting, is more effective than many scenes in Chaplin in which the little tramp cries over some fairly conventional object of pity (like, say, a blind girl selling flowers she cannot see) and the effectiveness here springs from the restraint. Though Keaton is a master of building comic sequences (as, say, in his exploitation of the diving suit's possibilities as monster costume, life raft, and slittable false belly), he has an even more characteristic ability to understate. The scene with the doors is beautiful primarily because it is short, simple, and self-contained. And one of the most attractive attitudes in which we find him is one of simple confusion when some accident has thwarted a process in which he is involved. Keaton's lack of understanding is exhibited more expressively in the passivity of his face while he searches for the cause of disaster and suggests in his motions the improbable hypotheses running through his mind to explain the difficulty than if he would have moved the comedy to a more blatant level by screwing up his face, scratching his head, muttering to himself. Keaton relies more on the audience's intelligence and attention than any other silent comedian, and he achieves, as a result, a closer rapport and greater effectiveness than others, while appealing at the same time to our esthetic appreciation of the economy of classic restraint.

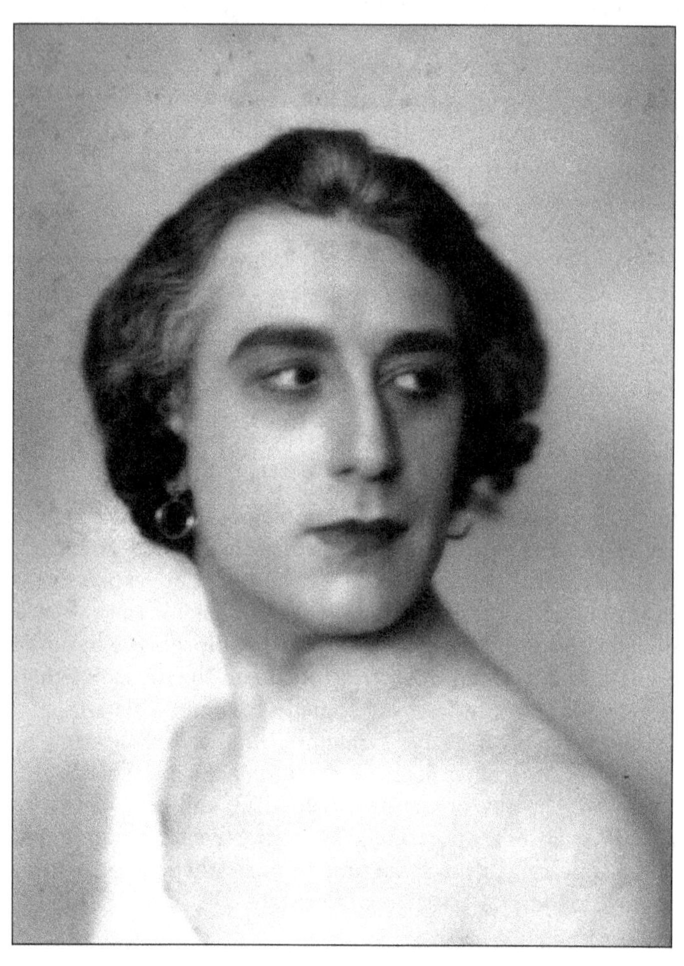

Director Abel Gance as Saint-Juste in his magnum opus,
Napoléon (1927).

La Roue
Arthur Lennig

The New York Film Festival of 1967 did not show only contemporary films. It also screened, with the cooperation of Henri Langlois of the Cinémathèque Française, a survey program of the works of Abel Gance, a filmmaker relatively unknown in the United States. Born in France in 1889, he began directing films during the First World War and completed his last feature in 1965. Unfortunately, the Museum of Modern Art Film Library and commercial distributors as well have never made available any of Gance's silent films—by far his greatest contribution—so that film critics as well as film buffs in general have suffered a large lacuna in their history.

Gance is one of those rare souls of the cinema: a man with a poetic sensibility, an intelligent grasp of theme and symbol, and a visually oriented technique as well. Sometimes the cinema offers directors who either can cut and group and light and stage fantastic sequences of little merit or who pay careful attention to theme but are not visually acute. Gance has both virtues, almost to the point of vice. In fact, he is somewhat of a madman. He enthusiastically throws everything into his work so that it seems an unholy alliance, an amalgam of Stroheim's naturalism, Griffith's poetry, Sjöström's use of landscape, and Eisenstein's montage. His visual style and his dramatic situations are "Grand," sometimes even purple, but, in spite of their exuberance and occasional tastelessness, a delight to any student of the screen.

For the most part Gance has received little critical recognition. Among his early works, his *La Dixième Symphonie*, a tale reeking of nineteenth-century romanticism and conventions of melodrama, is of some interest. Also almost entirely ignored is his *La Roue [The Wheel]*, which he began in 1919 and released in 1923. Running well over three hours (the print shown in New York at the film festival ran 2½ hours without titles and with some episodes missing), *La Roue* has many of the qualities of a nineteenth-century French novel and the length, alas, of a British one of the same period. The film, according to one of the rare comments on it, is "one of the monstrosities of the cinema, but an extraordinarily important monstrosity." (Bardeche and Brasillach, *The History of Motion Pictures*, p. 164.) The observation is astute. The film is long, occasionally tedious, but filled with poetic images and lyric passages, tragic moments and precise yet rapid editing far in advance of the usual production of the early twenties. In fact, it in many ways steals some of the thunder from Eisenstein and his fellow Soviet directors, for at moments the film is as full of montage as any Revolutionary epic.

The story of *La Roue* is both complicated and yet at the same time elementally simple. It is the naturalistic yet poetic and indeed tragic saga of a railroad engineer who rescues a child from a wreck, brings her up and, along with his own boy, eventually falls in love with her. Both are appalled by their attraction, and their attempt to work out their complicated emotions is the central subject of the film. Its other subject is not only the conflicting motives and torment of human tragedy but also the mechanical energy of railroading itself.

As *La Roue* begins, Gance's face appears on the screen staring at the camera and blinking slightly as double-exposed images of railroads move in the background. It says, in effect, here I am, a film master, and here is my vision. And a vision it is.

Gance is interested in energy, in the sheer naturalistic relationship between man and his machines. His preoccupation with signal switches, water-towers, steam and smoke places the story in time, in the industrial period, thereby giving it an amount of versimilitude which in a sense saves the film. It reinforces and extends what could well be a modern version of a Greek drama with all its curses, ironies, retributions, atonements, sufferings, *dei ex machina,* and elementality.

The film begins with a *tour de force* of editing: a train-wreck. Due to an open switch, one train plows into another: cars hurtle, people struggle and die, hands thrust themselves up from the litter of wreckage, smoke billows from the careened cars, a young woman appears hanging upside down, and men rush around trying to help. The whole scene has the intensity and pace of the Odessa Steps long before Eisenstein supposedly discovered montage. Off to the side of the wreck is a little girl. She is cross-cut with a flower, but an odd flower she will be. Beautiful but unconsciously and unwillingly deadly, this sweet girl will bring joy and then torment and, finally, tragedy to those who love her. The engineer takes the little orphan home, puts her in a crib with his own boy. The scene fades as the two children clutch each other.

Years pass. The son is now a violin maker who can also play and she is a beautiful Griffith-like maiden, all blonde and innocent. The two are very fond of each other, and in a fantasy sequence Gance shows them in a medieval setting, she as a princess strolling among formal gardens, and he as a prince serenading her on a stringed instrument. But the idyll fades to reality as they find themselves in the engineer's shack by the side of the tracks.

A rich man, and somewhat of a libertine as well, is attracted to her and finally speaks to the father. As the suitor is told of her past, Gance provides a reprise of rapid shots of the train wreck and of the engineer's saving her and bringing her home. She is shown in the garden and, as the father speaks, we see her cross-cut with a white rose. She appears in other scenes of innocence as well: seated at a well, talking to a bird—all reminiscent of nineteenth-century sentimentality but without Griffith-like coyness and mincing. Gance is perhaps extravagant and exaggerated here, but still not gauche. The girl may be a little one who is a dear, but she is not quite a Little Dear One.

The father, anxious he may lose her, tries to make himself appealing. He dresses up, combs his hair, and puts on a semblance of a suit, but she merely laughs at his different mode. It is a scene of extraordinary effect, creating a kind of *frisson.* This almost perverse, yet somehow noble, scene of the wooing of the daughter by the father is compounded when the father peers out through the window at her. She is on a swing. He stares at her black-stockinged legs and her high dress. Closing the window, he still can see through the glass. Finally he pulls down the curtain and then lifts it, again staring at her legs.

Soon after, Gance, with his always brilliant sense of the visual, contrasts a romantic shot of the boy and girl sitting in the window with a similar shot of the engineer and the rich man discussing the possibility of marriage. In despair of his loss, the father starts up his own locomotive and lies down on the tracks, but before he can kill himself, his friend interferes.

The father agrees (to save his own self from what could be an incestuous act) to let the girl marry the rich man. The brother bids her a sad farewell, leading the pet goat on a rope to the station. She boards the train on which her father is the engineer. Again feeling suicidal, he pushes the throttle full speed ahead. Intercut dials of the increasing speed, whirring

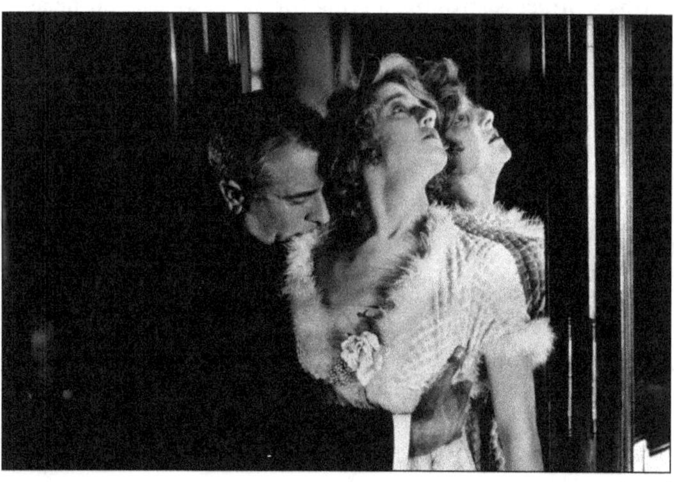

Writer-director Gance's silent railway extravaganza,
La Roue [The Wheel] (1923), with Pierre Magnier as Jacques
de Hersan, a wealthy cad who makes a loveless marriage with
Ivy Close as Norma. Orphaned in a train crash, she had been
adopted by a train engineer who works for Jacques.
(Films Abel Gance)

rails, the shaking of the carriages, the swift blurs of signals, his agonized face, add immeasurably to the effect. But the assistant turns down the throttle and the train pulls safely into the station.

Gance has made the locomotive and the whole railroading atmosphere a dynamic setting for his saga. But the locomotive too is a modern harbinger of tragedy, an agent of fate, bringing the girl to the man, taking her away, and eventually blinding him. It is, in short, the source of all his delights and troubles. The locomotive, then, is the modern means of destiny; it is God almost, controllable to some extent, but uncontrollable also.

The next scene shows her riding in her wedding carriage, it now all decked with flowers but more a hearse than a joyful vehicle. The boy is now home alone and one day looks amongst the family history and finds that she is not listed as his sister. The father explains, by means of flashbacks, and then a slow iris closes on the two unhappy men.

Fate continues its tragic progress. One day while the father works on a steam hole in the locomotive, the assistant falls momentarily asleep and shoots live steam into the man's eyes. Partially blinded, he is now ruined like the Oedipus of old by another engine of fate. The camera now becomes subjective and, in a series of out-of-focus and double-exposed shots, shows how the world looks to him.

Shortly after, the girl comes back to the house to see her father and brother, but is not greeted warmly, since both are afraid to be kind, so that they do not go too far.

The father, barely able to see, decides to kill himself and jumps upon the engine before his former assistant can interfere, and turns it on full speed. The engine roars into a bank of earth, strewing daisies across its front. The shot is poetic but a trifle gauche too, with all the daisies, but the father survives the crash. He is doomed to live.

Finally he and the boy move to the mountains in a small shack and there in a kind of exile (Oedipus at Colonus) try to live out their blighted lives. But there he cannot forget; her face still haunts him. Fate again intervenes. The daughter and the rich man go to a resort nearby, where the husband dies. Unfortunately, the boy accidentally slips down the side of a cliff and hangs onto a branch. A rapid montage of his life occurs before his grip loosens and he plummets to his death.

Two extraordinary episodes occur. She goes to the side of the cliff and throws, one by one, sprigs of flowers, a gesture romantic, extravagant, and yet emotionally compelling. Soon after, the father, almost blind, makes a wooden cross and, led by his limping dog, climbs the hill and erects the cross on the promontory. Here are Oedipus, Sisyphus, Prometheus and Christ combined. He wears a coat much like a robe, thus underlining the biblical overtones.

From here on the film becomes less controlled and more prolix, though relieved even at these wearisome moments by Gance's exasperating but fantastic imagination. The girl now lives with the father and is shown in a white vignette, with snow falling and melting on her long blonde hair, an angelic vision.

Gance then shifts to a circle of children dancing around a burning fir tree on the slopes of the mountains. The father sits at the window, a model locomotive in his hand, watching in his dim vision the children swirling in their celebration of life. Gance is too slow here, too reluctant to omit some shots, and so mutes his profound, almost cathartic point by overemphasizing it. Finally, after a number of other shots of the children walking on the ice, climbing, dancing, the old man drops the model locomotive and then his pipe. From behind him an open window looks out on the vista of superb mountains. As a cloud floats over the circle of children, he dies. Dense clouds fill the valley and over them appear the superimposed shots of the locomotive.

Gance mixed realistic, indeed almost documentary, shots of railroading with a theme broad and complex. That he could integrate these diverse materials at all is a tribute to his skill. But Gance is too rich, too full. Like von Stroheim, he could not stop, but continued to pack more and more in—or rather added more and more—and by so doing fantastically enriched but also debilitated his vision. The film is much too long; it is wearisome but at the same time dignified and poetic. A monstrosity but a beautiful one.

Napoléon
Arthur Lennig

Gance's *chef d'oeuvre, Napoléon,* appeared in 1927. This gigantic film, running over four hours, was originally intended to tell the whole life story of Napoleon. But Gance's fertile, grandiose and rather disproportioned imagination urged him on to further embellishment so that finally after a few years' work he could go only as far as the Italian campaigns. The script for the remainder of Napoleon's life was sold to another producer.

Gance was not content, however, to make his epic film in the usual way. Mechanically experimental, he decided that he could capture the sweep and splendor of his vision only by using three screens, thereby anticipating in some ways the three projectors of Cinerama. But unlike the American invention, Gance's process was not a mere gimmick, but an attempt to create a form appropriate to the content. Sometimes he used the triptych as one scene, but, we are told, he also broke it up so that Napoleon's face, for example, would be in the center while the two side panels would contain a long line of soldiers. Even in the one-screen version shown at the New York Film Festival, Gance's effects were still impressive, one of the few visual and ideological efforts in the Grand Style.

Napoléon is not the story of a man. It is the story of a God. And this story is brilliantly and reverently told. It has all the revolutionary fervor of Eisenstein's *October,* the tightly packed narrative of *The Birth of a Nation,* the grandiosity (not in sets but in content) of a *Siegfried,* the mystical

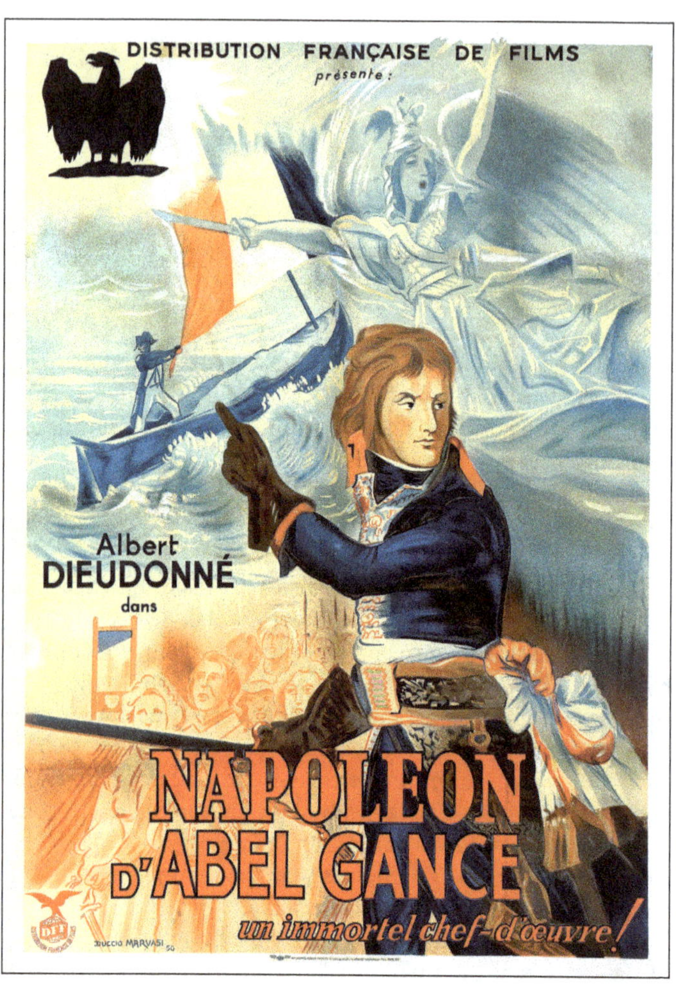

Original poster for Abel Gance's 1927 epic,
Napoléon (DFF/Gaumont–Metro-Goldwyn).

overtones of a Dreyer, and the powerful and audacious myth-making of a *Triumph of the Will.*

Gance's romantic nineteenth-century vision is not, however, the kind to appeal to an age enamored of the non-hero or antihero. Therefore the film fell oddly on the eyes of a New York audience which was in the process (at least in the American offerings) of seeing films debunking the establishment, decrying patriotism, and offering such dubious subjects as the unedifying spectacle of *Portrait of Jason.* Nor are the usual films in the commercial theaters much different. The main characters tend to be weak *(The Comedians),* dishonest *(The Fortune Cookie),* cowardly *(The Americanization of Emily),* aggressive and obnoxious *(The Blue Max),* or murderous *(Bonnie and Clyde).* The one trouble with *Napoléon*'s content can be summed up by the frequent hilarious reply of a foppish character in a Restoration play: "Sir, 'tis not the fashion."

Napoléon may be extravagant, exaggerated, overlong and overdone, and even ridiculous at times, but it has an inner strength, a belief. It creates Napoleon as a real hero, as a character of great strength and courage. The film does not debunk. It doesn't show the emperor with a stomach cramp or a pimple on his nose. It shows him as a man, an heroic man.

Gance was influenced by Beethoven—the musician was almost an obsession with him—and shares that composer's vision of what man is (a creature capable of deserving the somber chords of the Fifth Symphony without any mockery). Gance, too, shared Beethoven's vision of Napoleon (up until 1803 when Beethoven crossed out his dedication of the Third Symphony to the French leader). Beethoven may have lost faith, but not Gance. Man to Beethoven and to Gance was an heroic being caught in the web of his own mortality, but still striving to climb to the pinnacle.

Napoléon, then, is a portrait of the French leader done with the full instrumentation of an orchestra. Gance doesn't use a guitar strumming tunes of simple sorrow lamenting the end of an affair or the problems of inequality or the inequities of the class structure. Gance presents a picture of man created before the sociologists, penologists, psychiatrists and their ilk smashed the idol of man into smithereens, to become a mere victim of environment, unbalanced schools, and lack of mother love. Man here is still a full being, a potential hero, not mere mechanism: he is not a victim of every force and master of nothing.

The tenor of our times is such that if the same skill that Gance used were lavished on Al Capone, if we saw him stealing from a local grocery store and not winning snowball fights with brilliant tactical ability, if he rode in a bullet-proof car and not on a horse into Italy, if he hurried down a garbage-strewn alley and not across a stormy sea in a lone sailboat, if he were cross-cut with a man in the street and not an imperial eagle, the film would have been lavishly praised. But poor Gance made the mistake of "old-fashioned" thinking. He made no compromise with cynical modernity. Napoleon here is the master-planner, the brilliant tactician, the shrewd politician, the brave man motivated by only the highest impulse: the Glory of his country.

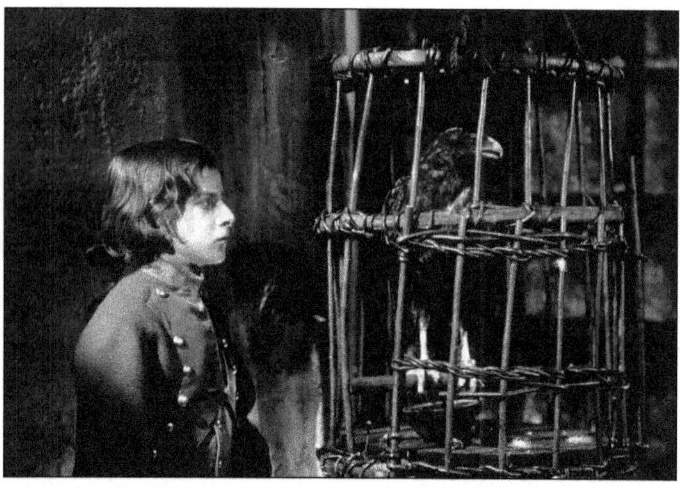

Vladimir Roudenko plays the young title character in Gance's *Napoléon*. The boy is contemplating a caged eagle that symbolizes his destiny as a conqueror and world leader as well as his ultimate downfall. (DFF/Gaumont–Metro-Goldwyn)

Not accident, but destiny pervades this film. Napoleon is often shown thinking about the future of the world. The first major instance shows him sitting in the mouth of a cave. There, with the mountains behind him and a broad vista before him, he muses. Later on, he stands upon a promontory and stares out across the sea. Waves break across the black rocks and then in a long shot he is shown with the afternoon sun's rays gleaming and enfolding his body in a splendor of luminosity.

The film's adulation of Napoleon reminds one of the moments in the Life of Our Lord; those picture books with Biblical text used at Sunday schools. But whereas many Biblical and so-called worshipful or patriotic films are almost always ridiculous, Gance's reverent attitude succeeds; his cosmic vision withstands the inroads of reality, mainly because of the vitality of his filmic techniques: his undoubted enthusiasm. He makes use of landscape, composition and movement to enhance and not detract from the primal importance of Napoleon, and creates a genuine mythos.

The beginning of the film, showing the young Napoleon at school, is indicative of Gance's method. Napoleon engages in a snowball fight with other children during a snowfall. With a moving, swirling and sometimes handheld camera, Gance captures the swirling flakes, the frantic action, the barrage of snowballs, the swarms of running children. An air of excitement, almost a newsreel quality, pervades the scene. The camera does not, however, as has been stated by some critics, become a snowball. As the fight continues, one of Napoleon's young enemies puts a stone in a snowball and hits him. Bleeding, the hero still fights on, a brilliant tactician even as a boy. As the fight ebbs and flows—all the boys with their three-cornered little hats—a shadow of the young Napoleon appears on the snow. The snowballs whiz back and forth, but the young leader remains: the young visionary in all his force. And this shadow stretches not only across the snow-covered field, but across the film, across history. One of the visitors to the school, having observed the boy's brilliant success, predicts he will go far.

Later, in the school room, the geography teacher is lecturing. The other boys are not paying attention, but Napoleon is, gathering up all the information that his shrewd and imaginative mind may someday use. Although the teacher makes some disparaging comments about Corsica, Napoleon praises his native land in his own copy book. Almost at the end of the lesson, the teacher announces that there is still another possession of France's: St. Helena. Napoleon writes the name in his book and then pauses, laying his plumed pen across the page. Such a moment—considering the outcome of history—is dramatically superb, though in actuality such a scene could not of course have happened. Napoleon may have been smart but he was no fortune teller. To the finicky admirer of the facts of history (or what Hitchcock refers to as a "plausible") such a scene may seem tremendously theatrical and "insincere," but if *Napoléon* is seen as the filming of a myth, as a "creative" rendition of a factual person, then this is one of its outstanding moments.

Shortly after, another episode reveals the curiously powerful dramatic powers of Gance. Napoleon keeps an eagle in a cage at school. Some of his schoolboy enemies release it. The bird flies away. Napoleon is irate and starts to fight with all the children because they have not told him who did it. As a result of his starting this fracas, the school authorities become angry at him: Who do you think you are, "you young scamp"? And he answers, "A man!" They lock him up in a chilly tower room. The boy sits on a large brass cannon. Outside, the eagle is seen perched in a branch, snow falling upon him. As the boy sits on the cannon, we can see the young leader, alone, high up in a tower by himself, the future master of the world. Although this shot would have been sufficient for most directors, Gance cannot leave this effective scene without adding more to it. And whereas in another director such an addition would be too much, would be hyperbole, somehow with Gance the scene succeeds. The eagle flies in the open turret window and lands on the cannon. And the audience has the privilege of seeing two eagles— Napoleon and bird—together.

Gance fills the film with passionately dramatic scenes. In the first part of the picture Napoleon visits an inn in Corsica. Some of the men in the tavern cry out that Corsica is Italy's, another that it is Spain's, another that it is England's, and then

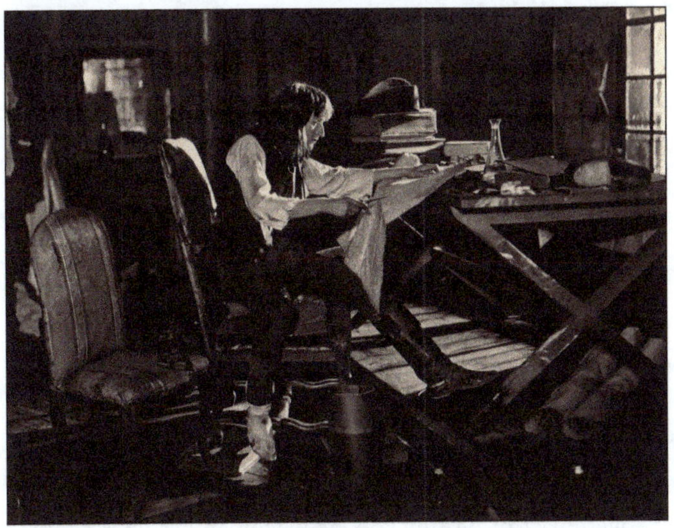

Albert Dieudonné, as the adult Napoleon working in his
study and contemplating his dreams of conquest.
(DFF/Gaumont–Metro-Goldwyn)

Napoleon stands up and says, "No, it is France's." The people
look at him in wonder. Suddenly a reward poster for Napoleon's life comes back into view. The men begin to attack him,
but he stares them down. The scene is certainly unlikely, for
an imperial look does not always hold back a cowardly crowd.
But Gance, unaffected by prosaic reality, audaciously cuts in a
shot of a splendid eagle. This scene captures the charisma that
the man must have had to have gone so far, from corporal to
emperor, in so short a time.

Shortly after, troops come to arrest him. Jumping on
his horse, he rides into town, climbs into the window of the
palace, takes the tri-color from the powers-that-be who are
in conference there, and tells them that they don't deserve the
flag. Pursued, he rides off to the sea, jumps in a sailboat, and
without sail hoists the tri-color and sails away against gigantic
waves, immense cloud banks, and the rays of the sun. It is
grand, almost unbelievable, but it works; it works magnifi-
cently.

Gance links Napoleon's stormy ride across the sea with the Paris convention. To add to the excitement he puts the camera on a swing and runs it back and forth in the hall, the faces rushing across the screen. Through cross-cutting, and then through superimposition of the waves of the ocean with the people, Gance creates a literal metaphor of a sea of faces. He shows that Napoleon governs not only the water but men and that soon he will be in control of both.

After arriving at Paris, Napoleon visits the deserted assembly rooms at nights alone. There in a series of visions he is offered power and says "Oui"; he gladly accepts the supreme rulership of France.

There are a few less grand moments. Napoleon meets Josephine and falls in love with her. But he just doesn't moon for her the way the average swain would do it. Instead we see her face superimposed over a globe of the world, as if she were part of destiny too, as if woman becomes another cosmic goal that must be won.

The film concludes with Napoleon's trip to Italy, where he in a short time transforms slovenly men into a fine fighting machine. Thousands of soldiers line up along the sides of the road to watch their leader ride through. One of the men says to his companions that he knew Napoleon at the boy's school (during the snowball fight days). As Napoleon comes by, the man takes a step forward and greets Napoleon by saying he knew him when. Napoleon orders the whole line of men one step forward and rides on. The implications are rich.

Like Griffith with his titles, Gance interlards the film with a number of captions labeled "Hist." for actual statements or actions out of history. But Gance has gone beyond facts. His film is essentially rhetorical; it is a kind of visual purple prose. In comparison to our age of understatement, Gance boldly bombards the eye with swirling movements, grandiose compositions and far-fetched characterization. At times all of this is too much, but at other times the style achieves the eloquence of a Shakespeare, as elaborate, complex and elevated as Elizabethan blank verse. Gance ascends "the brightest heights of invention" often enough to have made one of the most audacious of all silent films.

Vampyr
William Donnelly

Aware of their isolation, the Scandinavian countries developed a style of almost totally visual filmmaking and managed in the late Twenties and early Thirties to reach a world market. Sjöström, Stiller and Carl Theodor Dreyer are the best-known artists of this period. Dreyer wandered through Europe searching for backing for his uncompromising and highly original films. Acclaimed almost from the start as one of the world's greatest directors, Dreyer made films notable for their handling of light, acting and montage.

"With symbolism we are well on the way to abstraction, for symbolism works through suggestion." —Dreyer.

A highly self-conscious artist, Dreyer was not content to make a thriller. Drawing on many sources, notably the German *Nosferatu* (1922), he concentrated chiefly on the creation of a mood of the uncanny. Allan Gray (the descendant of Jonathan Harker in Bram Stoker's *Dracula,* the novel on which all early vampire films were based) is an English traveler in a strange country. A visitor in a country house, he has a strange experience in a nearby building: sees shadows cast by no one visible, and strange apparitions. After this experience the story itself begins. The daughter of an old man is being preyed on by a vampire. The girl's doctor is an accomplice of the vampire. Her father is killed by one of the vampire's shades. A servant sent for the police is brought back dead, drained of his blood. Gray witnesses these events with increasing horror. He is called on to donate blood for the girl. The girl recovers enough to menace a young servant. Gray and

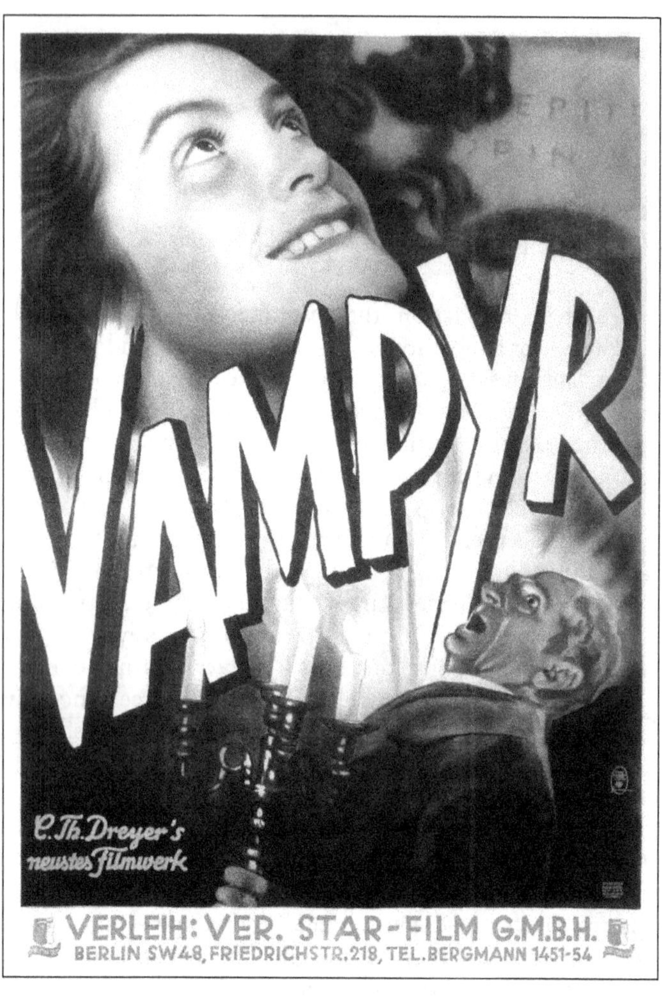

Original German poster for Danish director Carl Theodor Dreyer's avant-garde horror classic, *Vampyr*, which was released in three languages, German, French and Danish (1932). (Vereinigte Star-Film GmbH)

another servant, after a dream vision in which Gray sees himself buried, find the coffin of the vampire and drive a stake through his heart. This frees the daughter of her illness and incipient vampirism. The doctor, menaced by an apparition of the enraged vampire, flees to a flour mill where he is buried in sifting flour.

Poe-like in its unreality to begin with, the story simply transpires without the standard literary devices of introductions of characters and explanations of relationships. Dreyer's main interest is the present and mood, not the unfolding of a story. His establishing shots are brief and fragmentary. He cuts away from important events without explanation after we have caught only a glimpse of something disturbing. Recurrent motifs, shots reiterated without explanation (a weathervane, a shot of a man pitching hay run in reverse) interrupt the action for symbolic rather than expository reasons.

Critics are wrong to insist that the film eschews the supernatural. The giant raging face of the specter of the stricken vampire at the doctor's window scarcely falls within the realm of the natural, nor does murder by a rifle fired by a shadow, disappearance, or bilocation of the hero. What the critics are trying to convey is that the atmosphere of the unnatural is so thoroughly established that the supernatural occurrences seem quite plausible. This film does not set up the dichotomy between the natural and the supernatural that so many horror films have attempted. This dichotomy attempts to explain supernatural events in naturalistic terms. (Remember Peter Cushing dictating his notes on the theory of vampirism into his dictaphone, the most absurd moment in *Horror of Dracula?*) What if a film does succeed in convincing us vampires could exist in a rational world? The film is no longer horrible. Dreyer solves this problem by giving us a world that is strange and fantastic from the start. Rhythm, characterization, order of shots, all are beautiful but strange.

Of all the artistic media, the film most nearly resembles the dream. And the best films often resemble dreams in their flexible handling of time, their ability to give strange emphases to familiar events, their oneiric freedom in changing scene. Indeed, the film's power to mimic the dream is so potent that films which do not share major aspects of the dream—wish-

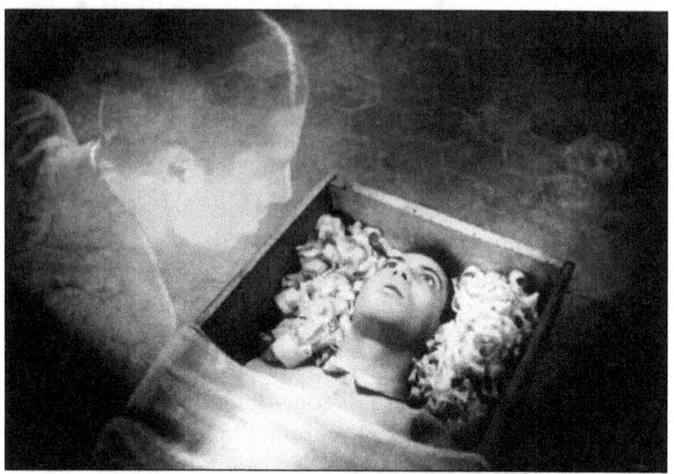

In Dreyer's *Vampyr*, Allan Gray (Julian West) is a student of the
occult whose fascination with vampires leads to strange experiences
when he journeys to a French village. Allan has a vision of himself
in a coffin; the film's subtitle is *Der Traum des Allan Gray/
The Dream of Allan Gray*. The nonprofessional actor, whose real
name was Baron Nicolas de Gunzburg, was a French-born member
of Russian nobility who later edited American fashion magazines.
He financed *Vampyr* in return for playing the lead role.
(Vereinigte Star-Film GmbH)

fulfillment, displacement, distortion—affect us as curiously
flat and disappointing. (Documentary filmmakers are simply
unable to cope with this inherent difficulty.)

Certainly *Vampyr* is not a perfect film. It is a self-conscious, "arty," incoherent, poorly-plotted failure, more a
series of impressive and evocative shots than a solidly-struc-
tured work of art. This much any viewer old enough to toddle
into the theater can see immediately. But we live in an age in
which the cinema is still much influenced by literature, and
we are accustomed to, and insistent upon, carefully plotted
"stories." It may be that we will outgrow this narrowness,
and that film will move into richer modes more hospitable
to its strengths. Despite its flaws, *Vampyr* is a valuable film
because as a piece of cinematic expressiveness it is still decades
ahead of James Bond. Viewed as cinematic experimentation,

as an exploration of the visual and psychological possibilities of film, *Vampyr* is not in the same league with any other horror film except, perhaps, *Repulsion*. Look at the distance Hitchcock has gotten out of a handful of the techniques Dreyer has exploited in this film.

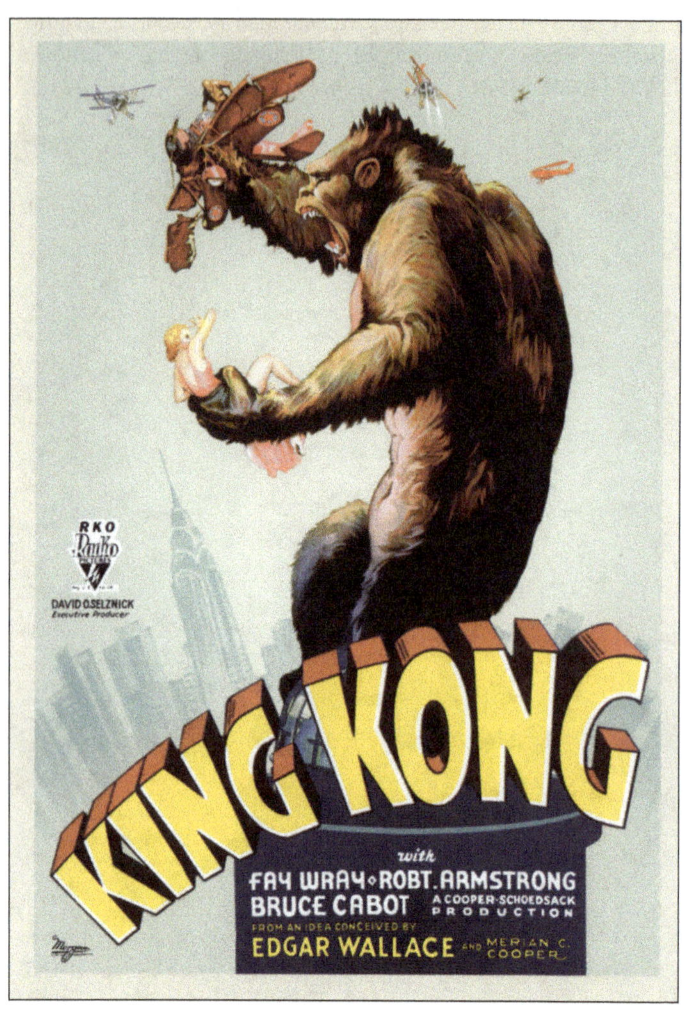

This original poster for the 1933 classic *King Kong* plays into the horror aspects of the film rather than the side of Kong that is appealing and makes him a figure of tragic pity. Audiences responded equally to both sides of the compelling character. (RKO)

Narrative, Fable and Dream in *King Kong*
R. C. Dale

The story of beauty and the beast is timeless. In antiquity it appears in many different forms, probably the most famous of which is the confrontation of Odysseus and Circe. Odysseus was wiser than his men: he resisted Circe's charms because he shared the common contemporary knowledge that witches had the power to enervate and destroy their lovers by secretly drawing off their blood in little bladders (according to Robert Graves, almost everybody knew that). But many other heroes fared less well, if we may trust the parabolic annals of antiquity, the Middle Ages and the Renaissance. One of the definitive victories of beauty, and the definitive version of the story, came from the eighteenth century: Mme. de Beaumont's fairy-tale called *La Belle et la Bête*. Eighteenth-century fairy-tales were closely allied to the popular form known as philosophical and moral (i.e., having to do with mores, manners) stories, thinly disguised fables with extremely clear messages. This whole tradition indulged itself in exoticism, eroticism, satire and social commentary. It eventually contributed a great deal to the later genre of the Gothic novel, which emphasized the first two of those characteristics and played down the others completely. *King Kong,* like its progenitors, the eighteenth-century fairy-tale and the Gothic novel, and like its sister, the horror film, is rich in implication and imagination.

Somehow, despite the fantastic goings-on in which the film abounds, it succeeds in casting a rare spell over most of its viewers, a spell somewhat similar to that created by the best of the Gothic novels, such as Lewis's *The Monk*. The film manages to bypass the critical, censorious level of the viewer's consciousness and to secure his suspension of disbelief with what appears to be great ease. A number of French critics have attributed this phenomenon to what they call the film's oneiric qualities, its pervasive dream-like control of some subconscious, uncritical part of the mind. Indeed, it does succeed in dreaming for us, and we are swept along with the dream as helpless spectators, as if the dream were our own. Every viewer's reaction is obviously his own, but few can resist completely the involvement that the picture offers. Most film estheticians agree that this oneiric involvement is inherent to cinema, but rarely so well established as in the case of *Kong*. It may seem odd that a film based on patently fantastic happenings should succeed so well where many films based in conventional reality fail. There are a number of factors to explain this odd circumstance. First of all, *Kong* has a basic cinematic subject, an almost completely visual appeal as far as the action is concerned. Almost half of the film has no dialogue; instead, it builds suspense and involvement with emotion-reinforcing music. The special effects are extraordinarily well-handled. We recognize the animals as miniature models animated by means of stop-motion photography, but we allow ourselves to be deceived by them almost immediately. The fact that a brontosaurus, as a vegetarian, shouldn't really be chasing after meat, may flicker across our minds as we watch the action, but that logical objection is soon quelled by the struggle on the screen: the action never fails to fascinate. But probably the most important reasons for the film's success at capturing us as spectators are that it carefully establishes a reality of its own; it employs extensive use of archetypal myth imagery that appeals directly to our subconscious, and it uses an extremely effective narrative approach to its subject.

To facilitate leading us into its fantastic reality, the picture presents us with a classically simple narrative structure. It has a brief prologue, an introductory part set in New York and on the high seas; a second, crucial, part set on Skull Island, home of Kong; and a conclusion that returns us to the original locale. The narrator secures our good will by setting the beginning of his tale in familiar surroundings—the docks of a great city. He then specifies the time—the present, 1933, the height of the Depression. As he sets the scene, he also economically presents the principal characters. They are introduced to us without any editorial qualification expressed through angular viewing, exceptional cutting, or music.

We recognize Carl Denham as the central character in this section (and presumably in the film, although that is not to be the case) through the simple narrative principle of concentration, of following. Denham reveals himself as a strong, independent, masculine character who knows what he wants and who is used to getting it.

What does he want this time? asks the reporter with whom we have sympathetically boarded the ship for an interview. The narrator knows that we won't resist an interrogative identification with the reporter in a situation like this. Thus Denham isn't just talking to people, he's answering our question; and we are pulled into the interview.

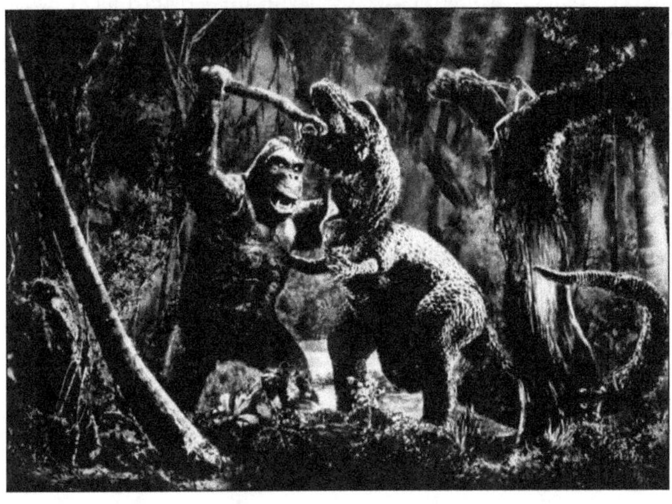

Kong does battle with a Tyrannosaurus rex in *King Kong* (1933) to save Ann (Fay Wray) while she sits helpless in the crotch of a tree. Directed and produced by Merian C. Cooper and Ernest B. Schoedsack, from a script by James Creelman and Ruth Rose based on an idea by Edgar Wallace and Cooper, *King Kong* has still-impressive special effects by Willis H. O'Brien. (RKO)

He wants to find a woman to go off somewhere (he's not saying where) with that odd, oversized crew on a vessel with enough explosives aboard to blow up the harbor. But why does he want her? Not because he likes women. "Do you think I wanna haul a girl around?" But he needs her. "I'm going out and find a girl for my picture, even if I hafta marry one."

The narrator cuts to women standing in a breadline, then to a girl standing, hesitating before a fruit stand. She reaches to steal an apple, but the owner rushes out and grabs her. Denham intercedes, takes her to a restaurant, restores her with food, and offers her the part in his picture. He tells her that he isn't bothering about her out of kindness or sexual interest in her, but can offer her "money, fame, the thrill of a lifetime, and a long sea voyage that starts at six in the morning."

The narrator has succeeded in provoking our curiosity and our interest by making Denham into a man of mystery and intrigue, but nonetheless a perfectly believable one. Like all the great creators of fantastic narrations—Mérimée, Lewis, Hoffmann—Cooper and Schoedsack lead us slowly and credibly away from reality. So far, they have centered our interest on Denham and his mysterious quest almost entirely through his own verbalization.

In the following section of the introductory part, the camera joins the microphone to intensify the mystery and to suggest without overt statement that we are slowly leaving behind civilization and the known. The photography becomes more muted and less obviously studio-shot, values of grey begin to appear, the lighting loses the uniformity of the soundstage. The ship enters a fogbank as barrier after barrier closes between the crew and civilization. They pass through a reef that forms another gate into the unknown, and finally reach the point of primitive isolation that is their goal.

Before we get into the great battle that forms the central part of the film, let us turn from narration to subject—to what is being narrated. The narrator, we remember, has been very careful to lead us slyly into his own world. He is equally sly when it comes to confiding in us what he really intends to discuss in this film. He tells us straight off, in the title card that precedes the first part, that we're going to see a story involving beauty and the beast. The card bears a putative Old Arabian Proverb that proclaims: "And lo, the beast looked upon the face of beauty, and it stayed its hand from killing. And from that day, it was as one dead."

Denham reiterates this apparent subject on numerous occasions during the first part of the picture. As they are sailing off into the unknown, he sees Ann with a little monkey, in a sort of prefigurative situation, and remarks: "Beauty and the beast, eh? If beauty gets you… that's the idea of my picture. The beast was a tough guy, too. He could lick the world. But when he saw beauty, she got him; he went soft, he forgot his wisdom… and the little guys got him."

Shortly after he utters those words, we get a glimpse of him directing Ann in a screen test aboard ship. She appears in an extremely diaphanous gown, the picture of fragility and femininity, submitting unquestioningly to his orders. He tells her to look up, higher, higher, until she sees something horrible, so horrible that it petrifies her. "You're helpless, Ann helpless. If you could scream—but you can't." At this point, certain peculiarities about Denham become pretty pronounced.

Denham, the apparent protagonist in the film, is very eager to obtain a girl—any girl—for his picture. He would marry one if he had to, and the marriage would presumably have no other purpose whatever. He picks a girl almost at random from the streets, a girl whose weakened condition and circumstances attract his attention. He photographs her entirely as an object and, in great eagerness to get right down to business, shoots her as she is about to be abducted by something monstrous, dangerous and undefined. Denham, as a master voyeur, is conducting an experiment in which he will be a recording observer—not an active participant. He has obtained a random example of femininity and now he intends to expose it to a vague, mysterious example of brute masculinity.

So much for Denham, the voyeur not interested in participating directly in courting and sex, who prefers to get his kicks vicariously and immaculately. But what of the narrator? Does he have any particular feelings about all this? Does he participate in this objectification and degradation of woman?

The answer, of course, is an unqualified yes. To begin with, he implicitly states his distrust of woman in the opening title (for which Denham can in no way be held responsible). Then he chooses to depict a breadline peopled exclusively by woman, suggesting their debilitated position in the effete American culture. Only by getting away from it, he further suggests, can masculinity have its day. In the last part of the film, back in New York, it is women who drag their reluctant husbands off to see the captive, figuratively castrated Kong. The narrator continually informs the picture with his own particular brand of misogyny. Between him and Denham, the film holds the almost total and certainly pervasive conviction that woman, like Circe, incapacitates man.

The complicity in outlook between the two runs the course of the picture, but there is a greater separation between the narrator and Denham in the first than in the subsequent parts, especially the central part. In the first part, the narrator observes Denham making his voyeuristic preparations and draws our attention as fellow witnesses. He also notes such details as the three crew members lined up vertically and rather phallically on a ship's ladder grinning expectantly at Ann as she does her stuff for the screen test. (By the way, that shot forms a very rare—perhaps even unique—example in this part of the phallic imagery that completely dominates the remaining parts of the film; it appears, significantly enough, exactly when overt voyeurism occurs onscreen.) In the first part, we consciously observe Denham laying his plans. Indeed, the narrator leads us deftly into the fantastic world of Skull Island by postponing visualization of it even after we have arrived there. As we peer over Denham's shoulder at the map of the island, we slowly become aware of the faint throbbing of drums in the distance. Then we rush to the deck to peer at indistinct forms in the far-off native village as Max Steiner's music sneaks in to increase our wonder and excitement.

The next day, we scan the beach and find it empty. Again, there is nothing tangible for us to reject, so we go along with the narrator. The music gets spookier as a landing party reaches shore. Amidst the sounds of drums and chanting, Denham suddenly stops, a look of excitement and wonder on his face. Only at this point does the narrator let us have a look at what is going on: the natives' ritual Kong dance. Although the dance itself is a bit on the silly side, the narrator doesn't allow us much time to think about it. Instead, he cuts back to Denham, who pushes aside some fronds and peeks through them at the dance. "Holy mackerel, what a show! If only I could get pictures before they see us." Thus the narrator again insists on Denham's voyeurism by forcing us to observe him rather than the action he is watching. The narrator is waiting for the right moment, the moment when he can get rid of Denham and make us take his place as direct witnesses of the action. The sequence also serves structurally as yet another prefiguration of things to come by showing us the natives practicing ritual sacrifice of a young maiden to the dangerous threatening force that they must keep locked out of their small society: the monster gorilla that inhabits Skull Mountain. The narrator thus implies without direct statement a sort of analogical extension of Denham's personal voyeur-istic inhibitions: society, no matter how primitive, must wall out the bestial impulse that Kong represents or be destroyed by it. Libido, the passionate and uncontrolled inhabitant of a mountain in the form of a giant skull, must be contained or society will perish.

The native chief reinforces Denham's recognition of Ann's sexuality. He offers to trade him six of his women for Ann, the "golden woman." Such a woman, he implicitly reckons, would keep Kong satisfied and out of the village for a good time. Denham, of course, won't accept the offer. After all, he is a gentleman. Or is that indeed the reason? It is interesting to note that the plot takes an important but almost imper-ceptible turn at this juncture. If we remember that the chief is proposing in effect to set up Denham's projected situation for him, we might wonder why Denham displays no interest at all in making some sort of deal with him about Ann. The reasons have to do more with narrative effectiveness than with demonstrating Denham's consideration for Ann.

But let us return with the narrator to the ship. On board after their visit to the island, Jack declares his love to Ann, and they kiss. Love-making scenes quite naturally bring out the voyeur in all of us, and this is the first moment in the film when we have actually been cast in that role. Up until now, Denham—in his mind, at least—has been doing that for us and we have been watching him do it for us. But now we are doing the observing without any intermediary other than the narrator, who keeps us at it for the next hour of nonstop involvement.

In order to do this, he must remove Ann from Denham's control, the control that a cautious man or a cautious society feels must exist over beauty or woman or the object of the libido. So the natives slip aboard ship, steal her off and take her ashore, up to the great gate leading into the land of unsuppressed desire. They chain her in an erotic crucifixion to two sinewy phallic stakes, and beat the gong that summons Kong to claim his sacrifice. The huge gate ponderously swings shut behind Ann, left alone and helpless in the land of the giant skull. The transition from reality to dream, from judgment to belief, from casual observer to vicarious participator on the part of the viewer has just been effected with consummate skill by the narrator. From here on, we are in the land of the libidinous dream, where everything is erotic in shape and in meaning. The great gate, for example, underwent one obvious and important modification for this film: when it was first built, for the Babylon sequences in *Intolerance*, it was closed by means of a huge gear system. In *Kong*, the gears are gone, replaced by a gigantic beam that slides across its front, slowly penetrating hoop after hoop in the gate and retaining wall.

The music begins to race, we hear a few tremendous growls, and Kong makes his appearance. The narrator cuts almost directly into an ECU of his eyes, as he leers lasciviously at Ann. Kong's intentions are obvious. He beats his breast and picks up Ann. Jack runs up, sees what's happening, and immediately takes over the situation. He leads the men into the jungle, admonishing them, "C'mon, fellas, and keep those guns cocked."

But what has become of Denham since the role of antagonist clearly has shifted to Kong? Despite his precautions for staying clear of the action, he is swept up into it. He loses the desired control of the situation, becoming involved in the necessity for rescuing Ann, which he soon gives up as hopeless without outside help. Kong is the realization of his wildest dreams, but Kong is too much for Denham, who loses control and flees, abandoning the viewer to his own fate. The audience replaces Denham as the voyeur in a situation that has got out of control, in a situation involving no more control than a dream. Denham dematerializes because of his very superfluity.

Thus the narrator has effectively involved the viewer, who is now immersed in his erotic dream. Every form assumes a strongly suggestive shape; a brontosaurus pricks his long, slithery neck above the surface of a swampy lake; Kong does battle with a cocky Tyrannosaurus rex, a huge snake, and finally a pterodactyl. He also battles members of the crew, who find themselves caught straddling a colossal log spanning a chasm. They hold onto the log for dear life, but Kong shakes them loose, one by one, and they hurtle screaming to the floor of the chasm and their destruction. To detail all the sexual imagery in this part of the film would amount to talking about something in practically every shot. The narrator has absolutely plunged us into his completely consistent and convincing dream. We are carried along by it without protest, no matter how extravagant it becomes, no matter how obvious the animation and rear-screening, no matter how showoffish the cross-cutting between various actions and locales; we are carried along because the narrator insists so pervasively on its inner reality that we simply cannot extricate ourselves from it.

During this part of the film, there is an absolute coincidence of dream symbolism and surface-level plot: each action builds suspense by delaying gratification of the beast's desires. As we advance deeper and deeper into the weird, wild landscape, over and beyond chasms, lakes, rivers, swamps, through thick banks of fog, farther and farther from the familiarity and security of civilization and exterior reality, we see that Kong is indomitable in his own territory. After each progressively briefer and more intense encounter, he beats his breast and bellows his defiance to the world. When finally he leads Ann up through his cave at the top of Skull Mountain and out an opening that forms the skull's eye socket, we know that the moment has come when the natural king of the natural world is about to take his natural prize—and we don't care how impractical that may be. He picks up Ann in his immense paw, leers most lasciviously indeed, and then slowly undresses her (the last part of this scene did not survive the censors' shears for long [it was later restored—Ed.]).

But a moment later it's all over for Kong. A pterodactyl distracts him as Jack and Ann escape by jumping into the lake far below. The narrator goes underwater to show them swimming together toward the surface. Kong's days as a would-be rapist are over; Jack and Ann have just been through ritual fertilization by water together.

Kong pursues them, eventually shattering the huge phallic bolt that is meant to keep him in his own element. With that symbolic act of castration, he bursts into civilization and his downfall.

Denham fells him with gas, an unnatural and thereby unfair weapon devised by civilization, then he brings him back to civilization itself, to be gawked at by the feckless crowd. The narrator returns us to our former roles as observers of observers, resuming the misogynic attitude he displayed in the

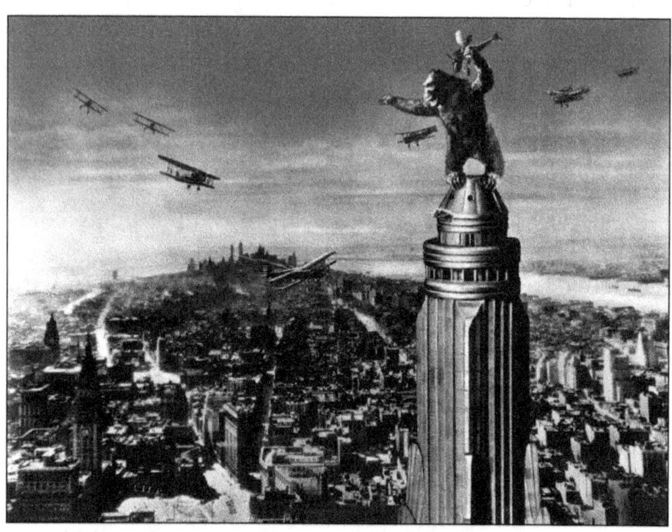

Kong on top of the world, trying to escape captivity before his tragic fall from New York's Empire State Building. (RKO)

first part. Kong, out of his element, is clearly intended to be the pathetic object of our sympathy. At no earlier point in the film has the narrator asked such indulgence for one of his characters. He certainly did not ask us to sympathize with Ann when she was at bay in Kong's world, but when the situation is exactly reversed and it is Kong's turn to be crucified, we see by comparison exactly how misogynic the picture actually is. In order to demonstrate the hopelessness of Kong's plight when he is in an unnatural realm, the narrator reenacts the high points of the chase on the island. Now Kong derails an elevated train that resembles the snake he conquered on the island; again he carries Ann up to an eyrie at the top of the world. But this mountain is not the skull bursting with libido; it is the symbol of restraint and control, the tallest man-made structure in the world, a tremendous lifeless monument whose very shape mocks its function. This time he does not bellow his victory, and he cannot overwhelm the airplanes as he did the pterodactyl in his own realm. He manages to knock off a few of them, but eventually their unnatural bullets penetrate his chest and he knows that he will die. He picks Ann up one final time, contemplates her, gently sets her down, and falls about as far to his death as any symbolic sex dream has ever had its dreamer fall.

The narrative in this last part has interspersed the techniques of each of the first two parts—conscious observation and dream. The narrator has felt no constraint to limit himself to either of the modes, since he has prepared us by now to accept both of them. But we cannot help noticing which mode he uses to end the picture: the crowd, panic-stricken shortly before, now mills about curiously to have a good look at civilization's victim. Denham, again master of the situation, becomes his brash, exploitive self. "Oh, no," he explains to the onlookers, "it wasn't the airplanes; it was beauty killed the beast." And the last shot in the film shows us Denham standing before Kong's lifeless body. He looks at him with contemplation written on his face—and his hands in his pockets.

Civilization has had its show, but not quite the one that Denham had set out to give them. He—and they—thought that it would be passive amusement, movieland, harmless voyeurism. But it turned out to be more than that for them: it turned out to be a participating, enthralling, engaging experience that threatened to destroy their protected, circumscribed, civilized existences. Nonetheless, civilization has managed to triumph once again over the impulses of the unrestrained libido.

And we, thanks to an unparalleled brilliance of narrative technique, have been through it all. Furthermore, thanks to the intricate interplay of narrative, we understand at the end of the film—while society does not—that civilization and its obvious representative, Denham, are the real culprits in this tale: they who would meddle with natural forces, who would entice them, deny them, remove them from their rightful contexts, and then destroy them in the name of preserving civilization.

No other fantastic film has ever even approached *King Kong* in overall effectiveness. Many have borrowed principles and have copied ideas, but no director has ever managed again to combine symmetry of plot, imagery, drama and narration so well as the men—the unrecognized and uncelebrated Cooper and Schoedsack—who put together this archetypal masterpiece of fantasy.

Footlight Parade
Joseph McBride

> A great part of my work has not been the work of a choreographer strictly speaking, because, for me, if I dare to say it, it is the camera that must dance.
>
> Busby Berkeley

Busby Berkeley's prolificacy in the Thirties was due largely to his collaboration with other directors; in only a few films did he also direct the story scenes. Usually he had a shoddy framework for his wonderful production numbers. *Gold Diggers of 1933*, perhaps his most famous film, is burdened with a so-so story only partially enlivened by Mervyn LeRoy's direction. But *Footlight Parade*, released later the same year, is different. James Cagney is cast as an obvious Berkeley figure, the director of stage "prologues." The other characters and the Warners' backstage plot are satirized; Berkeley appears to have worked in close harmony with Lloyd Bacon in planning the story scenes.

The structure fits the satirical attitude: there is but one production number, and that on a small scale, in the first half of the picture; in the second half there are three, each literally within seconds of the other. The girls in Cagney's troupe change in their bus as it speeds through town, siren blaring, from theater to theater to theater. The Berkeley trademark of a curtain opening on an impossibly huge "stage" number never fit the story's tone so well, and hence was never so amusing.

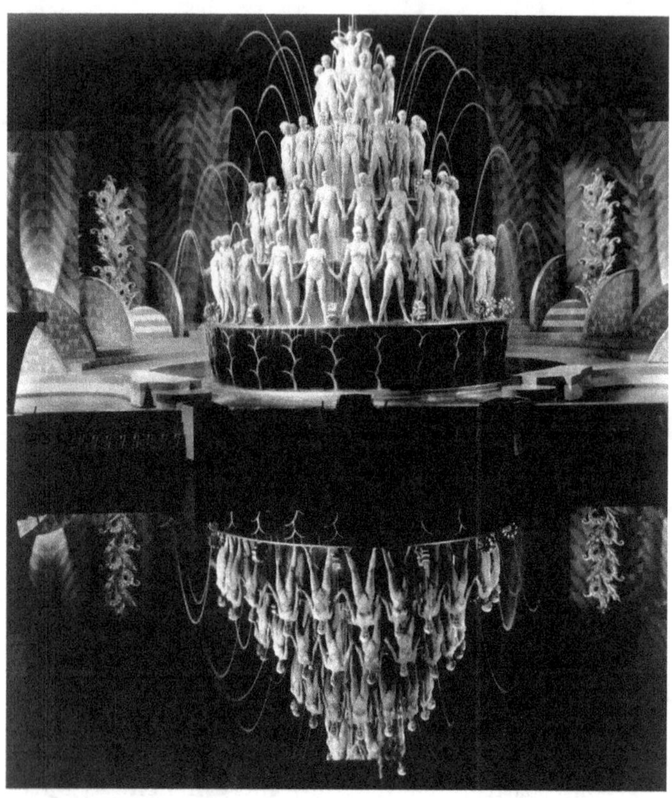

The "By a Waterfall" number in *Footlight Parade* (1933) is perhaps
the most extravagant of musical director Busby Berkeley's many
lavish and outlandish numbers that jocularly belied their conceit of
being mounted on a stage. (Warner Bros.)

The style of the story falls into several patterns. The money
problem, as in the *Gold Diggers* series, provides the dramatic
impetus. The film opens with Cagney learning that talking
pictures are forcing small-scale stage shows out of business,
and that the only solution is to travel with a large production. "Instead of forty people our musicals will have eighty!"
he says in a quintessential Berkeley statement. Cagney (as
Chester Kent) is having trouble keeping solvent; he gambles
on super-productions, and finally wins. (Berkeley's musicals
were Warners' gamble which brought that company out of its

near-fatal Depression slump.) Cagney/Berkeley bursts comically with ideas; the slightest hint sends him into a tap-dance illustrating a doctor-nurse routine, a cat he finds on the street inspires him to a "pussycat-tomcat" number, and even a coffee pot sends him into creative ecstacy: "Say, how about a great big coffee pot... the boys come out, the girls come out—and the audience goes out." Telephones are always ringing, the financiers are always nearby, his wife is divorcing him, a gold digger bilking him and his secretary (Joan Blondell) pursuing him. Berkeley's self-parody is comparable to Fellini's in *8½*. He even plays a part in the film—as the dance director who says he can't use Dick Powell.

Powell this time is not a starving songwriter but a sponge in the keep of a Margaret Dumont-like matron. Ruby Keeler begins as a schoolmarmish secretary, but winds up as the star of the show when she has her hair redone. Gone is the tartness of Aline MacMahon, replaced by the idiocy of a mutinous stage manager, an effete censor, and the snobbish, phony gold digger. The show is in extreme confusion, the dancers always rehearsing, Cagney always trotting around the building as only Cagney could trot. The soft-shoe routines he does during rehearsal and in the "Shanghai Lil" number take humorous advantage of his peculiarly stiffened shoulders and back.

The odd amalgam of stage and screen common to the early Thirties and exploited in the hardboiled films of Howard Hawks, Raoul Walsh and Michael Curtiz is here at its most taut: cuts always seem to come on lines of dialogue, ringing telephones, opening doors or people walking into the frame. The camera follows the characters around the room— they always walk *fast*—and the talk seems to consist largely of commands. Lewis Milestone was one of the first American directors to grasp this method of turning dialogue into action, in his 1931 *The Front Page;* he hit on the simple device of having the characters talk as rapidly as possible. In Walsh's *The Roaring Twenties* (1939), much of the excitement comes from the way the camera moves around with Bogart and Cagney as they talk. Hawks and, later, Orson Welles further developed styles of overlapping dialogue.

Footlight Parade abounds in wipes, up, down, sideways and of the windshield-wiper variety; the wipe, oddly enough, has much the same effect as a rapidly opening door. The wipe underscores the rapidity of the film's constant shifting from rehearsal scenes (there's always a chorus line going) to confrontations in the halls and offices. The wisecracking, insulting dialogue common to the gangster genre and here at its fastest pace was turned to great advantage in the verbal slapstick of the Marx Brothers and Preston Sturges. This style added immensely to the flavor of the gangster and backstage films, which by nature had to spend much of their time indoors. A gangster movie with slow, deliberately delivered lines and slow camera movements *(The Public Enemy)* seems almost to betray the style of its genre. "My camera moved all the time," Berkeley said recently. "For me that's the meaning of the expression 'motion picture.' It's images in movement." Berkeley liberated the moving camera from its basis of dialogue and counterpointed his images with music and singing, developing with Clair, Hitchcock, Renoir, Mamoulian and Vidor (and others) the authentic uses of sound film. He learned early that "the camera is the only spectator," and created strangely beautiful fantasies. Berkeley is a man of pure spectacle, or, if you will, abstraction.

Placing the short "Sittin' on a Backyard Fence" number early in the film whets the audience's taste for the larger numbers which bring the film to a close. "Backyard Fence," done on a small set with a small number of girls, is necessary for balance: with all the numbers at the end, the film would seem like two pictures spliced together. The expressionism of this number (slanted *Caligari*-like buildings, giant milk bottles, cat costumes, a painted Moon) foreshadows the unrestrained fantasy of the later numbers. Another Berkeley/ Bacon device prepares the audience for the last half hour: story scenes are played under music to be used later in the production numbers. Cagney plays "Shanghai Lil" at the piano while trying to think of ideas for the show, and the same music is played by the strings when he puts his arm around Joan Blondell. "Honeymoon Hotel" plays under Blondell's return to her apartment—but when the snobbish Miss Rich enters, the music shifts to the melancholic "Shanghai Lil." Powell teasing

Keeler is accompanied ironically with "By a Waterfall," and Blondell is wearing a "Shanghai Lil" sailor suit when Cagney reels in drunk with Miss Rich. This imaginative structural device helps greatly in uniting story with spectacle.

The three big production numbers take place at the Jupiter, Mercury and Diana Theaters—Cagney says, "Looks like we're in the laps of the Greek gods"—a humorous tribute by Berkeley to the classical influences on his style, most clearly seen in the "Waterfall" number, shifting geometric images of swimming wood nymphs. John Thomas, in an excellent article on Berkeley ("The Machineries of Joy," *Film Society Review,* February 1967) points out that Jung considered the whorl pattern, or mandala, the basic integrating image within the human psyche. Thomas argues that Berkeley's variations on this pattern account for much of the appeal of his style, reflecting "an age so disorganized that mechanization could be seen as a desirable goal," and at the same time set his limitations. Berkeley shows in the first big number, "Honeymoon Hotel," that his style was based just as much on straight-line patterns, the style, in fact, of the tracking shot. "By a Waterfall," the most lavish of all his numbers and the one he found the most difficult to create, mixes whorls with shifting patterns of straight lines (one of the most characteristic is that of a row of girls appearing one by one in front of the camera, here static but in *Gold Diggers of 1933* moving). The final number, "Shanghai Lil," is again largely diagonal, starting with a long trucking shot of Cagney and climaxing with crane shots of marching soldiers, another image germane to Berkeley's style. "Honeymoon Hotel" emphasizes faces and is, naturally, more intimate than the other two in its odd comic-strip way; "Waterfall" is dreamlike abstraction of movement; "Shanghai Lil" begins slowly with faces speaking and singing in succession and builds to a rousing martial climax louder and more dynamic than anything in the previous two numbers.

After the long trucking shot along the street with Powell and Keeler's feet as they approach the Honeymoon Hotel and start to sing, the scene changes to a series of panning closeups of the hotel workers singing rather scabrously about their duties, from the leering doorman to the boy who brings the "cider" to the house dicks who wonder why everyone's name is Smith. The fast rhythm of the music makes the syncopated walking of the couple and the maid seem almost balletic, as is the motion of the pairs of husbands marching into the washrooms and the long lines of hands pulling them into the boudoirs—and the hands hanging out "Do Not Disturb" signs. Berkeley has marvelous fun with the symmetry of the hall, climaxing the pattern with a shot of the entire set (two floors) seen in cutaway. The number ends directly with a pan from Powell and Keeler in bed to a magazine next to the window blowing open to a picture of a baby. This is the funniest of the numbers and the quickest, a sort of teaser for the more lyrical ones to follow.

"If this doesn't get 'em, nothing will," Cagney whispers at the start of "By a Waterfall." Berkeley recalls, "The day I had the idea, I let Jack Warner know about it and he told me I would ruin even the Bank of America." This incredible number, one of the most ambitious in the history of the musical, is clearly intended as a sexual dream. Powell falls asleep in the woods and Ruby Keeler runs off to cavort with nymphs sliding down an Edenic waterfall. After a shot of water streaming against the back of Keeler's head, enveloping her in a halo not unlike the tiaras of Grecian statues, Berkeley poises a girl on a rock—and only when she dives and shatters the surface do we realize that the camera is under water, a hallucinatory effect drawing us into the dream. Lines of girls swim back and forth horizontally, then a long triangular train of girls paddles majestically toward the camera from the top of the frame. Another classical shot, worthy of *Olympia* (another hymn to the human form in motion), focuses on two long lines of girls lying on their backs in the water; a diver in the extreme foreground raises her arms vertically, the lines meet b.g. to match the pattern of her arms, and she dives into their midst, swimming through the breaking and re-forming lines. More underwater shots, then a cut to a whorl shot; the camera tracks back to reveal a girl poised in the foreground ready to dive, then further back to show the setting—a huge water palace geometrically constructed and lined on all sides with diving girls.

Berkeley cuts to overhead patterns as the girls dive and the whorl contracts and expands into floral patterns of dazzling

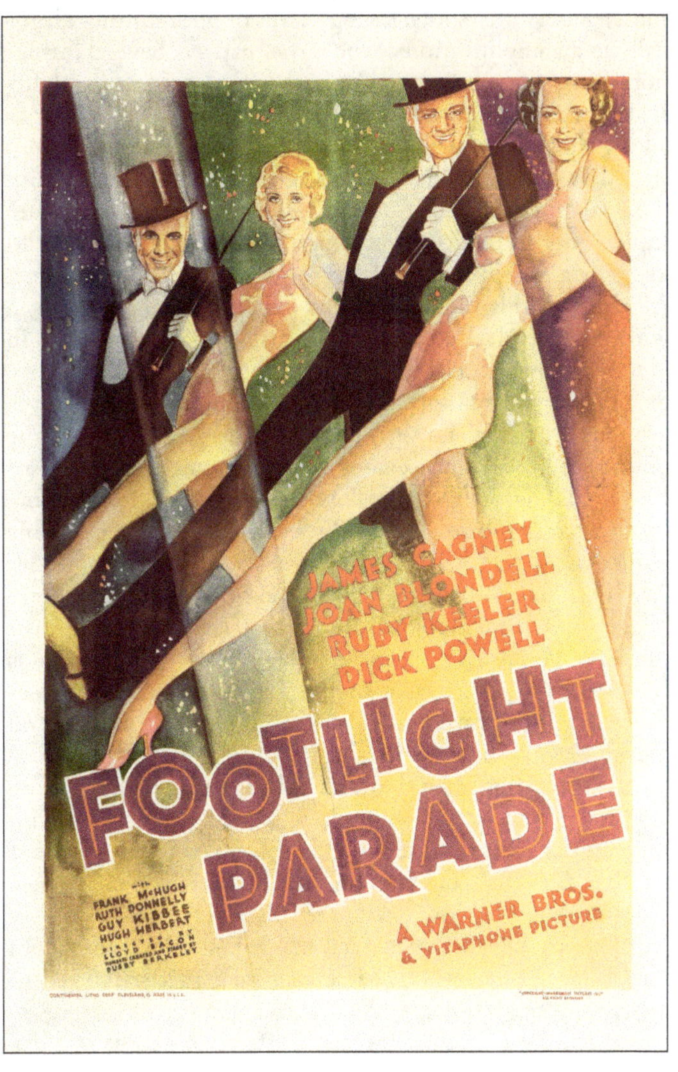

The poster art for classic films was sometimes as striking as the films themselves, such as this original art deco poster for *Footlight Parade*. (Warner Bros.)

precision, the lights in the tank changing from eerie shadows to bright lights, a breathtaking use of tonal montage. Closer shots, underwater shots, then patterns of lines shifting diagonally in an amplification of the earlier pattern. Several formations of straight and curved lines, then a cut to girls revolving around a giant fountain. Berkeley cuts from a medium shot to a long shot to a closeup of the girls, then to another closeup from the opposite side: then to on extreme long shot with the fountain reflected in the water of the foreground; a full shot of the fountain, then a high shot as the girls start to kick their legs in several patterns—swinging, jackknife, etc. All through this sequence choral singing has been mixed in with pure musical accompaniment; no vocal closeups as in "Honeymoon Hotel," but rather an abstraction of the beauty of Woman. Harmonious motion seen from a distance and the group movements and singing create a rarified contrast to the brash sexuality of the previous number. A small coda scene of Keeler tossing water to awaken Powell, the camera craning up to a nest of birds, gracefully ends this most remarkable sequence.

After this, "Shanghai Lil" would be an anticlimax were it not for the melodramatic power of Cagney taking over the lead singing role when his male star for the number is revealed as a phony planted by a rival. The story rescues the pacing—the final benefit of the integration of story and music. Cagney pushes the singer onto the stairs to the set, but tumbles down the stairs himself; the scene begins, as in "Honeymoon Hotel," with a long trucking shot along with his feet; this recreates the suspense dissipated by the previous number, since the audience does not know which of the men is going to carry through with the song. As the camera moves past people at their tables, each one half-speaks, half-sings a line about the mysterious "Shanghai Lil"; after a static scene of Cagney singing at a table, the pace gradually increases as a long trucking shot moves past the faces of people at a bar, singing a line each about Shanghai Lil. A series of Sternbergian shots of a brothel, crisscrossed by slats and bars, follows as Cagney searches for Lil. Sailors enter and fight Cagney, the scene choreographed like a musical number. Then the last slight pause in the rhythm: Cagney finds Lil (Ruby Keeler) and they start, slowly, to tap-dance.

From then on the scene becomes increasingly dynamic. A bugle calls the sailors to their ship, the camera craning up the stairs left as the sailors march down right and finally halting at the very base of the floor as the men march around it. The sailors march in patterns, anticipating the style of *Triumph of the Will;* pans of marching men are intercut with extreme closeups of faces shouting orders. Chinese girls join the marchers, and the whole group forms overhead patterns of that great trio, the American flag, President Roosevelt, and The Blue Eagle. Lil joins Cagney disguised as a sailor. A long crane movement sweeps along with the marching men, gaining on them and forming its own abstract pattern of movement. Berkeley tracks in on Cagney flipping a pack of cards for Lil, showing her the ship to America sailing in animation. After a shot of the two marching off to join the rest, the number ends. With backstage scenes of Chester Kent's triumph the movie ends.

With a single-mindedness and individuality rare in the history of the movies (he speaks of his effort to make "something new, something surprising, something never seen before"), Busby Berkeley created an inimitable body of work. Today everything is against him; he is "camp." Audiences feel constrained in enjoying his films wholeheartedly. This is a shame, of course, but some people don't want to be entertained. And if this doesn't get 'em, nothing will.

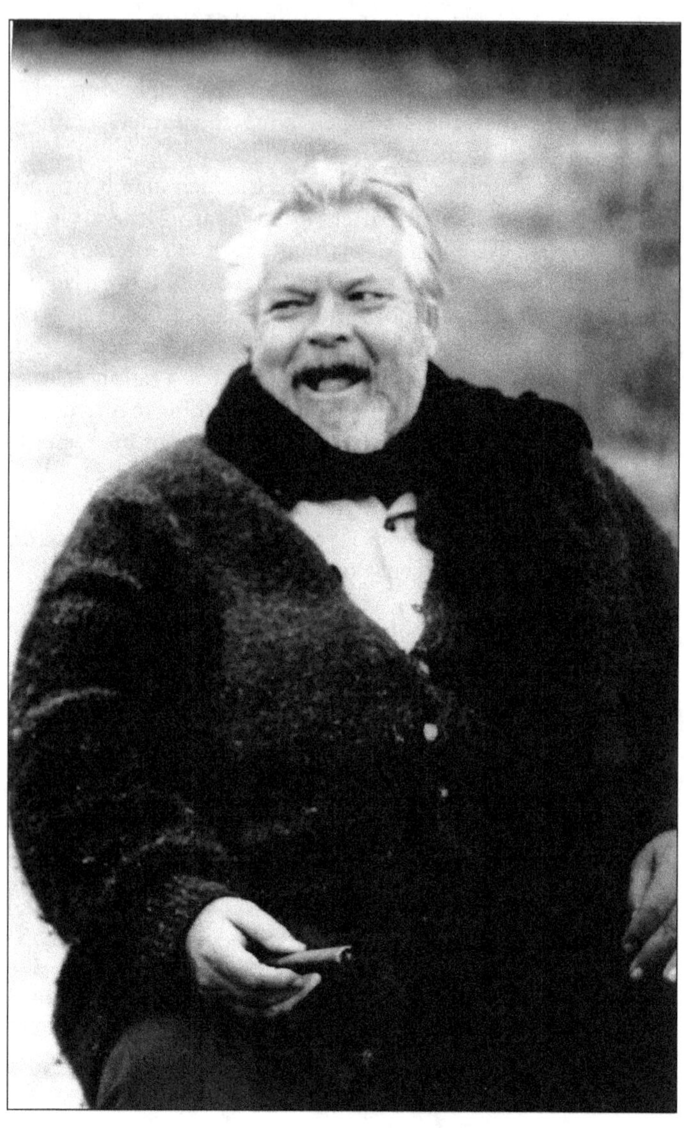

One of cinematographer Gary Graver's favorite portraits of Orson Welles during their collaboration in the later stage of his career. Here he is filming his satirical drama about the "New Hollywood," *The Other Side of the Wind* (begun in 1970 but not completed until 2018, after his death). (Graver)

ORSON WELLES

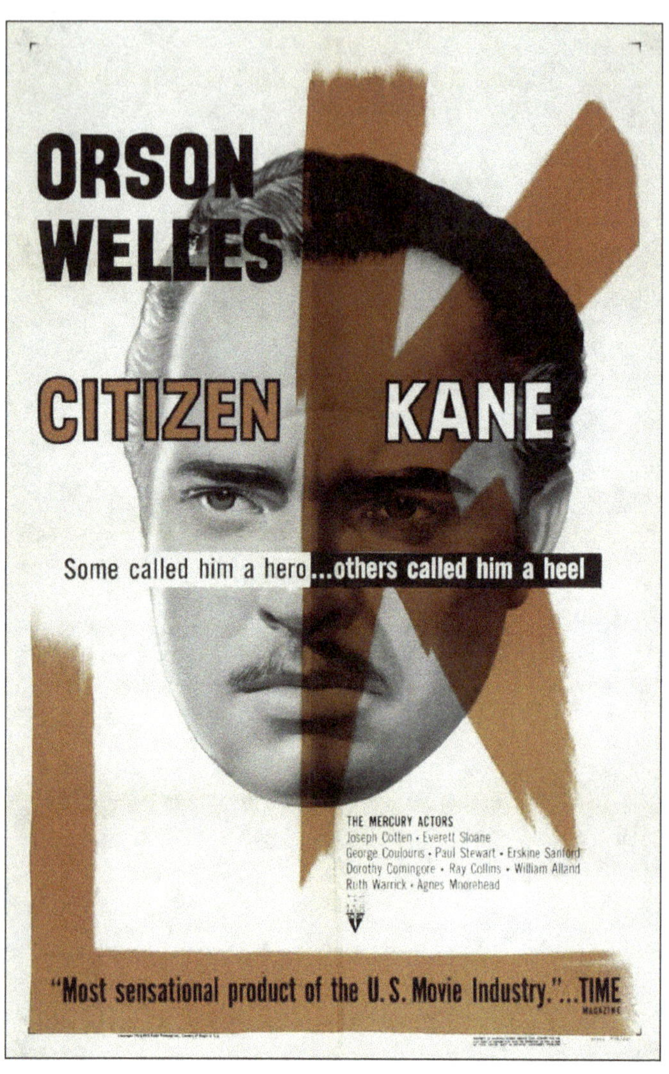

Because of pressure from the Hearst Empire on newspapers and theaters (no major chain originally would play the picture), *Citizen Kane* (1941), despite glowing reviews (novelist John O'Hara in *Newsweek* called it "the best picture he ever saw" with "the best actor in the history of acting"), did not make a profit until its 1956 reissue, for which this poster was used. (RKO)

Citizen Kane
Joseph McBride

Citizen Kane is a tragedy in fugal form; thus it is also the denial of tragedy. Kane's finally ineffective actions are run in counterpoint with the drama of the reporter who reconstructs his life. The arrangement of the scenes of Kane's life follows the progression of the reporter's viewpoint. Kane's fall, as we see it with the reporter, is constructed in non-Aristotelian terms. His end, in fact, comes at the beginning of the film. The negation of the idea of classical chronology insofar as it applies to Kane implies a deterministic suspension of the laws of cause and effect. Kane is presented as powerful, is indeed powerful; but he is also, in the paradox of the time scheme, powerless. Thompson, the reporter, is seen in Aristotelian terms, as having the power to change, but he too—final irony—is trapped in the time of the film. Neither of the two is present with us in the parenthetical opening and closing views of Xanadu.

Orson Welles's use of time counterpoints Kane's apparently effective actions with the audience's foreknowledge that those actions will fail and that he will remain as he was shown at the beginning of the two hours: destroyed. Kane's death at the film's inception occurs in a fantastic, dreamlike context to which the audience has no orientation. The jump-cut from the death to the newsreel continues this disorientation from mimetic reality. Though the newsreel shows the events of Kane's life in their relation to historical time, placing Emily's death in 1918, his death in 1941, etc., it is only when we are shown the reporters conferring in the projection room that we are placed in a coherent time system. Now the film's present tense, the prosaic, anti-romantic aspect, is introduced. A system has been created in which all of Kane's actions are now in the past tense—and hence no longer of any effect. The events of his life as we will see them exist in a limbo of moral futility.

Since we have been given immediate knowledge of the character's end, a reversal of conventional dramatic chronology which has a profound effect on our consideration of the nature of Kane as a hero, we must know when in his life he is doing what he is doing. In *8 ½*, in which the events depicted are themselves dreamlike, the viewer does not know the specific time in which the events are occurring to the protagonist, other than the now of the film. Dream and actuality are inseparable. *Citizen Kane*, on the other hand, depends on the viewer's awareness of the exact placing of each event in the locus of Kane's life. Most of the time shifts in *8½* come as cuts; most of the flashbacks in *Kane* come as dissolves, a distancing device making us aware of a rhetorical use of time.

Guido in *8½* is alive and triumphant at the end of the film. Kane is not. He has no Aristotelian existence except in the opening sequence, that of his death. The single event over which Kane has power, in the dramatic terms the film establishes, is that over which in actuality he has the least control; a damning irony. Kane is a prisoner of time, a temporal phenomenon—to which he gives mute testimony in his accumulating mountains of useless objects. His mother's stove standing in the vast storeroom and linked in a camera movement with a headless statue of Venus is not his mother but only a symbol of her memory. Rosebud is not his youth, but an emblem of it; his youth is lost, and Rosebud haunts his mind. In Proust's words, "Life is composed of a series of isolated moments, given meaning by their temporal relationship to the memories of the man who experiences them." In the context of *Kane,* this applies equally to Kane, to Thompson and to the audience. Let me suggest that time itself is the hero of *Citizen Kane.*

When the newsreel ends, we see the beam throwing it to the screen, then hands turning off the projector, which halts with a whir. It is as if the movie world has been declared void—but only "as if," for *Citizen Kane* continues. Welles

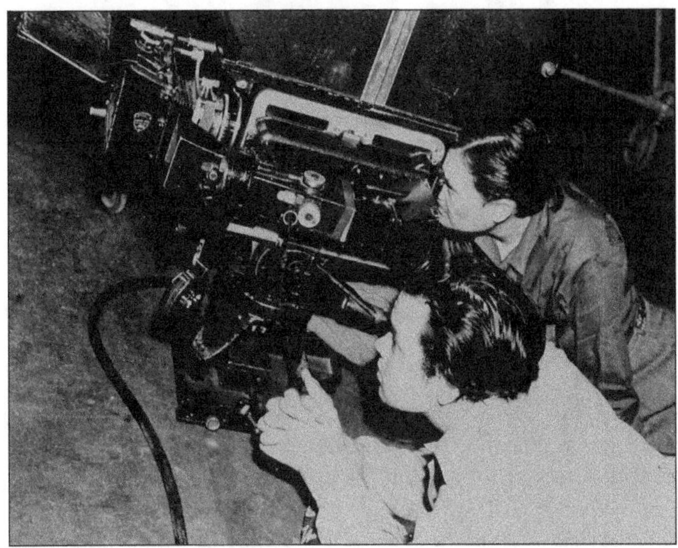

Welles's collaboration with the great, innovative cinematographer Gregg Toland on *Citizen Kane* played a large role in that 1941 film's artistic success, and Welles rewarded Toland by sharing his end credit card with him. Here we can see how Welles and Toland cut holes in the raised floors of sets to achieve their favored low angles; in the photo below, Welles is conferring with Toland (back to camera) as he prepares to shoot the room-smashing scene. (RKO)

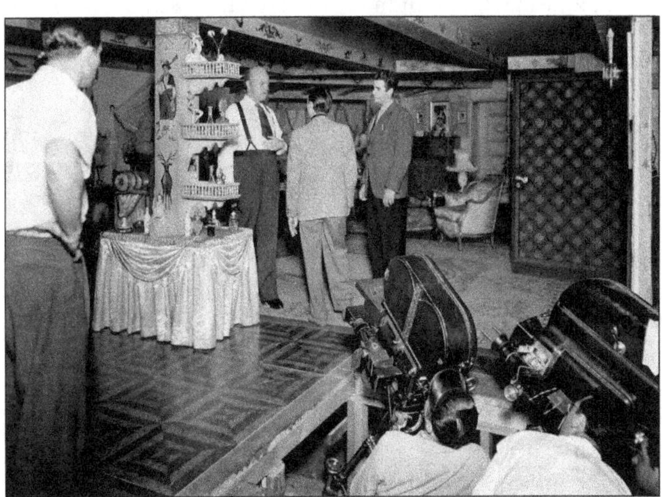

wants to shock us out of our acceptance—necessarily—of the newsreel as truth about Kane, and wants to further shock us by showing a man, Rawlston, the newsreel editor, standing and waving his arms in the very light with which the newsreel has just been shown. Welles keeps Rawlston's face in shadow, as he does that of Thompson throughout the film, to emphasize the distance necessary to the artist's inquiry. We see Thompson and are thus able to "identify" with his viewpoint, but we never see him completely, and are thus forced to temper our sympathy with irony. Kane's face is completely in shadow at his most selfless moment, when he reads the Declaration of Principles and signs it, pausing before he says "Kane" and giving an odd emphasis to the word. The shifting reportorial attitudes of Kane, Leland and Thompson form a running ironic motif about the possibility of presenting truth "objectively." All three are artists *manqué.*

Rawlston tells Thompson, the author of the newsreel, "It isn't enough to tell us what a man did. You've got to tell us *who he was.*" Overriding Thompson's protests and the wisecracks of the other reporters, among whom, without makeup, are Joseph Cotten (Leland) and Erskine Sanford (the old editor, Carter), Rawlston sends him out in quest of the meaning of "Rosebud," Kane's last word: "Maybe he told us all about himself on his deathbed." To which another reporter calls out, "Yeah, and maybe he didn't." Intrigued, or rather forced, to speculate on the meaning of a word or an action, the artist goes in closer search of the possible implications of the clue. In the course of seeking development for his image, he finds both contradiction and support for it, gradually modifying it and then abandoning his search just short of finding the definitive solution to the problem. The reporter goes as far as he can—within feet, in fact, of Rosebud—but never does reach it. *Kane* is a paradoxical statement about the nature of artistic truth; one artist, Thompson, fails; another, Orson Welles, succeeds. Both, however, reach the same conclusion.

"With me," Welles said in a recent interview, "the visual is a solution to what the poetical and musical form dictates. I don't begin with the visual and then try to find a poetry or music and try to stick it in the picture. The picture has to follow it. And again, people tend to think that my first preoccupation is with the simple plastic effects of the cinema. But to me they all come out of an interior rhythm, which is like the shape of music or the shape of poetry.... The danger in the cinema is that you see everything, because it's a camera. So what you have to do is to manage to evoke, to incant, to raise up things which are not really there.... And the interior conception of the author, above all, must have a single shape."

The rest of the film is colored by what we have seen in the newsreel, the first statement we have received about Kane. The reporter's subsequent inquiries are for him and for us a kind of criticism of the magniloquent *News on the March*. (And of the documentary approach?) What we saw in the newsreel undoubtedly happened to Kane; he did live in the castle we are shown, did make the speeches we see, etc.; but we are not yet able to go beyond the surface to comprehend the totality. Cocteau called film the art which shows death at work. Time is suspect in *Kane*, and each moment in it has its

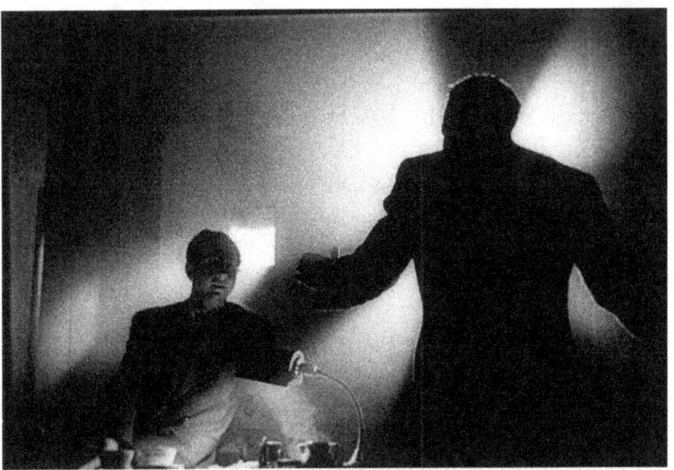

"Find out about Rosebud!"—Newsreel editor Rawlston (Philip Van Zandt) challenges reporter Jerry Thompson (William Alland) in the projection room, the first scene Welles shot for *Citizen Kane*. (Frame enlargement; RKO)

significance only in the context of all the other moments, past and to come. What is on the screen at a given moment is not definitive but is part of a state of mind shared by the author and his audience. The newsreel's function is similar to that of the chorus in a Greek tragedy. Welles sketches in the broad outlines of the myth quickly so that the viewer can concentrate on the search for cause. Kane's "effects" we see in two forms; in *précis* in the newsreel, more fully in the subsequent parts of the film. The reiteration has an ironic effect. Our prior knowledge of Kane's fate makes us aware of the consequences inherent in his actions *as* he carries them out. The tension is sustained in a fusion of suspense and mystery: suspense in that we (with Thompson) have information of which Kane is unaware and which enables us to concentrate on what might happen next; mystery in that we are trying to discover Rosebud.

Significantly, neither of Kane's closest friends, Leland and Bernstein, appears in the newsreel. The script called for them to be present in the shots of Kane's wedding to Emily, but Welles wisely omitted them. "All I saw on that screen is that Charles Foster Kane is dead—I know that, I read the papers," Rawlston jokingly comments. What we see obviously is the product of a man who has no personal acquaintance with Kane's life. All Thompson has done is read the papers and look at the newsreel footage. But for a brief section of "bootlegged" footage of the elderly Kane being wheeled through his rose garden, the newsreel has shown us only what Kane did for the public's eyes. The bootlegged footage, like the one sequence in *Rear Window* shot outside of the hero's perspective, helps to ensure our awareness of the perceptual strategy involved. We even see Kane trying to smash the camera of his own photographer after his wedding to Susan. A title in the newsreel fills the screen with the paradoxically true and false words, "Few private lives were more public."

Thompson's search is chronological, and he changes during the beginning-to-end frame of the film, a period of something more than a week from Kane's death to the end of his research into Kane's life. The climax of Thompson's drama comes as Bernstein breaks into his comment about Leland having nothing in particular the matter with him, just—"Just... old age." Thereafter Thompson is less and less detached, and finally he is repelled by the callousness shown by Kane's butler. He is seeing himself as he had been at the beginning of the search. Like Kane and Leland, Thompson is an innocent cruelly brought to recognize corruption. Time itself is seen as a corrupting force when the young and old Kane, the young and old Leland, the young Thompson and the old Bernstein and Leland are juxtaposed.

The counterpoint between Thompson's dramatic growth and Kane's futile attempts to change the course of his life contributes subconsciously to the irony of the film, just as the absolute symmetry of the film's construction maintains a constant ironic counterpoint to the utter lack of order in Kane's life. To give just one example of the hundreds of symmetrical devices, the photograph of Kane, Emily and their son used in the paper when the mother and son die in an automobile accident appears in the newsreel immediately after Kane and Emily strike a pose for their wedding picture. Then, much later, we see the photograph being taken—the moment before Emily sends the boy home in the car and tells Kane that they are going to Susan's apartment; where Kane will decide to end the marriage. It takes dozens of viewings to become conscious of this kind of subliminal metaphor, though one does sense its operation. We feel what Gertrude Stein called "the pleasure of concentrating on the final simplicity of excessive complication."

In the doggedness of Thompson's search for the meaning of Kane's last word and in the final futility of the search, Welles is mocking the audience's hope for a pat solution to Kane's life. Leland mocks it: "Rosebud? Yeah, I saw that in *The Inquirer.* Well, I never believed anything I saw in *The Inquirer.* Anything else?" Thompson alone of the reporters who gather in Xanadu recognizes that, finally, there is no solution. A woman reporter tells him that if he had found out what Rosebud meant, it would have explained everything. Facing the camera though still in shadow and with the camera receding from him, he says, "No. I don't think so. No. Mr. Kane was a man who got everything he wanted and then lost it. Maybe Rosebud was something he couldn't get or something he lost, but anyway it wouldn't have explained anything. No, I guess Rosebud is just a piece in a jigsaw puzzle—a missing piece."

Then the missing piece is filled in, but what may we make of the completed puzzle? Welles's camera leaves Thompson for majestic tracking shots over the vast pile of objects Kane has spent his life in accumulating. Then, from the high shots of the pile, we move into a privileged shot: Rosebud, Kane's sled, filling the screen, burning. Dwight Macdonald is a typical viewer in stating that he gets "a big thrill" out of this shot, though he can't explain why. With the shot we achieve a visual catharsis, an epiphany in which we see finally the true nature of Kane's futile situation. We see the "solution" for which we and the reporter have been searching, and we realize that it does in fact solve nothing. Thompson is dignified by our realization that we had to see Rosebud to reach his understanding.

But is it possible, as some feel, that the reporter's speech is ironic, that seeing Rosebud makes us realize that there is an explanation? Yes, insofar as the image is emotionally satisfying. Yes, *but.* Our emotions are never pure in confronting *Kane,* though they are finally, in Gertrude Stein's terms, simple. As psychoanalysis, *Kane* would be simplistic and Rosebud an inadequate conclusion. But a work of art is not a philosophical treatise. It does not explain anything; it demonstrates. The "solution" the film offers is its lucidity. We are shown all the reasons for the character's behavior and are then forced to consider irrationality itself as a reason. If Welles had not shown us Rosebud, we would have continued to think that there could be a solution, and that Thompson is merely unable to find it. We would be left to conjure up our own "solutions." By presenting us with the most satisfying possible resolution—recalling Kane's expulsion from his mother and his use of the sled as a weapon against Thatcher, his guardian—Welles makes us recognize that not only Kane is under scrutiny, but the very validity of rational explanation. In itself, a shot of a sled burning signifies nothing; but in context, as the resolution of a pattern of leitmotifs, the shot completes the work, closing it off from interpolated meanings and allowing us to consider the film as its own solution. Welles does not restrict our vision by showing Rosebud; on the contrary, if he had not shown it, the film would have been meaningless.

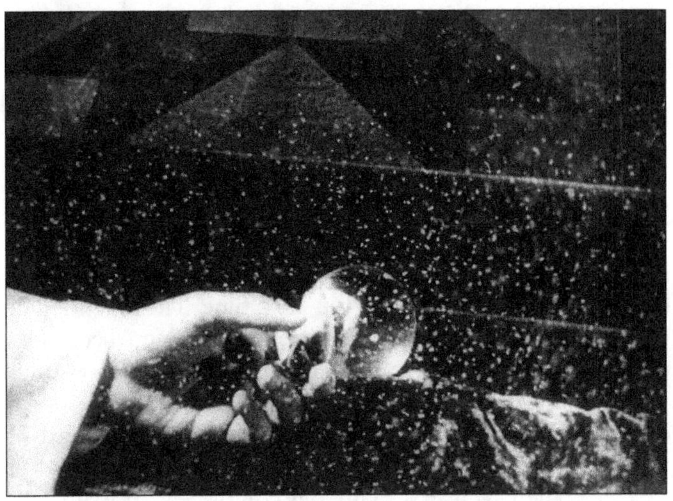

The expulsion from Eden (although a troubled place) frequently recurs in Welles's films; here the young Charlie Kane (Buddy Swan) reacts to being sold to a bank by his mother (Agnes Moorehead). Also in this dreamlike flashback at his Colorado home are banker Walter Parks Thatcher (George Coulouris, at left) and the boy's father (Harry Shannon). (Frame enlargements; RKO)

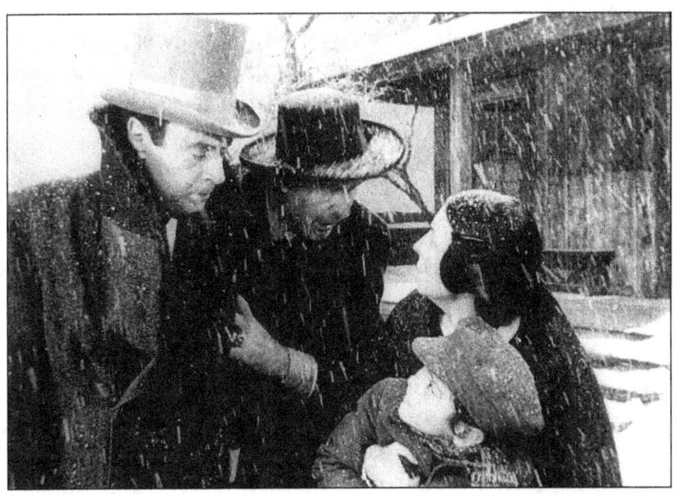

Though the author himself is prone to apologize for Rose-bud—"It's a gimmick, really, and rather dollar-book Freud"—we should trust the tale, not the teller, and consider also the shots following those of the sled: smoke rising from the castle and dissolving into the dark sky, a dissolve to our initial position behind the "No Trespassing" sign, and then a dissolve to Xanadu seen again from behind the giant "K," altered now by the darkness of the window behind which Kane died, dawn light faintly shining on the clouds around the castle, and the smoke rising from above it. We are forced finally to hold two opposed ideas in the mind at the same time. The repetition of two perspectives from the enigmatic opening sequence makes us acknowledge that though Kane's situation has been illuminated, the evidence is still open to consideration, We must continue to look at the film. As Robin Wood observed of the psychiatrist's explanation of Norman Bates at the end of *Psycho:* "The psychiatrist, glib and complacent, reassures us. But Hitchcock crystallizes this for us merely to force us to reject it. We shall see on reflection that the 'explanation' ignores as much as it explains." Hitchcock then shows us Norman, whom we "understand," sitting wrapped in a blanket, irretrievably irrational; and then the car withdrawing from the swamp. Similarly, the last sequence of *Kane,* under which merge the two counterpointed motifs of the musical score—the "power" motif in brass and the "Rosebud" motif on the vibraphone—resolves the situation into perfect ambiguity.

The title itself expresses the central paradox. "Citizenship," alliance with effective human society, is the goal to which Kane/Cain vainly aspires. He speaks the word "citizens" twice, at the times in which his purest societal impulses are manifested, but moments also of the highest irony: when he is reading the Declaration of Principles—"I will also provide them with a fighting and tireless champion of their rights as citizens, and as human beings"—and when he is delivering his campaign speech to "decent, ordinary citizens." Welles undercuts the spirit of Kane's high-minded speech by cutting to Leland on the words "the working man and the slum child" and to Bernstein and his unsavory associates applauding after the words "the underprivileged, the under-paid and the underfed."

Citizen represents the heroic, effective aspect of Kane; *Kane* represents his foredoomed, determined aspect. Our heroic conception of Kane as a tragically flawed character marching through time to his doom is tempered with an understanding that he was not in complete control of the events of his life, that some force has ordered them. Thompson's presence further emphasizes this tension, as do the use of deep-focus photography, the recurrence of low-angle shots and the virtual absence of closeups, strategies all of which tend to integrate the character into the milieu. The title is associated with Kane's lost innocence when Rawlston tells his reporters, "When Citizen Charles Foster Kane died, he said just one word—" and Thompson says "Rosebud!" In private he was a fugitive and a vagabond; in public he was Citizen Kane.

Thompson's cockiness has been supplanted by humility. He now has an empathy with Kane which was only perfunctorily expressed in *News on the March*. By vicariously experiencing the events he represented in his newsreel, he has come to understand that Kane was more than "an emperor of newsprint." In a speech included in the final version of the script but not in the film, Thompson has this to say to a reporter who asks him what he has discovered: "Well—it's become a very clear picture. He was the most honest man who ever lived, with a streak of crookedness a yard wide. He was a liberal and a reactionary. He was a loving husband—and both his wives left him. He had a gift for friendship such as few men have—and he broke his oldest friend's heart like you'd throw away a cigarette you were through with. Outside of that—" This is best out of the film since it merely verbalizes what is so powerfully made felt through the sight and sound of the ending scenes. But it is a hint of the film's method, the constant ironic undercutting of the audience's search for a solution.

It might be assumed that the events of Kane's life included in each of the narrators flashbacks—Thompson's newsreel, the Thatcher manuscript, Bernstein, Leland, Susan and Raymond—are grouped together not by chance but for metaphorical reasons. Such is the case. The newsreel shows the public Kane. Thatcher's section has to do entirely with his "surrogate motherhood," his taking Charles away from Mary Kane, his giving Kane a substitute sled, Kane's retaliation by means of his newspaper, and finally Thatcher's taking of the newspaper from Kane.

Bernstein is childlike. His flashback shows an idealized Kane and contains most of the triumphal moments of Kane's career. Of all the characters in the film, Bernstein is the best-disposed toward Kane, who demanded nothing from him but camaraderie. The structure of Bernstein's section equates him with the newspaper, the projection of Kane's best, when non-destructive, and worst, when manipulative, societal impulses. Bernstein and Leland repeatedly are seen facing each other in profile across the frame, and their radical opposition dramatizes the difference between the emotional demands they make on Kane. The last time the two are together, on the night of the disastrous opera, Bernstein faces Leland and tells him in a strange and moving tone, "I guess that'll show you." As the script indicates, the line is delivered "with a kind of quiet passion, rather than triumph."

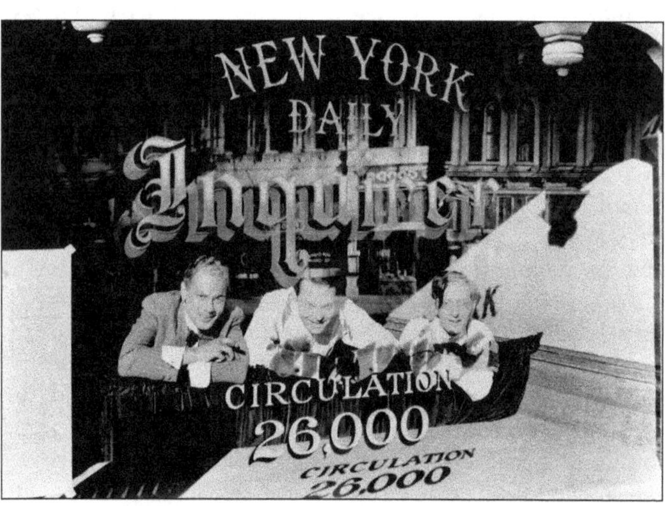

Welles's Kane in his early days as an enterprising newspaper publisher at the *Inquirer* office, flanked by his employees Jed Leland (Joseph Cotten), who eventually becomes disillusioned and leaves him, and his ever-loyal business manager, Mr. Bernstein (Everett Sloane). (RKO)

Leland is equated with love, with the crisis, that is, of the maturing process. In the enclosure of his flashback, conditioned by his choral explanations, we witness Kane's attempts at love from the idyllic beginning of marriage (in Bernstein's flashback we see Emily only in long shot, but in Leland's we see the marriage in all of its phases, in the breakfast montage) to the meeting with Susan, the confrontation with Gettys in Susan's apartment, the resultant rupture from Emily and from Leland, the marriage to the "singer," and finally Susan's and Kane's humiliations in the opera. In the next section, Susan's flashback, we will witness the catastrophic effects of the events in Leland's section. He is the punctuation between Kane's attempts at love. His face is held in a lap dissolve over the start of the breakfast montage, and again over the end of the montage: "It was a marriage just like any other marriage" is his comment. Again, when he tells about Kane meeting Susan, his face is held for several seconds over the rainy street. His speech in Kane's behalf is the middle link in a series of sound transitions from Susan's singing for Kane to Kane delivering his election speech. Finally, when Leland walks away escorted by two nurses, there occurs the most profound device of the film: he vanishes into the picture of Susan.

Leland is never seen with a woman, though there is a hint of an infatuation with Emily: "I can tell you about Emily. I went to dancing school with Emily. I was very graceful.— We were talking about the first Mrs. Kane." The script did in fact contain a scene set in a brothel in which Kane tries unsuccessfully to interest Leland in a girl. He ignores her and challenges Kane about his dragging the country into war. Leland personifies Kane's loving impulses, and his flaw is candor. He tells Kane what he thinks about Susie, and is punished, like Cordelia in *King Lear*, like Falstaff, for loving too freely and simply. Kane tells lies, overreaches, creates a myth about himself, and finally crushes the alter ego who questions the human value of that power. Leland's presence emphasizes the limits of Kane's ability to love. He plays Abel to Kane.

In the closing moments Welles gives us his simplest metaphors for Kane's condition. The screeching cockatoo flies past the camera as Susan leaves Xanadu, and we see Kane standing in shock at the door of her room. He pivots mechanically back into it, and Welles cuts to a low-angled shot of the rest of the motion; Kane moves like a marionette, a feeling intensified by the formalizing device of changing the angle of a continuous motion. The lowness of the angle abstracts him into a shape, non-rational, a phenomenon of milieu, just as had the extreme long shots of him walking in Xanadu's halls. This moment is the most explicit expression of Welles's deterministic view of Kane.

And immediately after this, as Kane is demolishing the room, there occurs a magical editing effect. The sequence is done in seven shots, recurrently from a distance to emphasize Kane's impotence. He smashes objects in the back of the room and then runs, almost exhausted now, toward the camera. At this point Welles cuts to an oblique shot from several feet farther back, and Kane's running form for a moment actually is smaller than it had been in the previous shot. It takes Kane about a second to regain his previous size on the screen: he bursts forward through the overlap and runs into the left foreground to rip a shelf off the wall. The editing has created a time warp through which Kane has to move in order to continue his effectless action: an actualization of the central metaphor of the film, Kane's entrapment in time, the barrier which restrains even his most violent attempts to act.

Appendix: Source and Script

Though there has been a surprising amount of pussyfooting around the subject, there can be no question that Kane was patterned primarily on William Randolph Hearst, as a reading of W. A. Swanberg's *Citizen Hearst* will show. Welles has confined himself to ironic comments—e.g., "Some fine day, if Mr. Hearst isn't frightfully careful, I'm going to make a film that's *really* based on his life" and "Kane would have liked to see a film on his life, but not Hearst—he didn't have quite enough style." However, it seems that Hearst greatly enjoyed seeing his life dramatized on the screen. It is reported that he owned a print and showed it to his friends. The son of a former Hearst executive told me that at the yearly conferences at San Simeon the executives would greet Hearst with "How's old Citizen Kane?" and that he would respond happily.

Apparently Hearst's somewhat half-hearted approval of Louella Parsons's attacks on *Kane* was in deference to Marion Davies, who understandably was bothered by the anti-romantic depiction of Susan Alexander and referred to the film as "that g-g-g-goddam *Citizen Kane*." Kane is of course an autonomous dramatic character, existing apart from any reference to Hearst, but there is value in noting where the characters of Kane and his prototype intersect and where they diverge. Interestingly, it is where they diverge that the film most resembles autobiography. Hearst, for example, lived with his parents until he was nineteen and continued to see them, but Welles's mother died when he was nine—a year older than Kane's age when Thatcher takes him from Mary—and his father when he was fifteen. Again Welles shies from the comparison ("I had no Rosebuds") but there are more points of contact than he will acknowledge.

According to *The Motion Picture Daily* of March 12, 1941, it was Joseph L. Mankiewicz who gave his brother Herman J. Mankiewicz the idea of writing a script based on the life of Hearst. Herman's treatment, entitled simply *Kane*, passed around Hollywood for several years, unsalable. John Houseman, Welles's Mercury Theatre partner, has described how the film came to be made:

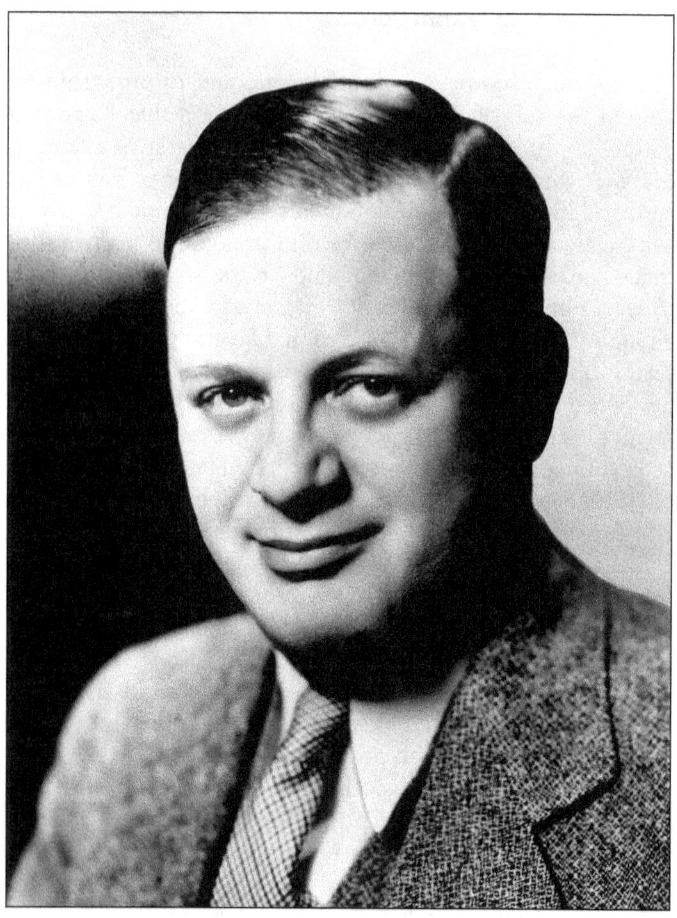

Herman J. Mankiewicz, co-author with Orson Welles
of the screenplay for *Citizen Kane*.

...we had done some work together on *Heart of Darkness*, which was to have been his first picture at RKO, and on something called *The Smiler with the Knife*. After I'd gone back East, Orson continued trying to find a subject. We had a mutual and very brilliant friend, Herman Mankiewicz, a celebrated Hollywood figure, who had recently broken his leg under tragicomic circumstances that I haven't time to go into. Having goaded each studio in turn into dismissing him, he had sunk to working on some of our radio shows. Orson arrived one night in New York, and over dinner told me that Mankiewicz had come up with an idea for a movie: a multi-faceted story about William Randolph Hearst in which Orson would play the title-part and direct. He asked me whether I would work with Mankiewicz as editor and collaborator on the script. I agreed and returned to Hollywood. After several conferences, at which Mankiewicz continued to develop his ideas, we moved him—nurse, plaster cast and all—up to a place in the mountains called Victorville, about a hundred miles from Los Angeles. There we installed ourselves on a guest ranch. Mankiewicz wrote, I mostly edited and the nurse was bored. Orson drove out once for dinner. At the end of three months we returned to Los Angeles with the 220-page script of *Kane*, later called *Citizen Kane*.

This is a delicate subject: I think Welles has always sincerely felt that he, single-handed, wrote *Kane* and everything else that he has directed—except, possibly, the plays of Shakespeare. But the script of *Kane* was essentially Mankiewicz's. The conception and the structure were his, all the dramatic Hearstian mythology and the journalistic and political wisdom which he had been carrying around with him for years and which he now poured into the only serious job he ever did in a lifetime of film writing. But Orson turned *Kane* into a film: the dynamics and the tensions are his and the brilliant cinematic effects—all those visual and aural inventions that add up to make *Citizen Kane* one of the world's great movies—those were pure Orson Welles. ("Interview with John Houseman," Penelope Houston, *Sight and Sound*, Autumn 1962)

Welles does play down Mankiewicz's contribution, stating that he was responsible only for "several important scenes" and for Rosebud. The script reads like a play, setting each scene briefly and following with dialogue and a minimum of scene indications. The scene with Gettys in Susan's room, for example, is eight pages of almost uninterrupted dialogue. There was a divided authorship of the script—Mankiewicz, Houseman, Welles, Joseph Cotten and Gregg Toland, the cinematographer, all contributed—and it seems fair to let the question rest and agree with Houseman that Welles is the author of *Citizen Kane* as film. [See my books *Orson Welles* and *What Ever Happened to Orson Welles?: A Portrait of an Independent Career* for more on the Mankiewicz-Welles collaboration on the script of *Kane*.—Ed.]

Though the structure of the film and its dialogue are not much different from that of the script, the revisions and omissions Welles made are uniformly excellent. The newsreel was to have opened with a shot of the Florida coastline, and to have followed with the scenes of Kane's career; Welles moved the metaphorical shots of the mountain's construction, the statues, the animals, etc., to the beginning of the newsreel. Before we see Kane in the film we see Xanadu, his grotesque self-enlargement, and before we see and hear of his life in the newsreel, we see Xanadu. The cut from Kane's death to the newsreel is Welles's addition, as are the shots of the projector beam after the newsreel—the script had called for a shot of a door, with "Projection Room" on it, to make the transition.

Welles's addition of humorous choreography, ragtime music and the little "Excuse me" ballet to the scene in which Kane takes over the *Inquirer* turns the episode into a vaudeville routine—note how Kane and Leland take off their hats in unison—an apt metaphor for the young Kane's attitude toward journalism. Welles omitted most of an awkward brothel scene, transposing "Oh, Mr. Kane!," which he was to have sung at the piano, to the party scene, which is such a concentrated expression of Kane's attempts at friendship. None of the actors, except, apparently, Cotten, was permitted to read more than his own scenes, and it is reported that the actors complained of Welles's constant on-set rewriting.

A particularly revealing example is his revision of Leland's first scene with Thompson. The script calls for the camera to move, after a few lines, from Thompson's face to Leland's, but Welles had decided to keep the reporter's face constantly out of direct sight of the camera. So we share Thompson's obsessive stare at Leland. Welles's transposition of the lines, "I can remember absolutely everything, young man, that's my curse. That's the greatest curse ever inflicted on the human race, memory" from a position later in the speech to the very opening of the scene has an important effect on our view of Leland—as an embodiment of Kane's past, the physical presence of his memory, a living Rosebud, perhaps Kane's living conscience as well—notions evoked by the motif of introducing Leland with the word "memory," a reinforcement of his choral function. Seen in this perspective, Leland's action in refusing to answer Kane's letter from Xanadu is the last refusal of Kane's conscience to accept his gesture of reconciliation. Leland's monologue is Joycean in its ironic caesuras (from "…we do believe in something" to "You're absolutely sure you haven't got a cigar?"), all the more so in the lines as Cotten speaks them.

Also to be noted in the transition from raw material to film are the subtle changes from Marion Davies to Susan Alexander and from Millicent Hearst to Emily Kane, the broader changes from Senator George Hearst to the ineffectual Jim Kane, the amalgamation of Jim Gettys from Charles Murphy, Mark Hanna and several other Hearst opponents, and the creation of Jedediah Leland from the personalities of several Hearst associates and, most strongly, from Mankiewicz's and Cotten's own personalities. Bernstein is modeled, even in appearance, on Dr. Maurice Bernstein, Welles's guardian.

The script makes several overt references to Hearst, including Kane's telling Leland, "Jed, how would *The Inquirer* look with no news about this non-existent war with Pulitzer and Hearst devoting twenty columns a day to it?" But only two are retained in the film, as an acknowledgement of the borrowing and as a legal disclaimer. The studio lawyers advised the redubbing of a line in the newsreel about Kane's having "Swung the election to one American president at least—so furiously attacked another as to be blamed for his death—called his assassin—burned in effigy" to "Swung the election to one American president at least—spoke for millions of Americans—was hated by as many more." Hearst's

Welles put Mankiewicz in first position on the writing credit for *Kane*, which scholar Robert Carringer, after studying the script materials, concludes was accurate. (Frame enlargement; RKO)

papers had run statements urging McKinley's assassination, and after it did occur some blamed him for it. As the narrator speaks the phrases in the film, we see a rally against Kane and the burning of an effigy; the phrases and the narrator's pause between them would seem to call for two dialectically opposed images, one of praise and the other of condemnation. (Welles had used a similar antithetical device moments before, gaining our unconscious sympathy for Kane's purposes: when the narrator says, "Kane urged his country's entry into one war—," we see the Rough Riders marching; when he says, "—opposed participation in another," we see crosses in a cemetery.) The two direct hints retained in the film of the parallel between Kane and Hearst are the newsreel's reference to Kane as "the great yellow journalist" and Rawlston's challenge to the reporters, "But how was he any different from Ford? Or Hearst for that matter? Or John Doe?"

The Magnificent Ambersons
Joseph McBride

Showmanship in place of genius:
a new deal at RKO.

Trade Advertisement, 1942

I.

There is a photograph of Orson Welles as an 1890s stage manager in his play *Moby Dick—Rehearsed*: the nose is caked with putty, the nostrils are arched, the black hat shadows the eyes, the gloved hand and its obscene cigar point at the apprehensive leer on his face. The man of the rhetorical theater, of an ending century. We see a tender Kane only in the brief Nineties scenes with Susan in her apartment and with Emily at the start of the breakfast montage. These scenes are a rehearsal for *The Magnificent Ambersons*, which places the crisis of Welles's work in the time of its genesis.

His boyhood resembled Kane's, but in some ways George Orson Welles was closer to George Amberson Minafer. Bred in genteel Midland towns, the boys were exceptional, George Minafer as the last of the aristocrats, Welles as an intellectual outsider. Both had pampering mothers, little parental discipline, and innate physical charm. Beyond that the factual parallel should not be pushed, though it should be noted that Welles's father, like Eugene Morgan in *The Ambersons*, was an inventor. His works included the army mess kit, a steam-driven airplane and a carbide bicycle lamp; the last of the

Amberson fortune is squandered on automobile headlights. "At the turn of the century," Welles recalls, "my father began making bicycle lamps because he thought there was no future in the automotive business. He made a fortune in spite of himself, inasmuch as the automobile manufacturers bought the lamps for their cars."

George Minafer is Charlie Kane given a decade's reprieve. Kane's snow scene is brief, tense, claustrophobic, punctuated by small, sharp camera movements. His childhood is over in minutes. George's Eden lasts years longer, and his expulsion is delayed for thirty minutes on the screen. The camera movements in his film are longer, more graceful, his snow scene more relaxed. George's innocence ends with a long iris-out, a tribute both to the passing of an age—the death of his father and the birth of the automobile—and to the conventions of an earlier, more graceful age of movies. As *Chimes at Midnight* is a lament for the conception of Merrie England, *The Ambersons,* Welles has said, is a lament "not so much for the epoch as for the sense of moral values which are destroyed."

After *Citizen Kane* Welles wanted to make *The Pickwick Papers* with W. C. Fields, but that Falstaff was already under contract to make the film with another studio. RKO still considered Welles's longstanding *Heart of Darkness* project too experimental, and he finally decided to write a script based on Booth Tarkington's novel, which had won a Pulitzer Prize in 1919 but had been almost forgotten in the interim. It had been filmed once before, as *Pampered Youth*, a 1925 silent directed by David Smith. Ben Alexander played George as a boy, and Cullen Landis was George as a young man. The New York *Times* noted that the *Ambersons* were "It" in their town and praised "an excellent fire sequence with a realistic blaze and an exciting rescue."

Welles had adapted *Penrod* and *Seventeen* for his "First Person Singular" series of narrated radio shows—Tarkington was one of his favorite authors—and on October 29, 1939, had presented his adaptation of *The Ambersons,* starring himself and Walter Huston. It is clear that when he came to make the film, in late 1941, he conceived of its soundtrack almost as an autonomous work of art. Robert Wise, the editor of Welles's first two features, recalls that Welles was nervous about recording some loops needed for post-synchronization on *Kane*. After the looping was done, however, he was so taken with the process that he decided to make a preproduction recording of the dialogue for *The Ambersons* and have the actors synchronize their lips and motions to it. The first day of shooting was a fiasco: the actors could hardly act, let alone synchronize. Wise says that everyone but Welles and the actors found the whole matter hilarious, and it was abandoned by lunchtime.

Unsuccessful though it was, the experiment in "radio sound" furthered Welles's work. There are precedents for almost every visual device in *Kane,* but the use of sound is Welles's true innovation. Others have learned from his camera movement, lighting, angles, use of focus, cutting and oblique exposition, but few have done much with any of the sound

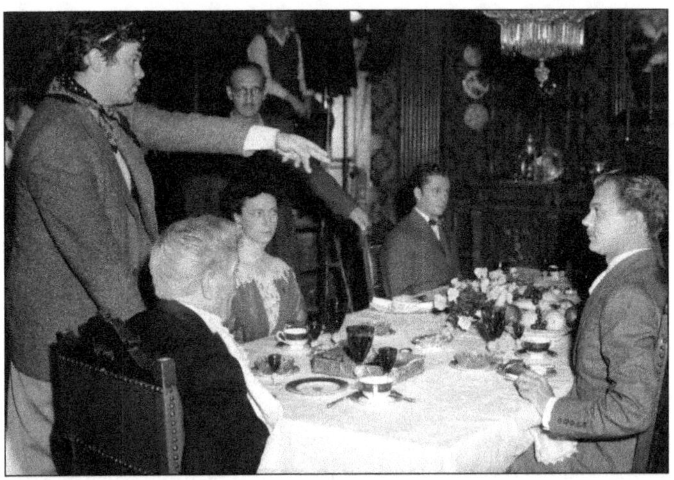

Welles directing his favorite scene in *The Magnificent Ambersons* (1942), the first to be shot for the film: the fraught dinner scene at which George (Tim Holt, seated near end of table) rudely attacks Eugene Morgan (Joseph Cotten, right) for helping invent automobiles. Also present are Major Amberson (Richard Bennett, seated left) and Fanny Minafer (Agnes Moorehead, below Welles). Assistant director Freddie Fleck, who directed some reshoots including the absurd happy ending, watches from the background. (RKO)

techniques he developed. Hitchcock is a notable exception. Other directors have experimented with aural montage and sound perspective, but few have exploited what Bernard Herrmann, Welles's composer, called "radio scoring" in a 1941 New York *Times* article. Herrmann explains that these are "musical cues which last only a few seconds… in radio drama, every scene must be bridged by some sort of sound device, so that even five seconds of music becomes a vital instrument in telling the ear that the scene is shifting." Herrmann conceived of some scenes in *Kane,* such as the breakfast montage, as "ballet suites," and Welles cut them to match the music. Herrmann worked closely with Welles on new uses of sound effects and orchestration, and in *The Ambersons* the two carried their experiments to a new degree. Ten- and twenty-minute sections are almost continuously underscored with music, and overlapping dialogue is made to serve new dramatic functions.

Welles wrote the script of *The Ambersons* in nine days, no doubt helped by his radio experience with the book. Shooting began on October 28, 1941. At night he was acting in Norman Foster's *Journey Into Fear,* a Mercury production for which he helped Joseph Cotten write the script. On Mondays he was recording radio shows for his *Orson Welles Show* series on CBS Radio, and [after Pearl Harbor was tasked by the U.S. government to go to Rio de Janeiro in February to make a goodwill documentary, *It's All True.* — Ed.] All this pressure, added to the studio's increasing uneasiness over *Kane*'s distribution problems, forced him to let Wise direct two short scenes for *The Ambersons.* Shooting was completed on January 31, and [after being briefed in Washington and spending three days working on the editing and recording additional narration with Wise in Miami — Ed.], Welles left for Rio de Janeiro on February 4 to shoot *It's All True.* He took along a relatively polished 132-minute cut of *The Ambersons* and continued to edit it in long-distance conversations with Wise [who was supposed to go to to Rio to finish the work with Welles but was unable to travel, supposedly due to war restrictions; meanwhile, Welles's business manager Jack Moss sometimes didn't answer the phone from Rio and threw Welles's detailed cables into the trash. — Ed.].

On March 17, 1942, RKO gave the film a sneak preview [in Pomona, before a largely youthful audience who came to see a Dorothy Lamour musical, *The Fleet's In.*—Ed.]. The audience found it slow and unintentionally comic; since Welles was away Wise was ordered to make changes. [Even after a relatively successful second preview in more up-market Pasadena, the panicked studio ordered drastic cuts as well as reshuffling scenes, especially in the second half of the film, and reshooting of scenes by Wise, assistant director Freddie Fleck, and even Jack Moss. The ending and the scene preceding it of Cotten and Anne Baxter in his study were directed by Fleck.—Ed.] Two more previews convinced the studio to release *The Ambersons*—now down to its present length of 88 minutes—and it was double-billed on July 10 with a Lupe Velez comedy, *Mexican Spitfire Sees a Ghost.*

In the meantime RKO had undergone a change in hierarchy, and one of the new studio head Charles Koerner's first moves was to fire Welles, order him to return from Brazil, and strip him of his contract and the footage for the abortive *It's All True.* His Mercury staff were ordered to vacate their offices by July 1, ostensibly to make room for a unit producing a Tarzan picture. *Journey Into Fear* was edited without Welles's approval. He threatened to sue but agreed to shoot a new ending for it and to recut the last reel. He was furious with everyone involved in the "mutilation" of *The Ambersons* and remained so. He said that "they let the studio janitor cut *The Magnificent Ambersons* in my absence." He claimed also that the studio had failed to give the film adequate advance publicity on the grounds that it was an irredeemable flop. Today he explains that "about forty-five minutes were cut out—the whole heart of the picture really—for which the first part had been a preparation.... The film has a silly ending... just ridiculous.... It bears no relation to my script."

RKO's advertising tried to mask the somberness of the story with sensationalism—"Scandal played no favorites when that high-and-mighty Amberson girl fell in love once too often!" read the New York ad on the day of the premiere. The film was not a success with the public [however, that was after it was pulled quickly after mixed results in different cities—Ed.] nor with most of the reviewers, James Agee in

Time an exception, and is only today beginning to be appreciated for the great—though flawed—work that it is. This troubled film, whose history has long been obscure and whose appeal to a mass audience is limited, has not yet been analyzed in depth. Like *Greed* and *¡Que Viva México!*, it represents only part of its director's conception.

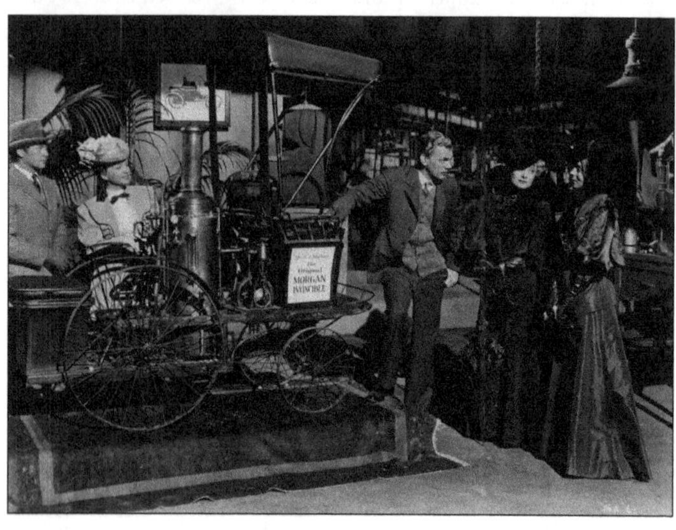

The bravura scene in Eugene's automobile factory was filmed the morning after the attack on Pearl Harbor, an event that helped cause the chain of catastrophes that led to the film's evisceration. From left are Holt, Anne Baxter, Cotten, Dolores Costello and Moorehead. (RKO)

II.

The transitions perhaps are what strike one most about *Citizen Kane*, but what one remembers from *The Ambersons* is the fluidity of each scene. The transitions in *Kane* draw attention to themselves and are the basis for the film's cyclical narrative structure; *The Ambersons* disguises its cuts and uses long sensuous dissolves to emphasize the inevitability, the flow, of the story's linear progression. This impressed François Truffaut, who wrote that "there are surely fewer than two hundred shots in this story which covers twenty-five years." Actually there are a great many more than that, but the fact that such a sophisticated viewer was deceived indicates the effectiveness of Welles's strategy.

For the effect of *The Ambersons* lies largely in the quiet frustration of the audience. Welles holds each shot a little longer than is normal; thirty seconds or a minute (or longer) is such an uncommon length for a shot that we are unconsciously drawn into thinking that it will last still longer. And when Welles does cut, for the most part unobtrusively, there is a slight disappointment—a nostalgia—that the scene is already over. To achieve this requires high concentration in each shot. The overlapping conversations, the continuous use of music, and the flowing motion of and before the camera achieve the grace and intensity needed for the effect. The fact that the collapse of a family and the deterioration of a town takes only an hour and a half and yet is so convincingly real is the final triumph of the film, which, unlike other films of "grow old and die" novels, does not satisfy itself with indicating nostalgia but actually creates it.

Griffith's *True Heart Susie* and Renoir's *Partie de Compagne* have this effect, as does *Jules et Jim*, which starts the year *The Ambersons* ends, 1912, and shows clearly its debt to all three films. The structure of Truffaut's film, as he admits, weakens in the last sections, as does that of *The Ambersons* for reasons not entirely due to the studio's recutting. To create a mood so buoyant as that achieved in the first half hour of each film and let it down gracefully into destruction proved too taxing for both young directors. And, as might be expected, Truffaut's comment on the style of *The Ambersons* is precisely correct: "This film was made in violent contrast to *Citizen Kane*, almost as if by another filmmaker who detested the first and wanted to give him a lesson in modesty."

The frame is edged with soft-focus in the early shots, which have the feeling of old photographs coming magically to life. Manny Farber complained that the first shots are no more than a succession of "postcards" connected by narration, but the flow of the section depends on this kind of time-compressing transition, disguised by the soft, whimsical music and Welles's skillful narration. Seen silently it would have less connection, but with the soundtrack the streetcar, the men in the bar, the rowboat, the stovepipe hat and Eugene modeling clothes go by in smooth and natural succession. Chiefly remarkable about this sequence, aside from its beauty, is its extreme economy, which is, of course, part of its beauty. The novel has a similar beginning—wry comments on the mores of the 1870s—but takes three chapters to get through George's childhood years. Given the advantage of being able to *show* the period evolving, Welles compresses George's first seventeen years into less than ten minutes. "The magnificence of the Ambersons began in 1873. Their splendor lasted throughout all the years that saw their Midland town spread and darken into a city. ..." In the first two sentences of narration Welles summarizes the rise and eventual collapse of the Amberson dynasty.

Welles's openings often contain a "synopsis" of the story that is to follow. *Kane* has its newsreel, *The Trial* its parable of the law, *Chimes at Midnight* the conversation between the two old men, Falstaff and Shallow, recounting their lives. These overviews serve a function similar to that of the chorus in a Greek tragedy: Welles sketches in the broad outlines of the myth so that the viewer can concentrate on its deeper implications. The use in *The Ambersons'* early scenes of the townspeople as a chorus and the designation of an old gossip as a "prophetess" could hardly make the parallel more explicit; nor could the story's relation to *Oedipus Rex* be more clear. Our prior knowledge of the fate of the characters makes us aware of the consequences inherent in their actions as they carry them out. By their very indirection, the poetic beginnings of *Kane, The Trial* and *Chimes* and the measured flippancy of *Kane's* newsreel—"The biggest private zoo since Noah"—heighten the tragedy that is to follow. What is left unsaid and what is treated playfully in the prologue to *The Ambersons* will echo throughout the slowly darkening remainder of the film.

Young George's two rapid rides through the town in his pony cart at ages nine and seventeen, separated by four short scenes, are perfect epitomizations of the later behavior of "Rides-Down-Everything," Lucy's name for him. Welles tells us that "George Amberson Minafer, the Major's one grandson, was a princely terror" as we see his cart gradually approaching the camera in extreme long shot. As he drives out of the frame left, Welles cuts to him driving left through a laborer's sand pile, then shows him driving away from the camera and through the town in three more shots. "There were people—grown people they were," the narration continues, "who expressed themselves longingly—they did hope to see the day, they said, when that boy would get his comeuppance."

As he did with Rosebud several times in the early parts of *Kane,* Welles mocks his own central motif. He cuts to a couple on the street: "His *what?*" asks the lady. "His come*up*pance," answers the gentleman in his most determined tones. "Something's bound to take him down someday; I only want to *be* there." This is one of the first indications of the slight variation in attitude between the novel and the film: Welles's distance from the characters is slightly greater than Tarkington's, a fact which no doubt accounts for much of the tittering of audiences unable to see the satire. When Eugene falls through the bass viol early in the film, Welles is telling how the instruments of the serenade will "presently release their melodies to the dulcet stars." Tarkington used the line with softer irony in referring to the popular songs of the day.

The second ride through the town is down from six shots to four, and the speed of the carriage is greatly increased: the cutting is more rapid, smaller portions of the left-to-right arc are used, and the effect is that George has indeed returned from college "with the same stuffing." The third shot, just after George has snapped his whip at another laborer, pans from ground level right with the carriage. The spinning hub veers close to the camera in a succinct visual metaphor for George's *hubris.*

Following this in the script was a scene in which George revisits the "Friends of the Ace," his boyhood club, and intimidates the members into re-electing him president because his grandfather owns, among other things, the club's gavel. This would have impeded the flow of the transition from George's carriage ride to the ball scene, and merely verbalizes what has already been expressed visually. (Almost all of the script's dialogue is taken from the novel, little of it rewritten in the finished film, but Welles freely omitted and relocated scenes and passages of dialogue.)

Welles's Hollywood enemies attributed the success of *Kane* to Gregg Toland, the great photographer who worked closely with him in planning the shots and the texture of the film. By the time *The Ambersons* went on the floor, Toland was working with John Ford in the Navy and the OSS's combat photography unit. Stanley Cortez furthered Toland's work with deep-focus, which is used in almost all of *The Ambersons'* shots. André Bazin has dealt at length with the psychological and dialectical advantages of giving equal focal stress to each object in the scene (with Toland's processes objects 200 feet from the camera are as sharp as those in the extreme foreground). The director can choreograph his scenes with great subtlety, changing the audience's viewpoint without resorting to the intervention of a cut. Bazin found that the deep-focus work of Jean Renoir, and Toland for William Wyler and Welles, represented a revolution in film style, an assertion of the integrality of space and time in direct opposition to the classical theories of montage.

Toland stated simply that it obviated the "loss of realism" due to breaking a scene up into "long and short angles." Welles has stressed the gain in ambiguity: "The public may choose, with its eyes, what it wants to see of a shot. I don't like to force it." The deep-focus effect minimizes the illusion of depth, and is thus comparable to the effect of Medieval painting, which in its flatness places equal emphasis on the character and the milieu. Cortez also achieved a black-and-white chiaroscuro reminiscent of period daguerreotypes and of Billy Bitzer's photography for D. W. Griffith. The counterpoint between the almost documentary immediacy of the exteriors in *The Ambersons* (in itself a kind of stylization) and the meticulous stylization of the camera movement, action and dialogue contributes much of the film's power. The recurrent use of low angles, though seldom as deliberately obtrusive as in *Kane*, places further emphasis on the characters' relation to their surroundings.

The resulting dominance of the city and the baroque furnishings of the mansion, and the implicit family-mansion metaphor, impart a strong determinism to the story. George could not have helped growing up that way ("They-couldn't-help-it" is Lucy's name for the woods inhabited by Chief

"Rides-Down-Everything"). Welles's meticulous use of settings—the idyllic snowy fields with only telephone wires intruding, the somnolent little town providing a backdrop for George and Lucy's carriage ride and the bustling, noisy city they later walk through (and the dirty metropolis George walks through alone)—all this carries the story of the town along with the story of the family. The film has epic quality, though it has been lessened by the recutting.

The constant use of the moving camera, most notably in the ball sequence, places further emphasis on the family's surroundings. In a Welles film the camera is a character. In his script for *Heart of Darkness*, his first RKO project, this is literally true—the camera was to have been Marlow. In *Kane* the camera shadows the reporter, whose face we never see completely. The camera is the audience, and the longer it moves without a cut being made, the more we are aware of its shifting relationship to the characters. The long take puts us into the scene. Like deep-focus, it helps to persuade us of the dramatic reality of the scene, and in respecting the integrity of space and time, it too asserts the unity of what is shown. Though the event—for example the long uninterrupted snow scene in *Kane*—may be highly dialectical in emotions and ideas, the integrality of the *mise-en-scène* functions as a metaphor for the inevitability of the actions' coincidence. Eisenstein said that a cut should occur when a scene has reached a point of unresolvable tension; then it will "explode" into the next scene. Welles prolongs the tension among the characters and camera as long as possible, to approximate the intimacy of a theatrical experience while retaining the cinema's freedom in changing point of view. This is the prime tension of his style; and, as Bazin has put it, "the paradox of the cinema is rooted in the dialectic of concrete and abstract." Welles notes that the ceaseless flow of actor-camera movement in his films "corresponds to my vision of the world: it reflects that sort of vertigo, uncertainty, lack of stability, that *mélange* of movement and tension that is our universe."

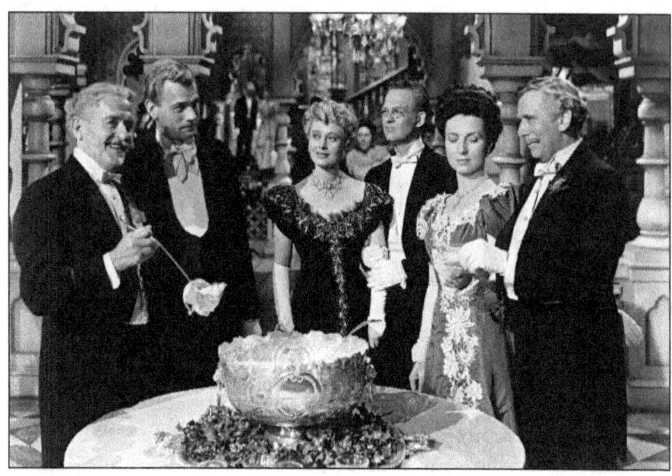

The ball in *Ambersons*, "the last of the great, long-remembered dances that 'Everybody talked about'" and the sequence Welles called "the greatest tour de force of my career": Bennett, Cotten, Costello, Don Dillaway, Moorehead and Ray Collins. (RKO)

III.

On George's return home, Welles tells us, "cards were out for a ball in his honor, and this"—slight ironic pause—"pageant of the tenantry was the last of the great, long-remembered dances that 'everybody talked about.'" The ball sequence lasts about ten minutes and is one of the most exhilarating in the history of the movies. After a distant shot of the mansion lit up for the ball, a slow dissolve reveals Eugene and Lucy, seen from behind, entering the house. The camera follows. The physical feeling in this shot is extraordinary: servants open the doors on either side, pulling hard against the wind and smiling broadly as they do it; Sam the butler bows and takes Eugene's hat; couples pass in front of the camera while in the background the party is in full gaiety (the camera all the time tracking in). And what to say of the other aspects of the scene—the sparkling, gently-swaying cut-glass chandelier, the vines and flowers set all around the hall, the dazzling gowns of the women, the opulent coats and ties of the men.

A cut to an opposite viewpoint starts a slow tracking shot toward George and Isabel's reception line. A lavishly decorated Christmas tree sweeps by on the left as the camera approaches Uncle John Minafer, a loud bumpkin telling the Major how he'll be laid out in this very hall "when his time comes," and telling George, "There was a time though in your fourth month when you was so puny nobody thought you'd live." This line is tossed off, but in it lies a key to George's megalomania, an explanation of the absurd affection Isabel will lavish on him until her death. On her deathbed she will ask George if he has had enough to eat and if he has caught a cold on the trip home. One is reminded of the first words of Mrs. Kane: "Be careful, Charles! Pull your muffler around your neck, Charles!" As she says the words Charles reflexively does pull his muffler around his neck. George's reaction to his uncle's untactful line here, however, is a fierce "M'mber you v'ry well indeed!" The first real glimpse of George as a young man gives him away. His arch, elegant profile is set against the left of the frame as the camera stops tracking, and his face shows the ridiculous arrogance that is to doom his mother.

Eugene is now greeting Isabel, and Welles cuts to a shot of the three faces: George's wary on the left, Isabel's smiling, Eugene's in profile on the right. Immediately, wordlessly, the tension is established. When Eugene tells George that "from now on you're going to see a lot of me—I hope," the violins off-camera start a gay tune. When Isabel introduces George to Lucy a few seconds later, the musicians are in the midst of a transition which becomes a high, plaintive note the moment after Isabel says "George, you don't remember her either, though of course you *will.*" Robert Rossen has remarked of Welles's ability to tell an entire story in a single shot; here Herrmann tells an entire story with a bar of music.

The rest of the scene is increasingly fluid: a long track back with George and Lucy through the ballroom which cranes up with them as they walk up the stairs (and shows a violinist in the foreground playing the plaintive tune), a dissolve to a tracking shot of Lucy's suitors criss-crossing in front of George and the camera, a cut to George and Lucy seating themselves on the stairs, a soft-focus wipe to the family gathered around a punchbowl. This begins a shot which was to have been an unbroken revolution almost entirely around the dance floor.

After the Major teases Eugene and Isabel about the bass viol, the camera tracks slightly back, panning right and then left as George and Lucy walk past the refreshment table. As they walk away from it a middle-aged couple approach, and at this point Wise cut several lines of dialogue about the town's latest delicacy—olives. "Don't ask me why they wanted it out," Welles says. "The result was a useless jump in an otherwise unbroken scene."

As it stands the camerawork is dazzling enough—a cut replaces the intended pan left from the couple to Eugene and Isabel dancing, but the camera still seems to dance away with them, stand still for George and Lucy's brief conversation, and then retreat as the two dance away on the wonderful exchange about George's ambition: to be a yachtsman. Chances are that the olive remarks caused guffaws at the preview, partially

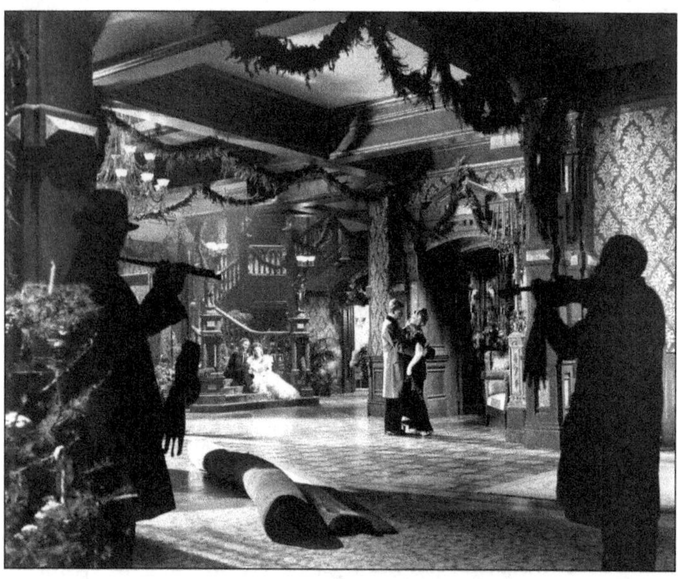

Isabel (Costello) rekindles her old flame with Eugene Morgan on his return to town in *Ambersons* as her son, George Amberson Minafer, and Eugene's daughter, Lucy (Baxter), watch from the staircase. (RKO)

because it is here that Welles's satire of his characters is most apparent. In the script, the couple's debate over the value of the delicacy goes thus: "…You're supposed to *eat* 'em…. I hear you gotta eat nine, and then you get to like them…. Well, I reckon most everybody'll be makin' a stagger to worm through nine of 'em, now Amberson's brought 'em to town."

The ball ends more quickly than we would like (the best example of Welles's strategy of frustration), on a slow Sternbergian dissolve from Eugene and Isabel dancing in the foreground to them dancing in the extreme background after the rest of the dancers have gone. Here Welles's use of sound perspective is at its height; we hear, distantly, George and Lucy talking, then on a cut we hear them at normal volume; the music stops, in the foreground Eugene thanks Isabel, and from the audience's side of the camera we hear Jack: "Bravo! Bravissimo!" Again we hear Eugene, then Lucy and George in the background. This linear use of three sound perspectives creates a remarkable illusion of depth, and the mingling of the voices in the subsequent leave-takings heightens the breathless tension of the scene. The choreography is similarly punctuated: Jack walks toward George, the camera panning left; Fanny runs in back of them; Isabel dashes in front of the camera. As the scene ends, Isabel is poised in the foreground between facing profiles of Lucy and George. The "flat" screen becomes surreally three-dimensioned.

Shortly after this, in the family argument in the hall, Welles uses sound montage for another kind of super-real tension as Fanny's, Jack's and George's voices follow each other in rapid irritated succession. Agnes Moorehead establishes Aunt Fanny's character as swiftly as she did Mrs. Kane's. The idiotic laughter that greets Aunt Fanny at almost every showing of the film is an indication of how much of this tortured woman she compels the audience to see. It is a beautiful and frightening performance, and it moves me greatly each time I see the film.

The script next contains a short scene of Isabel in George's room saying goodnight and asking why he doesn't like Eugene Morgan. "I don't say I don't care about Mr. Morgan—I don't say I care about him," is his answer. This scene is best out as—again—it verbalizes what has been made clear in the mother's and son's expressions and in the compositions of them with Eugene.

The snow scene which follows offers a humorous contrast between the grace of the sleigh (which soon capsizes) and the grotesque rumblings of Eugene Morgan's "broken-down chafing-dish." The scenes of Morgan starting the car with George's reluctant assistance are played out against a stylized backdrop which includes houses, fences and telephone wires. The automobile is still a diversion in this scene enacted in the purity of the snow—in one of the cut scenes George argues that people don't take their elephants visiting with them, so why should they take their automobiles?—and the riding song epitomizes the spirit of the scene as well as did "Oh, Mr. Kane!," which also marked the end of a carefree era. The novel had the riders singing "The Star-Spangled Banner," but Welles mercifully lifted a song from a later chapter:

> As I walk along the Boy de Balong
> > With an independent air,
> > You can hear the girls declare,
> > "He must be a millionaire. "
> *Oh*, you can hear them sigh, and wish to die,
> > And see them wink the other eye
> At the man who broke the bank at Monte Carlo!

The slow iris-out begins as the car and the singing diminish into the distance. The script has the film opening with an iris-out and the snow scene closing with a simple fade: the shifting was a brilliant idea.

IV.
The *allegro* movement of the film is over, and the gradual darkening begins. With a fade-in we see the mansion doors (which had opened on the ball scene shortly before) but now there is a wreath on one and Eugene's shadow on the other. The music stops abruptly as the door clicks shut behind the Morgans—indoors the neighbors and relatives are filing around a coffin. Placing the camera in the coffin's position was done notably by Carl Dreyer in *Vampyr* (1932), but of

course for a different effect. Here it serves to nullify our feelings—if any, since we have hardly seen him—for Wilbur, with whom, in Truffaut's theory about the subjective and objective uses of the camera, it is now impossible to identify.

A film in which the camera actually plays a character, as in Welles's Conrad script or in Robert Montgomery's *The Lady in the Lake*, is the exact opposite of the subjective film, which depends on the audience's identifying with the feelings of a character. And the only way to identify with a character, Truffaut concludes, is to see him. A classic example of the subjective camera is the little boy's interview with the psychiatrist in Truffaut's *Les Quatre Cent Coups:* the camera holds on the little boy's face for the whole interview, and we see his feelings. Welles takes this basic filmic rule and makes it part of his own style. When young Kane receives a Christmas sled from his guardian, for example, the camera tilts from his face to a grotesquely angled view of the towering Thatcher. In the same shot we see Charles and view Thatcher from the boy's angle—feeling as well the guardian's power over the boy. Another example is the long dolly shot in *The Ambersons* along with George and Lucy's carriage. We see the characters' feelings ("identify" with them), but the ceaseless variation of the distance between the camera and the carriage also distances us from them. This distortion, a contrapuntal actor-camera movement, a montage within the shot, explains the mixture of compassion and irony omnipresent in Welles's films.

Our attention is not on Wilbur in his coffin but on the family around it—and particularly on Fanny, who moves toward the camera and is then shown in great closeup, her face streaked with tears, more for herself than for her brother. A pointed little chorus follows on a dissolve from Fanny's face: two grim townsmen, staring into the camera as the mourners had done in the previous scene, one of them saying, "Wilbur Minafer—quiet man—town'll hardly know he's gone."

Missing before this chorus, evidently through Wise's cutting, is the first of a series of four shots intended as a motif solidifying and lending inevitability to the film. (Since they were "abstract," however, the shots were a logical choice for the cutting-bin.) Fanny's face was to dissolve into the

Amberson-Minafer cemetery plot, "a scene of stone only—not a tree or shrub in sight." In the background is a white marble column, taller than any other in the area, inscribed "AMBERSON." In the foreground is a granite block with the inscription "MINAFER"; the graves of the two families are between the two stones. Wilbur's headstone is close to the camera, heaped high with flowers and inscribed with his name and the dates of his birth and death. [After reading this, Welles told me he had omitted the cemetery motif because it was a cliché.—Ed.]

The scene of the two men staring into the camera, taken from a low angle (grave's eye-view) and showing the men in formal (funeral) dress against a daytime sky, is not in the script. So it apparently was meant to follow the shot of the gravestones. And it, in turn, had evidently dissolved to the second shot of the motif: the same scene, months later, after a rainfall. "The headstones are wet and the graves surrounded by puddles reflecting the sky. Some of the dirt has been washed off of Wilbur's grave, and on it is only a small bouquet." Though the gravestone scenes followed each other in the script, it is clear that Welles intended the chorus to fit (excellently) between them in the film.

The cemetery motif, which was to follow the deaths of Isabel and the Major as well, does what the rocking cradle of *Intolerance* fails to do. Eisenstein wrote that Griffith translated Walt Whitman's lines "not in the structure, not in the *harmonic recurrence of montage expressiveness*, but in *an isolated picture*, with the result that the cradle could not possibly be *abstracted into an image of eternally reborn epochs* and remained inevitably simply a *life-like cradle*, calling forth derision, surprise or vexation in the spectator [italics his]."

Welles's device, however, *was* integrated into the montage structure—each time the plot is seen it has aged with the weather and twice it has acquired a new tombstone. Its harmonic recurrence has the opposite emotional effect of the cradle.

The famous kitchen scene is the next retained in the released film. Welles seats the audience across from George as he stuffs himself, Fanny prodding him about Eugene's involvement with Isabel at the commencement, from which he has just returned. The camera makes two slight pans, one at the beginning and one at the end of the scene, and the effect is of eavesdropping on a confusing and revelatory confrontation between a person masking her emotions and another oblivious to them. We share each hesitation and gesture with the characters, prodded by no editorial device. The implication involved in showing the scene to us in its totality is that the hesitations are equally as important as the gestures. The *mise-en-scène* is highly baroque: a clutter of pots hanging in the background, a giant stove in the left rear, long black shadows across the ceiling, a clutter of serving dishes, pitchers and plates in the foreground. George stuffs himself relentlessly.

Welles has given an erroneous impression of this scene: "The actors were rehearsed for five weeks before we started the film. And on this scene at least four days, except that this scene was never written. No word of it was written—and we discussed everybody's life, each one's character, their background, their position at this moment in the story, what they would think about everything—and then sat down and cranked the camera, and every actor made up his lines as he went along. The scene lasts 3½ minutes or something in its entirety and was written by the actors as we went along. I'm very proud of them for it. It has an extraordinary effect, entirely due to their preparation for doing it."

A study of the novel and the screenplay contradicts Welles's remarks: with a few differences, the scene comprises the first part of chapter sixteen in the novel. Jack (a Falstaffian character whose name in the book is George Amberson) does not appear in this scene in the book; his lines are taken from a speech of his in chapter sixteen and from one of George Minafer's in chapter sixteen. And the scene was written out in the script—it covers pages 64 to 68—the only improvisations were the occasional lines about George's eating: "Quit bolting your food.... Don't eat so fast, George.... Want some more milk? No, thanks.... You're going to get fat.—Can't help that!" But Welles is correct in his praise of the actors: the scene *seems* off-the-cuff because of their skillful interweaving of set dialogue and impromptu remarks. Agnes Moorehead again sets and changes her tone with great concentration, and

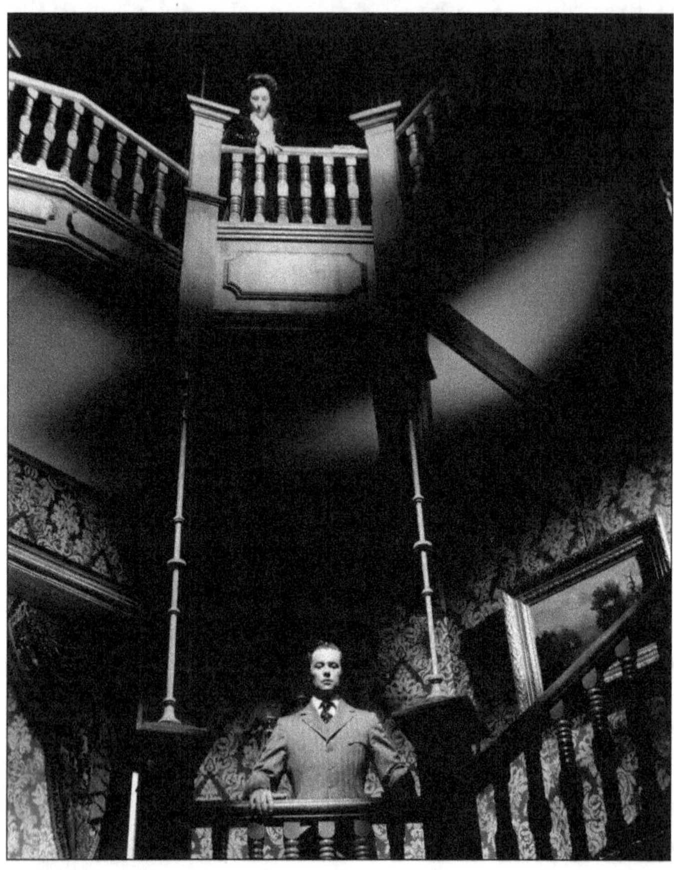

The staircase scenes in *Ambersons* are highly charged expression-
istic evocations of social and familial hierarchies, serving as stages
for some of Moorehead's most powerful moments in her great
performance as Aunt Fanny Minafer. She is seen here looking down
on her headstrong nephew, George. (RKO)

the slight stiffness of some of Tim Holt's and Ray Collins's
deliveries actually adds to the verisimilitude of the scene.

The scene ends with a fade-out on Jack's "I really don't
know of anything much Fanny *has* got—except her feeling
for Eugene" and a cut to a blacksmith hammering steel in
Eugene's factory. But apparently there have been cuts made
between these scenes. In the script George, looking out the

window (as he now is on the fade-out), shouts "Holy cats!" and dashes outside to look at a row of excavations on the mansion lawn. He stands in the rain, furious; Jack arrives a moment later to shield him with an umbrella and to defend the Major's decision to break up the lot for housing. This was to fade to George's buggy and Eugene's car parked outside the entrance of the "MORGAN HORSELESS CARRIAGE" factory. From *there* Welles intended to make the cut to the tracking shot of the group inside the factory.

The loss of the excavation scenes—and of later scenes which touch on the Major's thrift measures—robs the film of some of its most acute points of family-town conflict. The factory scene, with its intense workmen pulling ropes and pushing automobiles, its cars on display and its process screen showing large machines in the background—all this clamor sets off most effectively the small focus of the scene: Fanny's anguished face turning slowly toward the camera as Isabel and Eugene reminisce about "the first Morgan Invincible," which stands behind them. A brief excised scene was to have shown George and Lucy getting into their carriage and joking about their "sentimental" elders.

After the next scene in the released film, the brief conversation between Isabel and Eugene on the mansion lawn, which Welles had intended to come three scenes later (see Appendix), George is shown driving Lucy through the town. Welles jump-cuts from their carriage following in the exhaust of Eugene's car to the carriage trotting steadily along the street; the music conveys the same jaunty feeling as the cut. This long trucking shot is a famous example of Welles's camera vs. character counterpoint. At the end of the shot the camera gains slowly on the carriage, and we can see that the dolly has been rolling on streetcar tracks [actually the camera was on a crane—Ed.]. Welles goes so far to acknowledge the camera's involvement in the scene as actually to show the wheel of the [crane] in the lower left-hand corner of the screen.

The camera halts; George gallops the carriage out of the frame right; the Major's buggy follows and a quick dissolve shows Jack and the Major in conversation inside the buggy. This procession of the generations—first the automobile, then George, then the Major—is an excellent visual metaphor.

The buggy scene seems truncated, and the script indicates that Wise trimmed it because of a reference to the excavations. After the Major's line about the town rolling over his heart and "burying it under," the following dialogue is missing:

Major: When I think of those devilish workmen digging up my lawn, yelling around my house —
Jack: Never mind, Father. Don't think of it. When things are a nuisance, it's a good idea not to keep remembering 'em.
Major: (Murmurs) I *try* not to. I try to keep remembering that I won't be remembering anything very long. *(Becomes mirthful and slaps his knee)* Not so very long now, my boy. Not so very long now. Not so very long!

The next scene retained in the film is the dinner-table argument, but the buggy scene was to have dissolved into a conversation on the mansion verandah. Bicycles and surreys flash by in the evening, disrupted by an occasional noisy automobile. George is brooding, oblivious to the conversation. The five new houses on the lawn have progressed, one already completed. Fanny tells Isabel that autos are a fad, "like roller skates." "Besides," she goes on, "people just won't stand for them after a while. I shouldn't be surprised to see a law passed forbidding the sale of automobiles the way there is with concealed weapons." When Isabel counters with a gentle question about her sincerity in telling Eugene that she had enjoyed the afternoon's drive, Fanny says that she "didn't say it so very enthusiastically," and that it "hardly seems time yet — to me" for anyone to get the idea that Eugene had pleased her.

A very uneasy silence follows, the only sound the creaking of Fanny's wicker rocking chair. "A series of human shrieks could have been little more eloquent of emotional disturbance," Tarkington notes at this point. Then Isabel notices that across the street Mrs. Johnson is spying on them from her bedroom window with a pair of opera glasses. With a laughing remark, Isabel goes inside. Fanny expresses thinly concealed reproach over Isabel's "queer" behavior, her violation of mourning "on the *very* anniversary of Wilbur's death!" George ignores her as she clangs the door shut, leaving him alone. Then follows the scene which, for all the beauty it must have had, [Welles was pressured by RKO to cut; the entire first verandah scene was cut before the Pomona preview.—Ed.]

As George sits brooding, Lucy "appears in old-fashioned transparency (the shadowy ghost figure from the silents). She throws herself on the steps at his feet." The visionary Lucy begs George to forgive her and assures him that she will never again listen to her father's opinions. George solemnly pardons her but, realizing that he has been talking to himself, swings his feet down to the floor of the verandah: "Pardon nothing!" Then he pictures Lucy "as she probably really is at this moment; sitting on her own front porch in the moonlight with four or five boys, all of them laughing most likely, and some idiot probably playing a guitar." He paces the stone floor furiously, muttering "Riffraff!" over and over. This was to have dissolved to the lawn scene.

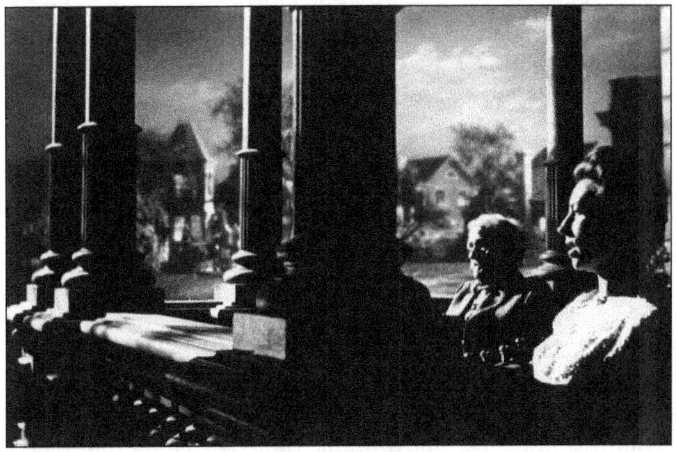

A frame enlargement, recently discovered by Roger Ryan, of the missing second verandah scene cut from Welles's version, another Chekhovian element in the original. Major Amberson and Fanny sit in the evening and watch the rapidly developing and decaying city while talking of their looming financial problems and Isabel's illness. (RKO/Roger Ryan/University of Michigan Special Collections Library)

V.

The climax of the drama, George's announcement that automobiles are "a useless nuisance," comes in the dinner sequence, the next retained in the film and reportedly Welles's favorite in the film. This is George's first formal step. From this point on he is determined to wreck his mother's romance. Chiefly remarkable about the argument is the brilliance of the montage: the first few shots keep George in the background, on the periphery of the conversation. He blurts out his line offscreen while Eugene and the Major are shown talking; Welles cuts to Jack withdrawing his hand from the table, then to Isabel holding her breath, her head slightly back and her eyes partly closed. Only then does he show George, who repeats what he has said and adds that "they had no business to be invented." After a reprimand from Jack (which in the novel is given by the Major, Jack being absent), George is shown in sullen isolation. In the background is a giant cross-bar shadow, similar to those which appear throughout *Kane*, at the most ominous moments: the opening, the breakfast montage, Susan's suicide attempt, the ending. Welles also made extensive use of this in *Othello,* which opens with Othello's funeral procession and Iago being thrown into a cage.

Eugene's speech about automobiles changing men's minds is remarkable not so much for the content of the words as for their effect on his and George's faces, which are shown in an exchange of several closeups. Eugene is agreeing with George that automobiles "had no business to be invented," but their faces say otherwise. Eugene excuses himself, leaves, Fanny darting after him, and on Jack's return through the door a moment later the camera pans from George on the left and Isabel on the right to a shot framing Jack (in the background) and George (now on the right). After another reprimand from Jack, George throws down his napkin and bolts for the door—the camera swinging right with his motion, Isabel rising at the same moment. Then a quick cut to George slamming open the door to the hall, where Fanny intercepts him. This rapid, precise cutting helps the acting and the carefully sculptured photography to establish George's increasingly angry mood.

The staircase scene which follows is one of the most effective crane shots in Welles's work. George follows Fanny ("It's always Fanny, ridiculous old Fanny—always—always!") through huge shadows; they halt on the first landing, the camera tilted slightly to the right as George shakes her. This is one of Agnes Moorehead's greatest scenes. She simultaneously conveys profound anger at George, envy of Isabel, transparent self-pity, and sympathy for George. She says that the romance "wouldn't have amounted to anything if Wilbur had lived," and he asks incredulously, "You mean Morgan might have married *you?*" She gulps—her head back, her fingers doing a nervous pirouette on the railing—and, with exquisite inflection, says. "No… because I don't know that—I'd have accepted him."

George dashes off, leaving Fanny terrified. As he grills the old gossip, Mrs. Johnson, the camera eavesdrops, reframing the characters five times in its almost complete revolution around the room. The transition from this scene is a visual shock like that of the screaming cockatoo in *Citizen Kane*: George in his dark suit strides out of the frame left—the white-dressed Mrs. Johnson stands outraged for a moment—then a cut to Jack's bath water streaming out of the faucet as he and it make similar groaning sounds. After George's portentous exit from the bathroom (Jack's comment, "For heaven's sake, don't be so theatrical!" is also the artist's humorous comment on his work, as was Kane's line, "I had no idea you had this flair for melodrama, Emily"), three scenes have been cut:

Isabel's door opens as George walks into the hall. He steps into a shadow as he hears her voice. She opens the door to his room, sees that he is gone, and returns to her room. He noiselessly goes to the stairs and up to the ballroom. The next scene is similar to famous shots in *Kane* and *The Lady from Shanghai:* "Moonlight, coming through the glass ceiling, floods the room. George walks to the center of the ballroom and stands there, reflected in the pier-glass mirrors that line all sides of the room." Like Kane he sees the endless reflection of his own ego, and this, his most acute moment of consciousness, is interrupted by Isabel's footfall and voice.

She stops on the stairs, and he has nowhere to go. Her timid attempts at wishing him goodnight are answered in perfunctory monosyllables. She walks away, and the scene fades to George unwrapping a framed photograph of his father the next day in the drawing-room. He whispers brokenly, "Poor, poor father! Poor man, I'm glad you didn't know!" He walks to the window and sits looking through the curtains. Through the gloomy silence Isabel's voice can be heard in a song:

> Lord Bateman was a noble lord,
> A noble lord of high degree;
> And he sailed West and he sailed East,
> Far countries for to see....

The words to this foreshadowing of Eugene's visit become indistinct, change to a whistle, to a hum, and then drift out of hearing. George stares out the window.

The next part of the sequence is retained in the released film: Eugene arriving, George watching from the window, George opening the door and ordering him to leave. "Perhaps you'll understand *this*," he says, and slams the door. For about ten seconds Morgan stands still, seen through the frosted glass. Then he leaves, and George goes back into the house, slamming the door of the entrance hall behind him. Missing here is a scene in the drawing room in which Isabel, still whistling "Lord Bateman," a kind of sound montage, finds George sitting in the gloom. Hearing the doorbell ring and then being told by the maid that it was a peddler, she asks George what the earlier "peddler" (George's explanation to the maid) had been selling. "He didn't say," George answers. A tense moment follows when Isabel notices the silver-framed picture George has placed on the table. She asks if it is Lucy but on approaching gives a long, just-audible "Oh!" George is silent, and she says, "That was nice of you, Georgie. I ought to have had it framed myself, when I gave it to you." She puts her hand on his shoulder, withdraws it and leaves. After a while George follows.

Dissolves were to connect two short scenes of him in the hall peering at his mother, who is waiting at the window of the drawing room for Eugene to arrive. A third scene shows him leaving his room as Jack rings the doorbell off-camera.

In the film as it stands, George walking away from Eugene dissolves into Isabel waiting (which was to have been the next shot in this intended sequence). The framed picture of Wilbur is prominently placed in this scene. Isabel rises and goes into the hall. Welles then cuts to Jack leading her through the hall to tell her what George has done. A ponderous upward tilt of the camera, underscored by a heavy musical chord and huge shadows, shows Fanny dashing down the stairs to keep George from disturbing his mother. After this a short scene of Isabel comforting her son in his room, a dark, pathetic moment in which she whispers, "You mustn't be troubled, darling," has been cut.

The letter scenes which follow are a gamble against stiffness, and they do not come off well, except for the brilliant device of dissolving a tilted shot of the empty hall (through which Jack and Isabel had walked moments earlier) between Eugene writing the letter and Isabel reading it. From internal evidence it appears that these two scenes were the ones directed by Wise when Welles was forced to speed his shooting schedule. The setup in Eugene's study is almost exactly similar to that of the next-to-last scene in the released film, and the lighting is similarly banal. The lighting in Isabel's room, more difficult because more heavily shadowed, is extremely bad but for the device of lights shining into her eyes to make them stand out through the darkness. Welles may have planned the camera placement—the dissolve from the hall to the room is a beautiful visual effect—but here it can be seen how much the film's texture depended on Cortez and on Welles's knowledge of lighting.

These scenes were shot with a second camera unit; compare also the mediocre lighting of the film's last three shots. The placement of the three key lights in Isabel's room is awkward: the one behind the window glares straight into the lens, the one from below left is useless for effect or illumination, and the one behind the door right is irrelevant and distracting. Certain elements in the letter scenes work well—the script is good ("Don't strike my life down twice, dear—this time I've not deserved it") as is the high-note scoring for the violins.

The distancing effect of the montage in the scene between Isabel and George as they discuss the letter makes this potentially mawkish scene quite effective. There are three camera positions: a medium shot of George, a medium shot of Isabel, and a formal long shot of the two facing each other across the frame. After beginning the sequence with a long shot of George opening the door and following it with six alternating medium shots, Welles has Isabel rise *in long shot* to confront George with the fact that Eugene has always loved her. The fourth in another series of medium shots shows her grieving over George's bewilderment at what she has done—and Welles shows her walking to George in long shot and cradling him, in medium shot. The camera tracks in as she tells him, "I'll write Eugene. He'll understand. It will be better this way. We'll go away for a while, you and I." One of Hitchcock's rules for the maintenance of emotion is to keep the camera on the character's face as he rises and walks: but the cutting here anticipates—makes inevitable—Isabel's motion and dissipates the excessive emotion it would otherwise arouse. The music should perhaps have counterpointed the action instead of swelling behind it; as it is, this very delicate scene just barely escapes sentimentality.

The script here contains a letter from Isabel to George, to be narrated the same way as that from Eugene to Isabel. But as her voice says, "and for all this pain you'll forgive your loving and devoted--" Welles was to have cut to George reading the letter and speaking the last word," —mother." Some of this letter is incorporated in the dialogue of the previous scene, the ending of which has been reworked. It was to have shown Isabel leaving the room in tears at George's assumption (which she of course takes as an order) that she won't see Eugene again. She tells him that she has never let him see her cry before, except when his father died: after she leaves, George examines himself in the mirror and recites Hamlet's speech beginning "'Tis not alone my inky cloak, good mother ... ," a self-conscious parallel on George's and Tarkington's parts which works passably well in the novel but would have been too much at this point in the film.

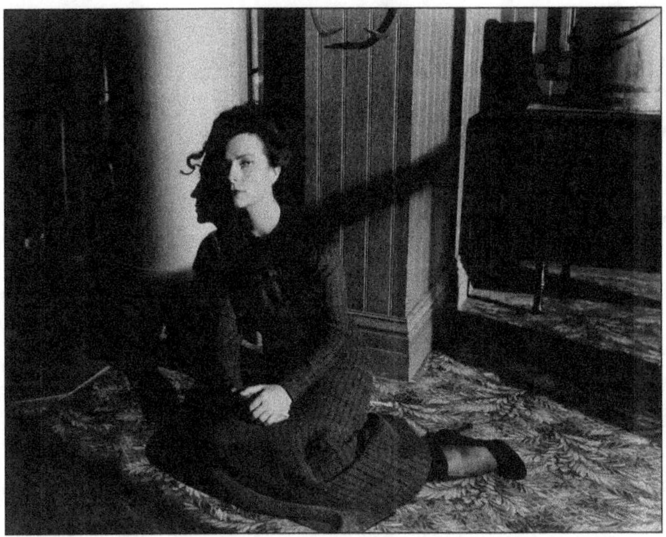

"It's not hot—it's *cold*"—Fanny sits distraught at the boiler in the kitchen of the Amberson mansion in this harrowing scene of her breakdown as she and George prepare to move out due to the loss of the family fortune. (RKO)

VI.

The long tracking shot along the street with George and Lucy, the film's next scene, is concerned not with a combat between two wills, as was their earlier trip through the town, but with Lucy's cool domination over George. Hence the camera maintains a *constant* distance from them. Welles's Stroheim-like realism dominates here—in the windows of the buildings behind them can be seen reflections of the buildings across the street, as in the earlier shot. But things are different: more people are on the sidewalks, the pedestrians' pace is faster, the traffic heavier. Several Model-T's are among the reflected vehicles. The earlier shot had included more residences than stores: in place of the earlier scene's homely hardware store are a drapery shop, a large bank, a movie theater, a drugstore. A warehouse has acquired a second story since we saw it last. On the boards outside the theater are posters for a Méliès movie—this is a tribute from one cinematic magician to another [actually the poster is not for a Georges Méliès movie but one by his brother Gaston—Ed.]—and for "Jack Holt in *Explosion.*" This is a reference to Tim Holt's actor father, a former stuntman who started his long Western career in 1919, fourteen years after this scene took place.

This shot is the oddest in the film. Some critics have thought that Lucy's rather puzzling indifference to George would have been better explained had the film not been cut, and this is true. Welles intended the scene to be in its present place, but it should be recalled that the last time Lucy had appeared was in the cut scene of George's "vision." At the close of that scene she was seen being wooed by four or five other boys, and if that had remained, her attitude here would be more easily understood. As the shot begins George asks her, "haven't you—," and she cuts in, "Haven't I what?" He drops the matter and it is apparent that Eugene hasn't told her about what has happened the day before (she wouldn't be speaking to George if he had).

But all that now exists in the film to explain her attitude are her comments about the quarrel they had had, and how they hadn't spoken to each other "all the way home from a long, long drive." It is hard for the audience to connect this with the carriage ride through town, which happened more than a dozen scenes earlier. Lucy teases George about the absurdity of their earlier behavior, and the confused audience is left to speculate over whether she has or hasn't heard about Eugene's expulsion after all. And when George walks away and Welles cuts to a closeup of Lucy which shows only the dark parts of her outfit—her collar, hat and muff—this tonal change, which would have been such a brilliant formal effect had the film retained its original structure, only provides more confusion. And when she faints in the drugstore. ... Since this sequence is intended both to counterpoint a much earlier scene and to refer to a scene which has been removed, it is unsuccessful.

After this [RKO—Ed.] omitted a short scene of the druggist recounting the fainting to his pals in the pool hall. Wise also cut the next three scenes and apparently reshot the fourth. The first was a night shot of the five new houses on the mansion lawn. In front of them a steady stream of automobiles passes, with now and then a bicycle or, at long intervals, a surrey or buggy passing by. The Major and Fanny are seen on the verandah in long shot, then more closely. Their dialogue is concerned with the Major's financial problems, which he had tried to remedy (without much luck) by having the house built, and with Fanny's and Jack's investments in the headlight company. The dialogue shifts to an ironic exchange:

Major: (Gravely) Isabel wants to come home. Her letters are full of it. Jack writes me she talks of nothing else.
No answer from Fanny.
Major: She's wanted to come for a long while. She ought to come while she can stand the journey.
Another pause.
Fanny: People are making such enormous fortunes out of everything to do with motor cars, it does seem as if—I wrote Jack I'd think it over seriously.
Major: (Laughing) Well, Fanny, maybe we'll be partners. How about it? And millionaires, too!

The scene fades to a chauffeur-driven car starting up the driveway of the great Georgian Morgan mansion. Another shot shows Lucy and Jack inside the car. Lucy doesn't quite understand when Jack tells her, "Here's the Amberson Mansion again, only it's Georgian instead of nondescript Romanesque; but it's just the same Amberson Mansion my father built long before you were born." She laughs "as a friend should," and they go into the house. An interior scene shows him teasing her about still being a belle of the ball, and about her recent refusal to become engaged to one of George's boyhood friends. She laughs, a little embarrassed.

Jack: Well, you're pretty refreshingly out of the smoke up here.
Lucy: (Laughing) For a little while. Until it comes and we have to move out farther.
Jack: No, you'll stay here. It'll be somebody else who'll move out farther.

Then the scene dissolves to Jack telling Eugene and Lucy that Isabel wants to come home from abroad, and that she ought to be in a wheelchair. As the film now stands, Lucy's fainting fades out and into a slow zoom shot (the only in the film) of Jack and Lucy walking up the steps of the Morgan Mansion. The dialogue is the archest kind of plot exposition: "Mighty nice of you, Lucy, you and Eugene, to have me over to your new house my first day back.—You'll probably find the old town rather dull after Paris." This looks like Wise's work. He had carefully removed all the scenes dealing with the new houses on the lawn, and as a consequence found himself with a five-year gap to explain (it is now 1910, and the fainting scene occurred in 1905, just before George and Isabel left for Europe). So he decided to shoot a new scene, which leads most clumsily into the completely static discussion in the Morgan library, a scene which probably fit well into the original film, but here is conspicuously slow.

After the short scenes of Isabel arriving at the station and being driven home ("Changed—so changed"), the script indicates a scene outside her second-floor bedroom. The Major querulously demands to see his daughter, and when he is admitted into the room Fanny asks George if Eugene can see Isabel. George abruptly refuses, and Fanny tells Eugene. He asks if he could only "look into the room and see her for just a second," but finally capitulates. These scenes were rewritten [and reshot by Freddie Fleck—Ed.] into the present one, which shows George refusing Morgan at the foot of the stairs, Morgan defying him, and then Fanny saying, "I don't think you should right now—the doctor said…" and breaking into tears. Jack agrees with her, and Eugene leaves, Fanny following him with her eyes.

This change of emphasis is unfortunate. Shifting the final decision, however inconclusively, to Fanny and Jack lessens one of the book's (and script's) most powerful themes, George's guilt over denying his mother's last request. The next shot is of George's face superimposed on the window as Eugene walks to his car: this seems to imply that George had *ordered* Fanny and Jack's decision, which would contradict the scene on the stairs. And if Fanny is denying Eugene's request only because of her own envy, why does Jack also deny Eugene?

The nurse's voice tells George that his mother wants to see him, and Welles immediately cuts from the superimposed shot of George's face to his actual face turning away from the window. This is a powerful effect, a visual shock that in its complete reversal of George's image shows how deeply he is shaken. (Compare this to the bullets shattering the mirror images of Bannister and his wife at the end of *The Lady from Shanghai.*) Achieving this effect allows Welles to understate the deathbed scene, which could otherwise have been mawkish. George shows more shame than grief, the grief having been shown at the window, as he listens to his mother's pathetic questions. "Dear, did you—get something to eat?" "Yes, mother." "All you needed?" "Yes, mother." When she says that she would have liked to have seen Eugene just once, George turns away in deep shame. Isabel's eyes strain to see him leave.

Her face dissolves into perhaps the most powerful shot in Welles's entire *oeuvre.* The slow dissolve, accompanied by the two contrasting musical motifs used in *Citizen Kane*—the deep brass of the "power" motif and the vibraphone "Rosebud" motif—reveals the Major sleeping fitfully on George's bed. He suddenly awakes, the music hinting that he has been dreaming, and rises in terror. The camera makes an hallucinatory pull slightly away from him, Jack crosses in front of him, the camera holds on the Major for a moment and then pans right as he totters off toward Jack, who by now has almost left the frame—suddenly Fanny throws her arms around George, who is standing in the extreme foreground with his back to the camera. "George! She loved you! She loved you!" George's face is not shown, just his back, and Welles again achieves the objective-subjective fusion of the reporter's scenes in *Kane.* The two tiny camera movements achieve such a strong effect because of their careful timing with the characters' movements, with the shock of Fanny's entrance, and because of the surreal, dreamlike compression of the scene: once the Major wakes, it is over in seconds. Like Kane's hand entering the frame to slap Susan, it is an epiphany.

A fade was to have shown the Minafer plot, Isabel's headstone bright and new and heaped with flowers, Wilbur's aged and with only a few. A dissolve was then to have flickered (as a fade does now) to the Major seated in front of an unseen fireplace, the light of the flames playing on his face. He stares straight into the camera, which is at a slight low angle.

"And now," Welles narrates, "Major Amberson was engaged in the profoundest thinking of his life...." Richard Bennett, whom Welles had brought out of retirement to play the Major and who died two years after the film was made, had trouble retaining his lines, and his eyesight was so bad that he couldn't read from a blackboard during the scene. *Collier's* reported that Welles had recited the Major's speech ("It must be in—the Sun—") on a record which Bennett then took home to memorize.

"I play it over," he explained to Joseph Cotten, "and I take portions of it and write them down and study them. I do it over and over, word by word."

"Are you getting them?" Cotten asked.

"Not a bloody blasted one of them!" cried Bennett proudly.

When the scene was shot Welles stood just outside the frame and prompted Bennett every few words. When the sound was processed Welles's voice was eliminated. This partially explains the pauses between the phrases which have such a moving effect when combined with the somber music, the slow track forward and the sculptural lighting on the Major's deeply lined face. The fade-out also flickers, an effect repeated several times during the film: the lighting on the character's face (here from the fire) is the strongest in the shot, so the dissolve or fade makes the face appear disembodied. This scene was to have dissolved to the Major's grave in the Amberson plot, underscoring the rapidity with which his death followed Isabel's.

As it stands the shot fades to the nearly-static scene of Jack's departure in the railroad station. The structure of the film after this scene has been changed completely. (See the Appendix for the order of the intended and actual sequences.)

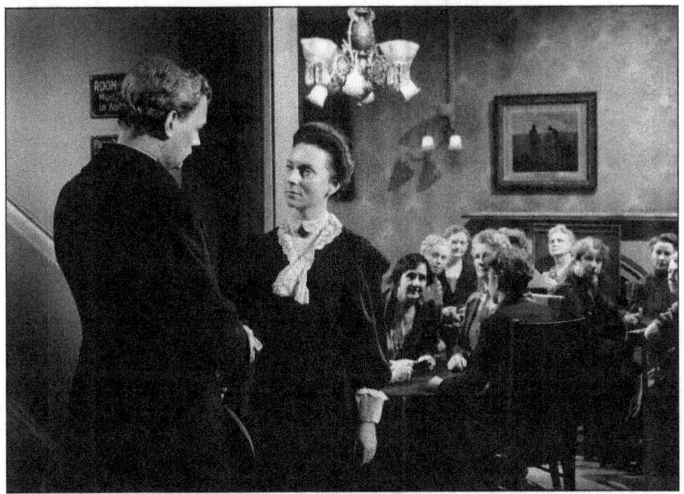

During production Welles came up with a new ending to replace Tarkington's (and the script's) unsatisfactory conclusions. After George is injured and hospitalized due to being hit by an automobile, Eugene goes to the shabby boarding house where Fanny has moved to economize. Welles referred to how this sequence, which was cut from the film by RKO, dealt with "the deterioration of personality, the way people diminish with age, and particularly with impecunious old age. The end of the communication between people, as well as the end of an era." (RKO/Lilly Library, Indiana University, Bloomington, Indiana)

VII.

The first thing to be said about the original ending sequence is that it was fluid. A static scene (the Major's death—and his grave) is followed by a violent scene (Fanny's hysteria in the kitchen) which is followed by a less-intense scene (George in Bronson's office), and so forth. The scenes as they stand now are jerky and have only a haphazard chronological continuity. The scene which suffers the most from this displacement is the quite beautiful shot of Eugene and Lucy walking through their garden. In its present place as the third in a succession of nearly static scenes it seems oppressively slow and, consequently, labored and coy. But as Welles intended it, as a letdown from the intense montage of George walking through the town, it would have been most effective.

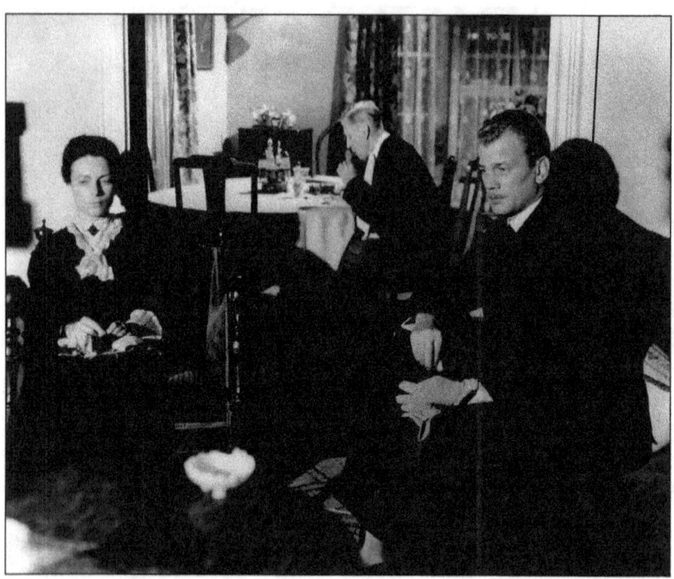

As Eugene sits with Fanny, oblivious to her emotions, they find it
hard to talk because of the lack of privacy, and because, as Welles
said, "there's just nothing left between them at all. Everything
is over—her feelings and her world and his world; everything is
buried under the parking lots and the cars." (RKO/Lilly Library,
Indiana University, Bloomington, Indiana)

Furthermore, George's job at the dynamite factory seems
to last an incongruously short time before he is injured in the
auto accident, which in turn is weakened in effect. As Welles
planned it, three scenes were to have intervened between
Bronson's office and the accident: Jack's farewell, the montage,
and the garden scene. The lapse of screen time involved, and
the passage of actual time implied, would have conditioned
the viewer's awareness that George has been on the job for
some time, as indeed he has: the script indicates that a year has
elapsed. The accident, in the novel's words, was "so common-
place and inconsequent that it was a comedy," but following
immediately after his "comeuppance," that moving shot of
him kneeling in the deserted mansion, the accident seems so
consequent upon his defeat that it is absurd. But the audience
doesn't have time to reflect on the silliness of its placement,

for immediately after the newspaper inserts reporting the accident come the campy ending shots. Strangely enough, of all the reviewers only Manny Farber in *The Nation* seemed to have been bothered by these last three shots, attributing the "hearts-and-flowers finish" to "blundering editing."

The thematic reversal in these last two scenes, not to mention the stylistic letdown, is appalling. After a scene in Morgan's study in which Anne Baxter prods a hypnotized-looking Joseph Cotten into striding out of the frame with her, we are asked to agree, as Eugene informs Fanny outside George's hospital room, that "everything's going to be all right." And, thanks to the meretricious direction, Fanny seems to have become Eugene "true love."

The book's rather protracted denouement had Eugene going to a medium and believing for a while that he had contacted Isabel, who tells him to "be kind." Then he returns home to see George, who asks his forgiveness. The script makes several changes, omitting the mawkish device of the medium: it shows Eugene in his office deciding to see George (in the book he reads the story of the accident on a train going east); dissolves to him telling the chauffeur to take him to the hospital and being told by the chauffeur that Lucy is already there; dissolves to the car arriving at dusk and from that to Eugene leaving the hospital later that night; and finally, after a dissolve to him pulling up to his door and saying goodnight to the chauffeur, shows him entering his library. He takes a diary from the drawer of his desk, unlocks the clasp with a tiny key on his watch chain, opens the book, picks up a pen and starts to write.

The book ends with the sentimental note that through Eugene, Isabel "had brought her boy under shelter again. Her eyes would look wistful no more." Fleck's ending has Eugene telling Fanny that through him Isabel had "brought her boy under shelter again and that I'd been true at last to my true love." On these last words the camera swings to Fanny's face, then back to include Eugene. The implication, reinforced by a sudden burst of music and a little sigh from Fanny, is that Eugene has loved her all along.

In the script the same last line closes the film, but with the order of the clauses reversed. This makes a world of ironic difference. The final shot is a closeup of Eugene's face as he writes (all the words played to show his reaction to them). We hear the scratching of his pen, and his voice narrating what he is writing:

> Dearest Isabel—your boy was hurt in a street accident today—run down by an automobile. I thought at first I wouldn't go to see him at the hospital, but of course I did. I thought it would be hard not to be bitter but I found it was easy—he looked so much like you, dearest one. As I came in, he lifted his hand in a queer gesture, half-forbidding, half-imploring, then let his arm fall back on the covers. He said, "You must have thought my mother wanted you to come so that I could ask you to—to forgive me." Lucy was beside him and she shook her head. "No," she said, "just to take his hand—gently." She was radiant… But for me another radiance filled the room—and I knew I'd been true at last to my true love and that through me you had brought your boy under shelter again.

No mention of Fanny, but a pathetic apostrophe to a dead woman. George's apology is the logical outcome of the scene in the mansion in which, kneeling, he begs, "Mother, forgive me. *God*, forgive me." But the final irony of the film—a much richer ending than that of the book—is that Eugene has gladly accepted the situation which has destroyed his life: Isabel's domination of her son, and George's consequent domination of them. [The boarding house ending Welles shot made this irony even more painful.—Ed.] As in *Kane*, the music under the credits—here the waltz theme of the early part of the movie, and there the jaunty "Oh, Mr. Kane!"—fulfills the crescendo function common to the closing scenes of all tragedies.

The power of individual scenes persists through the chaotic structure of the present ending sequence. Foremost is Agnes Moorehead's great scene in the kitchen and hall of the deserted mansion. Welles rehearsed her over and over until she actually was in hysterics when it was filmed. As George drags her through the hall, shaking her back to her senses, the camera tracks rapidly back with them through three rooms and into the dining room, gaining increasingly on them and finally pulling away to distance us from a scene of an intensity seldom equalled on film.

The dissolves of George walking through "the strange streets of a strange city" are done with the camera playing George (in the script he was to have appeared, seen from the back, in the first shot of the series; the camera moves faster than he does, tracking in so close that his body forms a dark screen for a dissolve): this objective effect reinforces the strangeness of the dirty buildings, telephone wires and rundown houses ("New Hope Apartments"). The script indicates a montage at least three times as long as that in the present film: shots of a cleaning and dye house, a funeral home and a lodge (once scenes of George's boyhood, the narrator says) have been cut, as has a short scene in which a carload of youngsters jeer at him as he walks down what had once been "Amberson Boulevard" and is now "10th Street." From the angle of the people in the car, George is seen muttering "Riffraff!" The camera pulls away slowly, then faster, "as though it is the car," leaving George a tiny figure in the darkness—another insult from the automobile.

This dissolves to shots of him entering the mansion, which in turn dissolve to a shot in which the camera wanders slowly through the dismantled house. It recapitulates the reception room, the kitchen, returns up the staircase, stops for a moment, pans down to the heavy library doors (behind which Isabel had learned of Eugene's expulsion), and after a short pause pans back and continues, even more slowly, up the stairs to the second-floor hall and to the closed door of Isabel's room. The door swings open and we see that nothing has been changed. Then this extraordinary shot was to fade out. [Welles evidently cut the shot, which may not have worked.—Ed.] During this part of the montage the narrator has been saying:

> The city had rolled over his heart and buried it under as it rolled over the Major's and the Ambersons' and buried them under to the last vestige.

Tonight would be the last night that he and Fanny were to spend in the house which the Major had forgotten to deed to Isabel. Tomorrow they were to "move out."

Tomorrow everything would be gone: the very space in which tonight was still Isabel's room would be cut into new shapes by new walls and floors and ceilings. And if space itself can be haunted as memory is haunted, then it may be that some impressionable, overworked woman in a "kitchenette," after turning out the light, will seem to see a young man kneeling in the darkness, with arms outstretched through the wall, clutching at the covers of a shadowy bed. It may seem to her that she hears the faint cry, over and over—

[The narration kept in Welles's version began with "Tomorrow they were to 'move out.'"—Ed.] Now the screen was to fade into the dark shot of the back of George's head, which, as the camera retreats, reveals him kneeling in his mother's room. After the narration which remains in the film ("… George Amberson Minafer had got his comeuppance. He'd got it three times filled and running over…."), the scene was to dissolve slowly to a shot of the old mansion, windows broken, front door ajar and "idiot salacity" smeared upon the pillars and stonework of the verandah. This was to fade to the garden scene.

VIII.
The mutilation of the film is, of course, unconscionable, but the first half is relatively intact, and in that and in the isolated power of the other scenes *The Ambersons* will continue to live. As Truffaut has said, "If Flaubert re-read *Don Quixote* each year, why can't we re-see *The Ambersons* whenever possible?"

The film as we see it is quite hectic, more melodramatic than it had been; Wise naturally retained the "plot" scenes at the expense of the quieter, more ironic shots Welles has called "the whole heart of the picture really" (the cemetery motif, the verandah scenes, the missing two-thirds of the town montage, the camera moving through the empty house, etc.). With the loss of the excavation scenes and other shots of the spreading town, the film concentrates more on the family than was intended, and the ironic bite arising from the Ambersons' gradual de-eminence in the town has been lessened. The exact pace of the planned film has become ragged and somewhat exhausting, but enough of Welles's overall conception remains for it to be apparent from the film itself just how great a work it was before RKO got cold feet. Today Robert Wise feels that no serious harm was done: "We had a picture with major problems, and I feel all of us tried sincerely to keep the best of Welles's concept and still lick the problem.

"Since *Ambersons* has become something of a classic, I think it's now apparent we didn't 'mutilate' Orson's film."

After his success with the recutting Wise began petitioning the front office for a chance to direct, which he received two years later.

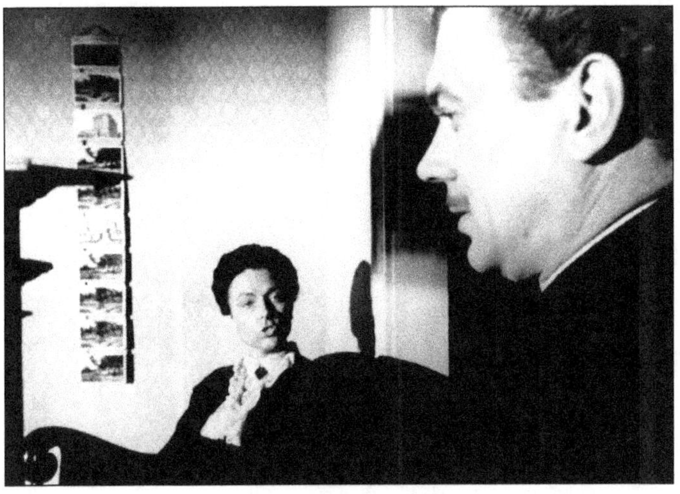

A frame enlargement Welles had made from the missing boarding house sequence, with Fanny's restrained distress evident to the audience, if not to Eugene, who reminisces about his love for Isabel. Welles told Peter Bogdanovich, "Sure, it was pretty rough going for an audience—particularly in those days. But without question it was much the best scene in the movie." (RKO/Lilly Library, Indiana University, Bloomington, Indiana)

He felt that the war had prevented the audiences' interest in the film's subject matter. Which war? The New York *Times* spoke for its public when it wrote, "In a world brimful of momentous drama beggaring serious screen treatment, it does seem that Mr. Welles is imposing when he asks moviegoers to become emotionally disturbed over the decline of such minor-league American aristocracy as the Ambersons represented in the late Eighteen Seventies."

Welles has talked of shooting two new reels to make the ending coherent, using the surviving actors as they are today, but admits that he is getting depressed by the number of his unfinished projects.

Appendix: The Original Structure of
The Magnificent Ambersons

This chart has been compiled by comparing the script and the novel with the film as released. As far as internal evidence can establish, the scenes in brackets were cut by Welles from the original script, and the scenes in parentheses were cut by Robert Wise from the finished film. For descriptions of these scenes see the text of this article. The final shooting script, 165 pages in length, is dated October 7, 1941.

SCENES

1. Prelude: streetcar scene, men in bar, Wilbur and Isabel rowing, Major's stovepipe hat knocked off by snowball, Eugene modeling clothes, mansion in the snow, the serenade, Eugene walking toward mansion, street chorus, Eugene at mansion door, [street chorus,] Eugene again at door, street chorus, Eugene driving away from mansion, Isabel and Wilbur walking the dog and snubbing Eugene, Jack in the barber shop, the sewing-room gossips, [street chorus,] young George driving through town in pony cart, street chorus, George fighting, George reprimanded on lawn, street chorus, George at seventeen driving through town in his cart.
2. [George halts outside the Amberson Block Building.]
3. [George with his old friends at a meeting of their boyhood club, the "Friends of the Ace," in the Building.]
4. The ball ("olive" remarks cut).
5. After the ball: [Eugene dancing with Fanny,] Eugene dancing with Isabel, George talking with Lucy, the Morgans leaving.
6. The Morgans start their car.
7. Eugene and Lucy talking about George—novel: in their hotel room; script: in stable while putting away the car; film: while driving home from ball.
8. George arguing with Isabel, Wilbur, Fanny and Jack.
9. [Isabel in George's room saying goodnight.]
10. Sleigh and car scene: iris-out.
11. [Exterior view of mansion—funeral procession parked outside.]
12. Wilbur's wake.
13. [The Amberson-Minafer cemetery plot: day of funeral.]

14. Chorus—not in script.
15. [The cemetery plot several months later.]
16. [Insert: George's college diploma.]
17. Exterior view of mansion in the rain.
18. Kitchen scene—partially improvised.
19. (Outside the mansion: George and Jack argue about excavations.)
20. (George's buggy and Morgan's car parked outside factory.)
21. Eugene, Lucy, George, Isabel and Fanny inside factory.
22. (George and Lucy outside factory.)
23. Eugene and Isabel on mansion lawn (in script this came between scenes 26 and 27).
24. George drives Lucy through town.
25. Major and Jack in buggy (end of scene cut).
26. (Verandah: George, Isabel, Fanny and George's vision of Lucy.)
27. Argument at dinner table.
28. George and Fanny argue on staircase.
29. [George outside Mrs. Johnson's.]
30. George confronts Mrs. Johnson.
31. George in Jack's bathroom.
32. (Isabel talks to George on stairs and in ballroom.)
33. (George in drawing-room the next day with Wilbur's portrait.)
34. (George, sitting in drawing-room, hears Isabel singing.)
35. Eugene arrives; George watches from window.
36. George orders Eugene to leave.
37. Eugene leaves; George watches.
38. (George talks with Isabel in drawing-room; they both leave.)
39. (George watches Isabel: two shots.)
40. (George leaves his room as Jack rings doorbell off-camera.)
41. Isabel leaves drawing-room.
42. She walks through hall with Jack; Fanny restrains George on staircase.
43. (Isabel comforts George in his room.)
44. Jack in Morgans' parlor as Eugene writes letter.
45. Eugene writes letter to Isabel.
46. Tilted shot of mansion hall.
47. Isabel receives letter.

48. George walks through hall to Isabel's room.
49. Isabel and George discuss letter.
50. [Isabel writes letter to George…]
51. […he reads it.]
52. George walks along street with Lucy.
53. Lucy faints in drugstore.
54. (Druggist in pool hall telling of her fainting.)
55. (Five new houses on mansion's old lawn.)
56. (Major and Fanny on verandah.)
57. (Car approaching Morgan mansion.)
58. (Jack and Lucy inside car.)
59. Jack and Lucy entering mansion.
60. (Jack and Lucy in hall.)
61. Eugene, Jack, Lucy in mansion library.
62. Isabel arrives with George at railroad station.
63. Isabel driven home in carriage.
64. Family gathered outside Isabel's room: Fanny and George discuss Morgan's arrival.*
65. Eugene arrives and leaves.
66. George waiting at window, watching him leave.
67. George at Isabel's bedside.
68. George's room—Major sleeping—Jack walks in—Fanny rushes to George: "George! She loved you! She loved you!"
69. [Cemetery—Isabel's grave.]
70. Major at fireside.
71. [Major's grave.]

Note: the following is the original ending sequence as it appears in the script.

72. George with Fanny in mansion kitchen and hall.
73. George in Bronson's office.
74. Jack and George at station.
75. George walks through town: dissolves of buildings; people in car jeer at him; camera follows him to mansion and then wanders through it; he kneels at bed; exterior view of mansion.
76. Eugene and Lucy in their garden.
77. George injured in auto accident.

---

* See text of article for discussion of scenes 64 and 65.

78. Accident seen as newspaper story
79. Eugene reads story in his office; leaves for hospital.
80. Dusk: Eugene arrives at hospital.
81. Night: he leaves hospital.
82. He arrives at his home.
83. He writes in his diary; closeup of his face. Fade out.
84. Credits.

The following is the ending sequence as it now stands.

72. Jack and George at station.
73. Eugene and Lucy in their garden.
74. George with Fanny in mansion kitchen and hall.
75. George in Bronson's office.
76. George walks through town: dissolves of buildings; he kneels at bed.[*]
77. George injured in auto accident.
78. Accident seen as newspaper story.
79. Eugene in his study with Lucy: two shots.[†]
80. Eugene and Fanny in hospital corridor.
81. Credits.

---

[*] Compare this with scene 75 in the original ending sequence above.
[†] Scenes 79 and 80 directed by assistant director Freddie Fleck.

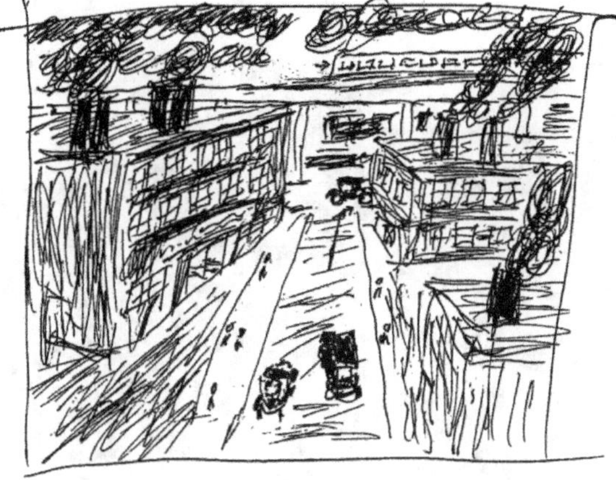

In 1970, Peter Bogdanovich showed me frame enlargements Welles had made of some of the missing scenes from his version of *The Magnificent Ambersons*. That's when I saw this frame enlargement of his last shot (before the end credits). Some of the stills Bogdanovich showed me exist, but this one evidently has been lost, so I drew it from memory in 2008.

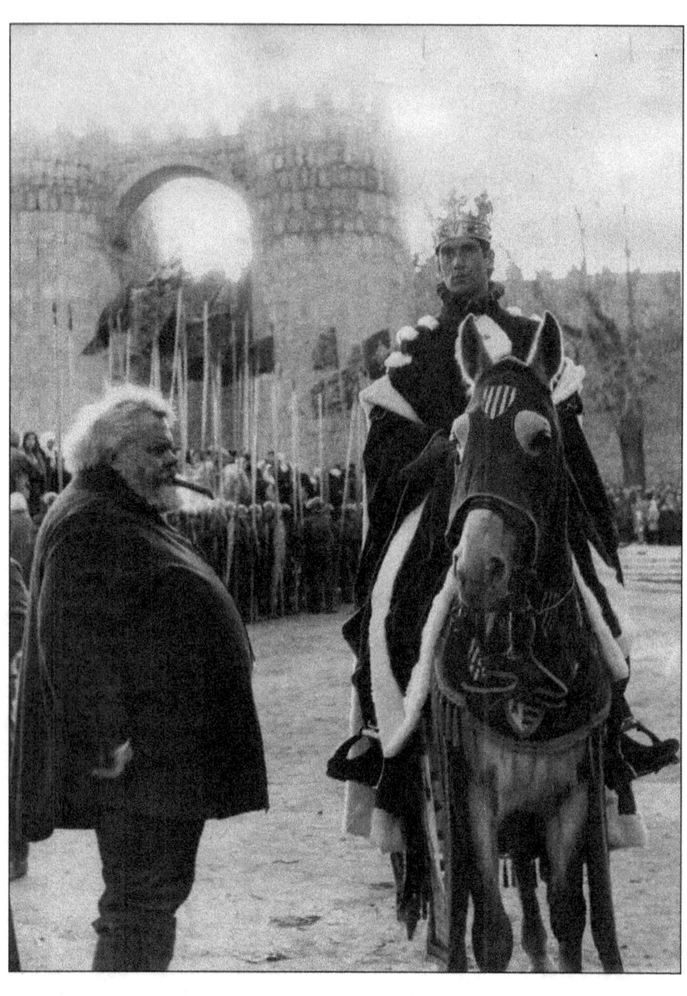

Welles directs Keith Baxter in his coronation scene as
King Henry V, formerly Prince Hal, in the director's adaptation
of history plays by Shakespeare, *Chimes at Midnight* (1965),
shot on Spanish locations.

Chimes at Midnight
Joseph McBride

To see Orson Welles's *Chimes at Midnight*, which has been masquerading in this country under the more prosaic title of *Falstaff*, I had to go to Chicago before it finished its five-day run and the Town Underground changed back into a nudie theater. Distribution elsewhere in the country has been just as scandalous. Though the film was a great success in Europe, the disapproval of a New York reviewer whose name shall not be mentioned here has discouraged a wide American release. I saw it three times in one night and twice again when it returned for an unprofitable two-week stand, but I am still unable to write an analysis worthy of *Chimes at Midnight*, which I consider to be Welles's masterpiece. For the present, let these brief notes express my love for it.

Welles's vision has lost its boyish vitality and has matured into an even more damning statement about the possibilities of innocence. He has achieved a world in which there is no distinction between comedy and tragedy. *Chimes at Midnight* has none of the earlier films' violent movements from exhilaration to dejection; its equipoise reflects an awareness on the hero's part that destruction is omnipresent and that love, though the only defense, is finally powerless. Falstaff battles this awareness throughout; his attempts to ignore it provide the comedy. Finally his very goodness, his complete candor, is his flaw. Not that it itself destroys him, but that it is unable to prevent his destruction. That is the tragedy.

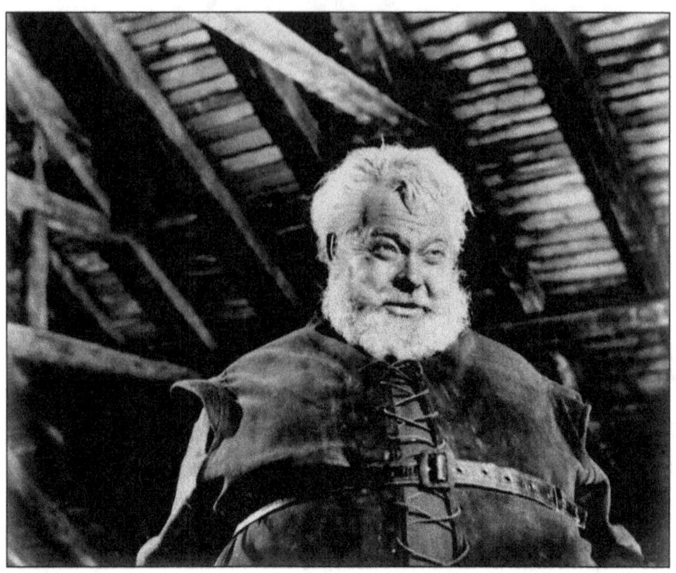

"Banish plump Jack, and banish all the world!"—Sir John Falstaff (Welles) gives his eerily prophetic and passionate self-defense ("If sack and sugar be a fault, then God help the wicked!") in a speech at the tavern in *Chimes at Midnight*. (International Films Española/ Alpine/Peppercorn-Wormser)

Hal's renunciation of Falstaff—"I know thee not, old man. Fall to thy prayers. How ill white hairs become a fool and jester"—is a moment of epiphany in Welles's work, the final expulsion of the man he calls "the most completely good man in all drama." The younger Welles subscribed more instinctively to the romantic aspects of the young man's setting out to conquer the world. His heroes then were luckier than Quinlan or K. or Falstaff. Welles dramatizes the Faustian split between instinctive evil and instinctive good which he sees in his own nature in terms of a corrupted power figure and another man, usually younger, who is in the process of recognizing his own corruption. The corrupted innocent (Leland, the younger Kane, George Minafer, O'Hara, Othello, Vargas, K., etc.) is naive, credulous, somewhat ridiculous. He searches out and confronts the man of power, who usually attempts to hide the secrets of his past, if not from others then at least from himself. Usually the innocent unmasks the man of power and is himself tainted in the process. A great deal of *Chimes at Midnight*'s pathos and irony comes from the reversal of the old and young men's roles. It is the old man, Falstaff, who is truly innocent, and Hal, whom he befriends and who finally must destroy him, the man of power.

In Welles's later films, most bitterly in the strained play-acting between Hal and Falstaff in the tavern scene which foreshadows the climax, the awareness of destruction is present even in moments of "respite." As a director matures his work becomes simpler, more direct, allowing room for deeper audience response; as Truffaut has put it, what is in front of the camera becomes more important. In *Chimes* Welles has merged his own viewpoint and that of his hero

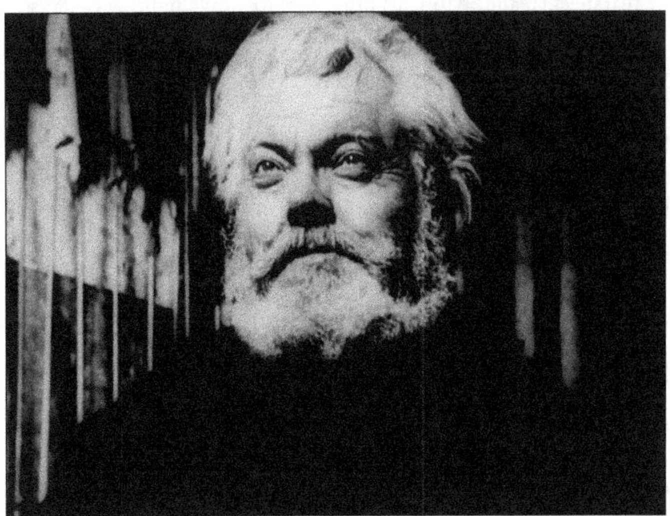

"I know thee not, old man. Fall to thy prayers"—Falstaff reacts to his rejection and banishment by King Henry V at his corona-tion. This was Welles's greatest moment as a screen actor, showing mingled heartbreak and pride at his surrogate son becoming king, even though the former reprobate Prince Hal must turn away his followers to demonstrate his worthiness to the world. It is the culmination of many such betrayals in Welles's body of work. (Frame enlargement; International Films Española/Alpine/ Peppercorn-Wormser)

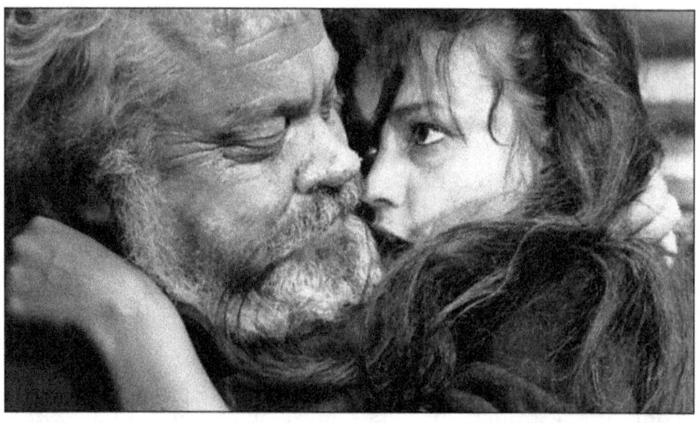

While offering solace to Falstaff in his old age, the prostitute Doll Tearsheet (Jeanne Moreau) urges him to "leave fighting o' days and foining o' nights and begin to patch your bare old body for heaven." This is one of three films in which Welles directed the great French actress, who said, "If he calls you and says, 'I need you,' then you say 'Orson needs me and it's something important.' His career is so strange because he's capable of such beautiful things and it's so hard for him now to make a film that you wouldn't be the little stone that would stop the machine from going, once he has the chance to make a film. I think that's why we all do react that way." (International Films Española/Alpine/Peppercorn-Wormser)

into a direct communication of emotion. His style no longer demands our attention for itself. Instead, much like Jean Renoir in *La Grande Illusion,* a similar story of the necessary betrayal of friendship, he simply presents people to us.

It had long seemed that Welles was capable of playing only cold characters, ones with masked emotions. We sympathize more with the author of *Citizen Kane* than with Kane himself. The emotions are expressed more through the *mise-en-scène* than through the characters' faces. With Welles's maturity as a director, however, has come an almost miraculous growth as an actor. Irony is omnipresent in *Kane,* but it is achieved at the expense of the central character. Falstaff is childlike and has little of Kane's sophistication, but he is more aware of what time brings. He tells Doll Tearsheet, "I am old, I am old," and "Thou'lt forget me when I am gone." It is unlikely that Welles as director or actor will achieve again so moving a scene as that of Falstaff's expulsion. With the author's consent we may feel superior to Kane, but we are never superior to Falstaff. He is naked before us. *Chimes at Midnight* is Welles's testament.

A CASABLANCA DOSSIER

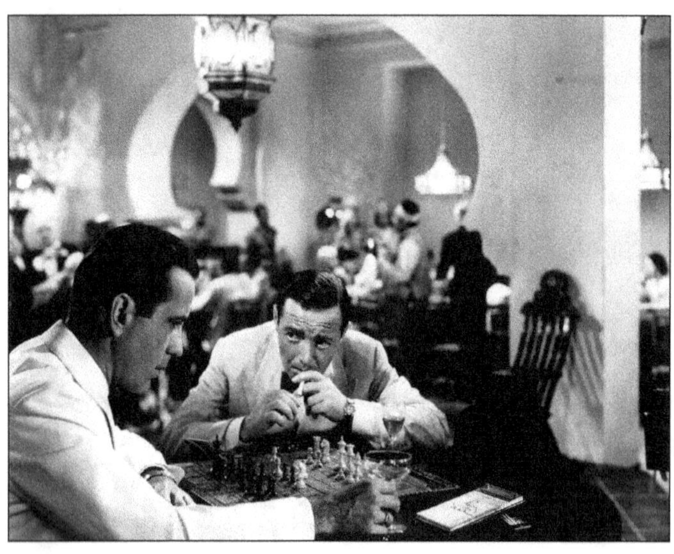

Humphrey Bogart as American expatriate café owner Rick Blaine shares a table in *Casablanca* (1942) with the petty criminal Ugarte (Peter Lorre), who asks, "You despise me, don't you?" To which Rick replies, "If I gave you any thought I probably would." The film won Oscars for best picture (producer Hal Wallis) and director (Michael Curtiz) as well as for screenwriters Julius J. Epstein, Philip G. Epstein and Howard Koch for their adaptation of the play *Everybody Comes to Rick's* by Murray Burnett and Joan Alison. Even though *Casablanca* was not regarded as a first-rate project during production, it eventually became a classic. (Warner Bros.)

Notes on the Production of *Casablanca*
Howard Koch

In recent years a sort of mystique has grown up among the younger generation around *Casablanca,* which probably has played more revival dates than any other film and is now being prepared for the musical stage. Students tell me of "*Casablanca* Clubs" in many colleges in which members are expected to attend a showing each time it is revived in their area. Some have reported seeing it as many as fifteen times. When I query them why this impassioned loyalty to a film made over twenty years ago, they give me various and inconclusive answers. Is it the blend of romanticism and cynicism? Is it the antifascist political theme? I'm not certain nor are they. For whatever reason, the young people have identified with *Casablanca* and its tough-minded protagonist, Humphrey Bogart.

When I look back on its unpromising genesis, I share some of their mysticism. *Casablanca* was one of those rare examples of a film conceived in sin and born in travail that managed to straighten itself out and lead an upright life. You could catalogue the most flagrant faults of Hollywood's belt-line system of production and find them all present in the making of this film. Yet *Casablanca* survived them all—and even thrived on them.

The original property purchased by Warners was a play called *Everybody Comes to Rick's* [by Murray Burnett and Joan Alison] that died on the road before reaching Broadway. I don't believe I ever saw a copy although Warners must have had one at the time. But it made a contribution—the locale,

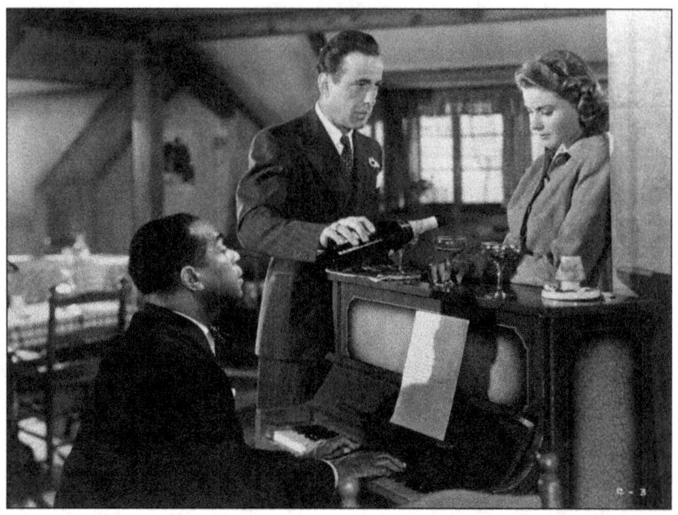

Rick's isolationist existence ("I stick my neck out for nobody")
is disrupted when his former lover, Ilsa Lund (Ingrid Bergman),
comes into his "gin joint" unexpectedly. Rick's friend and loyal
piano player, Sam (Dooley Wilson), is wary of Rick's new involvement with a woman the jaded café owner feels betrayed him.
(Warner Bros.)

Casablanca—that turned out to be an important one in the light
of subsequent history. The studio wanted Ingrid Bergman for
the leading female role but she was "owned" under the terms
of a long-running contract by David Selznick and had to be
pried away by the lure of a good story that would advance her
career and her box-office value to the Selznick Organization.
Having nothing on paper to submit—he knew it would be
futile to submit the original play—Hal Wallis, the then head
of Warner production, astutely dispatched Julius and Philip
Epstein, two talented and fast-talking screenwriters, to Mr.
Selznick, relying on them to improvise at least the appearance of a story important enough for his star. According to
their own confession, they had no story whatsoever but they
talked so fast that Mr. Selznick agreed to lend Miss Bergman,
probably on the theory that where there was so much smoke
there must be some fire. However, it was a pyrrhic victory for
the Epsteins. They had fooled Mr. Selznick but they couldn't

fool themselves. They had a locale, a few assorted characters and some fragments of situations but nothing to hold them together—no story—and they were facing a close deadline.

At this point the Warner management called me in to help. The Epsteins confessed to Hal Wallis that the "story" with which they had entertained Mr. Selznick was actually a feat of verbal legerdemain without any real substance to provide the basis for a picture. Since the scheduled shooting date was only one month off, when the stars' high salaries would begin, this news produced one of the crises so prevalent in Hollywood. The studio's policy in such circumstances is to assign an additional writer or writers. Since I was under contract and had just finished an assignment, I was summoned to the front office and told to get to work on a film which had a gilt-edged cast waiting in the wings and a very capable director, Mike Curtiz—in fact, everything that could be desired for a first-class production except the central ingredient—a story.

My collaboration with the Epstein brothers was entertaining and, to a degree, productive. They came up with all sorts of amusing lines and incidents for the various characters that were to people Rick's nightclub while I tried to fit the bits and pieces into some kind of dramatic continuity. However, after a week or so we were unhappily aware that, while we had some interesting elements, they didn't add up to a workable story. It was as though we were building a house and we had the bricks and timber but no blueprints, no guide to the eventual structure. At this point we had to face the fact that our collaboration was not producing the desired result and time was running out. Both the Epsteins and I were willing to bow out—more than willing, anxious to avoid what seemed like an impending disaster. The Epsteins, more experienced in the ways of Hollywood than I, acted with more dispatch. They asked to be transferred to another assignment and the front office granted their request.

[The Epsteins, identical twins who were known for their witty dialogue and skill in adapting plays, had volunteered to work on U.S. government films during World War II and were summoned to Washington, D.C., by Frank Capra to work on his *Why We Fight* series of Army propaganda films with five other writers. The Epsteins kept writing *Casablanca* while in

D.C. and eventually left to continue working on the feature in Hollywood. According to Aljean Harmetz's 1992/2002 book on the film, *Round Up the Usual Suspects/The Making of Casablanca*, Koch was writing behind the Epsteins, revising their material, and they revised his. But they never worked in the same room together. Koch acknowledged to Harmetz, "The major work was done by the Epsteins. They were on it the longest." Four other writers worked on the script at different stages, most importantly Casey Robinson, who revised the love scenes during production, without credit. And many of the story and character elements came from the play by Burnett and Alison, whose work was rarely acknowledged by Koch or others. — Ed.]

The morning I heard the news [about the Epsteins going to Washington] was not one of my happiest moments. There I was, a young, very junior writer holding a bag that, while not exactly empty, contained a miscellaneous jumble of characters, ideas for scenes and atmospheric bits. In those days any Hollywood writer earning less than a thousand a week was not usually entrusted with doing the screenplay for a production with important stars and a budget over a million dollars — and my salary at the time was considerably less. In the movie world there is no substitute for success and no acceptable excuse for failure. The prospect, to put it mildly, was not pleasing.

Where the story finally came from I don't know. The next three weeks — or perhaps they were months, I'd lost all track of time — were a nightmare of which I remember only fragments. In desperation I decided to forget there was no story line and just start at the beginning, writing scenes as they came to me and using the Epstein material wherever it fitted in. I had only the vaguest notion where each scene was leading, hoping only that it would lead to another scene and another and that the sum total, if I lived that long, would add up to a film that wouldn't be bad enough to end my brief career in Hollywood. In three weeks of day-and-night work something emerged — some sort of backbone on which to string the characters and incidents. I was too groggy by then to know whether it was good or bad but Mike Curtiz liked it — or maybe he just didn't have any choice. By the time the

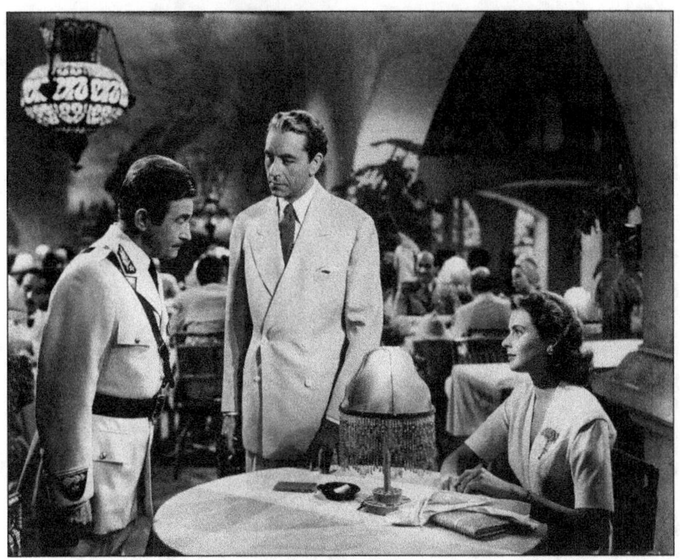

The suavely cynical and corrupt prefect of police in *Casablanca*, Captain Louis Renault (Claude Rains), toying with Resistance leader Victor Laszlo (Paul Henreid) and Ilsa at Rick's Café Américain. (Warner Bros.)

production date confronted us, I had the first act completed — about thirty or thirty-five pages of screenplay — and to my astonishment, it seemed to be building, creating its own tensions. Since the continuity was fairly well worked out, it was enough to start the wheels turning. But two more acts to go!

From then on it was a race between me and the camera and I soon found that the camera was recording scenes faster than my fatigued brain could invent them. Before long my slight lead was whittled down to a day or two. There were even several occasions when the company was on the set waiting for pages to rehearse a scene. Jack Warner, who watches such things, began sending me memos reminding me that any day on which the cast had no material to shoot would cost the studio thirty thousand dollars.

Fortunately I had the help and encouragement of Bogie and Mike Curtiz. Bogie would invite me into his dressing room

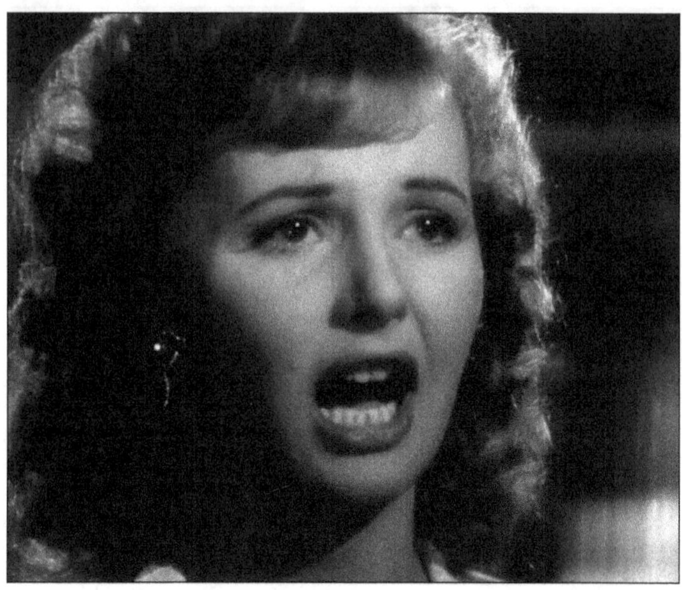

Madeleine Lebeau, an émigré French actress who plays Rick's spurned mistress in *Casablanca*, helps lead the stirring rendition of the French national anthem, "La Marseillaise," in competition with German officers singing "Watch on the Rhine." (Warner Bros.)

with his usual "relax and have a drink." We would talk and sometimes a genie popped out of the whiskey bottle—and off I'd go to develop the idea into a scene. Mike was comforting in another way. When I'd tell him some idea wouldn't work, it wasn't logical, he'd say in his Hungarian idiom, "Don't worry. I make it go so fast on the screen no one notices." The situation was further complicated by the fact that Mike Curtiz leaned strongly toward the romantic elements in the story, whereas I was more interested in the contrast among the characters of cynicism with political idealism. Somehow, against all the rules, the results of these disparate viewpoints meshed, and perhaps it was this very mixture which gave the film its special character.

Anyway, we argued and compromised and wrote and rewrote and staggered through to the finish. After the editing the producer and director said that we had an exciting film.

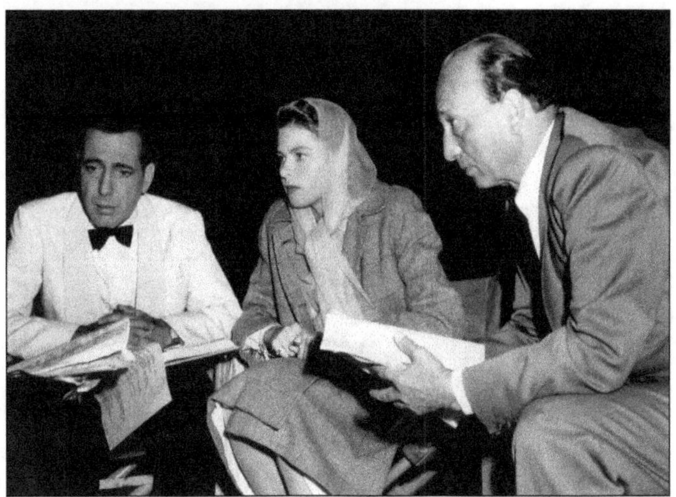

Director Michael Curtiz with Bogart and Bergman
on the set of *Casablanca*. (Warner Bros.)

I didn't believe them. I didn't even trust the audience's warm
reaction on opening night. I saw only the faults, the things that
weren't on the screen, at least in the way I had imagined them.
When a year later it received the Academy Award [it won
three Oscars: for best picture, director, and adapted screenplay (for the Epsteins and Koch)], I was by this time inured
to miracles. It was only some years later at a revival of the
film at London's National Film Theatre did I see *Casablanca*
for what it was—a slick and fast-moving melodrama, expertly
played, that owed much of its impact to ideas and images that
were moving people in the throes of a world conflict. President Roosevelt and Prime Minister Churchill added the final
link to the film's good-luck charm by selecting *Casablanca*
for their historic meeting.

Now as I look back on those hectic days, I still wonder
how the film emerged from the chaos of its birth. Being somewhat of a mystic, as I previously confessed, I like to think it
grew by itself out of some affinity with the hopes and dreams
of successive generations of young people and, no matter who
owns it today in a legal sense, *Casablanca* really belongs to its
youthful fans.

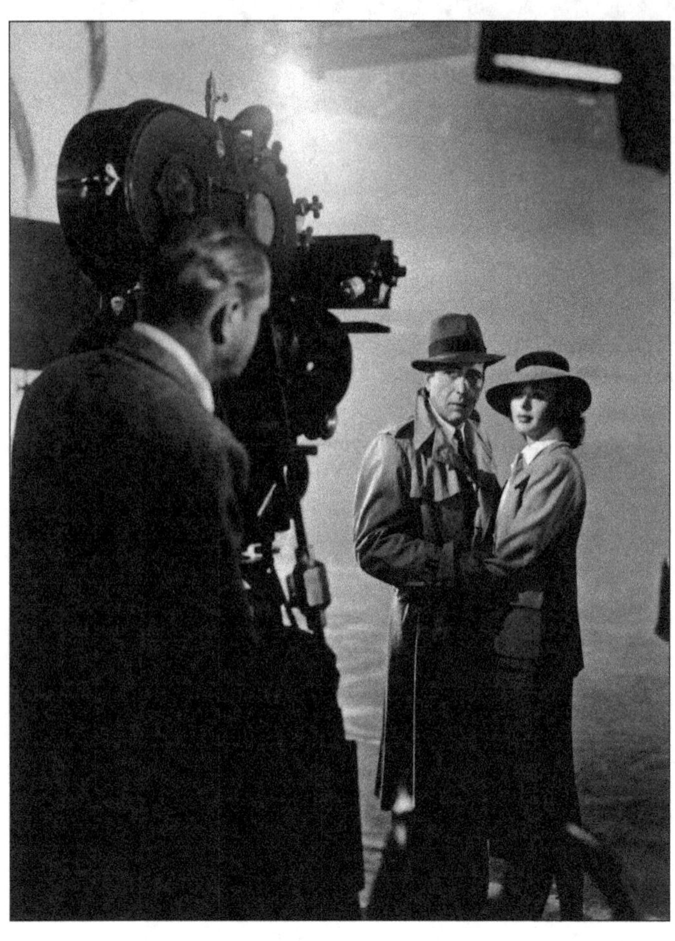

Cinematographer Arthur Edeson filming the last embrace of Rick and Ilsa in *Casablanca*. Edeson was nominated for an Oscar for this film, following his earlier nomination for the classic 1930 war movie, *All Quiet on the Western Front*. Edeson often served as his own camera operator. (Warner Bros.)

Excerpts from the Original Treatment
Howard Koch

Lois should not believe Laszlo is dead when she meets Rick in Paris. Laszlo is in a concentration camp. She can do nothing further for him, and believes he will never get out alive. In the brief period of her love affair with Rick, she is able to forget her unhappiness; then, when Laszlo escapes, her loyalty reasserts itself. She makes her decision to stand by Laszlo, who's been through hell and needs her now if he ever needed her. She doesn't see Rick again to explain, because she doesn't trust herself with him, and also, if he knows the truth, he will stay in France, in danger of his life, since he is a marked man by the Nazis, who are now coming into Paris.... This seems more credible than the "mistaken death" and humanizes Lois, who is in some danger of being a little too virtuous.

There is also a danger that Rick's sacrifice in the end will seem theatrical and phony unless, early in the story, we suggest the side of his nature that makes his final decision in character. It would be interesting to have Renault penetrate the mystery in his first scene with Rick when he guesses that the cynical American is underneath, a sentimentalist. Rick laughs at the idea, then Renault produces his record—"ran guns to Ethiopia," "fought for the Loyalists in the Spanish War." Rick says he got well paid on both occasions. Renault replies that the winning side would have paid him better. Strange that he always happens to be on the side of the under-dog. Rick dismisses the implication, but throughout the picture we see evidences of his humanity, which he does his best to cover up.

One very good such incident is the scene when he lets the refugee win at roulette, at his own expense. Why not make this a much bigger situation—for instance, it might be the way he rescues Annina and her husband from Renault? The Prefect has named a price for the visa too high for the couple to pay. In his most gracious manner, he suggests to Annina that she can pay in another way. In desperation, Jan gambles in an effort to stretch their small savings into the needed amount. He is losing. Annina comes for advice to Rick, who enables Jan to win at roulette, thus defeating the intention of his friend Renault. The Prefect, when he learns, should not resent this action of Rick's, but accept it as a sporting loss—and also as proof of his argument that Rick is a sentimentalist. There should be no rupture of friendship between Rick and Renault. The Prefect should never be serious with Rick except about one thing—that Laszlo does not escape. That would cost Renault his job, and the Prefect likes his job.

Much suspense will be gained if Rick and Lois, at their first meeting in the cafe, do not reveal in front of Laszlo and Renault that they've known each other before. Lois should have no idea that Rick is still in Casablanca. He is the man she would avoid at all costs, since it will reopen a conflict which she has resolved in favor of her duty to her husband. We see that their eyes hold when they first see each other, but they are clever enough to conceal their reactions from the others. When Renault, who is seated at their table, introduces her and Laszlo to Rick, he and Lois act the part of complete strangers in acknowledging the introduction. In the brief conversation that follows, Lois says nothing and Rick strolls over to another table.

Renault also excuses himself, and Lois, trying not to give away her excitement, takes the opportunity to ask Laszlo to take her home. But at that moment he spots Berger at the bar and tells Lois to stay at the table until he comes back.

Laszlo stands next to Berger as he orders a drink. Berger engages him in conversation on the pretext of selling him a ring, then in a lower voice he informs Laszlo that the police didn't find the Letters of Transit on Ugarte when they arrested him. Knowing that Ugarte trusted no one but Rick, it is probable that the Letters are in the possession of the owner of this cafe.

We cut to Lois' table as Rick sits down beside her. From the first moment they're alone, they drop all pretense of being strangers and we become aware of Rick's bitter hostility and Lois' nervous restraint. He takes a cynical pleasure in barbed references to her relationship with Laszlo. "So it's Laszlo's turn?" "How long will *he* last?" "Is he really your husband or is that a convenience for the moment?..." Then Rick baits her with sarcastic remarks about places in Paris, like the Belle Aurore, that have evidently had some previous sentimental association to them both. Lois is hurt by his attitude, but has the courage not to defend herself by making any explanation of whatever she did that has embittered Rick.... Why doesn't she explain? Because by telling the truth, she would have to admit she still loves Rick, and why put them both through that again, since under the circumstances their love is completely futile? Better if Rick even hates her, than to revive his love only to say good-bye again, since she means to stick to her husband... Finally Rick, in his effort to torment her into telling the truth, orders Sam to play "As Time Goes By." Obviously the song recalls a romantic memory now too painful to face. She rises, leaves Rick alone at the table, and starts toward the bar.

• • •

Lois and Laszlo come in. Rick asks Laszlo if he was followed. Trained to detect pursuit, the Czech replies that he believes the police are no longer trailing him. Why they're not, he can't imagine. Rick smiles. He just wanted to be sure.... Then he tells Laszlo he's changed his mind about selling the passports. If Laszlo will get out the money... The Czech is taking his money out of his wallet, counts out the amount agreed on, while Rick produces the Letters of Transit. As they are about to exchange, the French Prefect steps in from the next room, blandly places the Czech leader under arrest on a charge of bribery to obtain the stolen papers... At the first impact, Lois is too astounded for speech, then she begs Rick for some explanation. He remains silent, but Renault, surprised that she doesn't know, smilingly informs her that the explanation is quite simple. Love, he remarks, has triumphed over patriotism—not an infrequent occurrence in Casablanca. Then Rick briefly directs her to go to the plane, which leaves in 15 minutes. He will join her there presently. At this she breaks into a fury of denunciation. Does Rick imagine that she is going to run away with him after his conscienceless betrayal of her husband? She can't conceive how she could ever have loved a man capable of such a monstrous thing. Never will she leave Laszlo. Where they send him, they'll have to send her....

Rick says not a word during this outburst, then he quietly suggests to Laszlo to point out to his wife that regardless of her feelings toward himself, it is impractical and foolhardy for her to stay in Casablanca. Laszlo is trapped, and knows that nothing can be done. He goes over to Lois, who is dissolved in tears. He tries to calm her, and tells her that Rick is right. To remain in Casablanca would be a fruitless gesture. In America she can serve France in the way she understands. We know that he is referring to his statement at the underground meeting. "If I fail to leave Casablanca, one other person has the information that will gain American support for the Free French cause..." Regaining her composure, Lois realizes she has no other course but to go. She kisses her husband good-bye. He turns over his wallet to her. "Where I'm going, I'll have no need for this—and the Germans would..." Then Lois turns toward Rick with a look of contempt and implacable hate. Without revealing any feeling on his part, Rick gazes at her as though he's imprinting her image indelibly in his mind. Then, without another word between them, she goes out the door.

Up to now the French Prefect has been watching the drama with an impersonal but absorbing interest. When Lois leaves, he is suddenly overcome with the humor of the surprising denouement. "You are a man, Rick, who can be counted on to do the unexpected." He rocks with laughter, but the laughter stops as he finds himself looking into the barrel of Rick's revolver. Renault is incredulous. Surely this is a joke. Rick replies grimly that as much as he regards the Prefect as his friend, it would be unwise to assume that the gun is not in earnest if Renault makes the slightest move ... The Prefect tries to cajole, to threaten, but it's no use. Over his shoulder, Rick tells Laszlo that he just has time to make the plane. When the Czech leader realizes the full import of Rick's strategy, he looks at the American with admiration and gratitude. "One day France, the whole world, will honor you for this." Laszlo turns and goes out the door.

> RENAULT
>
> Ricky, this is not going to be pleasant for either of us—and especially for you. I'll have to arrest you, of course.

> RICK
>
> When the plane leaves, Louis. In the meantime we might as well be patient... Here, let's go on with this.

He motions to the chessboard. Renault has to smile. Rick backs up, keeps the official covered with his gun as the Frenchman approaches the board.

> RENAULT
>
> It was my move, I believe. (*He studies the board*) Mmm—a very difficult position.

He moves a piece, then backs away as Rick advances to the board, still covering his friend with the gun.

> RICK
>
> That doesn't leave me but one move. (*He makes it*)

Again the Prefect advances to the board, studies it.

> RENAULT
>
> There is no move. The Kings can't get out. We're checkmated.

> RICK
> (*grimly*)
> I guess the game's finished.

At this moment the plane carrying Lois and Laszlo roars over the roof of the cafe. The gaze of Rick and Renault sweeps the ceiling. The SOUND of the plane diminishes.

RENAULT

Ricky, I was right. You <u>are</u> a sentimentalist.

FADE OUT.

Love and Death in *Casablanca*
William Donnelly

If I don't do it someone else will.

Only when the spirit has vanished from the faith does the skeptical scholar step in to analyze.

And *Casablanca* is a mildly campy sacred text.

And I am going to say things about it that should make the ghost of Peter Lorre, murmuring with sensually apologetic voice and heavy-lidded eyes, appear behind me and stab me with a jeweled Levantine dagger from the Sidney Greenstreet collection.

What am I going to say?

1. The film is a bad film.

2. It is a corny international allegory.

3. Rick's relationship with Sam and with Captain Renault is a standard case of the repressed homosexuality that underlies most American adventure stories.

If you came in late and haven't seen the film, let me give you a whispered earful of the plot so you can sit back and enjoy.

Rick/Bogart is a famous bar owner in Casablanca, a jumping-off place for refugees from the Nazis. And he is cynical and bitter and doesn't want to get involved. He's cynical because Ilsa, his new girlfriend, abandoned him in Paris as the Germans marched in. He can't understand it. Sam, his Negro pianist, is the only one who knows the story, and Sam refrains from playing "As Time Goes By" because that song wounds the old heel and he rages and starts lisping whenever he hears it. The only way to get out of Casablanca and to America is to buy an exit visa from Captain Renault, the chief of police. The usual price for the girls is a night in his boudoir. All others pay cash. Enter Victor Laszlo, a refugee underground leader, and his wife Ilsa. ILSA! Rick plays it cool. He happens to have some improbable letters of transit deposited with him by Peter Lorre, who dry-gulched a couple of German couriers to get them. Will Rick give the letters to the Laszlos so they can escape to lead the underground from abroad? Major Strasser arrives from Berlin to see to it that Captain Renault does not let Laszlo escape. But don't worry, Rick is sulky because Ilsa didn't tell him she was already married back in Paris.

Confrontation scenes between Strasser and Laszlo, Rick and Strasser, Laszlo and Rick, Ilsa and Rick, Renault and Strasser, Renault and Rick, etc. Mix in Sydney Greenstreet as the big daddy of the black market and owner of a competing night club. Climax. Ilsa threatens Rick with a pistol to help her somewhat ineffectual hubby to escape. Moved by the depth of her revolutionary fervor, Rick kisses her. She suggests that she stay with him but that Laszlo be sent to America. Overcome by idealism at the airport, he sends her off with her hubby on the clipper, telling her through clenched teeth that he doesn't really love her and explaining that Laszlo needs her to help him carry on the good fight. Then he shoots Strasser (cheers). And sells his bar to join Renault, who, moved by this demonstration of idealism, decides to give up his slothful billygoat existence. Fade: Rick and Renault lighting out to the territory to zap the Boche.

Okay. Why is it a bad film? Because it isn't a film. It is a play. A good play, but nonetheless a play. Its basic action takes place in those confrontations. Despite some transitional footage that's more or less cinematic, we quickly perceive that this is not Casablanca but Hollywood, and the significant events are all going to be improbable talks within the confines of one or two sets, with entrance lines, exits, cues, speeches.

Now the wit and cynicism of the lines make this theatrical experience enjoyable, but I would urge that we are quite aware that we are seeing a filmed play, and that we appreciate the film as a set of acting jobs. As a result, it doesn't have the immediacy and power of vicarious experience. Few films made in 1942 did. Sound had been around for only ten or fifteen

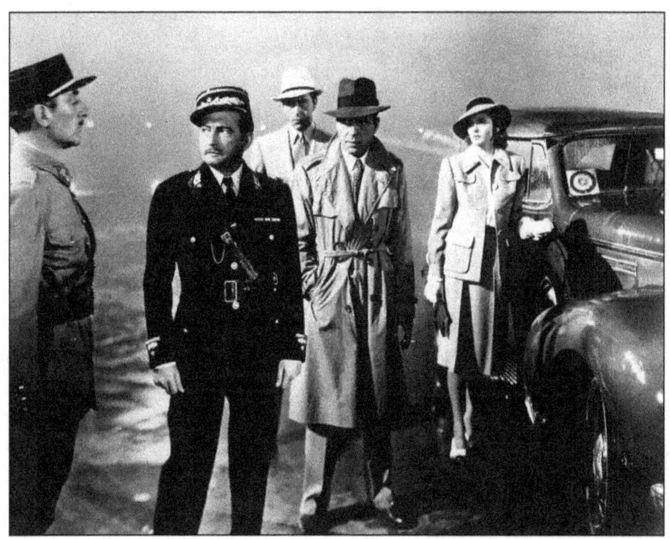

"Louis, I think this is the beginning of a beautiful friendship."
The celebrated ending of *Casablanca*, with Rick and Renault,
succumbing to their latent idealism, letting Victor and Ilsa escape
at the airport. (Warner Bros.)

years and film was still trying to find out how to deal with
it. To a sophisticated modern viewer some of those dialogues
seem a bit hokey. Too much verbalized emoting. But of course
you have to have that in a talk film.

So the film isn't as good as it seems. Isn't as enjoyable as
our pleasure at it tells us, Now when a critic maintains points
like that, he'd better be careful. It's possible that his theory is
leading him astray.

I've said repeatedly that the cynicism of the play is what
makes it attractive, and I won't quote a handful of witty gems
I have underlined in the playscript because I think that the
screenplay deserves a complete reading. It is available in John
Gassner and Dudley Nichols' *Best Film Plays 1943–44.*

Nor is it the cynicism alone that makes the film attractive.
On another level it is a political allegory of the reluctance of
the United States to enter World War II, as a result, probably, of the disillusion following its involvement with France
in World War I. Now of course the film isn't pure allegory;

everything that happens isn't politically symbolic, and I don't want to beat this into the ground.

The date is December, 1941. Rick, America, is embittered with idealistic politics. He will covertly aid, but will not commit himself. Renault is Vichy France. Strasser, Nazi Germany.

> *Renault:* If you are thinking of warning him [Ugarte, North Africa, about to be captured and murdered by Strasser], don't put yourself out. He can't possibly escape.
>
> *Rick:* I stick my neck out for nobody.
>
> *Renault:* A wise foreign policy.
>
> *Señor Ferrari:* My dear Rick, when will you realize that in the world today, isolationism is no longer a practical policy.

There's a lot of this sort of talk. The seating of Ilsa and Laszlo in the bar as far apart as possible is referred to as a problem in geography. Rick's bar is a microcosm. Germans and French try to out-sing each other in their national anthems. The staff of the bar are former bankers and professors. Rick treats them with cold generosity but wants to know nothing of their underground activities, and without his help they are merely clowns. The comic Russian bartender is preparing a new American drink called a Mickey Finn so that he will know how to tend bar in America. A German swaggers up, peremptorily drinks it down and collapses.

In this microcosm Rick even controls the symbolic wheel of fortune in his gambling room, using its economic power to punish and reward without direct commitment on his part.

No need to go on with this. *Casablanca* (and I was tempted to say that all we see of Casablanca is Rick's, and that literally Casablanca is "White House") was made in 1942, and part of its appeal then, and now, is the way in which it seems to make a case for America's stumbling entry into World War II, "too little and too late," as the phrase went then.

On a personal level, Rick gives up his romantic, self-centered cynicism because he is impressed by Ilsa's desperate loyalty to a Cause. And of course the allegorical level helps to keep the personal level from seeming trivial. But the film escapes from triviality on another level, and if you've heard this all before, tiptoe out for popcorn and come back in a paragraph or two.

Leslie Fiedler made an annoying but convincing discovery about the American adventure novel. He'd flirted with it in a *Partisan Review* article called "Come Back to the Raft Ag'in, Huck Honey!," but he gave us the whole thesis in 1960 in *Love and Death in the American Novel.* I am going to give you a précis of the theory from *Time* rather than my own summation, lest you think my summary was tailored to fit *Casablanca:*

> Fiedler argued that the peculiar kink in American literature was an obsession with death: and that, in turn, inhibited a mature approach to heterosexual themes. As a result, literature fastened on a sublimated homosexual ideal, a kind of interracial buckskin-buddy system of innocent dreamers, running toward what Huck Finn called "the territory ahead." Actually, Fiedler said, the dreamers were fleeing from women.

Particularly, I might add, women who were idealized as untouchables: virgins, other men's wives, etc. Now, Ingrid Bergman was that kind of untouchable symbol in the forties, the Joan of Arc of her age.

But I suppose you are way ahead of me. Where is the deep, meaningful relationship in the Rick, Sam, Ilsa triangle? What is really bugging Rick? Why is it so satisfying when the misogynist and his antitype, the contemptuous womanizer, go off arm-in-arm to kill, renouncing the idealized woman? Let me give you some lines as a sort of paint-the-number set so that you can do it yourself completely:

> The scene cuts to Sam playing—he is in the midst of a number—then back to Rick and Yvonne, with Sam alone spotlighted at the piano, while Rick and Yvonne stand in the gloom. Yvonne, who has never taken her eyes off Rick, finally blurts out:

Yvonne: Where were you last night?
Rick: That's so long ago. I don't remember.
Yvonne (after a pause): Will I see you tonight?
Rick (calmly): I never make plans that far ahead.

• • •

Renault: Rick is completely neutral about everything. And that takes in the field of women, too.

• • •

Renault: He is the kind of man that.... Well, if I were a woman and *I* ... (*tapping his chest*) were not around, I would be in love with Rick.

• • •

Sam: Boss. (*Receiving no answer*) Boss, ain't you going to bed? (*Receiving no answer*) Don't just sit and look a hole in that drink, Boss. (*Receiving no answer*) Pour it back and come to bed.
Rick: Not tonight, Sam. Tonight I've got a date with the heebie-jeebies.
Sam (scared): Boss, no. Listen to me, Boss. (*He comes quickly to him*) I've been with you a long time now. She's bad luck. You was doing fine until she come. Boss, let's get out of here.
Rick: I've got a date with the little green men, and pink elephants dancing in the moonlight in the Place Concorde—and a ferris wheel at Montmartre, and the lights at Belle Aurore, and the rotten smell of flowers in the Bois.
Sam: (pleading): Boss, we'll take a car and drive all night. We'll get drunk. We'll go fishing and stay away until she's gone.

The film ends as Rick asks for payment of a bet he has made with Renault (Claude Rains). Rick wagered that Laszlo would escape from Casablanca.

Renault: It might be a good idea for you to disappear from Casablanca for a while. There's a Free French Garrison over at Brazzaville. I could be induced to arrange your passage.
Rick: ... You still owe me ten thousand francs.
Renault (smiling): And that should pay our expenses.
Rick: Our expenses?
Renault: Uh-huh.
Rick (seeing him in a new light, pleased): Louis, I think this is the beginning of a beautiful friendship.

As the plane disappears in the fog and a lot of furtive eye-wiping takes place before the lights go on, let me make a couple of concluding comments.

About the cynicism and the political level of the film: both of these are very rare in American films. (Billy Wilder is an exception; and Stephen Farber in *Film Quarterly* has noted the presence of the Love and Death motif in *The Fortune Cookie*.) If the film is uncinematic, it is only typically uncinematic, but its sophisticated mode, its restraint in dealing with the war in an era in which John Wayne set the standard for that sort of discourse in film, is remarkable and commendable, and its richness, double entendre and irony is simply phenomenal. So it is a bad film only in absolute terms, and relative to other films of its time it is extraordinary.

As for the Love and Death stratum: I believe it is there, and I suspect that Fiedler's insight may come as much from watching American Westerns as from reading American novels. Apparently this renunciation of sexual maturity for a life of action is one of the most potent stories we can tell ourselves, and it is one which can readily be adopted by film because it has inimitable potentialities for handling action.

Possibly we have overemphasized the technical aspects of the development of film; perhaps film was born not because celluloid strips became available, but because we needed a new mode for the kind of stories we wanted to tell ourselves. And perhaps these basic stories should not be dismissed as incidental. It may be that we sorely need more of the kind of analysis we find in Fiedler, confronted as we are with the incredible mass and popularity of our film heritage.

In any case, I think to look at *Casablanca* critically and analytically is a rewarding experience, and one that goes deeper than cultish nostalgia.

Recent Films

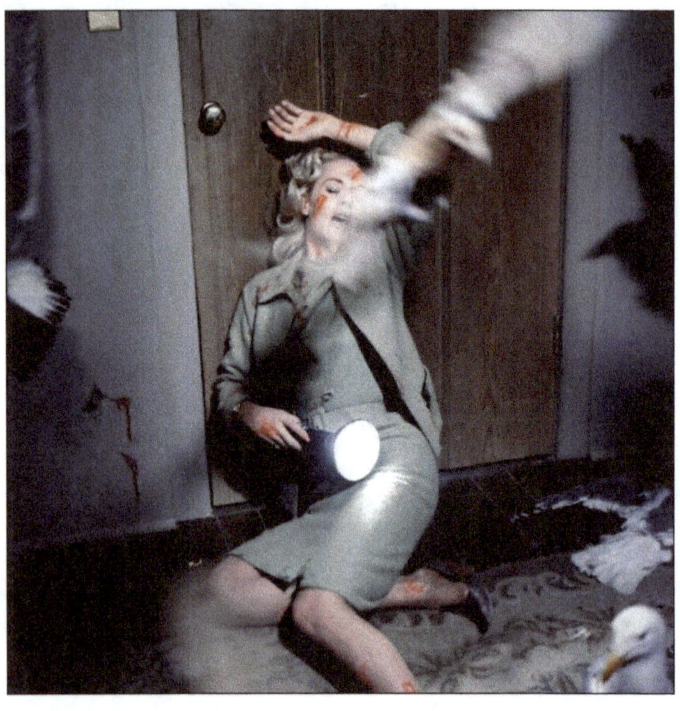

A rare behind-the-scenes look at how the birds' attack on Melanie
Daniels (Tippi Hedren) was filmed for Alfred Hitchcock's
The Birds (1963): you can see the arm of a bird handler throwing
one of the live birds at her in this scene that caused the actress great
distress. (Universal)

The High Forties Revisited
Andrew Sarris

While reminiscing about "The High Forties" in the *Sight and Sound* of Autumn 1961, John Russell Taylor complains about the "sheer unavailability" of Forties films in Britain. The sheer unavailability of films everywhere is a recurring problem for aspiring scholars. It would be helpful if the various governments of the world appropriated funds for the preservation and systematic exhibition of all the feature films produced within their boundaries. (Something is wrong—and pleasantly absurd—when an American must visit Paris to see *Scarface.*) International exchanges could be arranged through the UN to acquaint critics in depth with a comprehensive world picture. Retrospective exhibitions of the complete output of key directors could be sent to every town and hamlet where any interest is indicated. Treatises, monographs and filmographies could be cleared and translated by an international agency for the propagation of cinematic information. Specialization in the backwaters of the cinema, e.g., *The History of Monogram,* might be encouraged by academic recognition in the form of honored chairs at burgeoning film academies.

Now that we have indulged the fantasies of film enthusiasts, let us return to grim reality. Anyone who wishes to check the verdicts of film historians must take what he can get when he can get it. Too often, he will settle for faded, mutilated, even dismembered prints as alternatives to complete ignorance. If he is concerned primarily with texture and continuity, he will find American commercial-ridden television more visible than visual. In the course of his excavations, he may become disheartened by the eerie loneliness of his calling and the low assay of gold to dross. Discovery may become an end in itself, and the deeper the excavations, the more pointless the attempt to communicate to the world on the surface level of comprehension. Instead of acquiring cultural respectability along the way, he will content himself with the grudging acknowledgments of kindred eccentrics. Yet, he will probably keep digging if only not to admit that a career has degenerated into an addiction.

Nonetheless, the cinema must justify itself at some point in the search. There is no purpose in crossing a desert if there are no mountain ranges beyond, and, consequently, if Hollywood in the Forties were not represented by the peaks of Chaplin, Welles, Ford, Hitchcock, Renoir, Ophüls, Hawks, Sternberg and others, the incidental absurdities of Veronica Lake and Maria Montez would not warrant much misplaced nostalgia. Fun is fun, but if the Forties are worth troubling about at all, they merit a degree of intellectual sincerity. Otherwise, too much time and work is involved. When Mr. Taylor expresses concern for young critics who have never seen *The Maltese Falcon* or *Cat People*, he fails to convey the full dimensions of the vacuum. Over four thousand films were produced in Hollywood between 1940 and 1949. If young critics were permitted to see three films a day from this period at the British Film Institute, it would require almost four years to complete the course in the High Forties. Even if one restricted the curriculum to the 2700-some-odd productions from the major studios, it would require almost three years to graduate. Considering the academic facilities available today, it is a bit unfair to chide the young for being unfamiliar with Val Lewton, an overrated cult property of the late James Agee. Besides, there is more to be gained by saving the Fifties and Sixties than mourning the unfortunate neglect of the Thirties and Forties, particularly when the older generation has failed thus far to produce an adequate critical history of the American sound film.

Despite his presumably good intentions, Mr. Taylor performs a disservice to the cause of revival when he observes: "But then with popular films it has always been, for the really

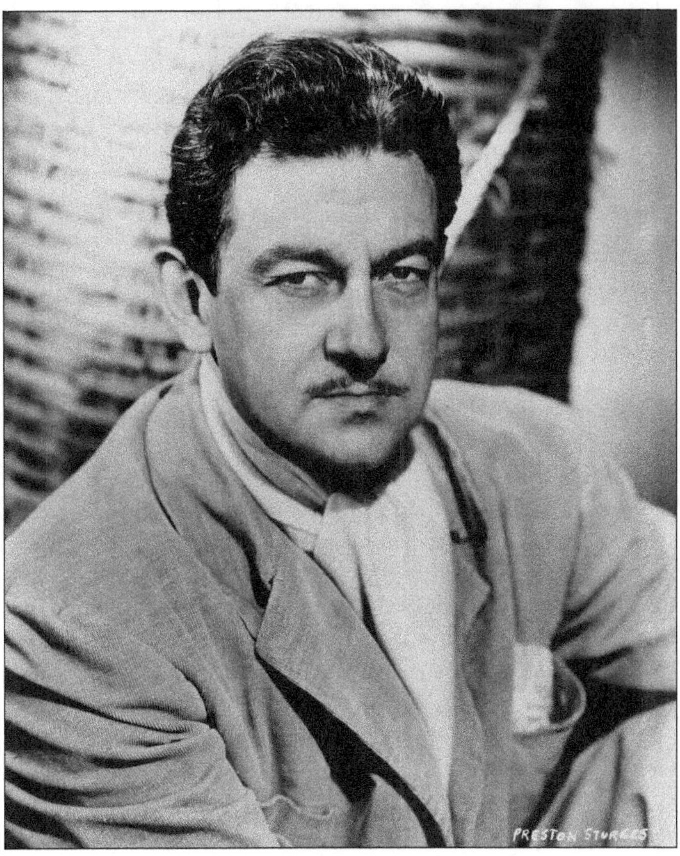

Preston Sturges, the kaleidoscopically witty writer-director whose amazing run of screwball comedies set the pace for the genre in the 1940s. (Paramount)

dedicated regular at least, not so much what they are as who is in them which counts." The operative word here is "popular," an epithet which justifies a suspension of value judgments by removing Hollywood from the stream of serious film history. The same tone of condescending frivolity can then be applied to *Citizen Kane* and *Cobra Woman*, and the Forties can be defamed by an undiscriminating adoration, the kiss, as it were, rather than the sword. Then also, as Louis Kronenberger has said of Oscar Wilde, "everything counts, and nothing matters." However, what does matter in the Forties and in every other period of the cinema is who is directing what, and subordinately, with whom. The illusion that stars transcend their vehicles is seldom sustained by retrospective judgment. Even the divine Garbo has tough going in her wheezier projects, and would her image be quite as lustrous today if it had not been for Cukor *(Camille)*, Lubitsch *(Ninotchka)* and Mamoulian *(Queen Christina)*? As for Grierson's guerrillas, the Marx Brothers, it is not surprising that their anarchic talents were best exploited by Leo McCarey in *Duck Soup.*

It has been argued in the past by some critics that the American cinema is a producer's rather than a director's cinema, and that the studio system standardizes the work of individual directors. Indeed, the gist of Mr. Taylor's article implies an inability to distinguish (or remember) individual films. Presumably, one can reach out at random and emerge with a typical film of the period with typical decor and typical background music. There is one practical advantage to such presumption, and that is prose relatively unencumbered by film titles. Mr. Taylor roams through the period with twenty-five film references, including the most casual citations and the captions for stills. These include in rough chronological order: *Rebecca* (1940), *The Lady Eve, Citizen Kane, Suspicion* and *The Maltese Falcon* (1941), *Bambi, Mrs. Miniver, Random Harvest* and *Cat People* (1942), *Madame Curie* (1943), *The Curse of the Cat People, The Miracle of Morgan's Creek, Double Indemnity, Cobra Woman, Dark Waters, To Have and Have Not* (1944), *A Song to Remember, The Body Snatchers, Sudan* and *Scarlet Street* (1945), *The Strange Love of Martha Ivers, The Dark Mirror* and *Strange Woman* (1946), *Up in Central Park* and *Siren of Atlantis* (1948) and *The Beautiful Blonde from Bashful Bend* (1949). Other references include two British films, *The Man in Grey* and *Gaslight,* if the latter is the Dickinson rather than the Cukor version; the last film of the Thirties, *Gone With the Wind;* two films of the Fifties, *The Asphalt Jungle* and *Moulin Rouge,* and Chabrol's *Les Bonnes Femmes,* the last an invidious reference. On *Night of the Demon,* Mr. Taylor has me. The only other person who has ever reported seeing it is Bill Everson, and he has seen everything.

Apart from statistical inadequacy, the list of references is eclectic if not downright bizarre. At least we can be grateful for the omission of such socially conscious standbys as *The Ox-Bow Incident* and *Crossfire,* but they may have been omitted out of respect. It might also be noted in passing that Robert Siodmak's interview in *Sight and Sound* appears to have colored impressions of the period. The duration of the period is never firmly established in Mr. Taylor's article. "The Forties came in with the war and went out with the New Look," we are informed, but elsewhere in the article, the Forties keep shrinking and expanding. Vincente Minnelli is treated as post-Forties although his first film was released in 1943, more than five years before Maria Montez impersonated the *Siren of Atlantis.* It is also difficult to understand why Judy Garland and Rita Hayworth are considered pre-Forties stars. Judy literally and figuratively grew up in the Forties, while Miss Hayworth, a contract vamp and second lead at Columbia in the late Thirties (vide *Only Angels Have Wings*), hit her stride in *Cover Girl* (1944) and *Gilda* (1946). One recalls the pin-up of her frolicsome pose in a negligee as one of the prominent artifacts of the war.

Almost every generalization Mr. Taylor makes can be refuted by a different selection of films and players, or even by unmentioned plot elements in the films he does mention. For example, according to Mr. Taylor: "The men—well, the men can be virtually ignored. Apart from one or two of the tough private eyes (Humphrey Bogart in the big pictures, Lloyd Nolan and Tom Conway in the series), they counted for little. Poor, weak, yielding creatures, lost in their shapeless, voluminous suits, they were trampled on by ruthless *femmes fatales* and sung at by high-powered feminine vocalists." Could Mr. Taylor have forgotten the startling number of betrayals and aggressions committed against the female of the species in the Forties? Bogart probably started it when he let Mary Astor "take the fall" in *The Maltese Falcon* even while she was embracing him. Alan Ladd delivered Veronica Lake (*Saigon*) and Gail Russell (*Calcutta*) to similar fates. Maureen O'Hara was John Garfield's pigeon in *The Fallen Sparrow* while Glenn Ford slapped Rita Hayworth out of a promising striptease in *Gilda* before sending Janis Carter to the gallows

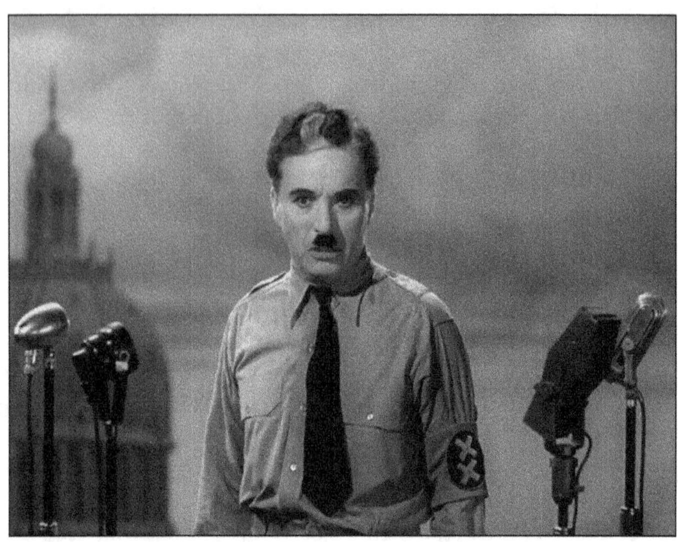

Charles Chaplin broke character at the end of *The Great Dictator*
to give his heartfelt anti-fascist plea for world peace and tolerance.
Chaplin, the writer-director-producer of this bold 1940 political
satire of Adolf Hitler, is playing a Jewish barber who becomes
mistaken for the lookalike dictator of Tomania, Adenoid Hynkel.
(United Artists)

in *Framed.* Dan Duryea rose to minor stardom by bashing
Joan Bennett for Fritz Lang in *The Woman in the Window*
and *Scarlet Street.* The war of the sexes reached a standoff in
Double Indemnity and *Duel in the Sun* where the lovers chose
lethal revolvers to demonstrate their mutual passion through
mutual perforations. Of course, one can prove everything
and nothing with random plot citations. On this surface level,
Hollywood has always had something for every taste except
the very highest and the very lowest. The studio discouraged
the former, the censors the latter, and the art of the cinema
was probably retarded in the process. We shall never know,
and it is a waste of time to speculate. Too many film histories
have degenerated into a discussion of metacinema, the cinema
which should or would have existed if governments, peoples,
banks, studios and producers had been more enlightened.

If I have backed into the Forties through Mr. Taylor's stimulating article, it is only to demonstrate the hazards of not seeing the trees for the forest. Whether or not there is also a question of unfamiliarity breeding contempt, I cannot say. The temptation to generalize a subject with as many variables as the weather is understandable, and Mr. Taylor cannot be singled out for admittedly pre-adolescent fancies recollected without revaluation. What remains disturbing is the implication that Hollywood need not be taken too seriously in retrospect. Most American (and, I suppose, British) intellectuals have been conditioned to curl their lips ever so slightly at Hollywood for such a long time that admirers of the American cinema may become too strident in its defense. If the conception of the best Hollywood directors as full-fledged artists is to counter the image of an automated industry unconsciously purveying popular myths, articles on the Forties or any other

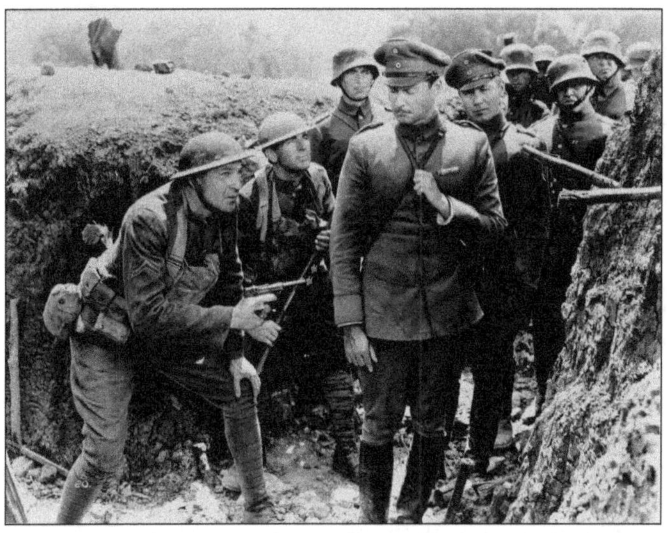

Gary Cooper won an Oscar for playing the legendary World War I hero Sgt. Alvin York in the 1941 Howard Hawks film *Sergeant York*. The film was such effective propaganda for American involvement in World War II against the Germans that it caused controversy among isolationists in the U.S. Congress.
(Warner Bros.)

arbitrary time span may do more harm than good. The chronological division of the cinema as one entity tends to perpetuate what may be called the pyramid fallacy of many film historians. This fallacy consists of viewing the history of cinema as a process by which approved artisans have deposited their slabs of celluloid on a single pyramid rising ultimately to a single apex, be it Realism, Humanism, Marxism, Journalism, Abstractionism or even Eroticism. Directors are valued primarily for their "contributions" to the evolution of a Utopian cinema efficiently adjusted to a Utopian society. Once a formal contribution has been made, subsequent refinements are downgraded. If Murnau disposed of camera movement, why should we honor Ophüls? Since most of the technical vocabulary, the zoom notwithstanding, was established by the end of the silent era, there has been a tendency to honor sound films almost exclusively for social content. The 1958 Brussels poll, which may have been the last gasp of the pyramid critics, cited only three sound films out of the top twelve, and of these three, *La Grande Illusion* and *The Bicycle Thief* were clearly content selections while *Citizen Kane* probably received mixed support from its formal and political partisans. (It might be noted that the recent *Sight and Sound* poll reflected the rising influence of the new French critics and film makers.)

The patent system of the pyramid generally holds that silent directors invented forms while sound directors perfected styles, and in the pyramid histories, particularly those oriented to realism, stylists are the drones of the cinema. It might be uncharitable to suggest that stylists are harder to analyze than inventors, and that it at least seems easier to define Eisenstein than to define Hitchcock. Actually, critics who are superficial about Hitchcock are usually superficial about Eisenstein as well.

One problem with the pyramid approach is that the base becomes rigid, and silent classics, especially, become encrusted with reverential moss. It is then almost as difficult to dislodge Pudovkin without disturbing Eisenstein as it is to move Stalin without compromising Lenin. Since new criticism is inevitably revolutionary, new critics may find it useful to smash the pyramid altogether and start with what they know first-hand.

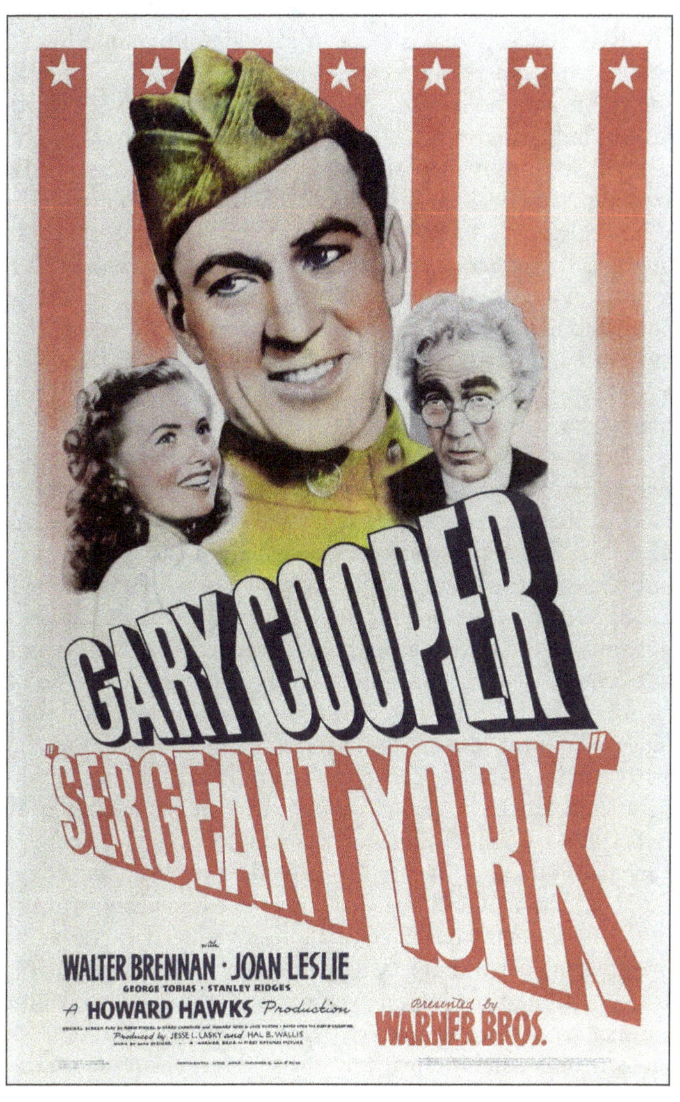

Poster for *Sergeant York* (1941), which became the biggest hit in the history of Warner Bros. up to that time.

Another hazard with the pyramid is that deviations from the apex are rejected even when acknowledged masters are involved. Indeed, what is most striking about pyramid histories is the number of directors who have allegedly declined, compromised, sold out, retreated from reality, evaded responsibility and otherwise gone astray. Some directors, of course, decline by any standards. It cannot be reasonably argued that René Clair in 1962 is equal to René Clair in 1932. What is tiresome about pyramid critics is their tone of moral outrage. In his *Sequence* attack on Hitchcock's Hollywood films, Lindsay Anderson seemed irritated even by the posh hotel Hitchcock patronized on his London visits. Perhaps the most remarkable pyramid denunciation of all time is Kracauer's criticism of German directors for being too esoteric for the masses.

What then is the alternative to the pyramid? I would suggest an inverted pyramid opening outward to accommodate the unpredictable range and diversity of individual directors. The time span of the cinema can then be divided into the career spans of its directors, each of whom is granted the options of a personal mystique apart from any collective mystique of the cinema as a whole. The inverted pyramid does not require a new manifesto. Critics and filmmakers have been moving in that direction for the past decade. History as biography is reflected in the increasing frequency of director retrospectives and in the popularization of director cults. Television has siphoned off a great deal of the sociological criticism with which the cinema was once afflicted, and the new medium may eventually provide a permanent home for the documentary. Not that the era of highbrow promotion is without its drawbacks. In discovering the cinema, it may become even more fashionable to abandon the movies. It is one thing to enjoy an evening at *Marienbad*. It is quite another to spend the next ten years wandering through its interminable corridors without the slightest desire to see the new Western down the street, particularly since *Marienbad*'s redeeming humor is derived mainly from Hollywood.

When the Forties are revisited via the directors of the period, it becomes apparent that Hollywood has the capacity to ride off furiously in all directions and that generalizations about "trends" are usually derived from insufficient evidence. In retrospect, the major directors of 1940 by almost any standard except the most vulgar would include: Charles Chaplin *(The Great Dictator)*, John Ford *(The Grapes of Wrath, The Long Voyage Home)*, Alfred Hitchcock *(Rebecca, Foreign Correspondent)*, Howard Hawks *(His Girl Friday)*, Ernst Lubitsch *(The Shop Around the Corner)*, George Cukor *(The Philadelphia Story, Susan and God)*, Frank Borzage *(The Mortal Storm, Strange Cargo, Flight Command)*, King Vidor *(Northwest Passage, Comrade X)*, Fritz Lang *(The Return of Frank James)*, Raoul Walsh *(They Drive by Night, Dark Command)*, Preston Sturges *(The Great McGinty, Christmas in July)*, Cecil B. DeMille *(Northwest Mounted Police)* and George Stevens *(Vigil in the Night)*. One could stretch a point with Garson Kanin *(My Favorite Wife, They Knew What They Wanted)* and Gregory La Cava *(Primrose Path)*, two likeable directors with elusive personalities. Even more dubious are William Wyler *(The Letter, The Westerner)* and Lewis Milestone *(Of Mice and Men, The Night of Nights, Lucky Partners)*, two overrated directors of the time with no personality at all. Although we have run through twenty-nine films, we have barely scratched the surface of Hollywood in 1940 from the point of view of the regular moviegoer.

The fun really begins down the line past the personalities and the stylists to the moderately competent and the expensively incompetent. The last step to the dregs is the inexpensively incompetent, and there only the most hardened movie addicts have ventured. (Their discoveries are often recorded in *Films in Review*, a publication which knows the credits of everything and the value of nothing.) Apart from such curiosities as George Abbott *(Too Many Girls)*, the one-shot [in the Forties] team of Lee Garmes and Ben Hecht *(Angels Over Broadway)*, and Edward F. Cline, the directorial appendage of W. C. Fields *(My Little Chickadee, The Villain Still Pursued Her, The Bank Dick)*, the lower middle range of directors includes: Busby Berkeley *(Strike Up the Band, Forty Little Mothers)*, Clarence Brown *(Edison, the Man)*, John Cromwell *(Victory)*, Michael Curtiz *(Virginia City, The Sea Hawk, Santa Fe Trail)*, William Dieterle *(Dr. Ehrlich's Magic Bullet, A Dispatch from Reuters)*, Allan Dwan *(Sailor's*

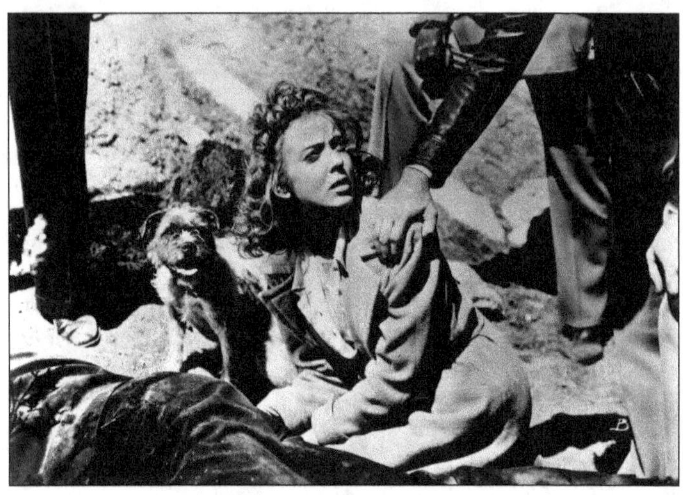

"Mister, what does it mean when a man 'crashes out'?"
Ida Lupino gives a heartrending performance in Raoul Walsh's
High Sierra (1941) as Marie Garson, the fugitive partner of gangster
Roy Earle (Humphrey Bogart), who has just fallen to his death
after being shot from a mountaintop by the authorities.
John Huston and W. R. Burnett adapted Burnett's novel.
(Warner Bros.)

Lady, Young People, Trail of the Vigilantes), Tay Garnett
(Slightly Honorable, Seven Sinners), Edmund Goulding *(Till
We Meet Again)*, Alexander Hall *(He Stayed For Breakfast,
The Doctor Takes a Wife)*, Henry Hathaway *(Johnny Apollo,
Brigham Young)*, Stuart Heisler *(The Biscuit Eater)*, William
K. Howard *(Money and the Woman)*, Henry King *(Little Old
New York, Maryland, Chad Hanna)*, Henry Koster *(Spring
Parade)*, Rowland V. Lee *(The Son of Monte Cristo)*, Mitchell
Leisen *(Remember the Night; Arise, My Love)*, Robert Z.
Leonard *(Pride and Prejudice)*, Mervyn LeRoy *(Waterloo
Bridge, Escape)*, Anatole Litvak *(Castle on the Hudson; City
for Conquest; All This, and Heaven Too; The Howards of
Virginia)*, Rouben Mamoulian *(The Mark of Zorro)*, George
Marshall *(When the Daltons Rode)*, Irving Pichel *(Earth-
bound, The Man I Married, Hudson's Bay)*, Henry C. Potter
(Congo Maisie, Second Chorus), Wesley Ruggles *(Arizona, Too
Many Husbands)*, Mark Sandrich *(Buck Benny Rides Again,*

Love Thy Neighbor), Victor Schertzinger (*Road to Singapore, Rhythm on the River*), Vincent Sherman (*Saturday's Children, Flight from Destiny*), Robert Stevenson (*Tom Brown's School Days*), Andrew Stone (*The Great Victor Herbert*), Richard Thorpe (*The Earl of Chicago*), Jacques Tourneur (*Phantom Raiders*), W. S. Van Dyke (*I Take This Woman, I Love You Again, Bitter Sweet*), Charles Vidor (*My Son, My Son; The Lady in Question*), James Whale (*Green Hell*), and Sam Wood (*Raffles, Our Town, Rangers of Fortune*). Now that we have approached the hundred film mark in 1940, we are considerably closer to the typical Hollywood film with which Mr. Taylor's article is concerned, but we cannot be sure even now that we have completed our preliminary research. If some bright new critic should awaken the world to the merits of Joseph Lewis in the near future, we will have to scramble back to his 1940 record: *Two-Fisted Rangers, Blazing Six Shooters, Texas Stagecoach, The Man From Tumbleweeds, Boys of the City, The Return of Wild Bill,* and *That Gang of Mine*. Admittedly, in this direction lies madness.

The only way to manage the year and the period and the Hollywood cinema as a whole is to concentrate on the top people, accept occasional dividends from the "intermediates," and forget about the dregs. However, it is irresponsible to palm off a random sampling of the three levels as characteristic of the period. It is also a mistake to assume that strong star personalities can carry the day very often against vile direction. Anatole Litvak was given James Cagney for *City for Conquest,* John Garfield for *Castle on the Hudson,* Charles Boyer and Bette Davis for *All This, and Heaven Too,* and Cary Grant for *The Howards of Virginia,* but all four films turned out heavy and turgid in the best Litvak tradition. On the other hand, Vivien Leigh and Conrad Veidt were well-mounted by Mervyn LeRoy in *Waterloo Bridge* and *Escape* respectively, Marlene Dietrich salvaged *Seven Sinners* for Tay Garnett, Robert Montgomery made Richard Thorpe look adequate for *The Earl of Chicago,* and Judy Garland furnished Busby Berkeley and Mickey Rooney with some class in *Strike Up the Band.* This is the realm of happy accidents, studio policies and the autonomous elements of artless entertainment. Here the intellect must combat the outrageous

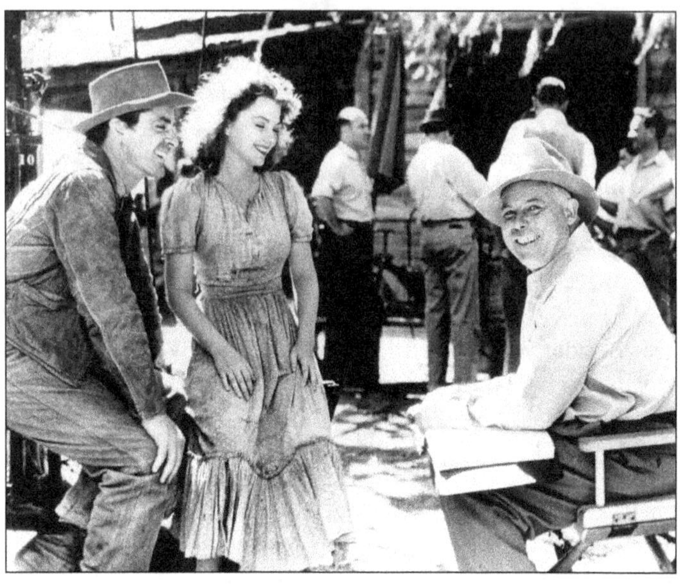

"Jean, we love you, but you're just not one of us," Fox executive Darryl F. Zanuck told French émigré director Jean Renoir after he came to Hollywood to resume his film career. But Renoir wanted to make authentic Americana and fought to film parts of *Swamp Water* (1941) on location in Georgia. Cast members Dana Andrews and Anne Baxter look on. (Twentieth Century-Fox)

responses of the nerve centers. I must admit that I prefer *Waterloo Bridge* to *The Return of Frank James* even though Mervyn LeRoy cannot begin to fit into Fritz Lang's shadow. There is at most one scene in the Lang which I can attribute to his personality, but the weakest Lang is still more interesting than the strongest LeRoy if only as a link in a longer and stronger chain of personal achievements. At least as far as movies are concerned, what we like is not always art. I suppose every critic has an unrecorded shame list of bad films he secretly enjoys along with a recorded pride list of serious films he secretly loathes. If the gap between what a critic really likes and what he officially admires is too great, he may overcompensate for his esthetic guilt by exaggerating the gulf between art and entertainment in the cinema. Worse still, he may suggest to his readers that pleasure is a response to bad art.

Hollywood's vaunted dream apparatus has never worked with quite the efficiency attributed to it by serious critics. Its strength in the diversity of its genres can be misleading. An inept Western or musical is not appreciably more enjoyable than a "serious" film. Only the most provincial audiences patronized the pulp Westerns during the Thirties, and few people viewed Betty Grable and Dorothy Lamour as the embodiments of grace and beauty. When one talks about the "bread and butter" Western, one is talking mainly about the Westerns of Ford and Hawks and the post–*Duel in the Sun* Freudian Westerns of King Vidor, Nicholas Ray, Raoul Walsh, Fritz Lang, Samuel Fuller, Budd Boetticher and Gerd Oswald. The Metro musical reached its flowering with Minnelli, Donen and Kelly, and on a lower level, Walters and Sidney. When one goes any lower, the Metro musicals become almost as much of an ordeal as the Fox and Warner atrocities. The mystiques of studio, producer, period and genre ultimately collapse before the mystique of the director, but the further one gets from art, the harder it is to make distinctions. The consistently superior craftsmanship of a Sandrich or a Schertzinger over a Taurog or a Tuttle requires an incredibly esoteric analysis to prove the point. If the point is not necessarily worth making, it nevertheless confirms the validity of careful distinctions at every level of the cinema.

The intermediate directors did come up with occasional surprises in the Forties whenever stars, scripts and technicians suddenly clicked in an unexpected way. In addition to the ambitious sleepers of Arthur Ripley *(Voice in the Wind, The Chase)* and the overdiscovered Val Lewton horror classics directed by Jacques Tourneur, Robert Wise and Mark Robson, there were more than fifty films which ran stronger than their directors. The bulk of these films were in the vehicle category, and the directors were usually specialists in dishing out the corn with a little flair. With actresses like Vivien Leigh, Margaret Sullavan, Bette Davis, Ida Lupino, Dorothy McGuire, Jennifer Jones, Gail Russell, Laraine Day, a little corn went a long way, particularly with a score by Max Steiner, Victor Young or Frank Skinner. There were often good actors like Cary Grant, Robert Montgomery, Charles Boyer and John Garfield to balance things out.

If there is one intermediate masterpiece of the Forties, it is *Casablanca,* the happiest of happy accidents. Again Michael Curtiz is somewhat more than moderately competent as a studio craftsman. Nevertheless, *Casablanca* emerges as a miracle of casting comparable to *The Maltese Falcon.* The idea of Humphrey Bogart, Ingrid Bergman, Paul Henreid, Claude Rains, Conrad Veidt, Sydney Greenstreet, Peter Lorre and Marcel Dalio acting together in a routine project suggests the incredible human resources of the period. The density of character acting in the Forties is so prodigious that the period is almost worth reviving just to see the various stock companies in action. Suddenly everyone seemed to be in Hollywood: Albert Basserman glaring at Maria Ouspenskaya past Walter Huston in Sternberg's *The Shanghai Gesture,* the Mercury Players breaking into each other's lines, the festivals of bit players erupting in eight Preston Sturges films for Paramount in four years, the Warners night people, not to mention the return of Erich von Stroheim, the arrivals of Peter van Eyck, Alexander Granach and Carl Esmond, and the revivals of Judith Anderson, Ethel Barrymore and Francis Lederer.

However, the waste of resources was equally prodigious. It was difficult to imagine then how absurd it would seem today to see Humphrey Bogart, Conrad Veidt and Judith Anderson cavorting in a tenth-rate espionage quickie like *All Through the Night.* We took such atrocities in stride because we had no idea that Hollywood was so close to sublimity, and that one day we would remember with awe and futile regret. It is not entirely middle-aged nostalgia which prompts veterans of the period to recall the Forties as the Golden Age of the stars. The Thirties had filtered out the unadaptable silent players while the Fifties witnessed the abolition of the studio contract lists. Consequently, the Forties had the best of both eras. It is difficult to recall many Depression deities who did not at least work in the Forties; it is almost as difficult to cite many current stars who did not at least begin their careers in the Forties. If a specialist in actors were limited to films of the Forties, he would miss Jean Harlow, Marie Dressler, Helen Hayes, Louis Wolheim, Osgood Perkins, Ruth Chatterton, Helen Chandler and Phillips Holmes from the preceding decade, in most cases through untimely deaths.

The few additions since 1949—Marlon Brando; James Dean; Grace Kelly; Audrey Hepburn, depending on the exact dates of her minor British credits; the male ingenues at Universal; the pallid blonds from Actors' Studio; the kooks and the curiously unattractive fashion models—have failed to keep pace with the needs of an aging star system. Hollywood's gradual hardening of the arteries is most conspicuously observed in this phase of the industry. It is perhaps more than a coincidence that on the directorial level as well, the older directors have continued to dominate the scene.

Even in 1940, the Hollywood cinema was aging at the top. Chaplin, Ford, Borzage, King Vidor, Walsh, DeMille and Dwan had directed their first films before 1920; Hitchcock, Hawks, Lubitsch, Lang, Wyler, Milestone and La Cava before sound; Cukor, Stevens, Kanin and Mamoulian after sound. Preston Sturges led off the writer-director movement in 1940, and there was a brief period of apparent rejuvenation. Orson Welles made his grand entrance in 1941, and was followed (at a considerable distance) by John Huston. Jean Renoir, René Clair and Robert Siodmak popped in from Europe, and Josef von Sternberg and Frank Capra of the pre-sound generation extended their careers into the Forties. Billy Wilder, Albert Lewin, Anthony Mann, Jules Dassin and Fred Zinnemann hit the circuits in 1942; Leo McCarey, another pre-sound figure, resumed. Douglas Sirk and Vincente Minnelli led off 1943, followed by Norman Krasna, Mark Robson and Herman Shumlin. Otto Preminger resumed a career which had been marginal in the Thirties, and he was accompanied by ancient veteran John Stahl. Budd Boetticher, Clifford Odets and Phil Karlson were admitted in 1944; Elia Kazan and Robert Wise in 1945 [Wise actually began directing in 1944—Ed.]; Joseph L. Mankiewicz, Dudley Nichols and Robert Montgomery in 1946; Max Opuls *(sic)* and Joseph Losey in 1947; Abe Polonsky in 1948; Nicholas Ray and Samuel Fuller in 1949.

When you add together the holdovers, the émigrés and the newcomers, Hollywood had enough directorial talent in the Forties to supply five golden ages. Even pioneers Griffith, Stroheim and Flaherty were available, Griffith and Stroheim as untouchables, and Flaherty outside the industry. Hollywood was still close enough to its beginnings and far enough

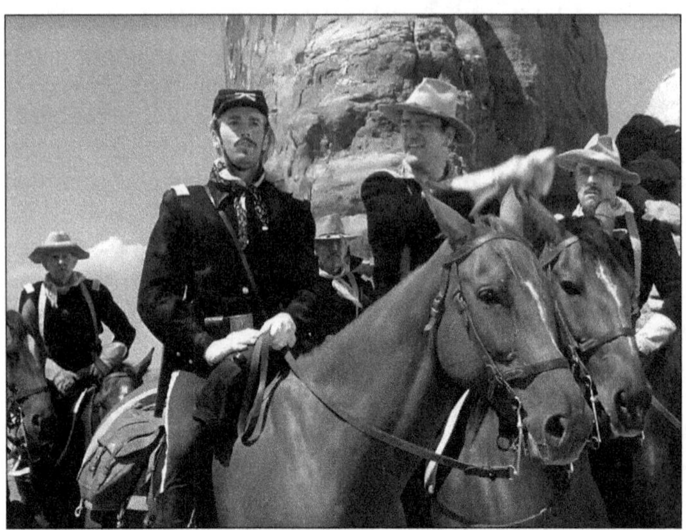

The tragic climax of John Ford's *Fort Apache* (1948), his and screenwriter Frank S. Nugent's revisionist study of the Custer legend.
Colonel Thursday (Henry Fonda), a glory-seeking martinet, has just
given the disastrous order to break a truce with the Apaches, split
his troop, and mount a charge to their deaths in what Captain York
(John Wayne) warns is an act of "suicide." York is throwing down
his gauntlet but is unable to stop the massacre. (Argosy/RKO)

from television to look forward with some confidence, but
everything seemed to go wrong at once. The anti-communist
drive expelled Chaplin, Losey and Polonsky, it now seems
forever,* and ironically, all Hollywood could salvage after
the storm had cleared were Edward Dmytryk, Carl Foreman
and Robert Rossen. One by one, Renoir, Ophüls *(sic)*, Lang,
Siodmak and Clair returned to Europe. Ford and Hitchcock
fell into disfavor with the critics and worked privately with
"minor" genres while Hollywood's man of all genres, Howard
Hawks, continued to be anonymously successful. Welles and
Sternberg joined Griffith and Stroheim in the ranks of the
untouchables. Preston Sturges was exiled; Ernst Lubitsch,

* In 1968 the formerly blacklisted Polonsky returned to Hollywood
to shoot *Tell Them Willie Boy Is Here*, his first film as a director
since *Force of Evil* in 1949. [Ed.]

Gregory La Cava and John Stahl died. The superficial ugliness of neorealism gave Hollywood a bad case of artistic jitters while British color fostered a professional neurosis. Above all, the critics went berserk on the pyramid of social significance. The wrong films and the wrong directors were honored. Propaganda was exalted above personality as was verbal solemnity over visual style.

By 1948, Hollywood itself was so disgusted with its output that it nominated *Hamlet* and *The Red Shoes* for Academy Awards with *Hamlet* winning. This was the year Opuls (Ophüls in less opulent Europe) was represented by *Letter from an Unknown Woman*, Welles by *The Lady from Shanghai*, Ford by *Fort Apache*, Hitchcock by *Rope*, Hawks by *Red River* and Borzage by *Moonrise*, to mention just the most glaring omissions from chronicles of the period. The fact that all six of these films and their directors were underrated at the time suggests the area where reappraisal is most necessary. One advantage in following directors instead of the commercial trinity of stars, subjects and studios is the higher yield of lasting art. It is one thing to recollect the mediocre joys of one's youth. It is quite another to justify expenditures for the mere preservation of the past in a tangible form. If it were possible to save all the films of the period, and then exhibit them in however haphazard an order, audiences could judge for themselves. It is quite likely, however, that a degree of selectivity will be required. After rummaging through hundreds of films of this period quite recently, I can find no sensible alternative to directors' retrospectives in organizing the period. The stars may be ageless, as Gloria Swanson reminds us in *Sunset Blvd.*, but they are not constant. Teresa Wright is scarcely bearable in Wyler's *Mrs. Miniver* and she is almost glorious in Hitchcock's *Shadow of a Doubt*. One could draw corresponding parallels for Montgomery Clift in Wyler's *The Heiress* and Hawks' *Red River*, for Zachary Scott and Betty Field in almost everything they did apart from Renoir's *The Southerner*. In retrospect, players who were wasted on bad directors lose ground to players who worked with the masters. Joan Fontaine (Ophüls, Hitchcock) finally triumphs over Olivia de Havilland (Wyler, Litvak). Anne Baxter (Renoir, Welles and later Hitchcock and Lang) and Joan Bennett (Renoir, Ophüls and Lang) are miraculously resurrected as directors' actresses while Bette Davis and Ida Lupino have to be rescued from the footnotes to their vehicles.

The emphasis on subjects is even more hopeless. Where are the topical films of yesteryear, and who cares anymore about the burning social issues of that time? *Home of the Brave, Lost Boundaries, Pinky, Intruder in the Dust, Crossfire, Gentleman's Agreement, The Ox-Bow Incident, Watch on the Rhine, All the King's Men, None but the Lonely Heart, The Searching Wind* and even *The Best Years of Our Lives* date badly, so badly, in fact, that the old question arises: Are there major and minor subjects, or just major and minor artists? Very often, it depends on whether cinema is considered analogous to painting or to literature, to abstraction or to representation. The alleged size of a screen subject is generally a function of the writing of the film, and unfortunately, writing is and always has been Hollywood's weakest cog. Much of the apparent absurdity of the Forties can be traced to the superficial impact of scripts. For one thing, films were saturated with propaganda, some hung over from the Depression and the Spanish Civil War, some improvised after Pearl Harbor, less after the beginning of the Cold War because of box-office resistance. Hollywood propaganda is unlike propaganda anywhere else. Instead of boy meets tractor, we have boy meets long-legged or big-bosomed girl who talks about nothing but tractor. The idea of Gary Cooper posing as a ban-the-bomb atomic scientist in *Cloak and Dagger* should have appalled any intelligent scenarist, but the possibilities of subliminal, star-associated ideology always seemed irresistible to the commissars and gauleiters of the swimming pools. The proceedings of the Un-American Activities Committee achieved their most hilarious effects in the analysis of individual films and sequences. It often came down to hack politicians arguing with hack writers about the content of commercials in the programming. Like all attempts at censorship, the political pressure on Hollywood was very silly and very harmful, but it is almost as silly to argue that Hollywood lost its soul as a consequence. After all, we still have the cinema of Stanley Kramer where no social issue is left to chance or central casting. A bigot in *Judgment at Nuremberg* must be played by the same unsavory character actor who mistreated a "One World" amputee in *The Best Years of Our Lives.*

However, even aside from the propaganda, Hollywood films have never read as well as they looked. The subterfuges to evade the censorship account for at least some of the ambiguities of the period. The spectacular mortality rate can be similarly attributed to the censor's insistence on some form of moral retribution, no matter how lurid. Hollywood still suffers from the Scribean script policy of the Thirties when each character was allotted one motivation and one motivation only. The relatively mysterious characterizations and moods of the Forties can be attributed in part to the vogue for psychoanalysis and in part to the stylistic revolution of *Citizen Kane.* Renoir's classic observation in *The Rules of the Game* that everyone has his reasons has become one of the premises of the modern cinema. Consequently, the gradual liberation of directors from the rigid moral allegories hammered out in studio-controlled script conferences give the films of the Forties a more personal quality than is found in comparable works of the Thirties. Nevertheless, only the top directors took full advantage of the period advantages.

It is now clear that Chaplin was moving into his deepest period in the Forties. As his public abandoned him, he revealed more and more of his personality. *The Great Dictator,* along with Renoir's *The Diary of a Chambermaid* and Eisenstein's *Ivan the Terrible,* one of the few profoundly political films ever made, expressed the ambiguity of Chaplin's personality through a revealing comprehension of both Hitler and the barber. *Monsieur Verdoux* unmasked Chaplin even further, too far, in fact, for the public to accept. The increasing bitterness of Chaplin's art as he became older is, perhaps, a key to the American cinema as well. In their various ways, Welles, Ford, Hitchcock, Hawks, and Sternberg became more confidential in their art, more indifferent to the critics and the public. Ford, for example, can now be traced more accurately from *Steamboat Round the Bend* through *Stagecoach* to the personal summit of his later Westerns rather than from *The Informer* through *The Grapes of Wrath.* Hitchcock's parabola shows a steady rise from *Shadow of a Doubt* through *Notorious* and *Under Capricorn* all the way through to *Psycho.*

His British period now looks like a primitive apprenticeship for the elaborate formality of the casuistic universe he was to create in Hollywood virtually unnoticed.

Some critics have attempted to organize the period and the American cinema as a whole in terms of studios, producers and technicians. Some of the more advanced visual critics have even started playing the photographer's game as an esoteric substitute for the director's game. There is just enough of a pattern in these areas to encourage a system, but research in depth, the relentless enemy of generalization, eventually wrecks the system. Subtract Gregg Toland from Welles and you still have a mountain; subtract Toland from Wyler and you have a molehill. Until 1945 Paramount had the fuzziest texture of any of the major studios. *Double Indemnity* looks particularly weak visually today vis-à-vis Fox's *Laura* and Metro's *Gaslight* that same year. Yet in 1945, the photography in Paramount's *Love Letters* and *The Lost Weekend* was superior to anything from the other studios. *Love Letters* can be explained by the temporary alliance of Lee Garmes and William Dieterle, but *The Lost Weekend* has no comparable variable [actually, John Seitz photographed both *Double Indemnity* and *The Lost Weekend* for director Billy Wilder—Ed.]. Studio identification was still meaningful in the Forties, but usually at the lower levels of production. The fact that Metro had the best lab work, Fox the best process shooting, Warners the best night quality is interesting but hardly crucial.

I am afraid it is impossible to generalize about a period represented by the polarities of Chaplin and Welles, Ford and Hitchcock, Hawks and Sternberg, Renoir and Ophüls, *The Southerner* and *Laura, My Darling Clementine* and *Notorious, Sergeant York* and *The Shanghai Gesture, She Wore a Yellow Ribbon* and *Under Capricorn, Monsieur Verdoux* and *The Magnificent Ambersons, Swamp Water* and *The Exile, They Were Expendable* and *Lifeboat, High Sierra* and *Suspicion, Air Force* and *Gaslight, They Live by Night* and *On the Town.* One advantage of the inverted pyramid is its sanction of alternatives. One need not be inconsistent to admire Chaplin and Renoir on the left, Ford and Hitchcock on the right, and Sternberg in the erotic center. It is also to be hoped that one is not compelled to choose between the masculine code of Hawks and the boudoir sensibility of Ophüls. Instead of standing up to be counted, we might try sitting down to better concentrate on the great art in our midst. In the foreseeable future it will be difficult to prove that the continuity of a director's career is more interesting than the surfaces of individual films. The sheer unavailability of films will haunt us for some time to come, but once the principle of directorial continuity is accepted even in Hollywood, films can never look the same again. If there is ever an organized program for reviving the Forties, it should begin with all the films of all the directors who have the slightest factional support. After that, the period can be thrown open to the wildest actor, genre and studio cults. Of course, it would be even more desirable to go back to the beginning of each director's career and follow through to the end, letting the Forties intersect where they may. For all serious purposes, the High Forties were nothing more than ten years in the lives of a group of directors.

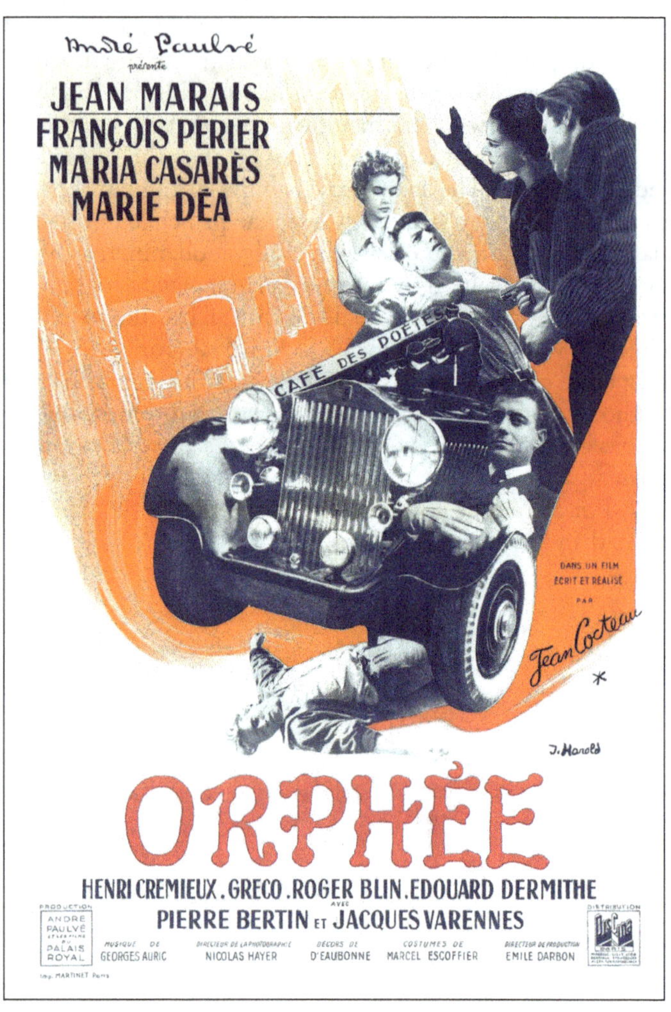

The poet, playwright, novelist, artist and filmmaker Jean Cocteau made the 1950 film *Orphée* as the center of his Orphic trilogy that also encompassed *The Blood of a Poet* (1930) and *The Testament of Orpheus* (1960). He wrote of *Orphée* that it "is not at all a dream in itself: through a wealth of detail similar to that which we find in dreams, it summarizes my way of living and my conception of life." (DisCina)

Orpheus: **Cocteau's Thanatopsis**
Jon Zwickey

Orpheus is surrealistic. Written in anthologies "surrealistic" becomes linguistic burrowing beneath authors' intentions through a narrow perspective of authentic man's witness to his meaning innocence. The guilt of meaning is the cross each beholder shoulders to go tell it on the mountain. Rejoice my brethren cross feathers are burdensome only when meaning becomes weighted with seriousness. Gravity maintains colossalest cross-main-pole tent you can imagine. Picasso said to Cocteau—OPIUM IS THE LEAST STUPID SMELL IN THE WORLD, IT REMINDS ME OF THE SEASHORE OR A CIRCUS TENT. 3 rings are 3 pyramids & the cross-fire on Calvary will not die. WHY HAST THOU FORSAKEN ME cursed the Phoenix approaching the pyre.

The film may sequentially divide into 17 bits corresponding to 20th century linear perspective. Ruth's drawing activates celluloid bits as film running time progresses from myth to nothing&ALL. Beyond linear's realm HERE is no advancement within the eternality of the circle formed NOW: timeless myth returned to timeless nothing. Linearly Orpheus' trip is expressed by the 3 pyramids & their connecting "reality" lines. The beholder's trip is not meaning accumulation but his "reality" destruction. The beholder's line is ideal & consequently too straight. *The Trip* of Roger Corman is ideally boring with quaint underground steals & profiting from sensational tail lines. Commercial "reality" opposes nothing&ALL; forming Yang Yin within the eternal circle. Will to power is male principle (Yang) manifesting desire for "reality's" security. Female principle (Yin) is the Princess: our death—nothing&ALL.

• • •

Two principles welding together (meditation as action) in conflict are not duality; but global configuration in proximity of ONE represented by the Yang Yin. Nietzsche (youthfully encountered opium as war medical corpsman—as did Cocteau) named the two principles Apollonian & Dionysian. Synthesis creates not a product but the annihilation of their difference: life & death yield the tragic course of their rendezvous. Complexity disfigured Apollo with a third principle—Socrates' "knowledge is virtue" veils the tragic Princess under embellished cares. Socraticists are offended by dancing seven veiled surrealists because death's kiss reveals nausea at first: nonsense is the illumination of ugliness by making it eat itself.

• • •

Heidegger (within the Black Forest) unveils the Princess not as the body's physical demise; but the SILENT CALL heard in the absence of windy baroque care. After Sartre's first mescaline trip (taken in a clinic) "reality" became Rococo initiating *Nausea* in an ego desiring nobility. Opening *The Doors of Perception* Huxley destroyed care's veil as Sartre had named the Princess BEAUTY (Being-for-itself-in-itself)—the death of *Being and Nothingness'* separation.

• • •

Freedom eternally interrupts the separation of consciousness from its object; yet Orpheus' veiling separation only reaches the pyre at the third pyramid pinnacle. There (Heidegger's HERE) the Princess says WE'RE FREE promising Orpheus FOREVER; since nothing&ALL's uncanniness negates time's sequential division.

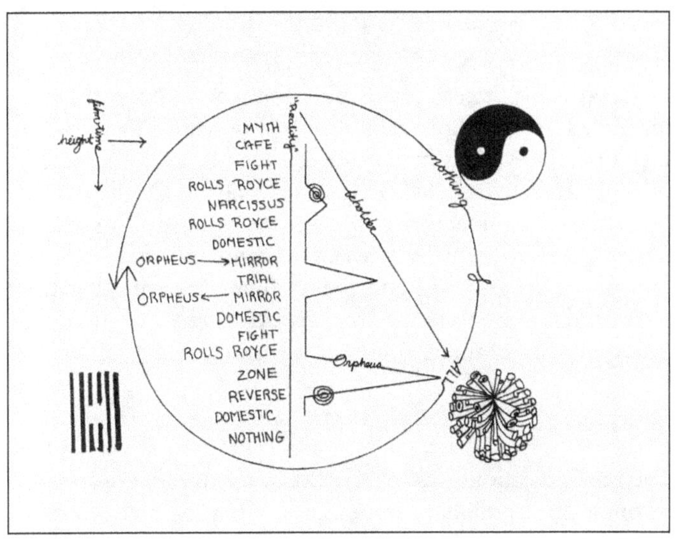

Diagram of Jean Cocteau's *Orpheus* for Zwickey's essay.

• • •

The Rolls Royce's radio names the 3 pyramids & Orpheus' reverse trip (right of third pinnacle) with horse-shoe precision—SILENCE GOES FASTER BACKWARDS, THREE TIMES. /film/

• • •

Apollinaire wounded (WWI) died two years later of head shrapnel [and influenza]. Cocteau imagined a radio to the unknown beneath his tunic bandage. The wounded poet relieved his pain with opium: the Horse says to Orpheus in Apollinaire's *Le Bestiaire*—
    MY STRICT AND FORMAL DREAMS RIDE UP
       TO YOU,
    MY FATE WILL MAKE ME COACHMAN FOR
       YOUR CAR
    WHOSE REINS, STRAINING IN VIOLENCE,
       WILL BE
    MY VERSES, PARAGONS OF POETRY.

• • •

In Cocteau's *Orphée* (play) the unknown contacts the poet through a Horse's hoof taps. In *Orpheus* (film) the Horse is 1 of 12 Rolls-Royces in Europe & the radio is the hoof. *The Glazier Heurtebise* (play) becomes one of Orpheus-Cocteau's intended memories within the Ruined Zone (film) where ALL are equally present in temporal flux—waiting for consciousness to intend them. Memories are other than pure lived experience: they are CHARRED by care-reason to become aware of them.

• • •

The poet's creations (less charred than memories) are revealed through an Apollonian appearance officially recognized as Orpheus. At the cafe Orpheus' fame alleviates detention's nuisance & requires the release of Rimbaud (HAVEN'T WRITTEN SINCE I WAS TWENTY /film/) from gang buster cops arriving at the cafe. Historical memory (Orpheus couldn't locate a cranium brush for Cégestes' face—cafe) precipitates Orpheus-Cocteau's awareness of difficulties encountered prior to TRUMPETED herd acquisition—IT IS THE PORTRAIT OF THE DONOR AT THE BOTTOM OF THE CANVAS; THE NAME OF THE PERSON WHO HAS BEEN RUN OVER, WHEN HE IS QUESTIONED AT THE CHEMIST SHOP. /Cocteau/ Cégestes (Orpheus-Cocteau's past) escaping from the cops is run over as black clad motorcyclists sacrifice *The Blood of a Poet*. Cocteau loved Raymond Radiguet whose youthful death reinforced the poet's belief that Radiguet was THE GLOVE OF HEAVEN. /Cocteau/ Orpheus receives the Princess' gloves (used for penetrating mirror entrance to the Ruined Zone) because Cégestes leaves them behind: Radiguet challenges Cocteau to join the heavenly eternity of Bach's SILENCE. Between the Princess' notes *(PRINCESS TO ORPHEUS:* I FORGOT, YOU ARE NOT A WRITER. /film/) is Cocteau's identity.

• • •

Notes of facticity—Cocteau born (1889) at Maisons-La-fitte—father died (1899) & kin to his friend Sartre formed an allegiance with his grandfather—first poetry reading (1906) organized by de Max—his *Le Prince Frivole* (1910) contained illustrations done by Alfred Jarry (pataphysi-cian & ether head)—traveled to Switzerland (1913) with Stravinsky after scandal over *The Rite of Spring*—ambulance corps (1914)—flipped aerial acrobatics (1915) with Roland Garros—with Picasso & others held party to celebrate Apollinaire's publishing *Le Poète Assassins* (1916) IT WAS CABLED THAT THE UNITED STATES OF AMERICA HAD DECIDED TO ELECTROCUTE ANY MAN WHO AVOWED HIS PROFESSION TO BE THAT OF POETRY /Apollinaire/—wrote the ballet *Phaedre* (1917) sets by Picasso & music by Erik Satie—Antonin Artaud (mesca-line & opium head) dropped out of *The Theatre & Its Double* to act in Cocteau's *Antigone* (1922) where Cocteau was the chorus—first opium "cure" & finished *Orphée* (1925)—second opium "cure" & book *Opium* (1928-1929)—filmed *Blood of a Poet* (1930)—Charlie Chaplin arranges for *Blood of a Poet* to be shown in New York City (1932)—premiere Cocteau's Oedipus Rex *The Infernal Machine* (1934)—on a bet traveled *Around the World in 80 Days* (1936) stopping at opium dens—manages bantamweight boxer Al Brown back to victory (1937)—filmed *Beauty and the Beast* (1946)—filmed *Orpheus* (1950) photographed by Nicolas Hayer, music by Georges Auric, cast: Jean Cocteau-Narrator, Jean Marais-Orpheus, Marie Dea-Eurydice, Maria Casares-Prin-cess, François Perier-Heurtebise, Edouard Dermithe-Cége-stes—writes *Hand of a Stranger* (1952) philosophy of invis-ible actual (title from *The Birth of Tragedy*'s last page)—Jean Cocteau died of a heart attack (October 11, 1963) leaving behind his film will *Testament of Orpheus* (1959).

● ● ●

The will which Orpheus-Cocteau burned in death was the WILL TO CARE: an anchor weighted with the superstition of "reality" forced the Phoenix to crawl toward the pyre. Untying the Gordian knot reveals death as "reality" (self structure) returning to nothing&ALL: DEATH IS THE NORMAL STATE FROM WHICH THE ANORMAL PHENOMENON OF LIFE EMERGES AND STAYS WITH US FOR A WHILE. /Cocteau/

• • •

How on earth to untie time's knot?

• • •

To express unearthly actuality Cocteau used "reality" against itself; he truly lied in the face of a lie. The delicate balance of negative poles achieves poetic potential relative to the field: the simple minded magazines (*Nudism* containing blank pages— film) Orpheus considers cute; but lacking challenge to reach our dynamo's total field. Death can not be totaled within the matrix where Christian Berard (created sets & costumes for *Orpheus*) died prior to production. The Princess is not physical demise: I AM THE IMAGE YOU HAVE OF DEATH. /film/ The image multiplies in the 3 face mirror: Orpheus Cégestes & Eurydice answer the Princess' identity problem through bearing witness to her being MY DEATH. /film/ Death is consciousness dropping out content ("self" & "reality") allowing expansion toward its actual nothingness—the ALL.

• • •

Yang & Yin's rendezvous is change annihilating the separating difference between consciousness & "reality"; such that freedom awaits the organizer's falling toward constraining consciousness to object of environmental facticity. At the third pyramid's height the Princess says to Orpheus—WE ARE FREE—Nirvana—mystical experience—CONSCIOUSNESS-FORGETFULNESS—(smoke).[3] Orpheus' fictional return from eternity's nothing&ALL required open freedom be choked off till a willing "self" began striving for IMMORTALITY. Temporal care springs man's ephemeral trap: coming down to time cherished ritual permanence (last domestic) bestowed fame & a son (Orpheus Jr.) limiting Orpheus' freedom.

• • •

1 of the 2 motorcyclists (Mother Miles) was up on motherhood & *Scorpio Rising* knew the angelic anger of Mother Chaos.

• • •

The Phoenix kin to Oedipus goes through his image of Mother Death—the flaming Princess. Eve's regality commits the only possible sin; where there are no CIRCUMSTANCES. /Tribunal/ The Princess' intervention (choking Orpheus' freedom) is love's Virgin (Cocteau undergoing opium "cure" discovered a nun attired nurse motherly—changing B & W Princess' dress). Mother returns our "reality" of living; but alleviating addiction to death traps as both the Sphinx *(Infernal Machine)* & the Princess commanded—CALCULATE, COUNT, LABOR AS I LABOR. /film/ Bestowing immortality violates fate & elicits punishment which is NOT AMUSING /Heurtebise/: the Princess (in *Testament of Orpheus*) is condemned TO JUDGE OTHERS /Heurtebise/ without circumstances ("reality") or awareness ("self") as ALL chaotically swims in her primordial womb.

• • •

The Princess (Cocteau's death image) appears—in *Thomas the Impostor* as ambulance unit member—in *Orphée* with 2 angels—in *Orpheus* with 2 motorcyclists—in *Testament of Orpheus* as the Trinity Tribunal. In *Orpheus* her entourage carry out her orders; but she is master chemist synthesizing fate yielding Orpheus' "reality" destruction & angelic companion Heurtebise. Heurtebise is *The Steppenwolf*'s connection (Pablo) with the Magic Theatre: Heurtebise is chauffeur of the Princess' Rolls-Royce containing Apollinaire's radio tuned into Picasso's studio. High on opium—ascending with the elevator toward Picasso's loft—Cocteau become hung up in the ascension—the "self" was vanishing—Cocteau struggling with the invisible imagined the elevator plaque contained the word Heurtebise. Cocteau's remaining

"self" grasping his angel's wings maintained will to subdue approaching CONSCIOUSNESSFORGETFULNESS till he reached Picasso's wisdom. IT IS A MIRACLE WE DON'T DISSOLVE IN THE BATH. /Picasso / After dissolving in union with the Princess (pinnacle third pyramid) she orders Heurtebise to choke Orpheus back to elevator existence. But Cocteau is committed to opium's pure breasts.
PRINCESS: WILL YOU OBEY ME?
ORPHEUS: YES.
PRINCESS: EVEN IF I JUDGE YOU? EVEN IF I TORTURE YOU?
ORPHEUS: I BELONG TO YOU. /film/
The sweet milk turns rancid in withdrawal; but returning to combustion within the pipe world reduces "the just's" words to TELLING SILENCE IT IS RUINED BY BACH. /Cocteau/ The ruin of "reality" is chaos (muses) providing accidental foundations of poet & his creation. WITH US, THERE IS A HOUSE, A LAMP, A PLATE OF SOUP, A FIRE, WINE AND PIPES AT THE BACK OF EVERY IMPORTANT WORK OF ART. /Cocteau/

• • •

Nietzsche's *The Birth of Tragedy* uses Wagner's *Tristan* as initiating vision. Cocteau created scenario & dialogue for *The Eternal Return* (1944-film) based on Wagner's opera. Cocteau's title refers to Nietzsche's conceptional ETERNAL RETURN replicated in Watt's *This Is It.* Sartre's first & unpublished novel reveals Nietzsche's tragic love for Cosima Wagner.

• • •

Aristotle demands a beginning, middle & end segment prior myth into Tragedy. The three pyramids satisfy the form & Heurtebise phones the cops precipitating Cégestes' death— Heurtebise is Ovid's mythical beekeeper on the level where Cégestes is Cocteau's Eurydice-Radiguet.

• • •

At the film's beginning Cocteau (as narrator) presents the myth of Orpheus; supplying the beholder with a vantage center. Cocteau presents the myth—Cocteau directs & edits the camera eye—what the eye sees becomes the beholder's scene: the beholder creates a glorious dream—his tragedy. For such a beholder the image on the screen will be his death. Tragedy is not a mere Aristotelian imitation; but a mirror supplying catharsis to those penetrating the vivid Apollonian appearance to its Dionysian wisdom.

• • •

A mirror presents an appearance on the surface hinting at imaginary space behind quicksilver. In *Calligrammes* Apollinaire typographically placed his name in an oval mirror frame. The poem frame & name read—IN THIS MIRROR I AM ENCLOSED LIVING & TRUE AS ONE IMAGINES ANGELS NOT AS REFLECTIONS ARE GUILLAUME APOLLINAIRE.

• • •

Man's essence disappears as he ascends in the Ruined Zone (behind mirror) where dead angels live (Cégestes) knowing not boredom's care. One is always in the proximity (radio) of the Holy; but Orpheus' access (unveiling actual) was attainable through Rolls-Royce or mirror trip. Orpheus' first trip lasting screen-reality-time minutes (Rolls-Royce— first pyramid—left side) begins in light & ends in darkness. Cross-cross cutting & negative photography facilitates day to night temporal elongation. The whole includes not only Yang & Yin or black & white or positive & negative but also the CHANGE (Princess' dress when entering the Zone with Eurydice). Does not Orpheus' trip reveal Kung Fu's negative eye as LIGHT whose sourcelessness allows omnipresence?

• • •

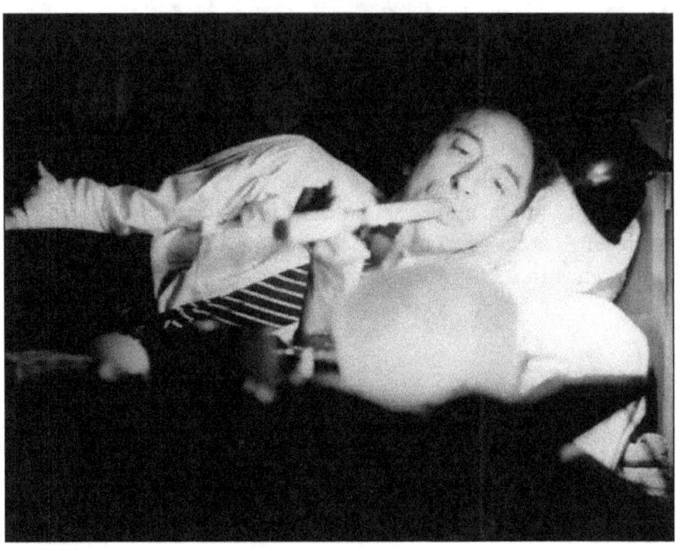

Jean Cocteau smoking opium.

The Rolls-Royce transports Orpheus, the Princess, Cégestes & Heurtebise to the Zone where they enter an old house. Orpheus is offered champagne by the Princess' 2 opium boys & then left alone as Cégestes is deathified. Orpheus has not yet deeply penetrated the Zone (first pyramid not reaching nothing&All) & placing his cheek against the Princess' mirror he is transferred (editing) to a beach. Not only did Cocteau destroy time sequence (Rolls-Royce trip) but he annihilates space continuity (house to beach no travel) as Orpheus rises to the first pyramid's pinnacle. "Self" love prevents his ascension to the pyre: cheek against beach water Narcissus clings to his essence. In fear & trembling Orpheus searches till he discovers Heurtebise & the Rolls-Royce. His guardian angel chauffeurs him to the world's solidified care; where inner maintaining concern for consciousness veils the QUESTION with care of one's public image (journalist meeting Orpheus returning). In "reality's" domestic world Orpheus journeys toward the police station to account for his presence at the café. Passing through the market he sees his DEATH but is unable to authentically reach her: the "reality" of girls wanting autographs is immortality's bad faith.

• • •

Meanwhile Eurydice is run over by Alfred Jarry's bicycle (*The Passion Considered as an Uphill Bicycle Race*) & delivered to the Andalusian hades.

• • •

Orpheus returns home & Heurtebise explains he must use the Princess' gloves (left by Cégestes-Radiguet) for entering the Zone. As Orpheus penetrates the mirror (800 pounds of mercury) the postman drops a letter in the postbox. The Zone's tribunal accepts Orpheus' testimony as a French court had allowed Cocteau's testimony on Jean Genet's behalf. The judges release Eurydice & Orpheus accompanied by Heurtebise after the Princess admits she loves Orpheus. The 3 returning through the mirror is followed by a CU of letter completely falling into postbox. The mirror manifests a time frame & the split (CU before & after) in the letter's fall into the box emphasizes the eternity of behind mirror time: $T = O$.

• • •

Eurydice & Heurtebise sit in the Rolls-Royce's back seat. Orpheus playing with the dash-mounted radio glances up & meets Eurydice's eyes in the rear view mirror—she disappears.

• • •

Outside the villa walls jealous poets & youths (from café) approach believing Orpheus is connected with Cégestes' disappearance. Orpheus' recent poetry was received via the radio & Cégestes has been manipulating the transmitter; consequently the Bacchantes are correct in discovering Cégestes' keying within Orpheus' poetry. As the jealous Bacchantes enter the villa yelling to drown out Orpheus' song (Ovid) Orpheus is shot. Heurtebise places the body in the Rolls-Royce beginning Orpheus' third trip before the police arrive. Even the bust suggests a time frame.

• • •

The highest pyramid requires the greatest courage & effort: following Heurtebise saving Orpheus' O.D.'d body from the cops Orpheus & Heurtebise perform a slow motion agonizing crawl (ceiling camera—floor set) to the third pinnacle. The death of Orpheus' consciousness touches fire's eternal moment: after the Princess & Orpheus are consumed in freedom Orpheus says—YOU BURN LIKE ICE. /film/

• • •

Orpheus' rebirth (Princess motivated—commanding his freedom be choked off) follows a BACKWARD trip toward "reality" (reverse of Orpheus' & Heurtebise's trip through the Ruined Zone—left side second pyramid—footage ½ different because Heurtebise faces opposite direction). The reverse footage annihilates (time frame logic) the film's existence between second pyramid beginning & the reverse's end punctuated with a wipe. The only other wipe is during the first Rolls-Royce trip (beginning first pyramid). Ruth has diagrammed wipes with pataphysical whirligigs (history of hypnotic spiral symbol traceable to Chinese thunder pattern whose origin is female cannabis bark design). The time frame formed by the whirligigs drops out time leaving Orpheus living in cafe & last domestic. Orpheus' remaining life is squeezed to eternity between the timeless myth & closing shot (Heurtebise & the Princess flanked by two motorcyclists—walking deeper into the Ruined Zone). The circle closes: nothing&ALL neither remains nor vanishes: the 360° pan which opens the café sequence becomes invisible at the beholder's center—the SUN.

• • •

Cross spectators in the meaning centrifuge are separated from their motionless central Zone containing ashes of ONENESS. THE PHOENIX, THAT FUNERAL PYRE WHO ENGENDERS HIMSELF FOR AN INSTANT, VEILS THE SCENE WITH HIS GLOWING ASHES. / Apollinaire from poem called *Zone*/ The regenerated head says to Socratic categorizers—KNOW THAT OUR WORK

IS ONLY ADDRESSED TO THOSE WHOSE WAVE-
LENGTH IS THE SAME AS OURS. /Cocteau/

revised 10 Gueules, 95 P.E.
Jon Zwickey

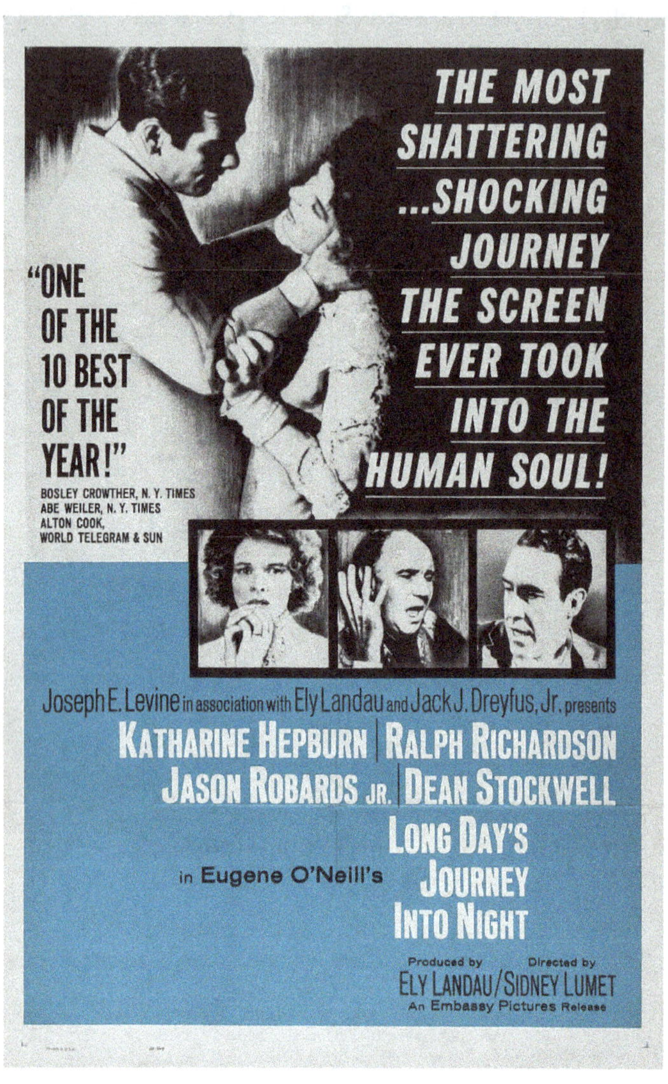

This original poster for *Long Day's Journey Into Night* (1962) seems uncertain about how to sell this faithful, uncompromising film version of Eugene O'Neill's devastating masterpiece to moviegoers. (Embassy Pictures)

Long Day's Journey Into Night
Michael Wilmington

I've got a theory on the way they make pictures based on stage plays.… Many filmmakers take a stage play and say "I'm going to make this into a film." Then they would begin to "open it up."… This technique overlooks the fact that the basic quality of any play is precisely its confinement within the proscenium. [So they] often go wrong and what they get is simply some dull footage that's been added to the play artificially.… What I did [in *Dial M for Murder*] was to emphasize the theatrical aspects.…

Alfred Hitchcock

Mike Nichols, while preparing *Who's Afraid of Virginia Woolf?*, remarked: "I don't want to make another *Long Day's Journey Into Night*. We're going to make a movie." Then, according to Warner Bros. publicity, he closeted himself with the "classics" of Truffaut and Fellini to study how they were made. Well, what did he want to make, another *400 Blows*? One really wonders why he didn't instead closet himself with Edward Albee to find out something about the play.

What he wound up with, anyway, is something that's probably closer to *8½* (though not on as grand a scale): a movie that's so conscious of itself as a movie, that it never has time to say anything. People come away from *8½* talking about the kinky surrealistic flashbacks, the bizarre gallery of faces, the opulent camera movement and composition—just as they come away from *Woolf* debating the merits of Taylor and Burton, and how daring it all was. They don't thrash over any insights they might have gotten, because there are no insights in these movies to thrash over. If Nichols communicated anything at all, it was simply the personality of an energetic, egocentric young director determined to get ahead; a child prodigy who smirkingly shows us how well-read he is, but fumbles when it comes to discussing what it all means.

Long Day's Journey Into Night, on the other hand, is probably damn near the best film version of a major play ever made. The people who don't like it say it's slow, stagey, derivative, the acting is too theatrical, it's "uncinematic." Well, it is slow (so is *The St John Passion*); the acting is somewhat more theatrical than we're accustomed to in films (though not in a bad way); and Sidney Lumet, when he undertook the project, obviously cared more about preserving and illuminating O'Neill's vision than developing one of his own (he didn't closet himself with the films of Eisenstein and Renoir and ringingly proclaim: "I'm not going to make another botch like *The Beggar's Opera*").

But is all that bad? Are those arguments to use against the film? If someone makes us a superb soufflé should we gripe because it isn't beef stroganoff? (We can if our tastes are in a rut.) A fast, zingy *Long Day's Journey* with elliptical cuts and flashbacks would be a perversion of the material; Lumet could have shown off if he wanted (his later films are certainly not devoid of gimmickry) but he wisely chose to stick to the play.

And the play itself almost demands this sort of treatment. *Long Day's Journey* is an almost unique theatrical document—the play as confessional. Watching it or reading it is like sitting down with a sensitive, disturbed friend, and listening to him pour out, with harrowing honesty, the most awful episodes of his life.

But there's an especially dreadful irony in O'Neill enclosing his confession in a stage play; because a great part of the tragedy of his family is probably that the O'Neills, a theatrical group which included two professional actors, found that they could never get off the stage; when we see them here, they're still trying to play roles, to disguise themselves.

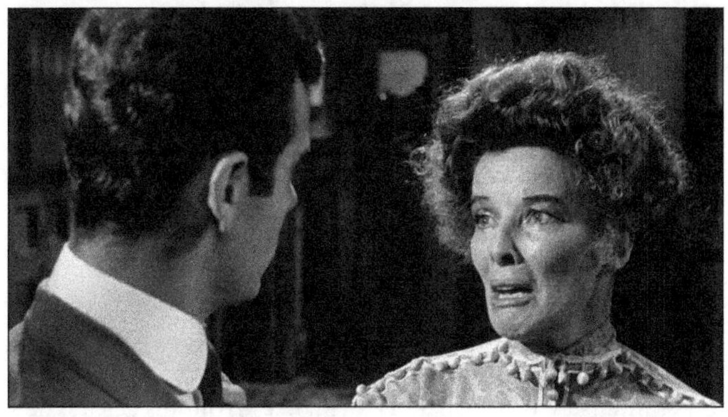

Katharine Hepburn as the drug-addicted mother, Mary Tyrone,
in *Long Day's Journey Into Night*, directed by Sidney Lumet
from the autobiographical play by O'Neill.
(Embassy Pictures)

Because of O'Neill's intense commitment, we feel with these
people, we laugh with them, suffer with them, and when they
try to clasp to their cheeks their pathetic little masks, we ache
for them. During the course of the day, these masks are eaten
away, the roles are eroded by drink, drugs, arguments, and a
chain of eviscerating sorrows, until only the naked horror of
their situation is left at the final curtain.

(As with most compulsive confessors, by the way,
O'Neill skimps when it comes to dealing with himself; his
proxy figure of Edmund has none of the hair-raising candor
of the other portraits. He's such an ingenuous tubercular angel
that he becomes really hard to take. But then what sensitive
person isn't also a bit paranoiac, doesn't tend to downplay
his own guilt? The picture of Edmund is the kind of flaw that
serves to point up the strengths of the rest of the work.)

Now I hope that those of you who read my *Marat/Sade*
review won't think I'm falling back on one of those handy
all-purpose arguments here, but the nature of the material demanded the "theatrical" restrictions Lumet placed on
himself. Since the Tyrones are play-acting for most of the
film, the slightly florid acting styles of Jason Robards, Ralph
Richardson, and Katharine Hepburn are a necessity (Bran-
doesque understatement would be totally out of place).

And to sacrifice the terrifying claustrophobic intensity of remaining in one house for all the action would compromise the final impact.

Are these restrictions necessarily "theatrical," by the way? Not unless you think theatre stops with Chekhov, Ibsen and the Greeks; Shakespeare and the German expressionists dissolve time and space as effectively as most movies. And the other weapons in the filmmaker's arsenal—closeups, editing, tracks, shifts in perspective—are all employed here by Lumet, extensively, and, for the most part, brilliantly.

One of Lumet's strong points has always been his ability to get intensely emotional performances from his actors; he's one of the few major film directors who rehearses extensively before shooting even begins. And if *Long Day's Journey* had nothing more to offer than the superb performances of Robards, Richardson, and, to a lesser extent, Hepburn, it still ought to be proof against the people who think it's a bad film. How often do we get performances of this caliber in roles of this scope anywhere, that we can so cheaply dismiss it all because it "violates" a few arbitrary "rules of form," "rules" which Alfred Hitchcock, one of the great contemporary masters of cinematic form, implies are ridiculous and artificial anyway. It's stage directors like Nichols who become so exaggeratedly exercised about defining the qualities of a "medium" that they're nowhere near mastering.

Robards' Jamie Tyrone is one of the glories of the screen, the definitive portrait of the Mephistophelian cynic who conceals a lost little boy—and it's sad that he's never been as good since. His technique in other movies often comes across as bombastic and over-theatrical; here it fits in perfectly with the role, and when Jamie, drunkenly sobbing, takes his brother in his arms and in a passionate frenzy of commingled love and sick jealous hatred, confesses that he wants to destroy him, it has all the stabbing shock of a revelation from a close friend.

Richardson is brilliant too, in a quieter way, and though Katharine Hepburn, as Mary Tyrone, starts on too high a level and begins to exhaust us about midway through the film, she still has moments that leave you limp; her final scene—drifting through the musty house with an ancient wedding gown, mind ravaged by drugs and age, but still clinging pathetically to the sweet frail pleasures of her girlhood—is a horrifying essay in self-delusion and pathos. The last lines of this movie—"I was so happy for a time"—carry a residue of pain and pity that is almost too much to bear.

Sidney Lumet himself regards this film as his masterpiece, and I'm inclined to agree with him; there are bits and flashes in his other movies that reach the kind of compassion and battering intensity which suffuse *Long Day's Journey* almost throughout (such as the one in *The Pawnbroker*, where the confused old man tries to talk about Baudelaire) but nowhere else is he simultaneously able to sustain this kind of extreme emotional environment and make it build and develop.

Perhaps he needed the discipline of sticking to a work that he so obviously loved; in his other movies, the greater freedom which poorer scripts and more loosely defined structure offered him may have spoiled him. And the type of acting that works so well for the theatrical Tyrones, desperately clinging to roles they can no longer fill, sits a little oddly on seedy pawnbrokers and Harlem toughs. His later movies (with the exception of *The Hill*) desperately need a restraint that would have been ruinous in this one.

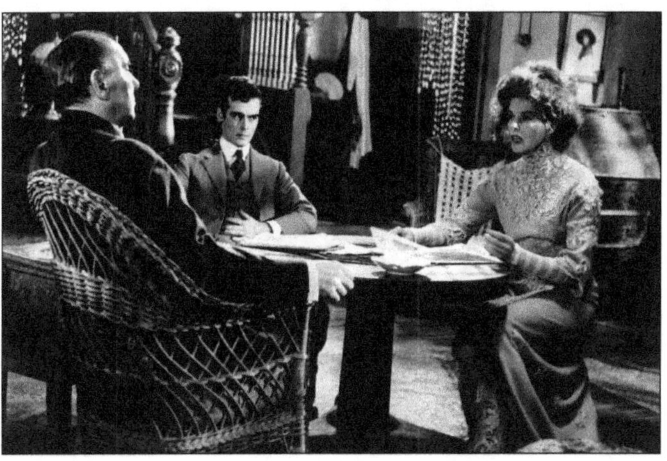

Dean Stockwell (as the playwright's proxy, Edmund), sits uneasily between his parents, James (Ralph Richardson) and Mary (Hepburn), members of the tormented Tyrone family in *Long Day's Journey Into Night*. (Embassy Pictures)

When I came out of this movie for the first time, I was shaking with an almost personal grief, and, when people later told me it was dull, uncinematic, "awful," I felt almost as if my own past sorrows were being held up to ridicule. *Long Day's Journey Into Night*, in its way, offers a kind of experience that's rare for the screen, a pathos that's so honest and overwhelming that it never leaves you quite the same person. It affects you deep inside, and leaves you with a feeling not of esthetic pleasure but of emotional turmoil (though it requires the most extreme kind of esthetic control to generate that turmoil).

Some people don't like this, just as they'd become embarrassed if their friends started suddenly confessing all their past troubles; the movie's plea for honesty, its condemnation of lies and role-playing, and its shattering compassion probably cut it off from a lot of people who may subscribe, in more ways than they realize, to the pathetic disease of the Tyrones.

The Brig: Jonas' Ballet
Jon Zwickey

Kenneth H. Brown's *The Brig* (play) was encountered in the academic *Tulane Drama Review* (23) which failed to provide student-intellectual accessibility of Barbara Garson's paperback *MacBird!* Falstaffian entertainment (Pres. as Ubu Macbeth) is unlike *The Brig*'s text which yields an impressionistic rendering of Goya's projected Marine Brig alchemically synthesized through Zola's possible imitating of Dreyfus' imprisonment.

• • •

The Color of Ritual, the Color of Thought (trilogy): *Divinations; Peyote Queen; Shaman* was Storm De Hirsch filmed & U. W. Film Society showed her *Newsreel: Jonas in the Brig.* That evening nouveau members (camp speed) were frightened to boisterosity by De Hirsch's camera movement & Jerry Berndt's film *Coming of Winter and Going of Spring.* The herd's fashion chews celluloid with a wicked projector's racket.

• • •

The Brig (film) was conceived & photographed by Jonas Mekas—brother Adolfas edited visual & sound [and Judith Malina directed with the Mekas brothers—Ed.]—from Living Theatre production of *The Brig*—with original players: Warren Finnerty, Jim Anderson, Henry Howard, Tom Lillard,

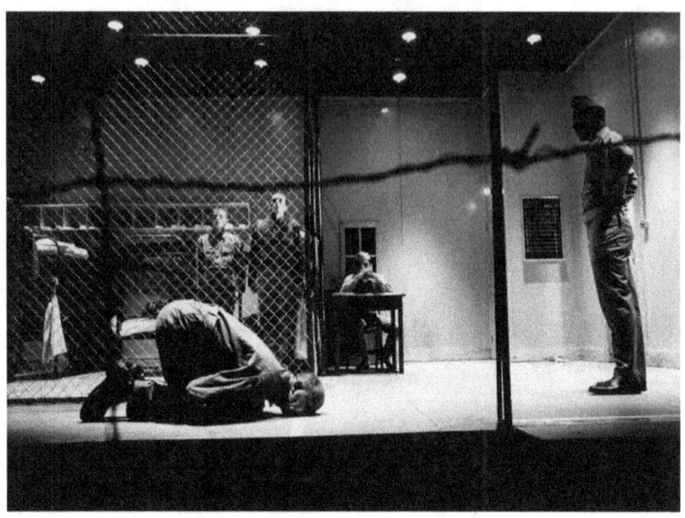

The Brig (1964), the film version of Kenneth H. Brown's play
about men in a brutal Marine Corps brig in 1957 Japan, drawn
from Brown's own experiences. Based on the Living Theater
production in New York, the film was directed by Judith Malina
(who also directed it onstage) and the brothers Adolfas Mekas and
Jonas Mekas (who was the cinematographer as well).
The documentary-style filming took place on the original stage set
with the actors from the play. (Film-Makers' Cooperative)

James Tiroff, Steven Ben Israel, Gene Lipton, Rufus Collins,
Michael Elias, William Shari, Viktor Allen, George Bartenieff,
Gene Gordon, Mark Duffy, Henry Proach, Carl Einhorn, &
Luke Theodore.

● ● ●

Stillborn administration controlled University theaters
produce comic melodic *Gypsy* or super classical *Hamlet*
& Broadway plays tax-deduction-dominoes with "play-
wrights." The Living Theatre was created & run (production,
direction, sets, secretarial, plumbing, etc.) by Judith Malina
& Julian Beck; dancing over the herd's comic classicism with
Picasso's *Desire*—Auden's *Age of Anxiety*—Gelber's *The
Connection*—Brown's *The Brig*. *SCHECHNER:* HOW

DO *THE BRIG* AND *THE CONNECTION*, PLAYS SO SEEMINGLY DISSIMILAR, RELATE TO THE IDEA OF YOUR THEATRE? *MALINA:*... THERE IS NO KIND OF EXPERIMENT WE WOULDN'T MAKE IF IT COULD MOVE US ALONG THE ROAD BETWEEN WHAT THE THEATRE IS NOW AND WHAT THE THEATRE IS TO BECOME. Yet theater doesn't become; since mammon's dime store culture register only accepts the herd's dysentery: the IRS closed the Living Theatre (October 1963) during the run of *The Brig:* storm troopers releasing rats in Parisian theaters has been U.S. Government refined.

• • •

THE INTERNAL REVENUE BUREAU, HEARING THAT THE LANDLORD WAS GOING TO CLOSE THE THEATRE ON TUESDAY, CAME IN WITHOUT ANY NOTICE AT THREE O'CLOCK THIS AFTER-NOON AND LOCKED EVERYTHING UP. /Malina/ ... WITHOUT EVEN THE OPPORTUNITY TO PLAY A CLOSING NIGHT. THIS, AS FAR AS I'M CONCERNED, IS BLASPHEMY. /Brown/ I WOULD SAY THAT THE KIND OF PLAYS WE DO HAS A LOT TO DO WITH IT. /Malina/ JUDITH WENT TO HER DRESSING ROOM, FOUND IT PADLOCKED, ASKED A DOZEN IRS MEN IF THEY WOULD OPEN THE LOCK SO THAT SHE COULD GET A TAMPAX. THEY REFUSED. I ASKED THEM, TWELVE MEN, MORE THAN A MINION, TO DO THIS. IT SEEMED TO ME THAT THERE WAS SOMETHING UNMANLY ABOUT NOT OPENING THE DOOR. THIS CONFRONTA-TION WAS TYPICAL OF REPEATED INCIDENTS THROUGHOUT THE NEXT THREE DAYS. /Beck/ IRS PERMITTED NO ONE INTO THE BUILDING. BUT THE AUDIENCE WAS ARRIVING AND THEY DID FIND WAYS INTO THE BUILDING, OVER THE ROOF, AND I OPENED A WINDOW AND THEY BROUGHT A LADDER AND CAME IN. AT ABOUT 9:45 THE SHOW BEGAN. IT WAS A PERFORMANCE WHICH WAS IN AND OF ITSELF AN ACT OF CIVIL

DISOBEDIENCE. IT WAS NOT A MESSAGE PLAY, NOT A PLAY OF PROTEST, IT WAS A PROTEST AGAINST A WHOLE LIFE IN WHICH EVERYTHING IS MEASURED BY MAMMON'S THUMB. /Beck/

• • •

Akin to Antigone's civil disobedience (I WILL SHOW YOU FEAR IN A HANDFUL OF DUST /Eliot/) the production of *The Brig* despite an edict to the contrary precipitated the State's vengeance. 25 were arrested (penalties of $5,000 &/or 3 years) as earlier Kenneth Brown (17 year old Marine) had been negatively rewarded (30 days in Japan's Camp Fuji brig) for returning 4 hours late. Authority's crab lice can't tolerate innocence remaining beyond all law.

• • •

Brown created *The Brig* first in poetry then as story & finally as anti-play. *The Brig* paraphrased—EACH PRISONER ... MUST BY NECESSITY NEGATE HIS REACTION, HIS NORMAL REACTION TO THE SUFFERING OF THE MAN NEXT TO HIM. THE MAN NEXT TO HIM KNOWS THAT IT IS NECESSARY FOR THE FIRST MAN TO NEGATE A NORMAL REACTION TO HIS SUFFERING AND LOVES HIM FOR IT. THE GUARDS IN *THE BRIG* ARE ABSENT OF LOVE, THEY ARE THE DEHUMANIZED MEMBERS OF SOCIETY. THEY ARE THE PEOPLE WHO HAVE BEEN GIVEN THE RESPONSIBILITY OF CARING FOR AND LEADING THE PRISONERS, OR THE LIVING THEATRES, OR THE LOWER MIDDLE CLASS, OR, IN THE PRESENT SCHEME OF THINGS, THE NEGRO. HOW BADLY THEY DO IT. /Brown/ *Playboy* upholds the Marine Corps (shipping Bunnies to Vietnam) & writes "Kenneth Brown is a camera and he paints horrible pictures."

• • •

The Brig reflecting Artaud's theory more authentically than the Marx Brothers is Theatre of Cruelty. Punishment inflicted through unreasoned cruelty expresses man's imitation of nature's indifference. Conveying the accidental nightmare-life requires not the Marine Corps copied; but destruction's INTENSITY artistically held before the beholder by perfectly cruel illusions. The Living Theatre's production of Brown's text combined with naturalistic set (brig) & actors seeking vividness through method, technique & biomechanical acting. IMMEDIATELY PRE-SET A KIND OF TECHNIQUE—EACH ACTOR REVIVIFIES A LIFE EXPERIENCE HERE AND NOW ON THE STAGE AS HE PERFORMS. /Malina/

• • •

Revivification is casual sequence destruction unveiling the accidental NOW; such a pataphysical awareness is either cruel *(Nausea)* or beautiful *(Doors of Perception)*. NOW is happening: *THIS IS IT* /Watt/ has no value other than what is revealed in it.

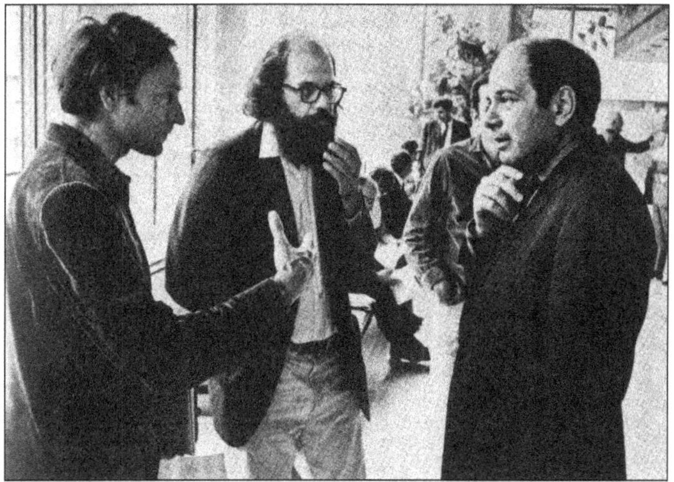

Jonas Mekas with poet Allen Ginsberg at the 1967 New York Film Festival with festival co-founder and film scholar Richard Roud.

• • •

Guns of the Trees is the revolutionary *Film Magazine of the Arts* censored by *The Brig*'s guards during the *Award Presentation to Andy Warhol* where the report from Millbrook was seen by Ginsberg singing *Hare Krishna* beneath Ringling leaves of the *Circus Notebook*.

• • •

BY NOW IT IS CLEAR EVEN TO A CASUAL OBSERVER THAT THERE ARE MANY DIFFERENT DIRECTIONS IN THE SO-CALLED UNDERGROUND CINEMA. YOU CAN'T LUMP THESE FILM-MAKERS TOGETHER. THERE ARE NO ONE OR TWO NAMES WHICH WOULD REPRESENT OR PROPERLY DESCRIBE WHAT'S HAPPENING. /Mekas/ GOD HASN'T WRITTEN WITH FIRE ON THE SKY THAT CINEMA (OR ANY ART) IS ONLY THIS OR THAT. ONLY THE HISTORY OF CINEMA IS FINITE NOT THE FUTURE. /Mekas/ "YOU MEAN," I ASKED HER, THAT YOUR VISION, YOUR EYES HAVE NOTHING TO DO WITH YOUR CONSCIOUSNESS? DOES YOUR CONSCIOUSNESS EXIST SEPARATELY FROM YOUR EYE? ... EVERY ONE OF OUR MANY SENSES IS A WINDOW TO THE WORLD AND TO OURSELVES." /Mekas/

• • •

Jonas Mekas-shoulder-harness-camera (De Hirsch's newsreel) developed intricate movement through revivifying precision. Blind Tiresias' cane became his appendage in the world as the brig situated camera became Jonas' prisoner.

• • •

Spectators watching the play destroy suspended disbelief through stage cognizance (illusion of "reality"). To annihilate over-educated disabilities Jonas created an illusion of a legit-

imate illusion. Flaherty's legit film is celluloid claiming to be illusion hinting at factual adherence accessible to the medium: documentary. Medium integrity of documentary footage congeals around the following 7 framing bars in *The Brig*—
1. No Shakespearean zoom through Globe to document production & not drama.
2. The opening titles indicate a documentary of Camp Fuji's brig—no actors list—no supers.
3. Edited in titles express time shift using 24 hour service time—no dissolves.
4. Extreme camera movement—Jonas allowed the shadow of himself & camera to appear—shooting till film ran out.
5. Approach-avoidance: no action CUs edited in.
6. Lighting & set are not arranged for each shot—maintaining the brig's fixed harshness.
7. Off mike voices indicate documentary tape recorder soundtrack procedure.

• • •

Poets believe the Universe's accidentality as each moment reveals marvelous mystery; if indeed there were another moment NOW. Yet poets work in time consuming "reality" where critic Tom Foolery demands medium integrity. The law of medium integrity renders a Grand Prize (Venice Documentary Festival—1964) to *The Brig*. The poet sees subjugation to the medium's history as a revolutionist views State authority. Civil disobedience is an edge of artistic creation: TO LIVE OUTSIDE THE LAW YOU MUST BE HONEST /Dylan/. To be beyond all law requires surpassing even that law: to be beyond medium integrity means not using integrity for its lawful purpose: to overcome the documentary (paralleling Brown's civil disobedience & staging *The Brig* despite IRS) requires presenting documentation imitating only itself.

• • •

The closing shots (Living Theatre stage followed by actors' credits) indicates the film is not reproducing the Camp Fuji brig. Nor did Jonas document a Living Theatre production of

The Brig; since camera movement & punctuated soundtrack alter original texture.

• • •

The beholder participates in a ballet of cruelty through feeling the camera's dance. The soundtrack counterpoints vision's leap with audio movement (microphone varies location & sensitivity relative to the camera). The experience is cruelty's transformation to lived lament—the swan song. There you are born circumspecting the brig—feeling absurd terror revealed as "reality" is stripped of necessity. Glowing hotly indifferent—you surpass the cruelty by burning the "self." You become a dancing Dionysian flight into the air—alive to the Universe's accidental "nature"; yet able to utter the noble unreasoned curse.

• • •

An ugly curse arising from its spontaneous absurdity becomes beautiful in the form's global configuration. Prometheus curses & *The Brig* places Jonas at his lament's center. Man's heart is the meat of the world.
AT EACH BEAT
IN THE EARTH'S ROTATING DANCE
THERE IS BORN ... "   "
A MOMENTARY CLUSTER OF MOLECULES
POSSESSING THE TRANSIENT ABILITY TO
KNOW-SEE-EXPERIENCE
        ITS OWN PLACE IN THE EVOLUTIONARY
        SPIRAL.

SUCH AN ORGANISM, SUCH AN EVENT,
SENSES EXACTLY WHERE HE IS
IN THE BILLION-YEAR OLD BALLET. /Homage to the Awe-full
See-er by Timothy Leary/

revised 8 Gueules, 95 P.E.
Jon Zwickey

For *The Birds*
Michael Wilmington

> In film you should not be permitted to reason, because the film should be stronger than reason.
>
> Hitchcock

I.

Analyzing a movie which has already been reviewed to death creates special problems. For one thing, all the reviews that have gone before tend to gather and become part of your subjective reasoning.

When I first saw Alfred Hitchcock's *The Birds* (five years ago, at a drive-in theater), I thought that the first half of the picture was quite slack, that none of the major characters was very memorable—but that the last half was terrifying. I was considerably more frightened by the birds' final attacks than by anything in *Psycho,* which is a better movie, and they disturbed me for days afterward.

This rather simple reaction of mine corresponds pretty well to the initial reviews of *The Birds,* which treated it as another frothy Hitchcock *frisson de terreur.* The second wave of reviews, however, from the big guns like Pauline Kael ("… a terrible movie… pointless and incomprehensible …"), Dwight Macdonald, and Stanley Kauffmann ("Hitchcock's worst in years") were almost universally derogatory, attacking the movie's logic, the acting, and Hitchcock's direction. They treated the film as if it was the botched hackwork of a fifth-rate neophyte. It isn't that bad, and the super-commonsensical Miss Kael to the contrary, it's not especially incomprehensible or illogical. Perhaps we can explain the ferocious tone of these later reviews by Hitchcock's peculiar standing in the film world. He's a director widely regarded as a major artist who's violated all the standard rules of "serious" filmmaking; he's also tremendously popular at the box-office.

Most critics, who delight in being connoisseurs, find popularity a little hard to swallow—it only becomes acceptable in retrospect, with people like Shakespeare, Dickens or Dostoevsky. That explains the acidulous and insulting tone of Stanley Kauffmann, for instance. (I read Kauffmann's attempts at criticism with the same enthusiasm I might take in dipping my head in a vat of suet pudding.) Kauffmann rudely calls Hitchcock "the Fat Boy." Simultaneously (and illogically), he accuses him of being a sadistic cynic and a secret sentimentalist, implies that he never was much good, but has been on the decline lately. And he wraps up the whole noxious thing with a fatuous misrepresentation of Hitchcock's French admirers.

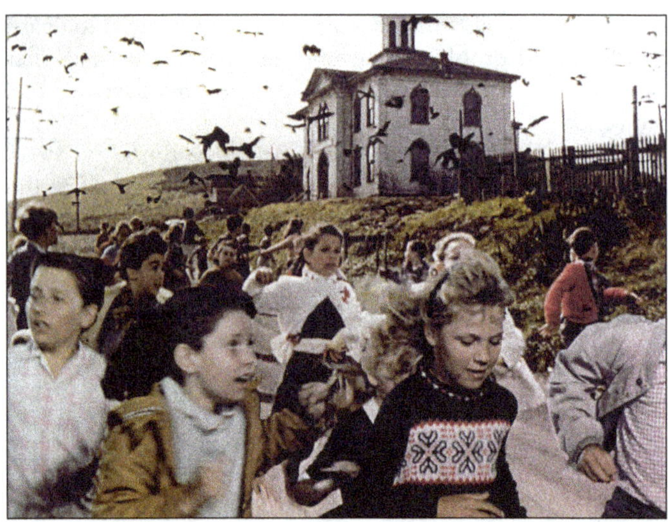

Hitchcock's *The Birds* was the state of the art in special effects in its time (1963). This scene of children running from a bird attack at their school in Bodega Bay, California, was combined with rotoscoped birds in postproduction. (Universal)

The last wave of reviews are mostly favorable, ranging from the usual ecstatic eulogies in *Cahiers du Cinéma* to Robin Wood's claim (in *Hitchcock's Films*) that *The Birds* is part of "an astonishing unbroken chain of masterpieces," and "among Hitchcock's finest achievements."

The audience I saw *The Birds* with in the University of Wisconsin Union were more in agreement with Kauffmann; they laughed and hooted derisively throughout much of the showing, and finally degenerated into yelling "jokes" at the screen. Particularly rabid were a couple behind me who, besides having their unattractive and smelly feet slung over the seats in front of them, were screeching the mild pun "Birdbrain!" at the top of their lungs, with birdlike regularity.

Now, after a while, I began to wonder about the audience's reaction, which appears to have been fairly typical; I've seen really bad movies where nobody complained, much less demonstrated their complaint in such a demented way. (At the incredibly inept *Riot on Sunset Strip,* for instance, which I saw with a fairly hip audience, the tone was one of affectionate derision, as if we all sympathized with the poor clods who had to make the movie.) Is it possible that the annoyance that so many people express for *The Birds*, which explodes into such manic behavior, is a coverup? Perhaps some of these people realize that if they really succumbed to the movie, they'd be experiencing a terror far more intense and far more disturbing than the customary cathartic release of violence and nightmare you get from, say, Polanski's *Repulsion,* which, instead of really getting at you, turns its masculine audience into voyeurs—peeping toms with esthetic passkeys.

II.

The Birds is a genre piece—a horror movie—and that's probably a big reason critics and the "hip" college audience I was with didn't like it: they felt it wasn't conforming to the rules of its own tradition. I think many critics like to classify horror movies like this: campy extravaganzas, good for a laugh; psychological murder stories, good for a few jolts; and stories in which children or civilians are involved in war, good for a few thousand words on the horror of the human condition. Of these three, the last is probably the most respectable—you can squeeze movies like *Night and Fog, The Bridge, Forbidden Games* and *Fires on the Plain* into it, which, among most non-*auteur* critics, have higher rankings than, say, *M* or *Freaks*.

But isn't it a little perverse to suggest, as these people do, that war is the main horror of the human condition, or the one worthiest of artistic expression? Most artists don't have much experience of war anyway—a movie like *Paths of Glory,* ostensibly about war, actually is about certain human emotions carried to an extreme and put in a war movie setting. Far from being realistic, the battle sequences in movies like this are dreamy ballets of violence. To me, *M* is a much better film than *Forbidden Games* not because I automatically rank Fritz Lang higher than René Clement, but because *M* is a more moving, rich, and memorable experience—and also because I'm a little suspicious of the easy emotional charge you get out of involving children, innocents, in a war environment.

So *The Birds,* as a horror movie, falls into the third class, the least intellectually respectable one: campy monster movies. The film probably would have had a greater critical reception if Hitchcock had played this up, parodied himself and filled the screen with little jokes to show he wasn't really serious. (It's extremely ironic that the critics who always complain of Hitchcock's lack of seriousness and depth seem to like him best when he's least serious. They prefer *The Lady Vanishes* to *Vertigo.*) But to say that *The Birds,* because its primary intention is to frighten the audience, is automatically a second-rate project is ridiculous—critics who cavil at Hitchcock for filming novels by Robert Bloch or Daphne du Maurier instead of, say, Dostoevsky or Kafka, are mistaking esthetic dilettantism for taste; what matters is what Hitchcock makes of his source material, the richness and depth he manages to bring to it.

And, anyway, suppose we applied that kind of sloppy critical shorthand to some other art—if we insisted, for instance, that *Troilus and Cressida* was a greater play than *King Lear* because Shakespeare had better source material to work with, or condemned Mozart for using frivolous librettos like *The Marriage of Figaro* and *The Magic Flute* instead of grappling with the relevant social issues of the day.

I guess it's natural for most critics, who by their very nature are artistic gourmets, wanting to pick only the most flawless treats, the juiciest, dampest plums, to think that artists reason the same way. But what matters in a van Gogh painting is not the sunflowers but van Gogh's reaction to them (and, finally, his communication of that reaction); if people really want to evaluate "cinema" as an "art form" they ought to stop judging it as a transcription from some other art form (novels, plays or even scenario-writing) and try to see it as an expression of the artist.

The Birds is not a light film, despite the deceptively nonchalant beginning—it seeks to involve us in an almost purely terrifying situation, to plunge us to the roots of chaos, torment and fear. Quite literally, it attacks its audience (as *Psycho* did in the shower murder scene, though *The Birds* has more in common with *North by Northwest*). There are three levels to this attack—fear of the irrational, shock from a sudden rupture of complacency, and fear of ourselves.

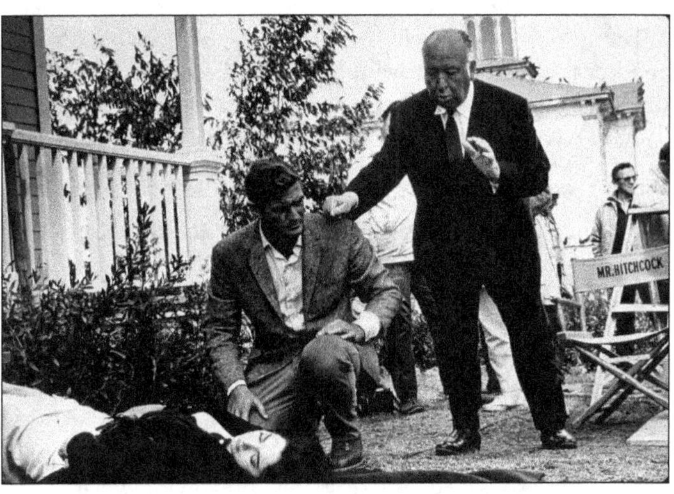

Hitchcock directing Rod Taylor as Mitch Brenner on location in Bodega Bay for *The Birds*, as he finds Suzanne Pleshette's character dead from an assault by birds. (Universal)

First, the irrational. Hitchcock makes no attempt at all to explain his fantastic premise, the attack on the residents of Bodega Bay by masses of previously harmless birds; in fact he makes fun of four or five assorted symbolic possibilities in the restaurant scene. The nature of these onslaughts is left up in the air—we can't reconcile them as science fiction or allegory, and it's difficult to accept them wholly as fantasy. We have to simply take them on faith, and they remain just beyond the rational—instinctual and nightmarish—to the end.

The second level, the disruption of complacency (which Hitchcock says is the theme at the picture) is what makes the film so fascinating structurally, and also what causes some of its failures. The average thriller is quick to whip up an ominous atmosphere, usually by flinging somebody's corpse onto the screen—but *The Birds* rambles on for quite a while as if it had nothing more on its mind than the usual banal romantic drama. Many people become impatient with this early buildup, but what the director is doing is creating a realistic, settled milieu, shaped by the attitudes of a group of characters who are almost offensively smug, but whose reserve and glibness hide a variety of barely observed neuroses and fears. The film would lose a good deal of its force if we didn't have these sections—when the attacks do come, they shock us almost as much as they do the characters (even though we've been prepared by the advertising and the shrieking birds under the credits) because we've begun to share their complacent attitudes.

Complacency is engendered both by the characters and their environment. The town of Bodega Bay, insular, provincial, surrounded by water, hills and trees, is almost the epitome of rural middle-class America. Perhaps no one who hasn't grown up in such a place can really appreciate its duality (city visitors usually regard such villages as either quaint or dull). Their special nature lies in the routine they create, a series of rituals both comforting and abrasive, patterns that grind down all the rough edges like a slowly revolving wheel. Like *Psycho, The Birds* in a primarily rural film, just as *Vertigo* and *North by Northwest,* Hitchcock's two previous films, were primarily urban. In this bland pastoral background, emotions are pushed to bizarre limits. Hitchcock isolates the characters in this milieu with extreme long shots, then detaches them through closeups and back projection, creating a sense of weird, almost neurotic uneasiness to underly the lackadaisical flow of Bodega Bay's existence.

The characters' self-satisfaction is underscored by this environment—especially Melanie Daniels (Tippi Hedren), superficially icy and reserved, and Mitch Brenner (Rod Taylor), a lawyer who makes glib wisecracks about a wife murderer he's defending. Brenner, at the outset, is almost a paragon of adolescent self-assurance, but if his relationship with his mother (Jessica Tandy) is reminiscent of the easy, jocular Cary Grant-Jessie Royce Landis alliance in *North by Northwest*, it also brings to mind those darker, more perverted Hitchcockian mother-son relationships in *Notorious, Strangers on a Train* and *Psycho*. The hints of buried neuroses in all the relationships, neuroses which the characters try to mask or rationalize, give the early part of the movie a great underlying edginess—which explodes into the concentrated violence and savagery of the last half. In addition there are a series of subtle, almost subliminal indications of something wrong, something within the characters that connects them to the birds. Deep down, these smug, seemingly self-confident people may carry the same twisted, self-destructive impulses which drive the Stewart and Perkins characters in *Vertigo* and *Psycho*. Perhaps, in some weird way, *they* are the birds.

It can't be just an accident that so many characters in this film have birdlike mannerisms—Tippi Hedren and Jessica Tandy, for instance, with their almost identical feathery coiffures, and the hawk-faced Rod Taylor, who is usually shot from below, looming above the women and us like a brooding bird of prey. Hedren consistently tilts her head like a reflective sparrow, and many of the minor characters have a flock of mannerisms—the bird shop proprietress, the hardware store salesman in his wire cage, the children at the school, and several of the people in the restaurant twitter, screech or peer like silent owls. Because of all this, several of the images take on an almost primally frightening force, such as the ones where Tippi Hedren is imprisoned in the car and the soundless glass telephone booth, a swirling storm of birds battering away outside. The film moves from the opening scene in the noisy but tranquil bird shop, with its rows of glittering cages, to these terrifying visions of caged human beings—in the booth, the restaurant, the school and Mitch Brenner's house, and because of the birdlike characteristics of the humans, these reversals have an eerie undercurrent of inevitability.

And this undercurrent is created by more than the connections between birds and people. Hitchcock's films almost always work on an instinctual, visceral level; he tries to make his images, as directly as possible, concrete expressions of an emotional state—which is why so many people accuse him of "manipulating" an audience. They're almost justified but, in a sense, what artist doesn't manipulate his audience? Wasn't Beethoven aware of the stirring effect of the rises and falls, the surging rhythms of *The Emperor Concerto?* And don't the quieter, more lyrical directors like Renoir and De Sica calculate their emotional effects? In the interviews he granted to François Truffaut, Hitchcock pretty consistently reduced each film to one simple idea, usually revolving around a sexual relationship. So *Notorious,* instead of being about spies and smuggled uranium, was about, according to Hitchcock, "the old conflict between love and duty.... Cary Grant's job—and it's a rather ironic situation—is to push Ingrid Bergman into Claude Rains's bed"; *Vertigo* was about "a form of necrophilia"; *Rear Window* about a "Peeping Tom"; and *Marnie* about "The fetish idea. A man wants to go to bed with a thief before she is a thief."

From the weight he gave them, it's obvious that these relationships are more important to Hitchcock than the simple mechanics of a murder mystery or suspense plot; they're what give his movies life and organic unity—the main themes around which he can weave variations to involve or frighten his audience. So what's important about the relationship in *The Birds?* (It's a mistake, I think, to see the Rod Taylor-Tippi Hedren affair as not central to the film, or as only an involved red herring in the buildup—simply because the attack of the birds is a cataclysm that strikes out at everyone, including children.) Seen by itself, *The Birds* has an emotional impact which is sort of mysterious—we're moved, but we can't really explain why. We're interested in the characters, even though (largely due to a streak of archness in Evan Hunter's screenplay) they seem shallow and sketched-in. Actually the portrayal of these characters is rich in nuance, though it's a nuance that's largely visual and emotional.

III.

Starting with *Vertigo* and ending with *The Birds,* Hitchcock made a series of four pictures which are really a kind of grand summation—both individually, and in the way they interact with each other. *Vertigo* and *North by Northwest* carry the two quintessential Hitchcock heroes—James Stewart and Cary Grant—to the logical climaxes of their relationships with women. The Stewart character, impressionable, voyeuristic, somewhat impotent, and ridden with delusions and anxieties, succeeds in destroying the girl he loves—but whom he loves only as a creature of romantic illusion, detached from the world (like Janet Leigh in *Psycho,* Kim Novak is almost like an adolescent's moviehouse dream of sex). Succumbing to his own inadequacies and weaknesses, he becomes destructive both to himself and the people around him, even the people who love him—and the great central metaphor of the film occurs in that magnificent and harrowing scene when, dizzy from acrophobia, he forces Kim Novak up the stairs of the belltower, railing at her for her deceit, only to watch her plunge a second time to her death. It's obviously a symbol of failed coitus, and though Hitchcock denies any conscious Catholic symbolism, it is significant that the girl falls, terrified, only after she sees a shadowy nun looming up behind the deranged Stewart.

In *North by Northwest,* the central character is Cary Grant, more sexually healthy than *Vertigo*'s Scottie but someone who, it's implied, must be punished for his complacency, insensitivity and glib lack of empathy for the people around him. He goes through a trial by fire in which he is gradually stripped of all his defenses, forced to fend for himself against a horde of outer forces that seem totally irrational and which, in fact, Hitchcock never bothers to explain. The spy ring in *North by Northwest* is comparable in its irrational destructiveness to the birds themselves, and, like the birds, it represents a danger not just to Grant but to Grant's whole milieu—aptly symbolized in the closing sequence with everyone madly scrambling around the presidents' heads on Mt. Rushmore. The climax of *North by Northwest* is in direct contrast to *Vertigo*'s: Grant pulls Eva Marie Saint up from the precipice into his upper berth, and the train plunges into the tunnel. (Success!)

Now, the third film of the sequence, *Psycho*, seems to offer some of the biggest clues of all, especially since it has so many references and allusions to birds. The central character, Anthony Perkins (who, with his shy, gangling courtliness, is like a younger and crazier Jimmy Stewart), is a schizoid motel keeper who works out his perverted sex drives by killing young girls while masquerading as his mother. In addition to killing and stuffing his mother, he also stuffs birds; a group of them line the walls of his parlor. Like many of the most striking and sometimes weirdly sympathetic Hitchcockian villains—Robert Walker in *Strangers on a Train*, Joseph Cotten in *Shadow of a Doubt*, Martin Landau in *North by Northwest* and Claude Rains in *Notorious*—Perkins is a latent homosexual with a strong mother fixation, and just as he becomes his mother when he kills, he also seems to become one of the birds. The soundtrack shrieks with Bernard Herrmann's birdlike pizzicatos during the murders, and the phallic knife, wildly plunging up and down, is almost like a beak.

It would be too much, I think, to make a quick birds-mother-sex-death corollary, and to decide that we've finally cracked the riddle of *The Birds*, that the end of the world is brought about by enraged homosexuals—but there are a few Freudian hints in *The Birds* too, such as the striking similarities between Tandy and Hedren, and it's important that we see the birds as a destructive, irrational force. Like Perkins in *Psycho*, the spies in *North by Northwest*, and the darker, voyeuristic side of James Stewart in *Vertigo*, they are a primal force of negation and chaos. Even more important, there are elements of these tendencies in the "normal" characters as well.

In this perspective the Taylor-Hedren relationship becomes clearer. If it most closely resembles the deep but outwardly sardonic Grant-Saint attachment, it is also charged with that same latent destructiveness, especially when Hedren submits masochistically to the birds in the attic; at that moment, she's nearly as equivocal as Ingrid Bergman in *Notorious*. The birds almost always go for the eyes, and that ties in with the sexual approach: scratching an eye is a

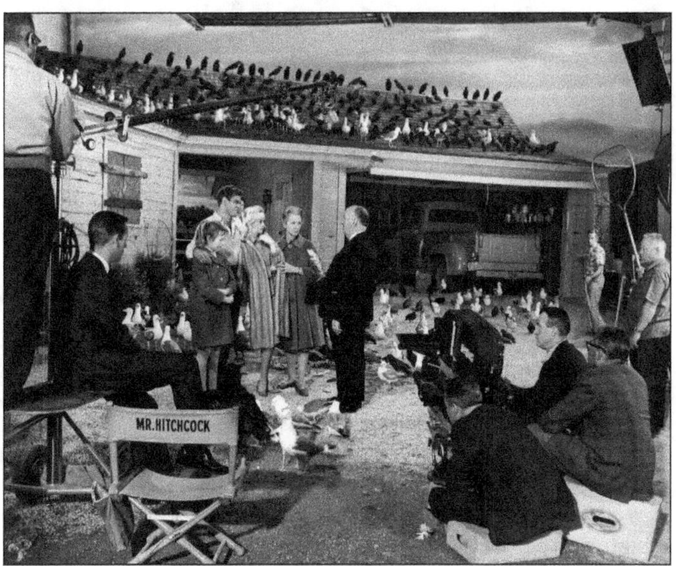

The apocalyptic, unresolved ending of *The Birds* being filmed on
a soundstage, with Hitchcock directing Veronica Cartwright, Rod
Taylor, Tippi Hedren, and Jessica Tandy. Cinematographer Robert
Burks is seated on an apple box behind the camera, in the checked
jacket. (Universal)

kind of surrealistic coitus symbol, as in Buñuel and Dali's *Un
Chien Andalou* (an image, incidentally, which Dali repeated
for Hitchcock in *Spellbound*). It also beautifully exemplifies
those destructive, voyeuristic aspects of sex which Hitchcock
likes to emphasize; in the *Psycho* shower murder, for example,
the two main images are the knife and the eye. After all, for a
voyeur what greater tragedy can exist than being blinded?

With this relationship at its center, a relationship that,
in its ultimate strength and endurance, becomes extremely
moving, *The Birds* moves to those final terrifying images
of a world gone mad, a world where all the complacency of
everyday living has been totally shattered, where no one is
safe. *The Birds* progresses from a playworld (both Truffaut
and Fellini have commented on the charming stylization of
the first part of the movie) to a world where horror and death
have been unleashed from the most simple, seemingly harm-

less source. From the bright, superficially ordered world of the opening, we have moved to a dark realm of savagery — to the aerial view of birds whirling down on a town plunged into fiery chaos; the three inexorable frozen closeups of the farmer with gouged-out eyes; and that incredibly moving last shot, with the birds mantling the entire landscape like a dark, undulating blanket, an omnipresent source of carnage and fear, quiet now but filling the air with thrumming of wings and an eerie hum while the four beleaguered humans move through to their car. We can see the monster clearly now, and most audiences, even the ones who ridicule the film, all but audibly gasp at this climax. The birds are the universal threat, the horror that lies just below our consciousness, hovers just above our heads; they are life, and life opens for an instant to let the people who thought they had mastered it pass safely. *The Birds* is a powerful and intricate film which doesn't quite yield its whole design on one viewing. It should be seen and re-seen for the grandeur and intensity of that last image alone.

Hawks at Seventy
Richard Thompson

...Howard Hawks' production *[Red Line 7000]* ignores its own first commandment, the text of which is pasted on a dashboard in the first scene: "Keep Brain in Gear at All Times." Yet the film does have commercial virtues. That is, it does have commercials. The color camera dwells long and lovingly on Ford cars (which win all the races), on Ford billboards, on a Pepsi-Cola machine, on Pure Oil emblems, Yamaha motorcycles and signs, Econo-Car rental leaflets and Benjamin stereo sets installed in the standardized bedrooms of a Holiday Inn motel.

It would have been better if the people at Paramount had kept their commercials free from the taint of dramatization, but the technique still has its virtues. *Red Line 7000* is the first melodrama ever made in which the hero is plainly identified by a "Pure" sign on his coveralls.

Newsweek, Dec. 27, 1965

...The plot, characteristically Hawksian, tells of the rough-and-ready guys who race stock cars and their turned-on track followers who cry, cheer and deliver romantic ultimatums that any dewy-eyed dropout might treasure. Scene after scene, brand names — Ford, Omega, Honda, Revell, Firestone, Grey-Rock brake linings—are dragged in like spare parts, as if to guarantee the authenticity of all that happens between location shots of screeching wheels and fiery crashes. "That was a close one... oh-oh, there's *another* one!" cries the agitated track announcer, valiantly promoting the idea that death lurks at every curve, as advertised, whenever a tachometer needle reaches the red-line mark for danger.

After the races, there are indoor sports at a Holiday Inn motel, played by a cast of hopefuls whose faces radiate the glossy anonymity of people in television commercials.... Both on the track and in the sack, *Red Line 7000* stresses the importance of luck—which must be the only hope for a movie put together with so little skill.

Time, Jan. 14, 1966

After Cornell, Howard Hawks built and raced cars and planes. Then he became a movie director in the American tradition—flying the camera plane filming stunts in *The Dawn Patrol,* designing the special bounceless camera trucks for *Hatari!,* and, generally, making films about men who flew planes or raced cars, and who were naturally sought out by aggressive, haunting, hip females. After learning his trade in this anonymous but personally satisfying underground, Hawks gained prestige, got to make A pictures, directed the two most profound studies of Bogart, and finally reached the pinnacle of directorial success: the new French critics pantheonized him along with Hitchcock as one of the greatest American directors; he had final control of his films (nobody re-edits them after he finishes); and he could pick up the phone in Africa, call John Wayne in Hollywood, tell him the idea for a picture in Africa, and have Wayne fly right out to do the film. He has done all the things a great director must do: created stars, created genres, created prototypical characters, created a style in the fullest sense of the word, and, like Shakespeare, managed to include something for everyone, so that he and his films are among the top moneymakers of that world which judges its faithful first as businessmen, then as artists—the Movies.

So now we come to *Red Line 7000* and one of the worst

sets of reviews a major director has received in the past ten years. ... What happened? Discarding senility as a possible answer (and anybody still discovering and building stars like Charlene Holt, and who not long ago made *El Dorado* with John Wayne and Robert Mitchum, is simply not all *that* old), we must address the two general problems *Red Line* presents: how it is different from other Hawks films, leaving even such staunch Hawksians as Andrew Sarris with quibbles and faint praise; and how it is like other Hawks movies—like enough, the reviewers see, to relegate the film to the drive-in trade. But before we get to the hardrock problems, we should examine the tradition Hawks has chosen, the racing car genre. Henri Agel has observed that Hawks takes the best elements of each genre and fuses them with his own themes; and we know that beyond the normal nature of Hawks' films as models for moral living, he sometimes makes specific films for didactic

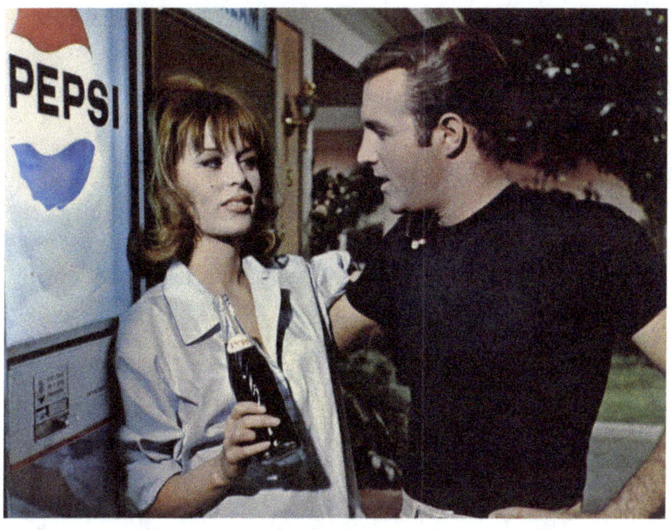

In this courting scene with Marianna Hill and James Caan, director-producer Howard Hawks humorously (and shamelessly) exploits production placement, which is integral to the commercial world of stock-car racing in his 1965 film maudit, *Red Line 7000*. (Paramount)

reasons. He made *Rio Bravo* as an answer to *High Noon*, commenting that a professional sheriff doesn't go around asking other people to do his job. I submit that Hawks has entered *Red Line* in a similar, though less direct, didactic exchange.

Hollywood makes two kinds of racing car pictures: the middle-class acceptable picture about titled noblemen and Ivy grads racing $25,000 Maseratis in culture-soaked Old Europe, designed to appeal to critics as something more valid than an action picture (for example, Hathaway's *The Racers*, with a star-studded cast of Real Actors); and pix made for those in direct contact with the car culture, the teenagers, these best exemplified by the complex mystique of the Mitchum-Ripley *Thunder Road. Thunder Road* has become a legend in America's popteen culture, and the legend has been extended and intensified by Tom Wolfe's zonk article on Junior Johnson, whose saga roars from a real-life *Thunder Road*, complete with identical social and political subplots, to the world of chromium-crass stock car racing in the New South, where it is not just a sport but a completely assimilated limb of Their Culture.

Hawks, who has never strayed from his commitment to casual (and as we'll see, causal) hipness, would hardly consider doing a picture about the highbrow Grand Prix world when its American-Hawksian counterpart exists in stock car racing; but on the other hand, lacking the social and political orientation manifested in Wolfe and *Thunder Road*, and being more a documentarist than a legend maker for youth-rebellion heroes, Hawks must make his own way. He chooses to make a practical, somewhat disillusioning statement of how it is in stock car racing without that legend stuff. He does. Then the reviewers complain that *Red Line* is laden with plugs for various automotive products, never realizing that most of the stock car racing world exists to sell car products and, like baseball and its $50-to-the-player-who-hits-this-sign at a game standards, stock car racing is a commercially exploited sport. Hawks, as a cultural documentor and sensitive modernist, *notes* rather than conceals this fact of modern sport. The reviewers who object might be more comfortable in another century.

As he gives us the stock car experience, Hawks also gives his documentary vein a workout, somewhat as Kenneth Anger does in *Scorpio Rising,* constructing a fictional documentary of life in a confined, narrowly limited culture. He shoots on the southern tracks rather than in a studio backlot; he includes the signs and ads and gimmicks of the racing world; and, asserting his constant contemporary strain, he includes the fetishes of the teen world: scooters, a frug band, sharp cars and clothes. Many reviewers intimate that Hawks seems to change his style in *Red Line* to forego, for the first time, his smoky-bar, cheap-liquor, wisecracking mystique of The Forties; but inspection shows that Hawks has always been *au courant* with his atmosphere: *Red Line 7000* (1965) is as far removed from the mood and cultural milieu of *To Have and Have Not* (1944) as *The Big Sleep* (1946) is from *Only Angels Have Wings* (1939).

What confuses observers is that Hawks uses parallel situations; since *Only Angels Have Wings,* he has had the man say "You better be good" to the girl as she sits at the piano; had the girl say to the man "I'm hard to get—all you have to do is ask me"; and even older than these, the cigarette bits. Just as Hitchcock appears in his own films as a trademark, Hawks uses cigarette bits; but he uses the presence and manipulation of the cigarette to reveal and advance the drama of characters as well—a monograph could be written on the subject—but the point is that Hawks is consistently modern in his situations, and the cigarette has replaced the more formal, less organically natural aside or subtitle as a device for showing feeling or relationship.

In the prototypical Hawksian drama, there is a mature authority figure. He is a professional who draws his heroic stature from his job, a job which is his entire role in life and by which he chooses to be identified and judged. He is surrounded by demi-heroes, trying to acquire full heroic status, or redeem it after a fall, or merely to act out their roles as hangers-on of heroes. As the drama unrolls in the job-world, the airport or race track or safari station, a woman appears, a professional, aggressive, competent woman, and she and the hero fall in love through a series of sharp-tongued sparring matches, feeling each other out while maintaining their hardboiled exteriors. The woman must adapt herself to the man's job, since it is the projection of the man into the world; and the man must understand the woman's human needs. This action, with a secondary plot, presents the education toward maturity of Hawks' films. His people are eminently practical. They exist in small microcosmic groups, and larger social institutions have no part in the drama—the moral issues are confined to the interaction of a few characters.

Using these personal conventions and forms, Hawks has concentrated on examining the heroic process. He examines the flawed, or immature, hero in *Scarface;* the pure agonistic hero in *Hatari!;* the hero compromised by conflict of old and new standards in *Red River;* and the Bogart-charismatic hero in *To Have and Have Not* and *The Big Sleep.* He generally places his heroes in unending odyssey situations, where the job is frustrating or cyclical, where a man draws heroism not from the kind of job but from how well he does it. This is Aristotle's real meaning of *vertu:* not a moral absolute, but a relative value, a virtuosity of all action and activity—Hawks is in his own way quite an Aristotelian. As a modern he is not as interested in specific action or goals as he is in style and roles. So: Is *Red Line 7000* different from Hawks' earlier work? Not by any standard yet revealed. They all share the pared-down, essential and simple visual style Hawks has been polishing since he left his von Sternberg-influence period; the color sensitivity common to all Hawks' color films; and the loose, straight-ahead narrative of *Rio Bravo* and *Hatari!* The presence of death is more emphasized here, but the material demands it; and Hawks, whose films are always direct reflections on Life and Men and Women, is no sentimentalist. He does not avoid the place of death in the life of people, particularly as his men, through the job metaphor (for Life), must constantly assert their role by challenging death, testing the exact limits of their skill.

The problem of ambition is more prominent in *Red Line 7000* than in other Hawks films, but in it Hawks views ambition as immaturity. The older driver, who has raced in Europe and acquired heroic cool, is not rabid for winning: in the racing world what is important is racing well, not coming in first. Just as in life, many things like luck, chance and prevailing conditions—the fates in a Hawks film—can keep the good man from winning; but the good man alone can keep himself from doing his best. Drivers of immature judgment race beyond the red danger line of the tachometer because they are ambitious; and by violating the code they bring disorder to a well-regulated moral world, a practical world with its practical channels for accommodating all human events, including death and love. This time, using the metaphor of the race track, Hawks presents us with a model for life, an exemplum of good and bad for moderns. We must all circle the track until we die, doing as well as we can without lusting for the sterling silver loving cup.

There is, however, a big difference in *Red Line:* we the audience and Hawks the director do not find the characters admirable; we do not like them nor identify with them as we do other Hawks characters. The nature of this dislike stems from Hawks' neat manipulation of the star system; this twist in turn comes from Hawks' disillusioned attitude toward the film. In *Rio Bravo*, Hawks uses stars. In doing so, in casting John Wayne for the lead, Hawks automatically acquires a character we know the moment he appears on the screen. A star, after all, is not merely the character written in the script; he is also John Wayne, a super-personality immediately and directly accessible to the audience. Wayne is not only an established person, he is already a super-person. We like him, we know how he acts, we already have a certain sort of sympathy for him. He is a hero and a god.

But in *Red Line 7000*, none of the figures is like this; and it would destroy a mystic and subtle theme of the *mise-en-scène* if they were. A staple of Hawks' cinema texture and milieu is his insistence on improvising with the actors, planning situations not around the plot, which is a mere excuse to Hawks, but around how Bogart and Bacall really look at each other and play cigarette games and ad-lib, actions which could not possibly be in the script. As stars, actors have complete confidence and ease in their relations with the other actors in the film: they are professionals even before the fact of the story makes them so. *Red Line* is about people who have not yet adjusted to the professional role, not yet acquired its bearing. They are not yet mature and not yet heroes *in the*

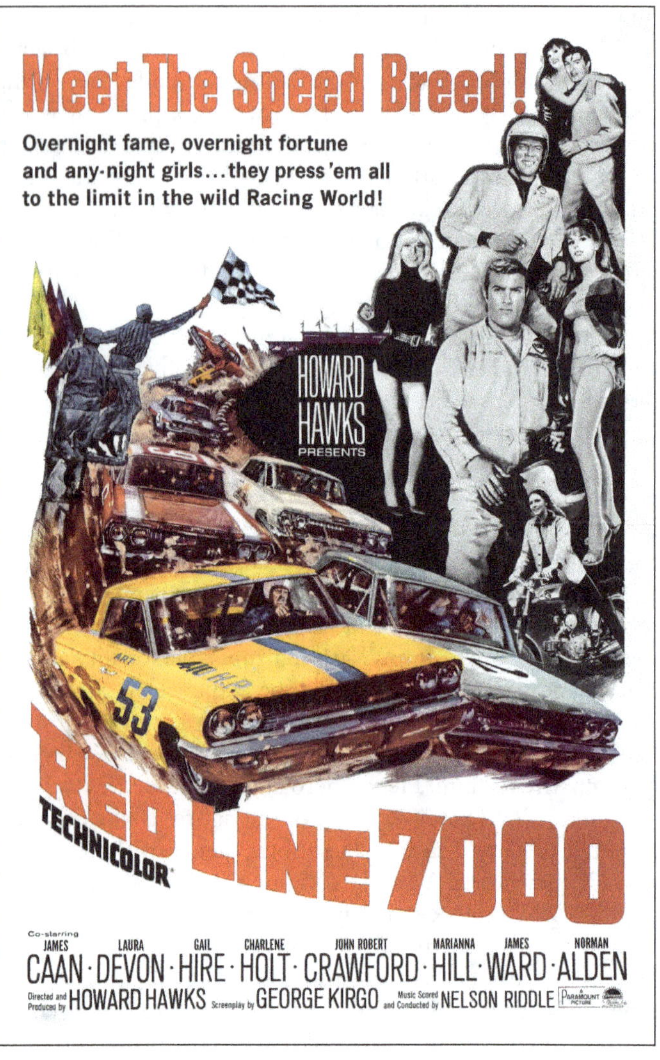

Poster for *Red Line 7000* shows how this late film by a veteran director was pitched uneasily to the youth audience as an exploitation movie. (Paramount)

story, and Hawks has reflected this in *Red Line* by casting actors whom we do not know as we know stars. These actors are not yet complete figures. They as actors are striving for completion of this role, just as in the terms of the film's story the characters are striving for a completion.

It would be absurd and foolish to cast stars in such roles; it would destroy the quietly mature pseudo-documentary approach Hawks employs. The virtue of Hawks' casting trick is seen throughout the film: contrast the embarrassingly adolescent bed sequence ("What were the other girls like?" "Uh … well …" "Tell me what the other girls were like, were they sexy?" "Yeah … they were … sexy"), which stunningly fills in the shallow characters, with any of Hawks' mature love scenes. Tension is created because the people in the movie are not what we usually find within the limits of such a genre, a tension which forces us to be more objective in what we see because we have no subjective identification with a star. A good example of Hawks' awareness of this tension is the tight balance he achieves between characters and event-experience in the courting-in-the-Mustang sequence, when the girl drives.

Usually Hawks examines and celebrates; in *Red Line* he only examines. Because he uses no stars, the dynamics of the film are strangely altered and somehow the emphasis seems to have shifted from the paternal figure, the one Hawksian professional hero in the film, to the failings of the immature figures, the defaulters from heroic stature. This emphasis is hard for us to follow because usually the drama would be cast in subjective terms of good and evil, whereas here we have it set in terms of immaturity. Though the film opens and closes on death and has for its climactic center a murder attempt, no central character dies or kills, as would be usual in this genre if done by another director. From one main female character in *Rio Bravo* to two in *Hatari!* and *Man's Favorite Sport?*, Hawks has put three in *Red Line,* and with the three male figures, created a back-and-forth web of parallel situations acted out with changing members of the group which, like a symbolic logic problem ("If Bill and Mary have one child, and Sally once divorced Bill, and Mary and Jim… "), serves to define each of the characters in terms of their relation to the others. It is possible that Hawks has created a surface for his contemporary moral drama so specific to the subculture it deals with, so tightly constructed in implicit rather than explicit meanings, as to render the film accessible only to the very sophisticated (though such a rendering is almost a functional definition of intellectual art, right?). However, my own feeling is that teenagers respond intuitively to a deeper and more intimate treatment of their situation; that serious moviegoers who read Hawks aright will find him here disillusioned in attitude though hardly diminished in skill, style or meaning; and that though not necessarily Hawks' best film nor the best film of the year, the qualities and forms of *Red Line* should be immediately evident to critics of *film* rather than to the arbiters of genres for occasional cinema-goers.

7 Women
Richard Thompson

Of all the rich personal heritages left by American directors, John Ford's is the least explored by subsequent generations of young directors, relative to Welles or von Sternberg, for example. Of all the directors who tried Ford's patterns and style (Waggner, Marin, Farrow, Grant), only Andrew V. McLaglen has been able to work meaningfully with them (*McLintock!*, *Shenandoah*, *The Rare Breed*), perhaps by hereditary right as the son of Fordian actor Victor McLaglen. Welles and von Sternberg are literal artists—their meaning, their style, their focus are right there on the screen to see and emulate. But Ford works in an artistic world much of which exists away from the screen, a world more evoked than pictured by the images. Ford's vision is the myth of American history and culture, which raises a problem of politics and fashion. Welles, Hitchcock, even von Sternberg with his exotic cynicism, take positions easily construed as antagonistic to that complex inadequately defined as "the mythic celebration of America"; the generation of intellectuals who would rather be Europeans than Americans have not come to grips with Ford as an artist because they refuse the ideas he stands for. Consequently, they lack the sensibility which must be exercised to comprehend Ford.

These people don't bother to see Ford films, let alone *7 Women*. Those who saw Ford's latest (and maybe last) film encountered another barrier, a blind which grew from *auteur* criticism and a confusion about material and method in an *auteur*'s work. It is too easy to find the identity of the material

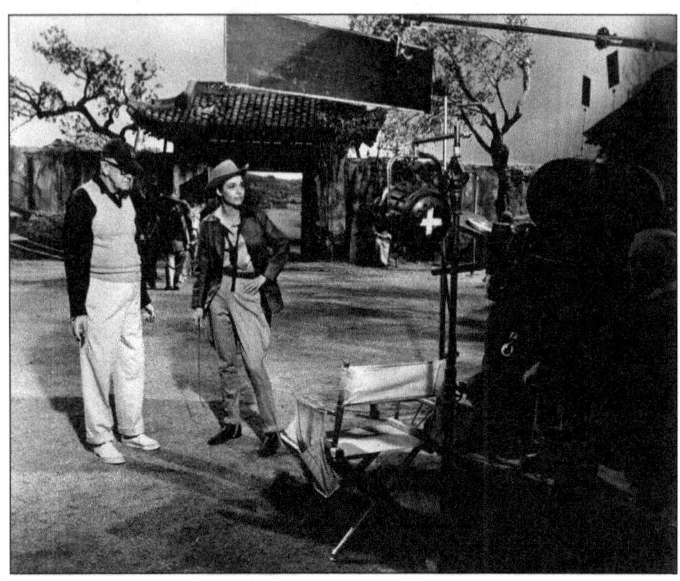

John Ford directs Anne Bancroft in *7 Women* as the atheist
Dr. Cartwright, who practices Christian values despite the
hypocrisy of missionaries in their Chinese compound during a time
of civil war in 1935. The film was mostly shot on this stylized set at
MGM to emphasize the mission's claustrophobia and failed attempt
to wall out the world. (MGM)

on the surface, rather than in the animating themes behind it,
or to assume that material and method are a single process.
7 Women disappointed the followers of Ford who expected
another broad epic summarizing Ford's feeling about a genre.
But the film is not epic, and if it belongs to a genre, the genre
is not one Ford has worked with in the past.

7 Women didn't fit the right patterns, so it was distrib-
uted, exhibited, and ignored by the reviewers as a B second
feature. It is actually the director's *tour de force,* shot in one
large studio set: the interior and exterior of an American
mission compound in China in 1935, a time, we are shown, of
civil unrest in a country of considerable barbarity. It is staged
as a character drama of contrast and conflict, acted in extreme
and intense individual styles. Ford chose to make a movie
about women for the first time [that's inaccurate; see David

Meuel's 2014 book, *Women in the Films of John Ford*—Ed.] at nearly the end of his career; the project wasn't forced on him, so why women? The story demands women, of course, but then, Ford chose the story. The women themselves aren't the Ford women we know; we never see them cooking, washing, socializing, taking care of their men, helping a new woman get settled, because unlike Ford's other women, who have or are getting a man and a home, these women have neither. Ford's other missionary types are more committed to God and to the service of others than our heroines—our missionaries seem shallow in their faith, using it to justify the lives they have chosen to lead.

The four sections of the film grow progressively blacker as Ford stresses his cultural and religious themes more than his historical ideas. The first part sets the scene: a Protestant mission staffed by Americans to bring the word of God and the ways of the USA to Chinese peasants; a few low buildings in a walled-off court; quiet browns and greens. The characters are dressed simply, as missionaries should be: Miss Andrews (Margaret Leighton), the middle-aged martinet who runs the mission austerely and authoritatively; her lifeless yes-woman, Miss Argent (Mildred Dunnock); Charles and Florrie Pether (Eddie Albert and Betty Field), middle-aged teachers who missed their youth by saving up to get married with the result that Florrie is with child at "a dangerous age"; and young Emma (Sue Lyon), very innocent and very good.

Ford quickly sketches the conflicts within this group. Miss Andrews must have her position of authority unchallenged. She resents the intrusion of worldly sex (the Pethers' pregnancy) under her sacred roof—mainly under *her* roof; but at the same time, she is having trouble keeping her hands off young Emma, devoted to her pupils, teaching them peace and love. Mr. Pether is in a tough spot: his wife embarrasses him constantly, demanding attention and sympathy; he himself, deprived of male dominance by Miss Andrews, wants to be a preacher if only to uncomprehending Chinese children. Mrs. Pether is histrionically enjoying her postponed late adolescence in the shadow of menopause. This foundation is laid carefully, formally, from a discreet distance; we see the action from a position outside. Things move slowly in the mission, in an established and unbroken rhythm, and the structure of this section corresponds. The drama is limited and specific, as the set is: Ford is dealing strictly with humans, not with the sea, the land, the air, forces the mission has cut itself off from. Already the film shapes up as an interior study.

The mission is waiting for a doctor to join their staff to operate the dispensary and care for Mrs. Pether. Part two opens with the arrival of the doctor, Dr. Cartwright (Anne Bancroft), neither the man they expected nor the sort of woman they can easily accept. She is worldly, earthy, outspoken, and unimpressed by Miss Andrews' authority and Mrs. Pether's hysteria. She is pointedly not religious: when one of the ladies calls on God for help with Mrs. Pether's delivery, Dr. Cartwright says she's seen thousands of deliveries in slum hospitals and God never lifted a finger to help any of them. She also smokes, drinks and curses ("You smoke too much."—"I do everything too much."). Part two culminates in open antagonism between the doctor and the headwoman, indicating that we are in for a politics-of-women soap opera story; but as the antagonism grows, intensified by Emma's admiration for the doctor's open character and ready humanity, part three closes in.

A band of refugees from the nearby British mission arrives (arrivals are significant in the mission, for they bring change and interrupt the rhythm), driven from their mission by the bandit hordes of Tunga Khan. Miss Andrews thinks that's horrid, but characteristically takes faith in the unreal protection of American citizenship: the savages wouldn't dare. The escapees bring with them a plague which suspends hostilities and makes a hero of the doctor: in the emergency, she effectively takes leadership of the mission away from Miss Andrews. The rapid action early in the section, when the victims of the epidemic are discovered and organized, gives way to the funereal pace and dark, sombre style of the third part's conclusion: the arrival of death and the destruction of the past as graves are dug and contaminated possessions burned. From this point on, tea can still be served at four, but nothing can ever be as it was. The drama hangs in a vacuum now, without the habits of the past to sustain it; it awaits the apocalypse of the future. Mr. Pether finally moves to action, takes the car, and goes to town to scout out the bandits and

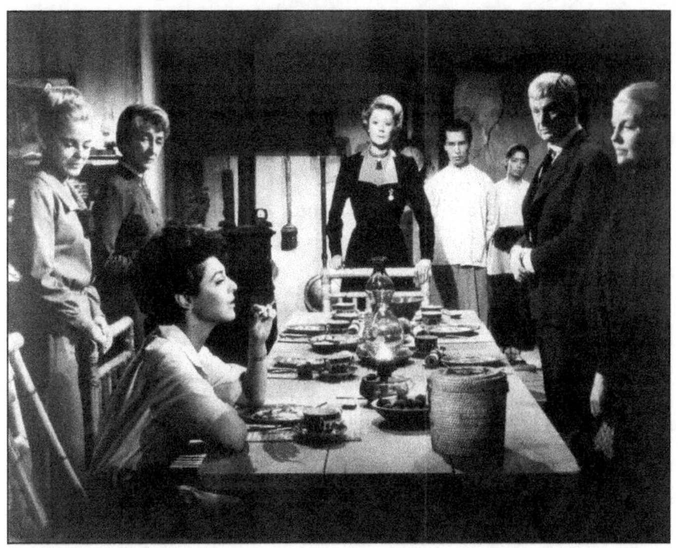

By smoking at dinner, Dr. Cartwright scandalizes and defies the autocratic mission leader, Agatha Andrews (Margaret Leighton, standing at end of table). Unlike in most other Ford films, the dinner rituals in *7 Women* are disruptive rather than reassuring expressions of tradition. Also seen (from left) are Sue Lyon, Mildred Dunnock, Hans William Lee, unidentified actress, Eddie Albert, and Betty Field. (MGM)

glimpse the future. We don't go with him; we stay inside the courtyard.

The final movement of the film opens as Tunga Khan (Mike Mazurki) and his bandits burst through the gate riding like Oriental Hell's Angels, speaking no English, and taking everything by right of force. They have killed Pether. They imprison all the white women in a storage shed. They drink, fight, dance, and kill. Though critics of Ford often find him unable to get inside his Indians, it seems that they, like the bandits here and the storm in *The Hurricane,* are more forces than characters in his dramatic movement. Anyway, the arrival of the bandits completes the destruction of the artificial world the missionaries have constructed. Through the bars of the shed, the women see everything they valued and built destroyed while they are unable to act in any way. Dr.

Cartwright alone remains functional, operating as the leader. She has won the battle with Miss Andrews on her own merits. Mrs. Pether's delivery begins in the shed under terrible conditions: no milk, no medicine, no tools. The final forceful intrusion of life is effected as all the women, cramped into a 12 × 12 room, are forced to watch a baby born.

Dr. Cartwright goes to Tunga Khan and asks for the supplies she needs. In a Tarzan and Jane sequence, the bandit agrees—for a suitable ransom: Dr. Cartwright. She accepts. Back in the shed, this is the final straw for Miss Andrews; she loses her grip on reality, damning the doctor as Scarlet Woman, etc., in spite of the fact that Dr. Cartwright has also bought the freedom of the other women. Miss Argent, the most faithful of Miss Andrews' charges, is horrified at the martinet's rejection of Dr. Cartwright's sacrifice and condemns her before all the others. As the women are freed on an oxcart, bumping away from the camera and the mission, into the night and the future, Sue Lyon completely understands the doctor's sacrifice. Ford sees her as hope: she is the one who, after the deluge, can find a value in Dr. Cartwright's liberating example. Back at the mission, Dr. Cartwright goes to the bandit, poisons their tea, and says, "So long, ya bastard." They both die. The End.

Juxtaposed with the flight of the fugitives and Sue Lyon's youthful hope, the death scene is treated in the best hardboiled manner: objective, quick, without theatrics. Strangely so, for in the film Bancroft's sacrifice is a religious one, one of the human miracles running through Ford's work, and an event which reveals the hypocrisy of the missionaries. Greater love hath no man... or woman; Bancroft has the necessary equipment for sacrifice: a grasp of the situation, humanity, heroic quality. On the other hand, the missionary ladies have no past, no future, no men or children or home—in Ford's terms, nothing to sacrifice. Bancroft is alive, whereas the missionary ladies have forfeited the changes and rewards of life for the monotonous security of the mission. The ladies know only the abstract, but Bancroft's experience with people is universal and adaptable.

Perhaps the most interesting aspect of *7 Women* is its use of sex motifs, occasionally scattered through other Ford works,

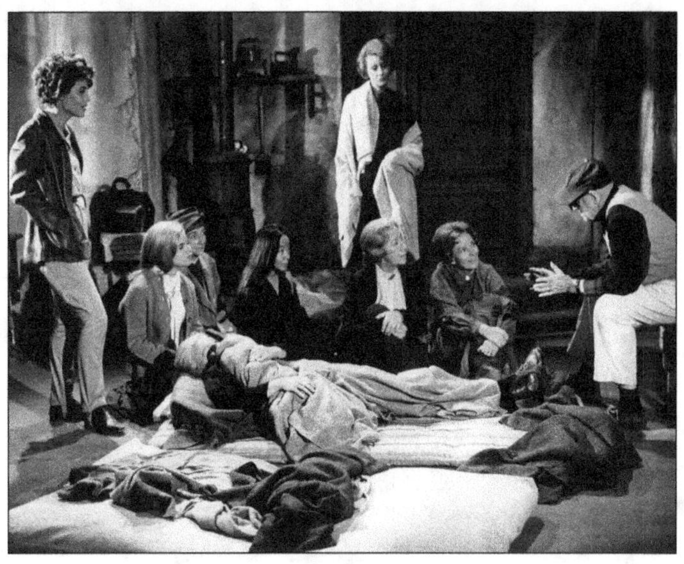

Ford directing the cast of *7 Women*: (from left), Bancroft, Lyon,
Dunnock, Field (lying on bed), Jane Chang, Leighton,
Flora Robson and Anna Lee. (MGM)

but abounding here. If is fascinating to see Ford's art accommodate them. The taste and economy of Margaret Leighton's designs on Sue Lyon, the wordless exchanges of Anne Bancroft and Tunga Khan's concubine, the unnaturalness and pathos of the Pethers' middle-aged youth, Leighton finally driven mad when Tunga Khan chooses Bancroft for his woman, and the political overtones of the bandits battling over Bancroft—these elements are projected in all their meaning as Fordian terms.

Ford's films generally center on a conflict of cultures or of social orders; with the introduction of Dr. Cartwright, the lines are drawn in *7 Women*. If Dr. Cartwright seems more sympathetic, it is because the Fordian vision is partial to emotions and actions drawn from real life rather than to intellectual responses founded on theory. The test of characters and values is how well they function in a situation of change and danger; Ford often stages this moral drama in terms of the old falling before the new, sometimes as the meeting of two

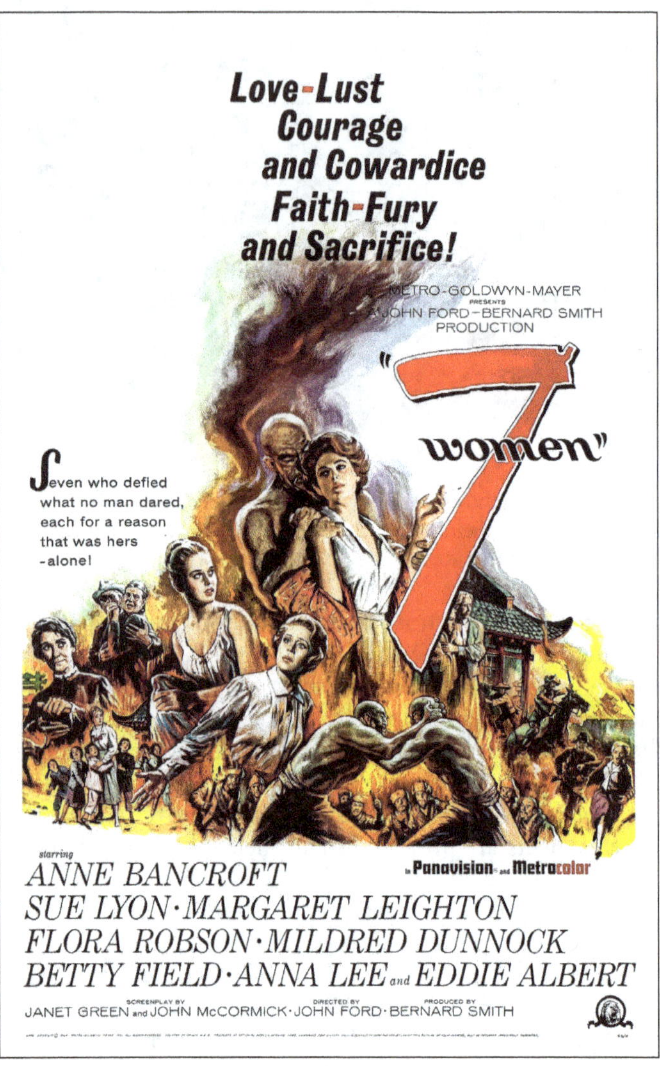

The lurid original MGM poster for *7 Women*,
unworthy of a great film.

equal cultures, but it has always meant order disrupted into disorder and resolved again into a new order. If we take this view of *7 Women*, there are certain exceptions to Ford's usual pattern which must be accounted for. The missionaries here take the part of the old and the doctor the part of the new. Usually, the old is replaced by the new because conditions have changed—progress; and both old and new have success because they have effectively met and adapted to the conditions around them—the land, the natives, the city, what have you. But here the missionaries have not adapted to anything. Instead, they have walled themselves off into an area where they can successfully impose very artificial standards. They are not an idealization, as is often the case, but an abstract. They are not really the past or the passing, but an evasion of the present; they attempt to control life. Throughout the film, Ford confronts them with manifestations of life they can't regulate and of the world they are avoiding: Mrs. Pether's pregnancy in the first part, Dr. Cartwright in the second, a plague in the third, bandits in the fourth.

Like Wayne (the old) and Stewart (the new) confronted by Lee Marvin (the test, disorder) in *The Man Who Shot Liberty Valance*, or Fonda, Wayne, and the Indians in *Fort Apache*, or even the natives, the Europeans, and the storm *(The Hurricane)*, Ford tests the missionaries and Anne Bancroft with the Chinese bandits. Ford makes the same arguments from the cultural and the religious level: that the missionaries are isolated, inner-directed, seeking to impose artificial standards not drawn from pragmatic experience and human feelings. Bancroft has no dogma, but has learned of life first-hand and can cope with its changes on a human level. She adapts, and so can she effect. Religion for Ford is always active, never static, and here (more freely perhaps because he deals with Protestants) Ford makes the same case: religion is for operation, not protection.

Above all else, the force of disorder still reigns at the end of this film. Bancroft's victory is Pyrrhic. More than ever, Ford seems an ideal director for Shakespeare—not the tragedies, which Welles defines, or the comedies, which seem better for Lubitsch or Tashlin, but the histories: both *Richard III* and *Henry V* cry out for Ford's epic scope and political vision of history through individuals.

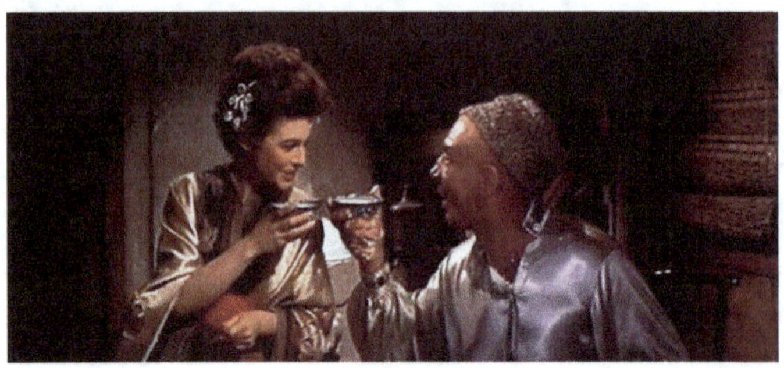

"So long, ya bastard." The stark finale of Ford's last feature,
7 Women, his valedictory after more than fifty years in films.
This line uttered by Dr. Cartwright to the bandit leader, Tunga
Khan (Mike Mazurki), as she poisons both him and herself was
written in pencil in Ford's shooting script by the director.
(Frame enlargement; MGM).

7 Women is Ford's most pessimistic film to date, culminating a progressive reappraisal of the myths he once celebrated and created. The dark vein of *Two Rode Together, The
Man Who Shot Liberty Valance* and *Cheyenne Autumn* is
now fully realized. Ford, of course, is The Old Order. Like
Duke Ellington, Ford goes his own way, following his vision
regardless of stylistic change around him. The sympathy Ford
expresses for the old-way heroes in his films of progress is
a personal sympathy. When Ford constructs a film with
disorder in control at the end, what does it signify for Ford?
For his art, and for films? For his view of America?

The Jewison Question
Michael Wilmington

I.

In an age and a country in which advertising is fast becoming a high art, it's hardly surprising to see the techniques of Madison Avenue being applied to older, more established forms; since Marshall McLuhan opened the door, I expect we'll see scholarly analysis of TV commercials any day now. *Valley of the Dolls* and, in a more sophisticated way, *The Confessions of Nat Turner,* are not so much novels as they are phenomena of promotion. But even better examples of how advertising and its techniques infiltrate the arts are in the movies.

In the Heat of the Night is a great example of how a movie can succeed because of clever packaging. If a box is pretty enough and has enough coupons, many people won't notice that their cornflakes are moldy. The film is not only a monetary success—some blatantly bad movies like *Valley of the Dolls* (again) and *To Sir, with Love* have also been blockbusters—but, more importantly, a tremendous critical one as well. It took the New York Film Critics Circle awards for best film and actor (Rod Steiger), was rhapsodized about in the trade papers, and picked up three of the major Oscars, best picture (producer Walter Mirisch), actor (Steiger) and adapted screenplay (Stirling Silliphant).

In a peculiar way, I think this movie has benefited from the *politique des auteurs.* American critics, most of whom are literarily oriented, have for years been denouncing American movie kitsch as feebleminded and unfit for an intelligent audience. When *Cahiers du Cinéma, Movie* and Andrew Sarris suddenly started applying high-toned analysis to directors like Cukor, Preminger and Fuller, directors dismissed as hacks years ago by the literate American cliques (who instead admired Huston, Zinnemann and Wyler), a real gloss was given to the kitsch. And the later cinematic success of former *Cahiers* critics like Godard, Truffaut and Chabrol demanded that their earlier critical efforts be taken seriously.

Now, recently, nearly every mainstream U.S. film reviewer has denounced or attacked the *auteur* theory. Still, I think that Godard & Co. made them a little kitsch-conscious, anxious to root out those qualities in American movies, hitherto unrecognized in their own country, which had aroused the admiration of Europeans. And it's really a bad joke that the director on whom many of them have seized is the crafty producer-technician Norman Jewison. (I think this must really delight the Hollywood "insiders," who have been attacked for years as pandering to knuckleheads, and are now being praised by those attackers because the same slick, vapid gimmickry has been applied to "serious" subjects: peaceful coexistence in Jewison's *The Russians Are Coming, The Russians Are Coming* and racial integration in *Heat.* Maybe the way Jewison hijacked these intellectuals for the Hollywood crowd will compensate for the way the *Cahiers* group kidnapped Hitchcock and Hawks for academia.)

II.

In the Heat of the Night is a good average movie, fast and entertaining if you don't think about it much. Unfortunately, on practically every level where the critics said it succeeded—sociologically, dramatically and as a detective story—it's a miserable failure. Even as a "slick" piece of Hollywood craftsmanship, it's not nearly as good as *El Dorado* or *Point Blank* or *The Honey Pot* or *Divorce American Style,* none of which got much of a tumble from the critics.

First of all—as a mystery story, *In the Heat of the Night* is an outrage: illogical, contrived and impossible to figure out.

Consider this: the killer is unmasked as a greasy counterman we've seen twice (both times doing a third-rate impersonation of Tony Perkins in *Psycho).* He has no connection with the plot except that a policeman, who discovered the corpse while he was wandering around that night, ate at his diner.

How does the movie's Sherlock (Sidney Poitier) pin the guilt to this obscure character? You'd never guess; he links him up with another obscure character—a girl who, in a long, vulgarly directed scene, admits to the town police chief (Rod Steiger) that she's pregnant.

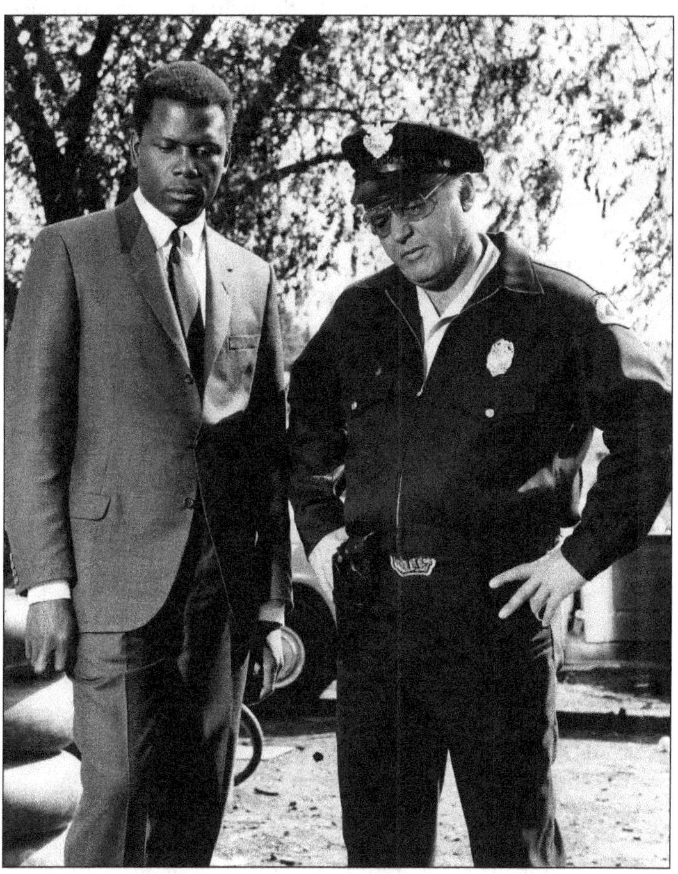

Sidney Poitier as Philadelphia Detective Virgil Tibbs gradually forms a professional bond with Police Chief Bill Gillespie (Rod Steiger) as they investigate a crime in his racially hostile Mississippi town in *In the Heat of the Night* (1967). (Mirisch Corp./United Artists)

Now follow this closely. As soon as he hears this confession, Poitier dashes off to nose out the local undercover abortionist because he's figured that the girl must be having a secret abortion that evening and that the killer must be the father. Our admiration at this truly incredible detective skill may cause us to gloss over two questions. One: short of a sperm analysis, how does Poitier know that the killer is the father? And two: why in the world would a girl who just admitted she was pregnant to everybody in sight, including her jealous brother, the town police chief and a detective from Philadelphia, be having a secret abortion?

But don't let all that worry you—the killer stumbles into Poitier's trap right on schedule. Before that, however, Jewison and scenarist Stirling Silliphant have come up with a whale of a red herring. It seems that somebody stole $700 from the dead man's wallet, so police chief Steiger arrests the wandering policeman who discovered the corpse because $700 was deposited in his bank account the day after the killing. But it turns out that the wandering policeman is really innocent: he won all that money pitching quarters over a period of six years. Think about that one for a while. (I should mention here that Poitier's figuring and the red herring are both quite logical in John Ball's original novel. But Jewison and Silliphant, or maybe the editors, were too interested in making a fast, loud, zappy movie to worry about whether it made any sense.)

III.

If *Heat* were just an illogical mystery, it wouldn't be as annoying; after all, *The Big Sleep* is sort of messy (even Hawks and Raymond Chandler couldn't explain what was going on in some of the scenes), and there are loopholes of logic in Hitchcock's *Vertigo,* one of the great films of all time. These movies work and succeed in different areas. *Heat* has other areas too, but unfortunately they're just as sloggily handled as the detective story; specifically, there are the "dramatic" sections, in which we're supposed to be watching the ripening of friendship and mutual respect between the Southern cop and the Negro detective.

Most audiences swallow that, and I really wonder why. The progression in the film isn't toward mutual respect at all; Steiger has professional respect for Poitier from the very first, but we're shown that the Negro irritates him, gets under his skin. Poitier never seems to respect Steiger at all, and why should he? Gillespie stumbles around arresting the wrong people and making numerous boners until the very end; Poitier does almost nothing wrong, though the movie does make a few feeble stabs at showing us he's "human."

So, at the end, what's changed is that Gillespie has become rather servilely fond of Tibbs (he's carrying his bags and simpering in a bad imitation of a porter), and Tibbs has learned to tolerate him enough to smile back. Isn't all this a sort of masochistic wish fulfillment of the average dull white liberal?

The film also has some pop sociology to offer, which is just as difficult to take, mostly because it's been so Jewisonized. At one point, Poitier and Steiger ride through a cotton field and we're treated to the spectacle of exploited darkies sweating and toiling in the sun. Hasn't the problem gotten a little more complicated than that?

The film's whole handling of Negroes is somewhat dense; whenever Poitier meets someone of his race they lapse into a sort of caricatured "soul brother" lingo that seems ludicrously forced. (Oddly enough, these scenes might have worked if they'd been played like the ones with the white Southerners, for comic exaggeration. But comic exaggeration of Negro characteristics is, in our present culture, out of bounds — only a Negro writer like Chester Himes can really get away with it. The white makers of *In the Heat of the Night* wouldn't want to risk alienating their audience, though the audience they're catering to is probably the white liberals. I doubt that many Negroes take this stuff seriously.)

If we remember that Norman Jewison made his reputation in Hollywood by directing Doris Day–Rock Hudson comedies (something Jewison, who obviously aspires to "serious" moviemaking, would probably rather forget), we can figure out the real theme of this film, as opposed to the spurious themes (the mystery, the sociology or the "mutual respect" idea). In reality, *Heat* is just another rehash of those earlier Frigidaire comedies; only this time Rod Steiger is Rock Hudson, and Sidney Poitier is sitting in for Doris Day. The idea, in itself, is faintly amusing, and Jewison might have had some fun with it (as Billy Wilder seems to have had in *The Fortune Cookie*) if he hadn't been so concerned with being straight and dramatic, qualities which pretty consistently elude him, especially in the "big" scene in Gillespie's living room, which seems to be constantly slipping off into homosexual farce.

IV.

Now the audience responds to this absurd representation of a human relationship for reasons which I think are extrinsic to the story or to Jewison's talent as a director of actors (he has almost none). The audience simply and directly responds to Poitier and Steiger, both of whom radiate an intense personal appeal regardless of the kind of role they play. (And that's the same reason for which a slightly less sophisticated audience responded to the Doris Day things.) It also responds, of course, because Poitier is a Negro, and by liking his films maybe they think they can strike a passive blow for civil rights.

Still, both of these men contribute performances which are below the grade of their best work. Looking at some of the other performances in the film, which range from pedestrian to awful—and continually consist of punching home "effects"—one can see why. Jewison is still exploiting the same heavy comic timing he mastered in his earlier work.

Poitier, who is very good when he is being quiet and understated, here comes off looking pompous because he's trying to understate an impossible character. He seems to be gifted with second sight and he comes out of several fights without a wrinkle in his suit. And the investigatorial genius he seems to be displaying with the mystery (which includes instant identification of an obscure species of fern) breaks down inexplicably at several points. This is, we are told, an experienced homicide detective from Philadelphia. Yet, knowing that he is an unwanted intruder in a hostile Southern town, he acts in the following boneheaded way: with a car full of murderous cretins chasing him, he gets out at what seems to be an abandoned factory on the edge of town and runs inside, evidently in order to make a phone call.

At the end of the film, Poitier has put himself in the following situation: he is operating a stakeout, without a gun, in a place that looks fairly cut off (I didn't spot a telephone) for the man he has incomprehensibly deduced is the killer. The same four cretins who, through no fault of Poitier's, bungled their last attempts, are still looking for him. Poitier has refused to tell Steiger where he's going, and he tells the kid who drove him there to go home. So what's he going to do with the killer when he catches him—walk him all the way back? Without a gun? At midnight? With two carloads of psychopaths looking for him? Of course we shouldn't worry about old Tibbs, since he's obviously superhuman, bulletproof and wrinkle-resistant, but maybe we ought to start worrying about those four cretins. They're dealing with a madman.

Everybody likes Rod Steiger in the film—and after years of seeing the Oscar go to people like Gregory Peck and Charlton Heston, we probably shouldn't complain that he picked one up this year. I like Steiger here too, but what he's doing seems to be an awful compromise, and I don't mean that in the snobbish sense that I'd rather see him doing *King Lear* or a sepia-tinted adaptation of Chekhov. Being excellent in junk is fine—Robert Ryan has made a career of it—but here a lot of the junk seems to have infiltrated Steiger's sensibility and affected his approach to the role.

His Chief Gillespie, as Pauline Kael observed (while praising the movie) is a comic performance, and it's a comic performance that's rigorously stylized. It may surprise traditionalists that a "method"-trained actor can display such razor-fine timing and control, but the trouble is with the dramatic parts. Steiger is fine when he's just kidding us along, popping his gum, and pretending to be a Mississippi cop. We know he isn't anyway because a sort of urban Jewish sensibility keeps shining through. Steiger has all the externals of the role down pat, and he uses them superbly to comic effect, but the internalization of the role—something at which "method" actors are supposed to be especially adept—is somehow missing.

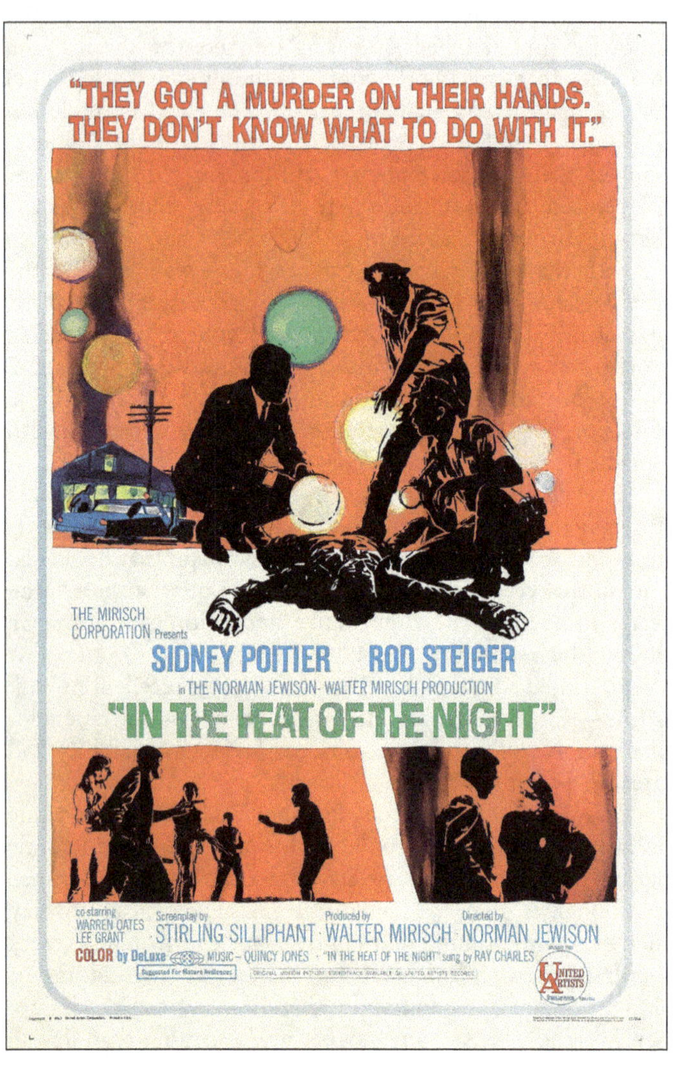

Original poster for *In the Heat of the Night*.
(Mirisch Corp./United Artists)

Because Jewison was so interested in punching home every scene, in wringing out every last drop of juice, we can't follow Gillespie's development; we're never clear as to where and why his attitudes toward Tibbs are shifting. Steiger plays much of the role at the top of his lungs, and then, in the dramatic scenes, his voice drops into an intense confidential murmur. But it doesn't work. It's like Laurel and Hardy trying to do a scene from *Waiting for Godot* right in the middle of *Swiss Miss.* Steiger is a good enough actor that he can carry us through the non-comic scenes, even though they make us uncomfortable; the less-talented people in the cast can't. Lee Grant and Beah Richards, for example, both come off looking grotesque.

V.

I could say a few hundred specific words about Norman Jewison's direction of all this, most of them bad, but that would be begging the issue. Jewison does have some talent, though I developed such an aversion for him back in the days when he was doing things like *The Art of Love* and *Send Me No Flowers* that I'm almost irrationally unwilling to grant him anything now.

He's like Blake Edwards, but not as good. Edwards' films, at their best *(A Shot in the Dark; What Did You Do in the War, Daddy?)*, are genuinely funny; he is a perfectionist of a trashy but ingratiating and controlled style. Jewison is a second-rate practitioner of that style who applies it to subjects he knows will go over big with most critics.

He has all kinds of fancy window dressing on his movies: Ray Charles, our greatest pop singer, sings the theme songs for two of them; the photography is good; the locations are well-selected; and Jewison does have a genuine talent for assembling casts, if not for directing them afterwards. Steiger, Poitier, Brian Keith, Alan Arkin, Steve McQueen, Faye Dunaway, Karl Malden, Rip Torn, Paul Ford, Michael J. Pollard, Warren Oates, Jonathan Winters, Edward G. Robinson and Jack Weston have appeared in his last four movies. If you have good enough actors they can carry you through a lot of sloppy or thoughtless direction, but in the end, as in this movie, the direction is going to defeat them.

It's ironic that Jewison is now the wonder-boy of Hollywood, since he built his career over the ashes of a genuinely gifted man, Sam Peckinpah, whom he replaced on *The Cincinnati Kid* several years ago. (Warren Oates, who does well as the deputy in *Heat,* was one of Peckinpah's budding stock company.) Peckinpah was fired off the set of *The Cincinnati Kid* for "perfectionism," an odd crime which we certainly couldn't accuse Jewison of.

The rumor is that Martin Ransohoff fired Peckinpah (who did the brilliant *Ride the High Country)* because he was so frustrated and infuriated with Tony Richardson's expensive antics on *The Loved One,* but of course couldn't can Richardson, whom the critics had decided was an "artist." Now, two years later, we find that Jewison is an "artist" too. Surprises never cease; who is the next "artist" going to be—Ken Annakin? Jack Smight? It's almost like the *politique* game, which I said might have benefited Jewison, except that here it's less a matter of tension within the movie than tension within the critic; he has to get a review in on time, and since Jewison has supplied him with all the external trappings of a good movie, since he's packaged the trash so beautifully, why not give him the old five stars?

The only thing that could have really saved *In the Heat of the Night,* which has the tone and structure, if not the unity and dramatic integrity, of *Pillow Talk,* is if, at the end, when Steiger delivers himself of that awful simpering smile, Poitier had suddenly given him the finger, yelled "Sock it to me, Black Power!" and let out a loud fart as he got on the train. Then Steiger could have sat down on the tracks, done a Stan Laurel bawl, and the Supremes could have come in on the soundtrack singing "You Always Hurt the One You Love." But the critics probably wouldn't have gotten it.

Color Motifs in Visconti's *The Stranger*
F. A. Macklin

Luchino Visconti has been supremely careful in his handling of Albert Camus' renowned novel, *The Stranger.* It is to the director's credit that he does not demand that the viewer recognize what he is doing; he does his work subtly and with gentle command. *The Stranger,* with excellent cinematography by Giuseppe Rotunno, is a film for the eye. The less attentive viewers may well miss Visconti's effects because they are not emblazoned; rather they are suggested—they are in hues and tones. Many viewers may find a lack of motivation in the film, and they may think it has failed, but the story itself is motiveless, and the courage of the film is in its not attempting to give decisiveness to that which is indecisive.

As in Visconti's direction of Lampedusa's *The Leopard,* the central figure is more acted upon than active. Many viewers were not willing to accept Burt Lancaster in quietude as the dancing swayed around him. In *The Stranger* Marcello Mastroianni (Meursault) is perhaps more acceptable as a numbed figure, but even he often seems oddly abstract in inaction. *The Stranger* is the story of a man who commits a chance, seemingly motiveless, murder; the film is the rendition of the events leading to the murder, and it focuses on the trial of the accused and the incidents prior to his execution. With Picasso-like emphasis on color, Visconti reveals the spirit of Meursault's life in changing tints and moods.

The film opens with Meursault's being led handcuffed through a milling crowd in a hallway; the scene immediately sets the feeling of oppressiveness—the heat and humanity as

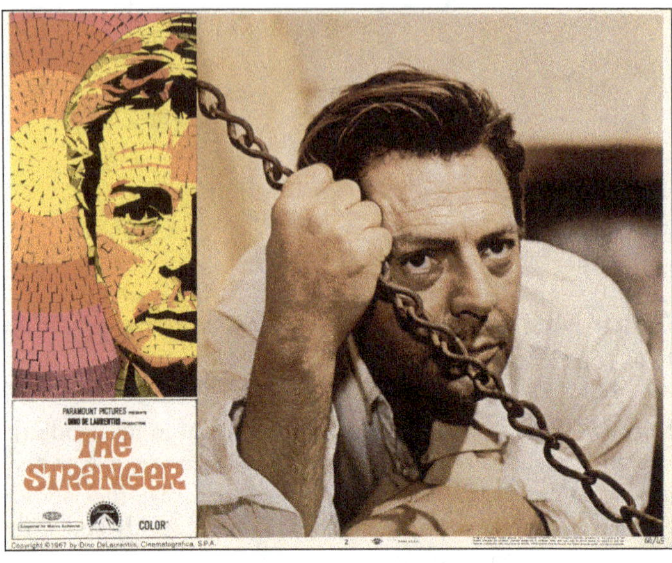

Original poster for director Luchino Visconti's 1967 film version
of the classic existentialist novel by Albert Camus, *The Stranger*.
(Paramount)

Meursault is pushed along. Visconti's beginning is different
from the book's. But the novel's opening line, one of the most
piquant in all literature ("Mother died today. Or, maybe,
yesterday...."), is not sacrificed; it is given later. Visconti
continually employs the language and specifics of the book,
though at his own pace.

When Meursault is brought before an examiner at the
beginning of the film (this scene begins Part Two of the
novel), Visconti's flashback technique is clearly and cogently
introduced. Meursault says, "My case is so simple." The scene
finds Meursault riding on a dull, hot, exhausting bus, as it
takes him to the rest home where his mother has died. Meursault is taken to a room where the coffin lies; the mood is one
of bright, white heat. His skin is white (its color varies in each
scene), and there is white light in the room. Behind his head
is the light wooden coffin, and the music is a slow tremble.
The eerie whiteness dominates. There are revealing closeups:
a large white coffee cup, a white wall, a white cigarette drawn

from a blue pack. Another blue object is a coffee pot. The few blue objects take on vividness in the terrible whiteness. There is the hazy, unfocused image, then focused, of the nurse and his mother's friends as they come to sit. Then a shot of the skylight, lighting up. Throughout the film, the images of dullness and isolation and freedom are beautifully edited. Things gain a simple beauty; they have impact. Visconti creates a flow of images, but always naturally, never with a forced or arty sense of construction.

As the people walk with the coffin to the burial place, even the tree trunks are painted white, carrying on the feeling of a world of bone, beautiful but perhaps sterile. There is a slow tedium, but always the lucid sense of image, as lucid and spare and ambiguous as Camus' prose. The shot of the white face of Thomas Perez, his mother's aged fiancé; he lolls back in a faint. Then the face of Meursault: "I still have memories of that day."

The feeling of chalk that was in the scenes at the rest home is washed away as Marie appears. (Anna Karina is Marie, and she is more human and less pretentious than in the Godard films.) Marie comes walking by the water, bouncy, smiling. Her black bathing suit is trimmed with orange and black belt and straps. She comes to Meursault, and they go out in the water and lie on a brilliant white and orange float—the water splashes up on them and she laughs gaily. (The sense of color of the float is as arresting as the orange smear that suddenly takes the form of an umbrella in Fellini's *Juliet of the Spirits*.)

When Meursault awakes alone in his room again a series of objects becomes focal: a chair, and on it the blue cigarette pack, the cigarette butts, and the clock. Time and habit dominate. Meursault arises from the bed and goes to the window. He looks down at the pavement; it has a blue cast to it. A group of men pass cheering, some in blue shirts. Above them, Meursault, behind the gratework looking down, is forever somehow imprisoned. When he goes to eat with a friend he exudes hunger; it is the one appetite he seems to have. Visconti finds the ideal representative for a minor character, the "little robot," from the novel—a stiff birdlike woman enters, orders her meal meticulously, and peers about. The closeup of her face reveals huge, watery, pale blue eyes behind her large round glasses. It is a vignette of superb eloquence. The feeling of frail, rigid, demanding humanity is perfect.

Meursault has dinner with his neighbor Raymond Sintes (Georges Géret). Again orange offers an odd, dull festive background. The spread on the bed and the material covering the headboard is striped; an orange-gold cast pervades. The pimp Raymond gets Meursault to write a letter to his girl friend damning her. Meursault has gotten involved without meaning to. When he leaves the room of his neighbor he is seen again through bars—in the railing; the camera then looks down through his eyes at the space plunging between landings—the islands of illusionary light.

When Meursault meets Marie for the second time in the film, there is again the great sense of people and isolation which Visconti creates. Marie and Meursault kiss, and as they do some sailors pass between them and the camera, but they pass on a natural promenade not even noticing the embracing couple. Marie and Meursault go to his room, and Visconti's brown period begins. Again there is a graphic portrait—done in white with vivid trim. She wears his white pajamas trimmed in brown; the walls are white, the background white, once more the large white cup. He wears a white undershirt, and their skin has a suggestion of brown—an earthen quality amidst the white world. Sudden shouting intervenes from above. Meursault leaves the embrace of Marie to see what is happening. Raymond has been beating his girl friend. Meursault comes upon police in light brown. It is an interesting note that the eyes of the characters in the ensuing scene are brown: the policeman's, Meursault's, Raymond's, the girl's. To pick colors out of context may seem presumptuous, but in context Visconti through the totality of brown suggests, almost subconsciously, a definite mood of sensuality and barrenness. Visconti evolves his brown spectrum further: Raymond is in red brown, the man who owns the dog is wearing brown; when Meursault stops to speak with him in the hallway there is a green cast.

The next time Meursault and Raymond communicate is on the phone. Raymond is afraid; he is being followed by some Arabs who want revenge for the beating he gave his girl friend. Raymond asks Meursault to go with him to a friend's house by the beach. Meusault agrees and says he will take Marie. While Raymond speaks on the phone, behind him is an ad for the Bastos cigarettes, which have appeared throughout the film—as though they are a symbol of civilization. The ad reappears when Meursault and Marie meet Raymond. Again there is water spray (as on the float) when Marie appears; this time from a streetcleaner's hose. The spray seems to represent Marie's vitality. The Arabs are following Raymond; they stand and watch against the advertisement.

At the beach Meursault is again hungry for food. "I'm ravenous," he says. As they eat the orange color is introduced once more. Marie is wearing an orange and white dress—one she wears for the remainder of the film. The shutters on the house are orange; orange posts support the railings. After the meal Meursault walks the beach with Raymond and his friend; Meursault trails after them dressed all in white, an outsider. Two Arabs appear; they are garbed in blue. One plays a pipe; the camera holds his face. A fight breaks out; one of the Arabs slashes Raymond with a knife on the face and arm. As the three Caucasians retreat up the beach to the house, they become smaller, and the water, bright and glazed with light, is prominent.

Meursault had taken Raymond's pistol from him, and he leaves the house and retraces his steps down the beach alone. The beach winks with spots of light—there is a sudden, flashing pocket of light. The white surf rolls in, and the music is intense. Meursault's skin has an orange tone to it. In the montage of heat and tension is the arresting shot of water spilling down the rocks. The flash of a knife; the flare of sunlight; it ricochets across Meursault's face.

The Arab is kneeling on his haunches; the camera focuses on his face. There is a shot of the pistol in Meursault's hand. He fires the pistol, and the Arab topples over. Meursault fires several times into the body.

The "accidental" murder committed, Meursault is imprisoned. The camera conveys the entrapment by a shot through the crossbar of his cell window out over the city and the blue sea. The lawyer (Bernard Blier) enters. His eyes are brown; he sits against an orange-tan background. As Meursault talks to him, part of Meursault's face is hidden by a wooden shelf

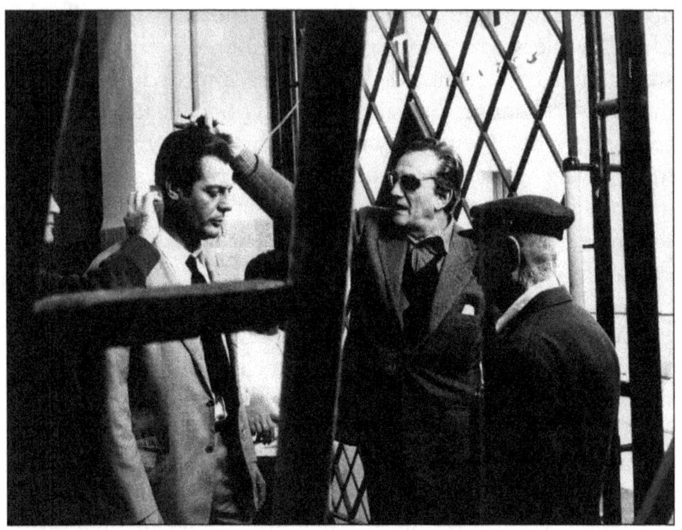

Director Luchino Visconti (with dark glasses) working with Marcello Mastroianni in his role as Meursault in *The Stranger*. (Paramount)

protruding from the wall with pans and dishes on it. It gives the effect of concealment; Meursault is seeing with, or perhaps revealing, only one eye. The shot makes an implication, but it is not at all intrusive. Meursault is brought before the examining officer. There is white on the left; on the right is a brown cabinet and a brown bookcase full of books. The curtains are white. The examining officer holds a crucifix: "Do you believe in God?" The camera moves in for Meursault's answer, "—No—." It is a technique Visconti uses in the crucial scenes of conflict to great effect: lingering on the edge of suspense, then leaping in to expose the character as he commits himself.

Marie visits Meursault in prison; again there is a manifestation of the barrier between humans. They are both, prisoner and visitor, behind bars, with a no-man's area separating them. The scene ends with the expressions of a youthful prisoner and his mother; the sense of loneliness and helplessness knows no age. There is a brilliant, beautifully edited transition. A flight of gulls over water, one gull soaring and swooping to powerful music. Then Meursault is shown huddled in a blanket in a bare corner of his cell. The contrast between the free gull and the caught human is a stunning one. Meursault covers the lower half of his face with the blue shroud.

The courtroom scene verbalizes several of *The Stranger*'s theses. The major one is the concept behind the murder. In answer to a question about why he went back to the spot where the Arab was, armed with a pistol, Meursault says, "It was a matter of chance." A friend later reiterates the fortuitous nature of the killing: "It was an accident. A stroke of bad luck." Much of the evidence against Meursault is sentimental, harsh, and irrelevant. The commentary in the courtroom shows the irrelevant values used in judging a man. There is a zoom shot of Meursault as the manager of the rest home where his mother died answers the question whether his mother felt Meursault betrayed her. When the manager answers "Qui" the zoom shot reveals Meursault's surprise. He seems an outsider, an outcast. The camera pans the jury and there is the sound of a babble of voices; when it rests on Meursault there is silence. The use of sound is another means for Visconti of showing the nature of the outsider.

Marie takes the stand wearing a yellow hat. She ends her testimony trapped and harming Meursault, and her tear-smashed face shows her agony at her failure. The camera probes the nakedness of the characters' expressions on the stand: Marie, the old man with the unattractively mottled face. When asked his motive for the murder, Meursault replies, "It was because of the Sun." The camera pans the reporters, halting on the face of a youth watching with open, thoughtful blue eyes.

Meursault is found guilty and placed in his dark cell to await death. His thoughts are given to us in a soliloquy. He thinks of death and is relieved when morning comes and he has not been taken to be executed. He is afraid and thinks, "I've never liked being taken by surprise." The chaplain visits the cell despite Meursault's refusals to see him. As the priest sits, there is a shot of his open hands rubbing in consternation and near prayer. The chaplain has blue eyes, and the darkness has a blue tint. The camera focuses on his earnest, moist face as he tries to communicate with the condemned man his concept of God. Meursault admits that he does want things, and when he says that the idea of God or happiness is like wanting a better-shaped mouth, there is the ironic shot of the priest's face with its scarred lip.

After the chaplain leaves and Meursault is again alone in the darkness, Visconti provides his consummate image in the spirit of Camus' work. Meursault's face is in the dark, but his profile takes form in the light glimmering on it. His face seems adrift in the darkness, as though the embodiment of a man's soul. An alien spirit in the great darkness on the screen. The ending of *The Stranger* is remarkable. The camera shows Meursault's hands being bound behind him with a rope. His face is perspiring. His eyes seem wet and sad. A tear falls from his eye down his left cheek. As he awaits the "howls of execration," there is the slightest trace, the faint quiver, of a smile—of acceptance—for a moment on his lips, and the film ends.

Visconti in filming *The Stranger* is true to the work as Camus envisioned it. It may seem an exaggeration to comment at length on the director's use of color and detail, but it is important to do so because Visconti has filmed *The Stranger* with an eye toward perfect, and complete, selection. Each detail stirs with impact, with feeling. Visconti has achieved an exact visualization of the novel; his use of color and movement has translated the classic work of fiction into classic language of film.

CAREERS

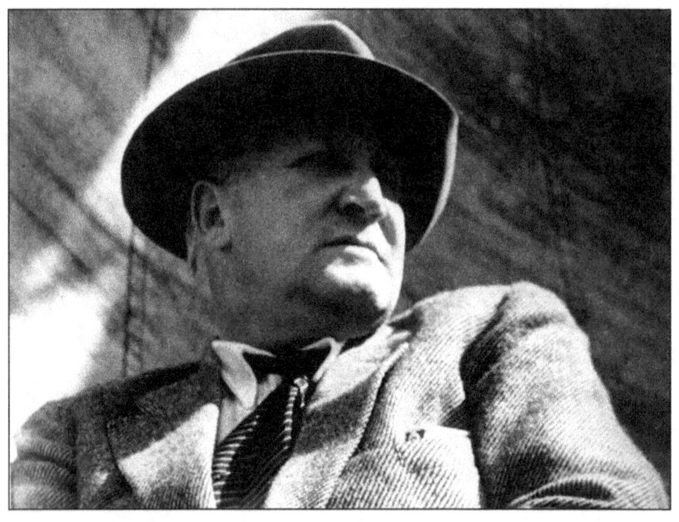

Robert Flaherty, widely regarded as the
"Father of the Documentary Film."

Robert Flaherty
Arthur Lennig

Perhaps there is no film figure more difficult to assess than Robert Flaherty. Not that his work is obscure or profound or subtle, but his name has been inalterably interwoven with various causes and movements about which a number of influential critics have become extremely partisan. To some, this father of documentary has become the watchword, the acme of perfection, the incorruptible man struggling against greedy and vulgar moguls. They have converted Flaherty into a symbol of one who went out to preach the Word, suffered a kind of martyrdom, survived his trials, and triumphed by becoming a venerated saint with annual homage at the Flaherty Seminars. Although documentarians make the pilgrimage and gather around like devotees, those critics and viewers who are less committed to Flaherty's work and ideas are apt to remain silent. Their caution is not ill-advised, for they know full well that questioning Flaherty's importance is like stirring up a nest of bees: stings are more likely than honey. But if the critic's role is to examine and evaluate, then he must put aside the personal affection he may feel for Flaherty or the role he attempted to play and discuss, instead, what Flaherty actually accomplished.

The problem in every art—and especially in the cinema because it developed so quickly from a mechanical invention into a means of expression—is to distinguish between what has historical importance and what continues to have esthetic value. The first man to paint on canvas, to use perspective, to use oils, to experiment with chiaroscuro, would be important historically, although the esthetic value of these milestones may be nil. Such a distinction between being first and being art (whatever ultimately "art" may be) has not been made frequently in the cinema, possibly because it is young or possibly because the people who choose to write on it have enthusiasms which transcend sober appraisal. But literature has such distinctions. Defoe's *Moll Flanders* and Horace Walpole's *The Castle of Otranto* are both firsts, and for that reason are important, but they are by no means as realized as works of Fielding or Jane Austen because of factors such as skill of narration, depth of character, structure and the whole problem of form. Similarly, Edwin S. Porter's *The Great Train Robbery* or Griffith's Biograph films are significant steps forward in the art of the cinema but do not reveal any particular esthetic merit. They are important for being first and should be shown for that reason, but they are by no means masterpieces.

To establish in cinema criticism distinctions between being first and being art is to incur all kinds of acrimony. These two areas have been too often muddled. Terms such as controversial, iconoclastic, obtuse and perverse are bandied about so that one wonders whether one is dealing with powers of judgment or the emotions of a football game. Flaherty, probably more than any so-called major figure, has had his cheering section. Only when myth and man, reputation and realization, and accomplishment, not intentions, are studied can Flaherty achieve his proper place in the *art* of the film.

Flaherty, according to his biography [by Arthur Calder-Marshall], *The Innocent Eye: The Life of Robert J. Flaherty* (["Based on research material by Paul Rotha and Basil Wright," 1963]), was—to put it bluntly—a rather ineffectual explorer of the Hudson Bay area who spent a few years wandering around the wastes of the Canadian north. He grew to know the Eskimo, purchased a movie camera, did filming, and, after a number of errors (including accidentally burning up his negative) returned with reels of film which he finally edited into *Nanook of the North*, released in 1922. This film immediately established him as a non-commercial man, as the father of documentary, and as someone working against the Hollywood grain of superficiality. *Nanook* was a first and, in terms of the other films released that year, one of the best. Whether it deserves to be ranked with the few dozen great films of the silent era, however, is another matter.

In April 1923, he set off for Samoa to do a film on the South Sea Islanders and returned on January 7, 1925, with footage which he eventually released as *Moana*. After *Tabu: A Story of the South Seas* [the 1931 film directed by F. W. Murnau after an abortive collaboration with Flaherty, who directed only the opening scene] and a few years of idleness, he set off for the Aran islands and finished *Man of Aran* (1934). His next important work was *Louisiana Story* (1948).

Flaherty, as his biography as well as his friends reveal, was an undisciplined person, a great verbal tale-weaver, an accomplished pub-crawler, and, apparently, quite a personable fellow. His adventures when he was in England during the thirties make good reading. To the effete, the orderly, the sophisticated, the cocktail party set, and the Terribly Serious, he seemed like some marvelously entertaining bear that floated by on an ice cake and did tricks. The men of Oxford and Cambridge gathered around amidst the bitters and listened to fanciful sagas of his exploring days. He was a bit of a Mark Twain speaking about adventures much farther north than the Mississippi and Hannibal. He played his rough Yankee role to the hilt and built an enviable off-screen reputation. He was a man, not a tricky merchant wheeling and dealing a financial empire, a romantic admirer of the simple, unspoiled life, not a purveyor of hokum. No one in his right mind could possibly be opposed to his intentions, but his realizations, unfortunately, are another matter. Sincerity, unless coupled with superb talent, cannot in itself achieve a masterpiece.

Flaherty's emphasis on people, not actors, on locale, not studio sets, on basic life, not civilized life, became particularly popular in the thirties. Although the intellectuals of the period reacted against the self-conscious experiments and art-for-art's-sake approach of the twenties, advocating social realism—the life of the worker, the poor, the undertrodden— Flaherty didn't quite fit. He was not wholly admired because his films avoided being "message" pictures. He did not depict the world as it actually appeared, nor did he have any social grievances. He was not interested in life as it was but life as it ought to be or as he imagined it had been. Furthermore, considering Flaherty's severe limitations as a tale-teller (on the screen) and his lack of awareness of what he was doing, there is doubt that he could have made a message picture even if he had wanted to. Certainly his attempts to work for the British documentary people and for the United States government ended in disaster.

Flaherty did not have any clearly articulated aim. But what he tried to do was to capture the essence of primitive life and to reconstruct its heroic aspects if they were no longer present. Nanook, for instance, spent his summers on tundra land, lived usually in a sod house, dealt with the trading store, used a gun, and did not really kill walruses the way he did. The Samoans seen in *Moana* did not make their clothing anymore, nor did they do much tattooing. The Aran Islanders had electricity and hadn't hunted sharks for generations. Flaherty "adjusted" reality. He tried to show the quaint aspects of primitive life, just as the tourist visiting Spain or Germany or Greece sets up his camera to avoid automobiles, Coca-Cola signs, TV antennae, and other tourists with cameras.

Nanook purported to be a film record of life in the north, but this was not true, as some explorers immediately pointed out. It did not depict life as it actually was; it was a rearrangement of life for the camera. But, by rearranging life before his camera, Flaherty also became responsible for its selection, organization, and esthetic construction. Unfortunately, however, he had little sense of film structure. He could make a shot, naturally, but he seemed to be unaware of the basic grammar of film. *Nanook* betrays this weakness; yet so foreign is the subject matter, and so winning is Nanook's personality that, coupled with our admiration and sympathy for this unspoiled, even heroic life, we ignore the failures of form for the originality of the content.

However, if the content is carrying the film rather than the form, how much can we attribute to artistry and how much to the basic material itself? A *National Geographic* story in stodgy prose is interesting not because of the skill of the

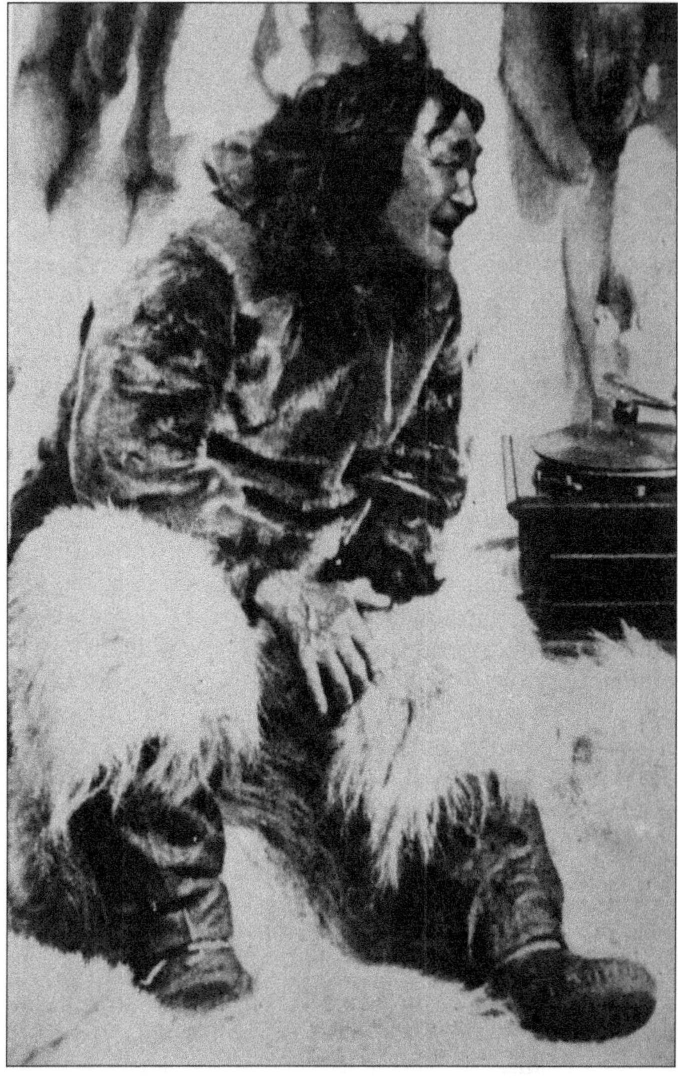

The humorous scene with Nanook (Allakariallak), the Canadian
Inuk hunter and fisherman, reacting to a phonograph at a white
man's trading post. This gag showing the clash of primitivism and
modernity in *Nanook of the North* has caused critical debate over
whether it is patronizing or satirical of colonialism, or both.
(Les Frères Revillon/Pathé)

writer (we grant that the writer or filmmaker knows enough to organize his material somewhat lucidly) but because of the content. The difference, then, between a report and a work of art is that the one could be done by almost anybody while the other could be done only by a specific person. One relies on fact to carry it through, the other on imagination. The one can be reproduced—providing the facts remain the same—whereas the other cannot, being the imaginative vision of a particular person. There is a difference between transference of information—using the medium to convey knowledge—and the use of the formal potentials of the medium. In literature we have a good example of such a problem. Stephen Crane was in a shipwreck and wrote an account for the newspaper which described the situation carefully and, in short, was faithful to the facts. Later on, however, he wrote "The Open Boat," which deals with the same incident but makes it live, not because it actually happened and was based on fact, but because it creates an esthetic reality. Unlike Crane, Flaherty does not shape his material; he doesn't bring to it the necessary control which a work needs to be considered art and not journalism. He did not have the skills and technique of a great artist, though he did have the integrity of one.

Flaherty tells a story (whatever there is of it) badly; he has no sense of architectonics, of structure, of pace. His work betrays that he simply does not understand the camera; he doesn't know how to move in for shots, or to contrast them to create mood or rhythm. A reading of his biography confirms this. He would shoot and shoot, not knowing what he was doing or where he was going. His wife confirms this:

> He made his pictures on the screen. For this he reversed the usual procedure in filmmaking: instead of thinking first, he shot first; and thinking came afterwards from the image on the screen. He gave up all scripting, pre-planning, all preconception. And this proved important, for it taught him the value of non-preconception.
>
> Non-preconception is a sort of abandonment, a letting-go, a surrender of the self to that which is

greater than the self, beyond the self, so that which is greater and beyond may be brought to light.

> Robert Hughes, *Film: Book I*
> *[The Audience and the Filmmaker]*,
> 1959, p. 63

Unfortunately, his wife found more "light" than most of his viewers. Not only was he faulty at building sequences within the film, but even at handling the individual shot. His irritating habit of panning almost constantly during *Man of Aran* (and not even panning well, so that his characters often disappear out of the frame and then as miraculously reappear—see the first few shots) makes the film at times a most sloppy visual experience. Admittedly, John Grierson thought just the opposite:

> No director has the same respect as Flaherty for the camera; indeed very few of them even trouble to look through the camera while it is shooting their scenes.... His own capacity for moving the camera in appreciation of... movements is an essential part of the magic. No man of cameras, to my knowledge, can plan so curiously, or so bewilderingly anticipate a fine gesture or expression.

> Grierson, *Grierson on
> Documentary*, 1946, p. 59

My only answer to Grierson's seemingly incredible opinion would be to request the reader to examine the shots of *Man of Aran;* they prove to a viewer less partisan than Grierson that Flaherty all too often does not anticipate movement but indeed is quite tardy in trying to keep up with it. Flaherty's editor for the film, John Goldman, almost went mad trying to select the few more accurate pans to use in the editing, and constantly cursed Flaherty for not taking more cut-away shots so that the action wouldn't jump from one take to the next. As Goldman said:

Flaherty's actual filmmaking took place not in the camera, not on the cutting bench, but in the projection room. Here he would sit running through reel after reel over and over again, panning for the golden nugget, and the only criterion for the recognition of this nugget was his own bare awareness.

During this long, tedious process there was no shape to the film, no beginning, no end.... There was no conscious thought directing it.

The Innocent Eye, p. 159

As a dramatic film director, I found his grammar and vocabulary, using those terms in a film sense, curiously limited.

The Innocent Eye, p. 160

Goldman said too that Flaherty had "no sense of the 'rhythm of film'; his delight was in the shot *per se,* not in the cumulative effect of shots arranged in a particular way." (*The Innocent Eye,* p. 157) His editor for his later films, Helen van Dongen, also confirms that Flaherty didn't know what to do with the material he shot.

Both of these editors brought a semblance of form to what they assure us was a kind of chaos. But the finished films still betray a basic confusion. It is not surprising that some of the discarded takes of *Aran* and *Louisiana Story*—reels upon reels, in fact—have been shown and admired for their beauty and sensitivity to nature; but all they prove is that Flaherty was more of a shot-maker than a filmmaker.

Because of Flaherty's severely flawed achievements, despite his employment of gifted professional editors, one wonders how Flaherty can be called a film Master, a major artist. In a *Time* magazine review of *The Innocent Eye,* the myth-making continued by comparing Flaherty to William Blake. If Blake's visions were sometimes obscure, sometimes, indeed, mad, his knowledge of the language was not. Blake knew English, knew meter, knew what effects he was after. Flaherty didn't. He was a poet with little knowledge of grammar,

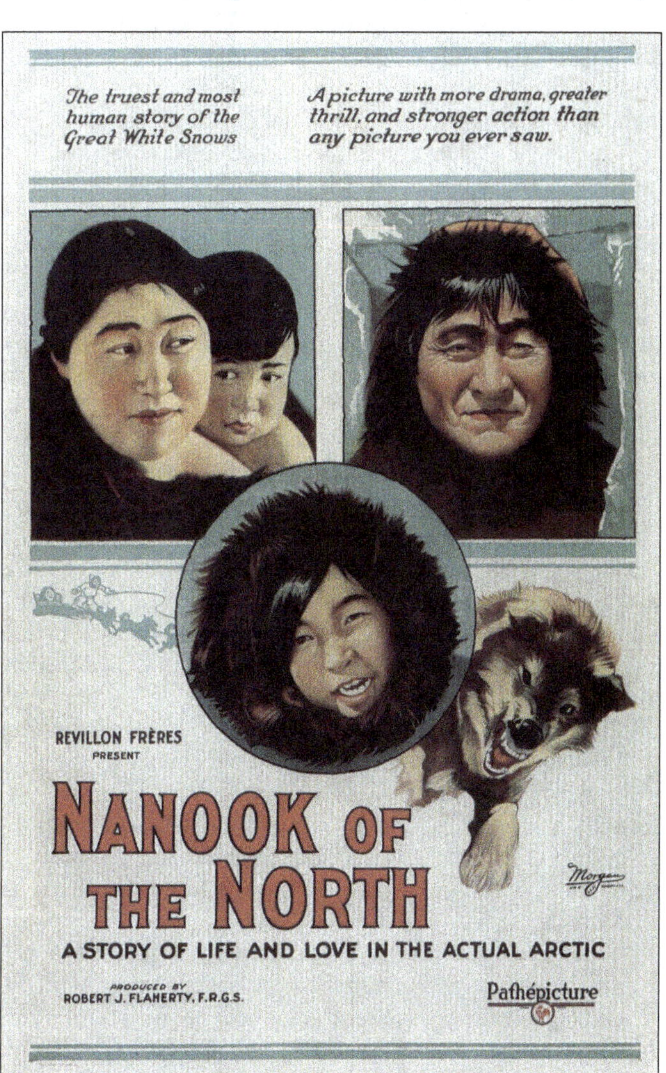

Original poster for the pioneering (semi-)documentary *Nanook of the North*, which became a surprise hit upon its release in 1922. (Les Frères Revillon/Pathé)

form and style. He would write and write and expect someone to cut his efforts into individual poems. But all the shrewd editing in the world cannot force material into a form which it lacks initially. Flaherty's eye may have been innocent, but innocence is a mixed blessing, a delightful quality in a girl, but ultimately a limitation unless it is coupled with an adult's experience and knowledge. The filmmaker needs innocence for freshness of vision, but he also needs the know-how to record and focus the vision. This control Flaherty never achieved.

Amidst all the praise that now in particular seems to be lavished on Flaherty, the criticism once directed at him has somehow been forgotten. In reviewing *Man of Aran*, C.A. Lejeune wrote that the film "is not a great picture, in the sense that *Nanook* was great.... *Man of Aran* has no story, not even the trace of a story...." *(The Innocent Eye*, p. 164) Graham Greene, hardly an obtuse observer corrupted by Hollywood, said, "Photography by itself cannot make poetic drama. By itself, it can only make arty cinema. *Man of Aran* was a glaring example of this; how affected and wearisome were those figures against the skyline, how meaningless that magnificent photography of storm after storm." *(The Innocent Eye*, pp. 165-66)

Let the reader not forget that Flaherty spent a long time on *Aran* and shot miles of film. The results, in terms of form, are very weak. Compare, for example, [Leni Riefenstahl's] *Triumph of the Will* (shot in six days) [after long preparation—Ed.] or the *Olympia*. The difference, really, is between someone who knows what [she] wants and knows how to get it and someone who doesn't.

It is clear that Flaherty was championed, and still is, not for what he gave us but for what he grew to represent. To men like John Grierson and Paul Rotha, both interested in the documentary movement, he loomed as a giant figure, the one man who had "made it," who had approached and indeed entered "the big time." Although Grierson himself did not entirely approve of Flaherty's work, he felt that Flaherty was a "soul-brother" and that anyone who criticized this big lovable man was criticizing a whole school of documentary and, indeed, truth and virtue:

[He] has stood uncompromisingly for everything that is fine in film. The story of his long fight with Hollywood is perhaps the best of all Hollywood stories, because it is the single one in which personal advantage has been sacrificed at every turn for a decent result.

Grierson on Documentary, p. 58

[When *Man of Aran* failed in Paris it was due to the] pessimism or inertia or stupidity of the commercial agent... (p. 134)

[*Moana* failed not because it was dull but because Hollywood liked only] garish spectacle and a redhot presentation of the latest curves. (p. 165)

And there's Charles Siepmann's comment:

Bob's films were denied promotion and distribution because they departed from Hollywood's prefabricated formulas for popular (i.e. box office) success.

Siepmann, "Robert Flaherty,"
Film: Book I, p. 73

Thus the intelligent filmgoer is pressured into liking Flaherty's works because they were not commercial successes. Their lack of story, dullness, and filmic ineptitudes are somehow transformed into virtues. But it is possible for the fair-minded critic to disapprove of Hollywood's tawdry values without necessarily building up Flaherty as a kind of noble opposition.

Flaherty is to be respected for trying to do something different, but to call him a supreme artist and put him in the ranks of Griffith, Eisenstein, von Stroheim and others is to be over-enthusiastic. Flaherty is the severely blemished artist whom the fair-minded critic—with no axe to grind—would like to admire more than he in all honesty can.

The documentarians have had their way with Flaherty and so the man and the genre have been married, for better or for worse, and have lived happily ever after. At least until now.

W. C. Fields and the Absurd World
Gerald Peary

Even the most adamant admirers of the films of W. C. Fields have found themselves on the defensive when the structure of these films has been questioned. There has appeared to be no way to argue against the standard attack—that the films are virtually plotless, that they are merely a series of clever vaudeville skits strung together without reason or connection.

"Nothing *happens* in a Fields film," adverse critics will say. "The picture ends about the same place where it began. The situation is the same; the characters are the same. "

It is interesting to note that identical arguments were used in another genre—as an attack on the plays of Samuel Beckett and other so-called "absurdists" when their dramas first appeared. It was only later that these strange plays in which "nothing happened" gained respectability, when it was realized that the apparent formlessness of the absurdist drama was really a revolutionary new form—a seemingly nonsensical, non-Aristotelian structure which legitimately articulated an absurd world in which literally "nothing" *does* happen and in which characters and situations remain forever and forever static.

The parallel between the films of W. C. Fields and the plays of the absurdists is not just coincidental. Although filmed obviously without philosophic intent, Fields's movies transcend their comic purpose and become, quite remarkably, a view of a world in every way analogous to that of the theater of the absurd. Regardless of the filmmakers' original intentions, it was the decision to place W. C. Fields at the center of

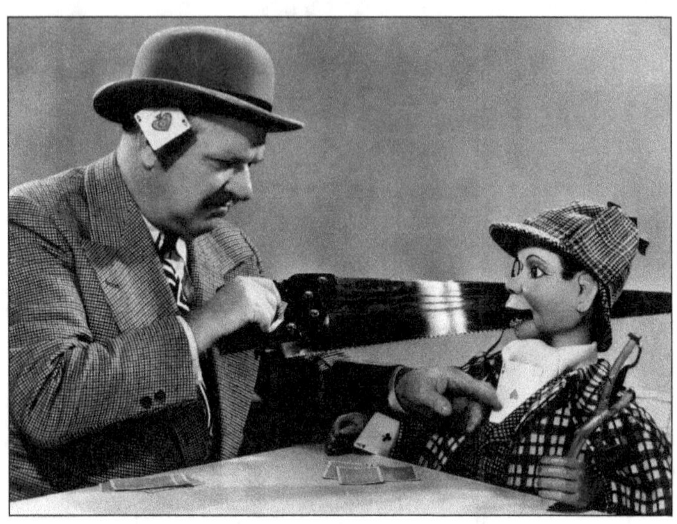

The absurdist worldview of W. C. Fields can be seen in many
forms, including his hostile reaction to his dummy co-star
Charlie McCarthy in *You Can't Cheat an Honest Man* (1939),
a stand-in for Fields's characteristic disdain for children. Fields had
a running feud with Charlie on ventriloquist's Edgar Bergen's radio
show. (Universal)

a film which dictated both form and content of an intended
project and forced the film into the world of the absurd.

Ionesco defined "absurdity" as "that which is devoid
of purpose." The character which Fields inevitably portrays
and the life pursued by this character certainly fit this definition. Every film finds Fields in the same position: "down
and out" in a meaningless and useless existence which does
not appear to have risen from anywhere nor be capable of
going anywhere. Life is always and inescapably the same.
Fields films, like the absurdist plays, take place in an "eternal
present."

There are always vague mentions (as in all of Beckett's dramas) of a previous existence apparently filled with
romance and adventure—battles with Indians, life among the
Eskimos or African aborigines. But these memories are so
ambiguous, hazy, and certainly permeated with half-truths,
that it is impossible to determine if they really ever happened.

In any case they have no relevance to the present state of Fields's character except in the slight reassurance they provide of a life which once seemingly was good.

The character Fields usually portrays is a comic variant of the ancient stock figure of the "braggart warrior"—the loud-mouthed adventurer who is really a coward and liar, the aging romantic who exuberantly pursues the young girl's hand, only, invariably, to lose out to the young lover.

But Fields's character, as he operates in an absurd world rather than the world of traditional comedy, has lost all his exuberance and does not believe for a minute that he has a real chance for love. The objects of his courtship are never the young, voluptuous virgins, but middle-aged, frigid little ladies who giggle at his colorful but innocuous speeches, or hardened *femmes fatales* with their best years behind them (typified by Mae West in *My Little Chickadee*) with whom he exchanges slightly risqué *double entendres* ("How's your ping pong?") but with whom he goes no further. As Fields states in *Mississippi,* "Women are like elephants. You like to look at 'em, but you wouldn't want to own one."

Sexual consummation, as in the plays of Samuel Beckett, has ceased to be a possibility in the Fields film. The traditional optimism of comedy symbolized by the sexual union of the deserving characters and the promise of a better world is replaced by "asexuality" as a symbol of a world beyond promise. Sex, like other all significant and meaningful actions in the Fields comedy, is reduced to words. Nor are the words themselves any kind of solace. There is no better dramatization of "lack of communication" than in the films of W. C. Fields. Except for the occasional streak of sentimentality tacked onto several of his films in which a "warm" relationship is concocted between Fields and his teenaged daughter or niece ("Good ol' Uncle Bill"), Fields walks through his movies in total isolation, mumbling to himself. He does not have even one friend in any of his pictures.

His own efforts to "break the ice" and be friendly are met with callousness (the brilliant scene with the waitress in *Never Give a Sucker an Even Break,* for instance). Likewise, Fields himself is often rude and suspicious of any friendship which is offered. His resistance to establishing dialogue makes sense. The kind of talk which passes between lesser characters in his films is so inane that attempts to communicate in themselves become absurd. There is no dialogue in Ionesco which so devastatingly pinpoints the babble which is called "conversation" than that in the Fields film.

An unforgettable example of this occurs in the great *It's a Gift.* Fields, a victim of insomnia, is lying in a hammock on the porch of the second floor of a three-story house. It is almost dawn and his eyes are finally closing. Suddenly he is jerked awake by a "conversation" between a mother (who is yelling down from the third-story porch) and her daughter, on the ground before the house. The daughter is about to embark on an errand, and the dialogue goes something like this:

"Mother, where should I go?"
"I don't care, honey. You go where you want to go. "
"No, I'll go where *you* want me to go."
"I won't tell you where to go."
"No, Mommy, tell me where to go."

Fields finally can take no more, as the conversation has moved from the inane to the claustrophobic. He interjects under his breath, "I'll tell you both where you can go!" The mother angrily responds, "I'm sorry, honey, I can't hear you. That awful man downstairs keeps *talking!*"

Fields, even more than Chaplin, embodies the idea of the absurdist antihero. Both Fields and Chaplin, like Vladimir and Estragon in *Godot,* are the tramps defeated by the world and left by the roadside, but both still retain vestiges of a previous existence of seeming worth and potential. Both maintain a facade of dignity in their dress—the too-tight formal jackets and top hats—which is undercut by their ludicrous behavior. Temperamentally, Chaplin never relinquishes the beautiful soul, which remains eternally optimistic and generous despite defeat after defeat. With Fields, sensitivity and sentimentality have been irreparably deadened. What is retained is a battered intellect, a superior if no longer totally rational mind which reveals itself through the incessant stream-of-conscious monologue that falls monotonously from the side of Fields's mouth and which (like similar speeches scattered throughout absurdist plays) produces the effect of the slowly unwinding machine repeating itself in rote fashion hundreds upon hundreds of times.

Critics have equated Chaplin's optimism with the unwavering hope of Beckett's characters. There is no connection. Chaplin's characters have a *right* to be optimistic. Their condition is subject to change; for, from Chaplin's political perspective, Society, the oppressor, can be changed. The tramp can become the aristocrat. And even if poverty is the temporary condition of Man, He can find meaning in life through love. Chaplin as creator is the perennial romantic. Beckett and Fields are, of course, post-love. Chaplinesque romance becomes vicious parody in Beckett. And is it possible to imagine Fields instead of Chaplin walking hand-in-hand with Paulette Goddard into the *Modern Times* sunset? Likewise, the world of the absurd and Fields's world are post-political. Social change means nothing and is not even worth considering. Man's life is innately absurd, beyond the salvation of enlightened society.

Finally, is life worth living? Chaplin, more in the spirit of early Thornton Wilder than of any of the playwrights with whom he usually is equated, answers emphatically, "Yes!" Life is exciting. Even at its darkest, it is filled with beautiful and touching moments. Fields, on the other hand, is far past searching for beauty or bothering to find meaning in life. If there is a word to characterize him it is "tired." His eyes are dead, completely expressionless. He rarely laughs or smiles in his "comedy" films. His conversation trails off incoherently; and even he himself is bored by what he is saying. He is happy only when standing at a bar, drinking and "bulling," temporarily elated only when, in true antiheroic terms, he acts briefly (if impotently) on his own deep-seated cynicism and cheats an idiot, strangles a child, kicks a baby, etc.

This then is the condition of W. C. Fields, exactly that of the characters in theater of the absurd: isolated, bored by himself and other people, beyond love, beyond politics, certainly beyond religion, skeptical of beauty, skeptical of sentimentality, incapable of finding any salvation in the world and unable, and finally uninterested, in changing his position.

But Fields goes on though there is no reason, even though what is ahead is exactly what is now and what has been before (thus the circular, non-progressive structure of his films), even if, differently from Chaplin, there is no possibility of a "happy ending," really of an "ending" at all. This, then, is what Beckett really is talking about, and Chekhov before him: "bravery in the face of absurdity," the unconscious philosophic essence lying beneath the masterful comic portrayals of W. C. Fields.

The Titans of Terror: Karloff & Lugosi*
Arthur Lennig

I.

Boris Karloff and Bela Lugosi—those names emblazoned on marquees throughout the Depression thirties and the hot- and then Cold War forties—were once, and for many people still remain, the Titans of Terror. Although they seldom appeared in the best theaters, their constant appeal to our strange Odyssean longings for adventure assured them of substantial followings and long, successful careers.

Their better films, those made during the thirties, would not compare well with more recent horror films if we were to connect an audience to an adrenaline and perspiration recorder. These older movies are curiously sedate and often naive. This is not necessarily a fault of their directors or content, for films of the thirties—at least most of the serious ones—are almost always paced more slowly. Audiences either took longer to understand things, or at least tolerated frequent

---

* *Titans of Terror is* the title of a book that Arthur Lennig and Paul Jensen have been working on for the past few years, long before the rash of rather superficial books on the same subject. "Our project may someday see the light, but if not, let the following pages at least be a gray monument to our eulogistic attempt." Lennig has concentrated on the introduction and on Lugosi; Jensen on the credits and Karloff. Some of the remarks on Lugosi have been considerably revised from *Classics of the Film* (1965). [The *Titans of Terror* book has not appeared, but Lennig published *The Count: The Life and Films of Bela "Dracula" Lugosi* in 1974 and revised and expanded it as *The Immortal Count: The Life and Films of Bela Lugosi,* in 2003.]

largos in the rhythm far more than present audiences. This restrained pace, however, has its advantages: it often achieves an air of oppressive dread.

These films are also hampered by their musical accompaniments. Those made in the first years of sound were unwilling to use music unless it had a specific source, and for this reason the two classic films, *Dracula* and *Frankenstein* (both 1931), are without any music behind the action. Compared to souped-up electronic scores, or hundred-piece orchestras perfectly timed to come to a crashing climax precisely at the opening of a door or at the revelation of a face in the moonlight, this musical silence can often be deadening, although at times this quietness creates its own gloomy effect.* Horror films made further into the thirties began to use orchestral accompaniment, but even that is comparatively quiet and sober. A few somber chords, a brief statement in the bass, suggest that maybe all is not quite well in the little Transylvanian town where bats are seen flickering against the sky or in the village of Frankenstein where weird flashings and curious buzzing sounds haunt the night air.

These older horror films may perhaps seem tepid to those of the modern generation for other reasons than their slow pace and lack of exciting music. They also contain very little violence. Although not consciously adhering to the tenets of the Greek drama which demanded that all violent action be committed offstage, these films reflect the less brutal, and, indeed, genteel taste of the thirties. Of course there is violence, but it is generally handled with some restraint. Chairs are not smashed over people's heads, nor are bodies disgustingly mutilated before one's eyes. We never see rotting corpses or dismembered bodies, nor do we see Dracula lapping up gushing blood. This is not to say that Dracula was on a low-

---

* In the original *Dracula*, the director attempted to get around the problem of background music by placing Dracula's first meetings with the Seward family at a Concert Hall in London. There the Court tells his attractive quarry that "to die, to be really dead; that must be glorious. There are far worse things awaiting man than death." These lines are underscored by the ominous chords of the orchestra. Unfortunately, it is the only scene with music, except for the credits, which are accompanied by music from *Swan Lake*.

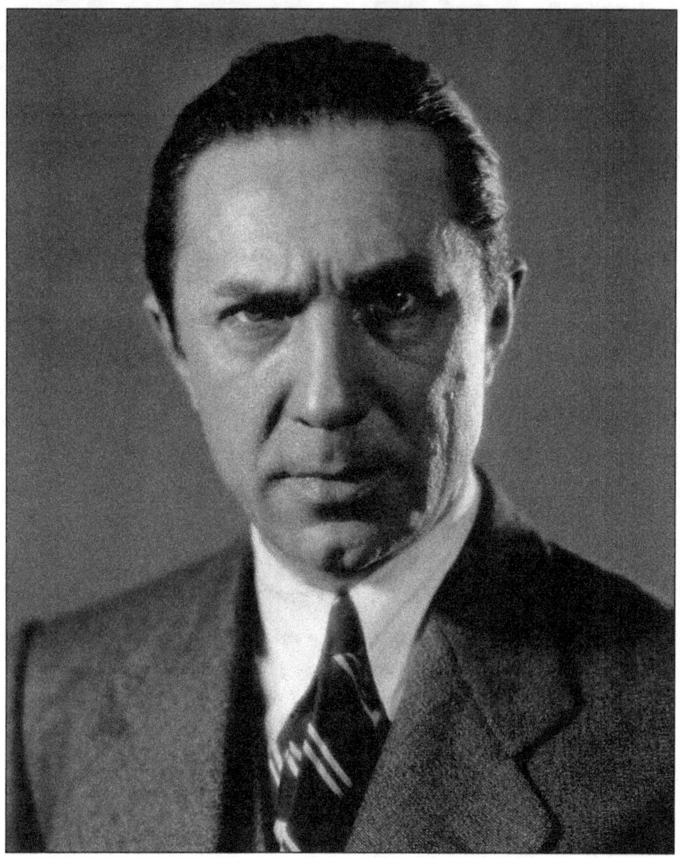

Portrait of Bela Lugosi.

protein diet, but that his actions are more circumspectly and less coarsely observed. Realities of spurting veins and clotted blood, of reeking pools and slow coagulations would have to wait, much like the basic and earthy facts of sex, until the more literal decades of the fifties and sixties. That the vampire's attraction for young women may descend below the neck is only vaguely hinted at in the original *Dracula.* Heroines in all these films remain clothed and even in the white dress or nightgown (always *de rigueur* for the genre), there is very little voyeuristic pleasure.

In terms of physical and aural shock, violence, and sex, then, the films of Boris and Bela are dated. As sheer visceral productions, they are about as effective as a maiden aunt's limping approach and asthmatic cry of "boo" to a little child playing on the rug. He hears her footsteps, knows her rather corny sense of humor, and is slightly bemused at her vain attempts to scare him.

If there can be any defense of these older films, it must be along different lines from those of mere shock. True, they can be defended as nostalgia. But they are more worthy than that. Some are masterpieces of mood and atmosphere, excursions into subtle realms of the weird. Besides their primary appeal of frightening adventure, they are also—though unintended to be so by their producers and directors—fascinating revelations into the sociology, philosophy, morals and even filmic techniques of the time.

Both Boris and Bela (their screen selves, of course) were the product of a still somewhat naive age that balanced the richness of the Gothic tradition with the realities of modern science. The Gothic aspects provided the myths: vampires, ghosts, alchemists, Byronic heroes, monsters created by man, and even the architectural trappings. Science, on the other hand, provided X-rays, cosmic rays, evolution, atomic energy and the unfading problems of broad experimentation versus ethics, of the scientific quest versus human values.

In the previous century and in the earlier part of our own, scientists were individuals with strongly moral and religious backgrounds who were aware of their cultural heritage of humanism. But soon science left behind the ethics and morality of the Biblical tradition and other old-fashioned concepts of good and evil. It no longer tried to reconcile itself with ancient prophecies or theological concepts. It didn't worry about "the soul" or life everlasting or even the concepts of love, honor, duty, patriotism, loyalty and all the other sticky nouns that still occasionally plague us. Instead, affected by relativism, it began to debate and then to ignore and finally to forget that rich past—a past full of superstitions and "thou shalt nots"—and became worshipful of the laboratory experiment and the statistical table. Whereas the earlier scientist was trying to unroll the mystery of God's universe and saw an almost religious quest in the very process of investigation, the modern scientist, though infinitely more efficient, is less "deep." His quest is much less passionate, his goal more circumscribed. He realizes that professionally he is far better off without feelings and emotions—what today could be described as "hang-ups." Lugosi's role as Dr. Vollin in *The Raven* is a superb example. He has been brilliantly functioning, but called out of his private world of experiment to operate on a young girl, he finds himself fatally attracted and ultimately distracted. Since she won't have him, and his brain must remain clear for thinking, he decides to torture her as she has tortured him. This is a perfect instance of the film's scientist being unable to reconcile his "human" side with his intellectual side. Lugosi could not adjust these two aspects of himself, being much too passionate in both. But the modern scientist is much more adjusted.

And so a new breed—which was foreshadowed in the Karloff-Lugosi films—has now taken over the world. Science has become the new faith; the white-coated men will bring not only physical salvation but psychic salvation as well. Even the drug-taking of today seems to be a curious mixture of the two drives. By means of chemicals one tries to get visions, to escape the self, and therefore in some way to find it. The goal is achieved not through contemplation, studied repose, insight, or mysticism, but chemically. Science has given us not only instant potatoes but instant vision. One of the results is of course the cool generation; they are in a sense a byproduct of the scientific approach which, in its extreme forms, seems to be more interested in eradicating emotions than enjoying or suffering with them. Not to be involved and therefore not to be hurt becomes the goal. And even sex—which was once idealistically the end result of love—becomes an end in itself. Love, the scientist realizes, can't be defined or measured or even explained. He lets it go and settles upon measuring blood pressure, sexual enlargement, and erogenous zones. Here at least a graph can be made and results published.

The problem of love doesn't enter too much into the horror films of the thirties except perhaps as a simple plot device. But a different kind of love often appears: a passionate involvement in a goal. Young Henry Frankenstein (Colin

Clive) in the original film explains that he is overwhelmingly interested in discovering the mysteries of life not so much for himself, but as a challenge. To him the creation of life was vindication of man as thinker and doer. But even so he is opposed in the film by his former professor, Dr. Waldman (played by Edward Van Sloan), who tells him that he has gone beyond the precepts of God, that man must not tamper with certain things which should remain mysteries, that this particular challenge should not have been taken up, for success would mean that Frankenstein has claimed for himself a role that belongs solely to God. One moment, which no critic or admirer of the film seems to remember, makes this point terribly clear. When Henry sees the hideous creature before him, hears him being tormented by the servant, watches its pathetic and somewhat malevolent face and its halted actions, he is overwhelmed with horror at what he has done. The old professor demands that the creature be destroyed, thus echoing in many ways the sentiments of the audience as well as the theme: that man must not go beyond his legitimate domain. Since that time, of course, the term "legitimate" has been vastly broadened. Ironically, the old professor is killed by the monster, but his death is even more symbolic in terms of later horror films and of twentieth-century life. Such spokesmen—and not without some justice—are now almost completely absent from the contemporary scene. When they do appear, they are old fuddy-duddies or crackpots and ranked at the same laughable level as anti-fluoridation fanatics.

The films of the thirties caught the transitional period during which science was having more and more impact on everyday living. The public, however, still brought up on Adam and Eve and "God's will be done," found this conflict fresh and new. This was the day before miracle drugs, extermination camps, atom bombs, shots to the Moon and other evidence of the "deductive" process. Today, despite science's mixed blessings, the public accepts progress as a matter of course. The scientist, in fact, is the modern hero. The brighter students are attracted to the challenge of science, to its financial rewards and to its lure of discovery. But, in terms of man himself, science is in some way the enemy. Cutting through

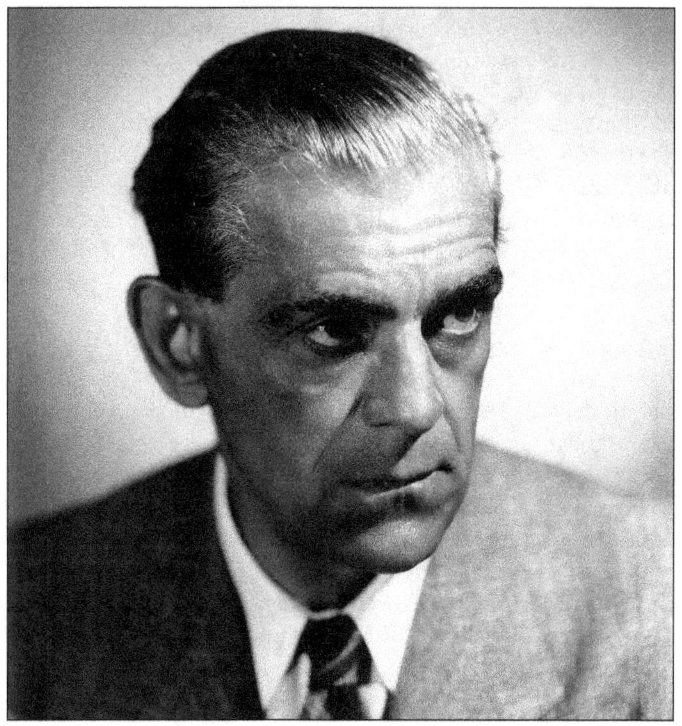

Portrait of Boris Karloff.

the murkiness of semantics, of our mixed motives, of our hypocrisies and pretensions, it questions all of our conduct. Those qualities which many humanists had thought admirable have been dispassionately examined and shown to be ignobly motivated. Man—that once-whole entity—has now been splintered into a creature formed by genes, environment, diet and a curious combination of body chemicals. Thus man in a sense has lost his soul, his sacredness of Self, and now is merely a preconditioned animal. Even love, whatever that may be, is now produced by Pavlovian conditioning, and passion is only the number of orgasms per week. To the modernists, Romeo is as strange and passé as the dodo.

The horror films of today reflect these changes. The modern scientist is no longer a passionately seeking Lugosi on some fantastic quest or a cruelly neglected Karloff who has discovered something of world-shaking import. Instead, their younger counterparts are colorless. The scientist drives to his laboratory from his house in suburbia, plays tennis on the weekends, tosses ball in the backyard with his children, and listens to his emotion-filled wife with some degree of tolerance. He is bland, efficient, hard-working, knowledgeable, and a crashing bore. He doesn't have the color of a Lugosi or even a Karloff. The modern scientist may be experimenting with genetics, readjusting genes, and creating test-tube life. (Shades of Dr. Pretorius, that urbane, sophisticated, and totally decadent "scientist" in *Bride of Frankenstein* who grows miniature people from "seed.") In contrast, the modern experimenter sitting home listening to hi-fi and reading a magazine is dabbling with the very secret of life, doing it matter-of-factly, carefully writing up reports and having the departmental secretary run off conclusions on the ditto machine. The larger issues have shrunk to blend in with these everyday aspects, and no elderly conscience walks through the white, fluorescent-lit, and air-conditioned corridors to acquaint the scientist with the dignity and implications of his quest.

The parson, hardly clear on his own religion, finds the questions of predestination, guilt and atonement, and original sin quite beyond him—echoes of a superstitious and constipated past. He is more likely to be screening Bogie movies for the students, talking at the local coffeehouse, and dispensing free advice on abortions. At the same time, the humanists are too busy enlarging their own lists of publications or struggling with moonlighting jobs to worry about the scientists. And so science is flooding forward unchecked, and worship of the Fact becomes the new religion. Philosophical grandeur is lost in a morass of environment, toilet training, and statistical tables. Who but fundamentalists, paranoids, squares, and assorted eccentrics would bother opposing the scientist now'?

Titans can exist only in an age which allows them, and so Bela and Boris—in their roles as scientists—are definitely of the past. Their like shall never come again. We must return to their era to find Byronic figures with depths to their souls and extreme emotional desires, to observe Promethean men struggling with the mysteries of the universe and thereby acknowledging that such mysteries exist, and to follow scripts quaint enough to imply the Faustian question of how far an explorer should venture. Such questions have not been outdated. They are, if anything, more keen today than ever before.*

In the frequently Faustian quest for creating life, creating a super ray, bringing people back to life, the role of Gretchen is not a large one. Women appear in horror films, but they are seldom of much importance. Often they function as a means of creating terror—the girl confronted with the monster or mad scientist—and sometimes she appears as a plot device, such as a nosy girl reporter *(Bride of the Monster)*, but for the most part the horror villains are a manly lot more interested in philosophical or metaphysical problems than in sheer romance. In the original *Frankenstein,* for example, the young doctor has neglected his girl; his only mistress is science. Although most of the horror villains do not care too much about women—at least until they encounter them during the film—their assistants do. They are close enough—with their limited intelligence and, frequently, handicapped body—to have regard and compassion for the girl and often cross up their "Master" at a crucial moment. In *The Raven* (1935), Lugosi is willing to kill the girl who has "tormented" him (although her torment was unintentional), but his maimed assistant (Karloff) vanquishes Lugosi and causes his death. In *Bride of the Monster* (1954), one of Lugosi's last films, again the assistant (Lobo) attacks Lugosi at the last moment, saving the girl. In other films, such as *White Zombie* (1932), the man partially responsible for transforming a girl he likes into a zombie repents of his act and therefore in a sense crosses Lugosi's "plans" for the girl. Ultimately, the one-time confederate kills Lugosi and the girl is rescued.

For the most part, women in horror films are a pest, a kind of necessary evil for the plot, but they are never really sympathetically depicted. Thus these horror films had a strong appeal for younger boys (before they were as sexually advanced or aware as today) because the films didn't like women any more than they did. There were no soupy or

---

* Bergman in *The Magician* revived—though infinitely more intelligently—some of these issues.

drippy scenes to interfere with the action. In this sense, the horror films were in many ways similar to the Westerns.

Occasionally, however, the so-called heavies did not ignore women entirely. Lugosi in *Voodoo Man* captures young girls but only so he can use their "will to live" to save his wife who has "been dead for twenty-two years." Such marital devotion by Lugosi is rare in his films and probably one can say that *Voodoo Man* was an aberration in the horror cycle. The screen Lugosi was too much of a "loner" to be saddled with a wife and children.

The one scene that often was looked forward to by audiences—and the one really valuable contribution the girl made to the film—was the "encounter." In *Frankenstein* this occurs when the monster crawls into the bridal chamber just before the wedding. This pattern of the girl meeting the evil reality appears in direct and muted forms throughout most of the films. In *White Zombie* the girl meets Lugosi right in the first few minutes of the film. In *Bride of Frankenstein* the shock of recognition is transferred from the heroine to a nosy neighbor woman who helps what she thinks is her husband from the burnt-down mill, only to see the Frankenstein monster before her. In some of the poorer films of the early forties, a Negro often encountered something mysterious and bulged his eyes in fear and terror. There must always be someone impressionable to react to the so-called horror.

Although recognition scenes still remain, other values besides the God-science conflict have disappeared. When Count Dracula meets a lovely young girl in the original film, he speaks of the abbey he has leased in England, and compares it to "the broken battlements of my own castle in Transylvania." The girl, intrigued by this strange Gothic love for the decaying and dilapidated, replies by quoting some lines of poetry to him. Significantly, Dracula and the girl first meet at a concert, while in *White Zombie* the girl plays Brahms and in *The Raven* the doctor plays Bach. Such a level of culture and style—even if the poetry isn't quite good or the music anything but old warhorses—is seen only in these vintage horror films. Today's vampire more closely resembles the Marquis de Sade than our distinguished and familiar Count, as he and the camera stare with nothing more than basic desire at the heroine's bulging bodice. Of course the vampire's victim has always been a sexual object, but she used to be desired for her beauty and temperament as well.

The older horror films have personality as well as intellectual passion; at least they contain characters who would be interesting to have over to dinner. Henry Frankenstein (as played by Colin Clive) is far more lively than the bland James Bond, and even crusty old Professor Van Helsing is far more interesting than many faculty members who come to mind. Certainly Count Dracula genuinely likes those wolves in the Transylvanian Alps, cherishes the old bottle of wine (though he himself slakes his thirst in less-vintage liquid), and has his guests drink from a silver goblet rather than a paper cup. With his marvelous bearing, delightful accent, and *Weltanschauung*, he radiates an old-world, if somewhat deadly, charm. As Dr. Vollin in *The Raven*, Lugosi is a keen intellect, a rapturous admirer of Poe. In *White Zombie* he is a master of the occult. As the scientist in *The Man with Nine Lives* or as a brain surgeon in *Black Friday* (1940), Karloff is a pleasant, kindly, cultured man.

Personality and perhaps even eccentricity are as absent from our films as they are from present-day American society. Everyone looks or acts like everyone else; even the non-conforming hippies have their common costume, language, addictions and politics. Lugosi and Karloff did not. They were individuals, with their own distinctive voices and faces; they resembled no one else, not even each other.

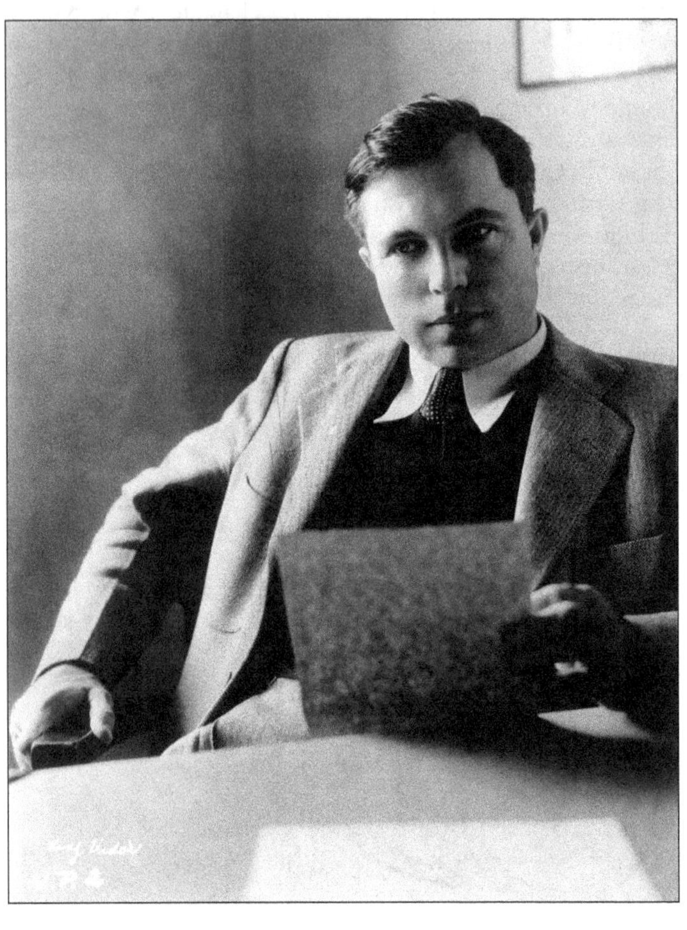

King Vidor at the time of his independent 1934 feature
Our Daily Bread, which electrified our Madison audience when he
brought it to campus. (Viking Productions/ United Artists)

A Random Sampling of Directors
William Donnelly

I didn't know Keaton was dying of throat cancer when I wrote him asking him to come to Wisconsin to speak. (I'd envisioned a couple of days of Keaton on campus because he deserved any honor we could give him.) But his death didn't kill the Wisconsin Union film committee's enthusiasm for bringing a speaker, and we built a series around Jean-Luc Godard. The big ripple in the New Wave canceled his tour at the last minute [Godard did come to campus later], but we already had the series by then: King Vidor, Shirley Clarke, George Stevens. A random sampling of directors: Vidor, a pupil of Griffith, one of the great innovating pioneers. Clarke, *magna mater* of the New York Underground who came to directing through dance films, ultimately a dancer, and a jaunty tough cookie. Stevens, one of the current Greats, a big-screen, big-star, big-film director.

A good sampling, and a random one. I keep saying that because what surprised me was that they were so much alike. I was coolest on Vidor, at first. I'd read about *Hallelujah* and *The Big Parade,* of course. But the only Vidor film I'd seen was *War and Peace,* and I remembered it as a handsome sprawl of a film, somewhat miscast, considerably overlong. I hadn't seen *Duel in the Sun* but had heard it dismissed as mawkish, slow, overlong.

Then I read a little more and found that Vidor was respected for the realism of his films and for their careful editing. *Film Culture* put him in the third rank in its famous American Directors number, and it's no disgrace to be there.

An amiable man, young for his years, King Vidor didn't have bad words for anyone. We tried to bait him into saying that Jennifer Jones was stupid, but it was obvious that he was very loyal to his stars and would say no such thing. Though he had made technological innovations that won him a rank near Eisenstein and Pudovkin in the silent era, he seemed to feel that his recent work was more interesting to people. He was proud of the stars and the scope of *War and Peace.*

The Big Parade beguiled the critics (in 1925) because of its lack of heroic posturing. Vidor had never seen war, but his battle footage was regarded as a touchstone. He was hailed as a realist. Looking at it today, one wonders where the reputation came from. His approach spawned a new kind of understated just-folks posturing. His innovations became the clichés. To us, the film looks contrived and conventional.

Still, one could respect him retroactively as an innovator, and there were other daring films on social themes. *The Crowd* dealt with anomie in urban civilization. *Hallelujah,* his first sound film, was made on location in the South with an all-Negro cast. He was happy to talk about how he dubbed in studio sound effects to supplant the lack of recording equipment in his location footage (a conscious strategy, also, to avoid studio interference). This innovation was one of the discoveries that freed the camera. Still, I felt he was strangely reticent about the film. Vidor may be worried about it because critics have objected to the picture of the Negro community it gives, maintaining that it reinforces stereotypes.

Our Daily Bread electrified the audience. Vidor showed a beautifully edited sequence in which determined farmers build an irrigation ditch. The gush of water into parched cornfields at the end of a beautifully paced buildup (timed, Vidor explained, with a metronome) touched a number of basic themes. That kind of painstaking work springs only from conviction. Vidor had been moved by a *Reader's Digest* story about farmers who worked cooperatively during the Depression. Obviously, he feels deeply about men at work on the soil. As a social philosopher, he is limited. He is moved by situations. And these are usually the situations which move the sentimental liberal. But his talk is anecdotal and human, even when he is challenged by more abstract questions.

His contribution, he feels, is his theory of film as music, as highly structured rhythm. On reflection, I decided that his emotional openness, his lack of commitment to or concern with complex philosophical or political problems made him an ideal representative for his audience. They too are generally of good will, more interested in the situation than its implications. Vidor is ahead of them, but not too far ahead.

He telegraphed Fellini on the opening night of *La Dolce Vita,* because he too had long wanted to make a film in which an innocent young girl is a symbol of purity. He was amazed that Fellini had hit upon the symbol. This film has been on his mind for some time and he mentioned it frequently. For Vidor an emblem like that is an adequate and original theme.

A man of feeling, then, painstaking when moved. An innovator, a man of integrity. (Rather than edit sequences out of *The Big Parade* he took it home and shortened it by removing single frames.) A man interested in social issues as they affect his emotions. A man moved by the landscape of America and by the people. And what if it's all a pose? After all, I only spent a few hours with him. Masks can reveal as much as faces.

Now Stevens. Less open. More talkative, but inclined to lose himself in abstractions. Inarticulate, but aware of it. An automatic smile that snaps on as if someone had switched a wire. Unbuttons the sleeve on his coat, rolls it up to make his watch visible.

Likes the good old days of shooting Westerns. An innovator: first one to use panchromatic film. Still a master of filters, lighting, composition. Films he had most fun on were silent Westerns featuring "Rex, King of the Wild Horses"; they packed back up into the mountains on horseback, left civilization behind. Like Vidor in love of American landscape. Like Vidor anecdotal in conversation. Tells the story of James Dean's death as if it were a short film. First sequence, Jimmy the star. Scenes of him hunkering up the back stairs of the studio to talk to fellow horse-lover, outdoorsman Stevens; bringing his Porsche to the set. Buddies, inarticulate together. Sequence of bad news at studio. Liz crying on stairs. Sequence of accident itself (flashback). Details of lighting of the scene. Action.

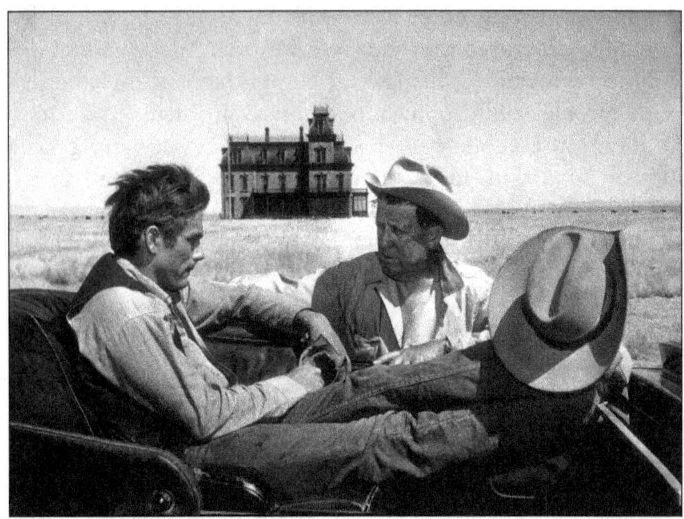

James Dean and director George Stevens, seen on location in Marfa,
Texas, had a troubled relationship during the making of the young
star's last film, *Giant* (1956). But Dean gives a great performance as
Jett Rink, the field hand turned oil tycoon in this epic film version
of Edna Ferber's novel about changes in Texas society over many
years of twentieth-century history. (Warner Bros.)

Convinced he makes films from conviction. Convinced
films made from films bad. Doesn't like idea of film being
a mass of conventions. Prefers to think of them as moving
records of reality. Feels that what will authentically move him
will move audience. Unable to defend *Shane* as a film growing
out of his revulsion at killing. Though he calls it his "war
film" and tells how he waited impatiently to make a statement
on his war experiences, when asked to reconcile stated theme
with action in film shoots out a cloud of abstractions like a
squid. Doesn't allow himself to be pinned down philosophi-
cally. Doesn't realize that *Shane* is one of the most archetypal
of Westerns.

Likes to work with social issues: *Giant* (racial discrimina-
tion), *A Place in the Sun* (abortion, class barriers), *The Diary
of Anne Frank* (Nazism). Did *The Greatest Story Ever Told*
to dramatize a compelling myth. Like Vidor in taste for films
with messages. Like Vidor in inarticulateness, although more

acutely, since he likes to talk. Like Vidor in sentimentality. (Talks about the heart and means it.) Unaware of largely conventional themes in his films. Loves his films and will fight for them (suing NBC for what they did to one of them).

These men articulate in their films. Have trouble with words. Specialize in emotions. Are sensitive to the temper of the age.

Clarke hasn't done enough to qualify as a great. One really good film, one poor one. Still, she's from a different plane. Started by making terrific short dance films. Filmed *The Connection,* essentially a play. Formed a company to go into Harlem to shoot from a novel about a hang kid, *The Cool World.* Did a remarkably fine job. Fought with the cops, fought with unions. Charmed the inhabitants. Spent a third of a million dollars on a film that offended the gentility of the critics. Lost money on it.

Showed up here in cowboy boots, hat. Small, peppery woman. Not much like Vidor and Stevens at first glance. Talkative, bright, college grad. But why the cowboy boots? Like Stevens and Vidor: a taste for adventure, for the unexpected. Not outdoorsy and inarticulate, but a lady with a red-hot social conscience. Feels that the film's message should mow 'em down. Vidor: "A film should have a message." Stevens: "Why make a film if you don't have something to say?" Clarke: "Look at this shit that's going on, you crumbs." A little subdued, now. Reckons her next film will have a conventional story so she can get distribution. (Wants to make a little money, too.) Buzzing with Underground gossip. Who's doing what? A booster for her gang on the Lower East Side. Dreams of Underground setting up its own distribution. Still admits she'd jump at a Hollywood offer.

[Now, in 1968, we note that her new film, *Portrait of Jason,* is most unconventional, that she has set up Underground distribution, and that there has been no Hollywood offer as yet.—Editor's note: Clarke was brought to Hollywood by Roger Corman to direct a 1975 crime comedy, *Crazy Mama,* but their collaboration fell through due to creative disagreements, and the film was directed by Jonathan Demme. Clarke played an independent filmmaker in Agnès Varda's 1969 independent film made in Hollywood, *Lions Love,* and

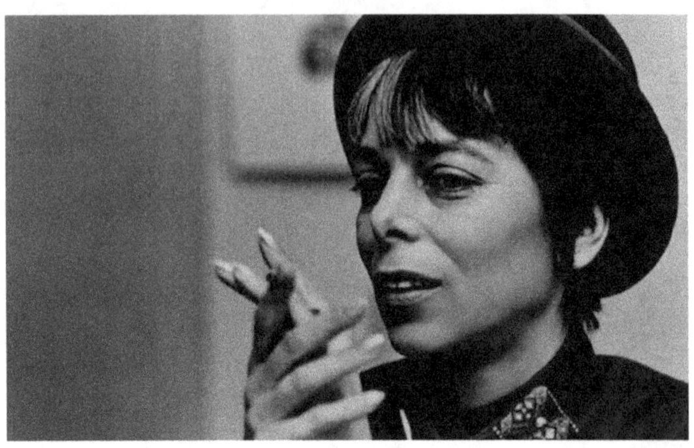

Portrait of Shirley Clarke.

Clarke was a professor of film at the University of California, Los Angeles, from 1975 to 1983.]

Good eye for shots. Doesn't hold shots too long, as does Stevens, doesn't carry over the slow emotional pacing of silent films like Vidor's. Still, can she ever win the respect of actors, New York bankers, critics, etc., as Vidor and Stevens have? A woman has a hard row. But you can't help but like her. She has plenty of reasons to be cocky. Same anecdotal approach to life. Same red-hot Americanism. Same taste for beauty in her shots. Same concern for rhythm. Same concern for people.

How to be a great director: love pace, composition, work, beauty, your country and its people. Feel, don't think. Have a taste for the Frontier: Harlem or Wyoming. And if you want to make money, find a potent emotional appeal in clichés.

Robert Rossen's Last Interview
Daniel Stein

[This interview was conducted in Robert Rossen's New York apartment on December 23, 1965. He died on February 18, 1966, at the age of 57. A hard-nosed and individualistic writer-director, Rossen began as a New York playwright and stage director. He entered movies as a Hollywood screenwriter in 1936, working on such films as *They Won't Forget, The Roaring Twenties*, and *A Walk in the Sun.* He later recalled that he was a member of the Communist Party "from about 1937 to 1947." After his directorial debut in 1947, Rossen made such critically acclaimed films as *Body and Soul* (written by Abraham Polonsky, who was later blacklisted) and *All the King's Men.*

[Rossen was one of the Hollywood Nineteen who were subpoenaed to testify before the House Committee on Un-American Activities in 1947, but he was one of eight who were not called. He was blacklisted and moved to Mexico after disavowing Communism but refusing to name names and taking the Fifth Amendment when called to testify before HUAC in 1951. In 1953, however, Rossen restored his career by acting as a friendly witness before HUAC, naming sixty people as Communist Party members. He told the committee, "I don't think, after two years of thinking, that any one individual can even indulge himself in the luxury of individual morality or pit it against what I feel today very strongly is the security and safety of this nation." Polonsky was not one of those named to HUAC by Rossen but said of his former colleague in 1997, "You wouldn't want to be on a desert island

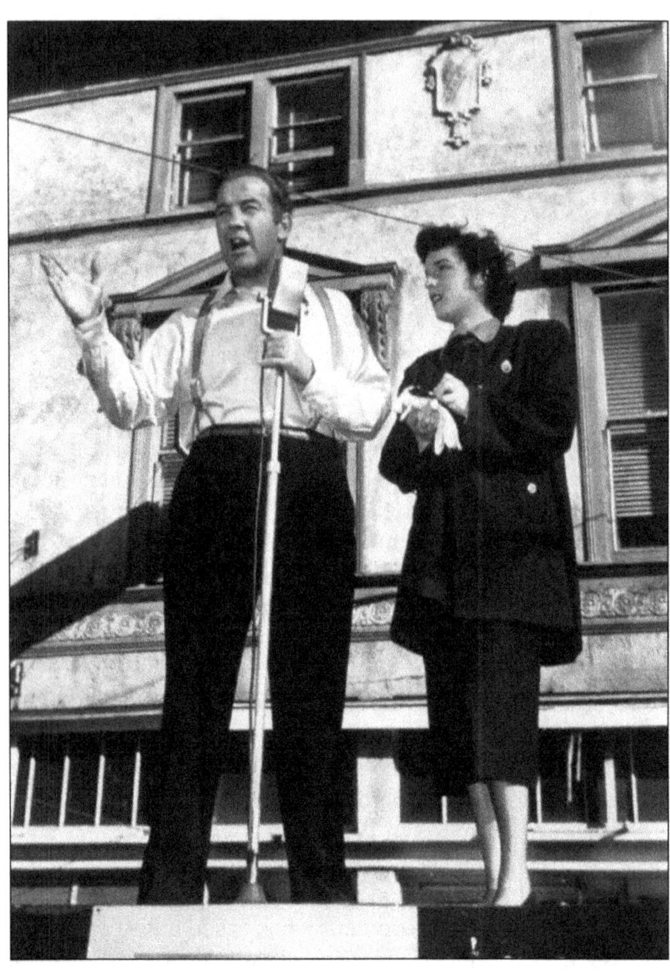

All the King's Men, based on the novel by Robert Penn Warren inspired by Louisiana politician Huey Long, follows the success and downfall of the populist demagogue Willie Stark. The film won Oscars for best picture and for Broderick Crawford as Stark and Mercedes McCambridge in a supporting role as his aide and lover Sadie Burke. Robert Rossen was nominated for writing and directing. (Columbia Pictures)

with Rossen, because if the two of you didn't have any food, he might want to have you for lunch tomorrow."

[Rossen eventually returned to prominence in the film industry; his last two films, *The Hustler* (1961) and *Lilith* (1964), are among his most highly regarded, but it took his death to make American critics look closely at his last film, after it opened to a more positive response in Europe. Rossen's son, Stephen, speaking to Victor S. Navasky for his 1980 book, *Naming Names*, said about his father's informing, "It ate away at him. I think it had a physical effect on him. It made him sick. He was one of those guys who took things internally." —Ed.]

Q: I'd like to start by asking about the East Side, where you were brought up, and so on. Do you find that the East Side experience helped you in making *The Hustler* and *Body and Soul?*
ROSSEN: Oh yes, very definitely. First of all I want to get clear about the East Side. When you say East Side what it usually means to people is that you lived in the lower East Side of Manhattan in Jewish neighborhoods and the ghetto, etc. I didn't have quite that kind of experience. I lived in the middle of Manhattan, on the East Side, and my experience was not a ghetto experience but it was worse. I never quite lived with Jewish surroundings, so I never had the sense of community that even if you lived in a ghetto you had. I was always living in a *Hustler* environment, you know, with Irish kids and Poles and Italians, etc., Germans…. I lived in Yorkville for a while, so that it probably gave me a clearer look at the impact of environment on character and vice versa than I would have had, because if I had lived in a Jewish neighborhood my concept of reality would have been within that community, which was in a sense almost a conformed community. Whether you were poor or rich it didn't really make any difference, but you were poor so certain things followed from that. But the very nature of the fact that you were in opposition to, and running away from, your own background, made you take a pretty hard look at it in order to determine how you would exist in that, what I call a pretty total jungle. You see the difference?

Q: Yes. I've read somewhere before that you are concerned primarily with character and the effect of environment and vice versa, and in an awful lot of your films this is a theme. But then again in some of your other films you go away from this theme, I think; I might be wrong.
ROSSEN: Like which?
Q: *Alexander the Great.*
ROSSEN: Well, you make an assumption that my preoccupation is primarily with the effect of character on environment and etc. It really isn't, because within that framework is... once character is formed in a certain way, certain other aspects come into play. In other words, let's take as an example *All the King's Men,* now, the background of Willie Stark or Huey Long, or however the hell you want to call him. The effect of character on him and his character on his environment, is very sharp. Because he lived—actually he was a redneck, which meant he was a backwoodsman. He wasn't a... well, within that came (a) his antagonism or hostility, his hard look at it, what it made of him, but also (b) was that the answer for him, which you would find in any relationship, character relationship like that, was the desire towards power and the absolute belief that had he power, if he had power—he would do things that would help people.
Q: This is a theme that, in a certain sense, comes back in *Lilith* too.
ROSSEN: Oh yes, oh yes, because the drive towards power never permits itself to be naked and always needs a rationale, whether it's, at least I think so, whether it's a rationale of a schizophrenic or a rationale of a Willie Stark. It needs it, it needs it, because it cannot face the fact that the need for power becomes primarily a subjective need. We like to think, like Lyndon Johnson likes to think that—I am positive he thinks that way—that his tremendous power or his drive towards power is for the good of the many. And how could he face the fact that Johnson's need and drive for rationale, etc., is... has become a subjective thing? I don't know what it was thirty years ago.
Q: But you also make a point in your films that this power tends to destroy itself and these people tend to destroy themselves.

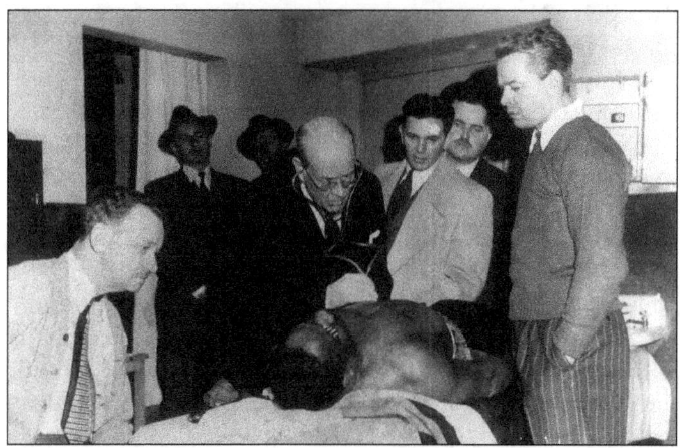

Body and Soul, an original screenplay by Abraham Polonsky, was made for the leftist independent Enterprise Studios and directed by Robert Rossen. John Garfield starred as a boxer struggling with the forces of corruption. As critic Glenn Erickson wrote, "One could populate a blacklister's graveyard with the number of participants in Rossen's picture knocked out of movie work by the witch hunts," including Polonsky, Garfield and Canada Lee (a former boxer whose character is dying from a ring injury here). (Enterprise/United Artists)

ROSSEN: Well, yes, yes, and isn't that true? I mean it's certainly much truer in a complex society. But then again if you go back to *Alexander*, which is not as complex a society, you find the same power in what he's doing; with him it's the other way around. Power was for him a natural and inevitable thing based on his own background, and his use of power constructively did not come until the last three or four years of his life, when he began to understand that power could be a constructive weapon.

Q: You made *Alexander* I think in '57.

ROSSEN: '55, I think; it was released in '56.

Q: This was a time when the spectacles were going out, and…

ROSSEN: It was before the spectacles.

Q: But was there any kind of conflict between what you wanted to do with this historical setting and what perhaps might have been demanded of you from the studios?

ROSSEN: No, there wasn't any conflict. The only pressures—and there were pressures I could have withstood, I suppose, if I had been strong enough at the time—were pressures on cutting the film, on getting it down in size. You see, *Alexander* ... *Alexander* originally is a three-hour picture. I wanted it done in an intermission. They got very frightened at the length. They finally wore me down. Now, actually, it's a much better picture in three hours than it is in two hours and twenty minutes, precisely for one reason. It unveils the guilts of Alexander towards his father, which are the subjective things, much more deeply, much more profoundly. For instance, his chase of Darius is not just a simple chase to kill the emperor of the Persian empire. The chase for Darius is tied up tremendously with his feeling that as long as a father figure is alive in royalty, he's got to kill him.

Q: Is this based on fact?

ROSSEN: This is based on whatever I've read, and I did, I'd say about two or three years of research, personally.

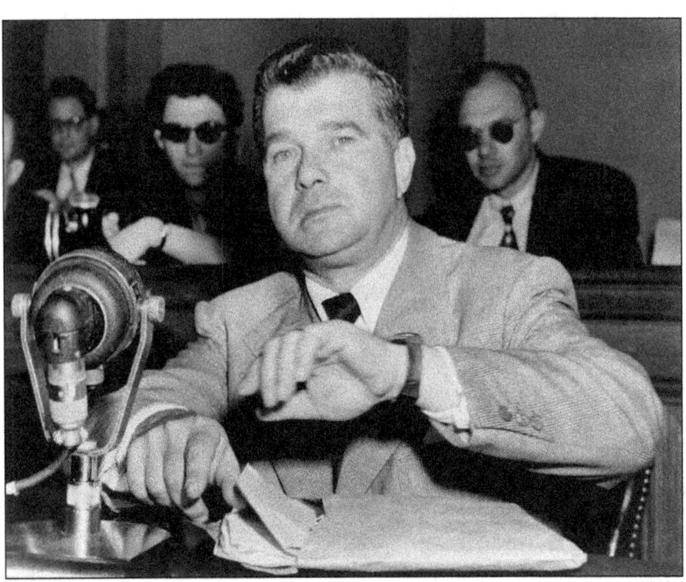

Robert Rossen naming names to escape the blacklist in his 1953 testimony as a friendly witness before the House Committee on Un-American Activities (HUAC).

Q: You were really drawn to the subject?

ROSSEN: Oh, yes, I was drawn to him completely. And this was a fact, you know, this man… For instance, Plutarch has it, but then there's so many other books on the Alexander thing, and Darius—he had to kill Darius, he had to, and if Darius had a wife, I think he'd have to go to bed with his wife. So he did the next best thing, he took one of his daughters. But the daughter story I don't quite believe. Even though it's hinted at and all that, I don't believe it. I think this has gone into the realm of legend, and in terms of legend, I think that every country in the East, practically, has a legend and claims Alexander as their either hero or god or what have you. Egypt does; the Indians still do, they call him "Esconda." Jews have a legend that he came to the gates of Jerusalem and was so impressed with monotheism that he spared Jerusalem. I mean this man is, you know… but I was fascinated. See, I don't think power—I think it's a matter of the words meaning many things to many people. So I think it's natural for people to want power, but then I think you have to really and truly decide what you mean by power. Is it the power to move people, is it the power to create things—you see?

Q: Is it for Willie Stark?

ROSSEN: Yes. And power is such a complex kind of thing, you see, because there are certain things in power, in the power thing, that are very human and very right and very neat, and people who have that… because power means, let's say, a girl gets on the stage and sings, and holds an audience by sheer force of her personality or voice. I mean, that's power at a given moment and a given time, but that power is a good power, that power is a creative power, that power is an expression of human personality, which is primarily what the hell we're all after and which we don't have now—and why we're so buggered up.

Q: Let me see…

ROSSEN: You were talking about *Body and Soul* and *The Hustler.* Those two particular pictures… they came very much out of my background. See? I once wrote a play about thirty years ago called *Corner Pocket.* And it wasn't done—I didn't want it to be done, everybody wanted to do it. It was a play about a poolroom. And it was about… oh, I spent from about

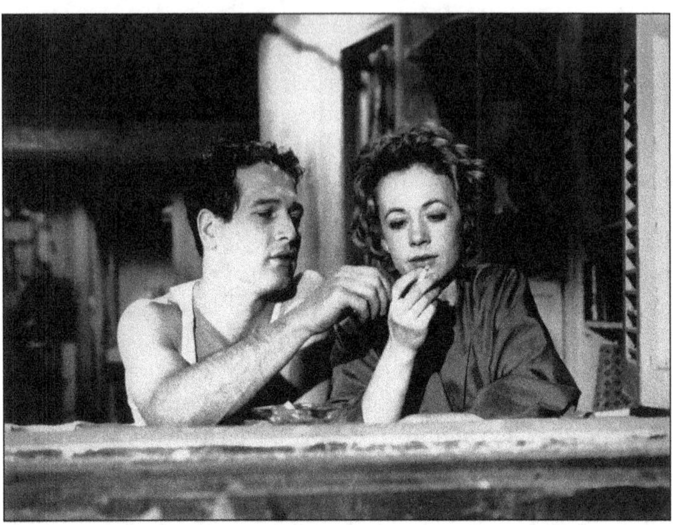

Rossen's gritty film *The Hustler* (1961) gave an iconic role to Paul Newman, the self-destructive pool hustler "Fast Eddie" Felson (which he reprised in the 1986 Martin Scorsese film *The Color of Money*, winning an Oscar for that film). Piper Laurie plays his alcoholic girlfriend in *The Hustler*, adapted from the novel by Walter Tevis. (Twentieth Century-Fox)

fifteen to about nineteen years old in addition to other things in a poolroom, and so obviously I was attracted to it. I was attracted to it—the aspect I was attracted to originally was not in *The Hustler*—that was another aspect. The aspect I was attracted to was, I thought pool halls or pool parlors or what have you, at a certain stage in the life of America, were a poor man's opium den. No place in the world where you could lie and be believed like in a poolroom; no place in the world where a guy who was running a laundry wagon, you know, and who was a shit on the outside, nothing… suddenly he walks in, he shoots a good game of pool, see, and he tells lies. He sits around, he bullshits, it's a place to stay in at three, four in the morning, it's a place to go to at eleven in the morning. That was the aspect of my play, but then I read this book [the source novel by Walter Tevis] and I… there were other things in it, which also were very valid, which I understood totally. I mean the best kind of pictures you can get or films that you

can make are films that you don't have to draw on intellectually at all, that come right out of your senses.
Q: It's hard to make a film like that with hundreds of people.
ROSSEN: Well, I didn't find it too hard. I've always done
films with a lot of people, for the most part. And—*Body and
Soul.* I used to fight around. And I knew Canada Lee before
he was an actor.
Q: Wasn't Garfield also a fighter?
ROSSEN: Sure. And Canada Lee was about, I'd say, second
top-ranking welterweight in the world before he became
an actor. So we all talked shorthand. It had to have truth if
nothing else. That aspect of the film had to have it. I knew
Garfield, well, ten or, more than that, fifteen years before that.
We used to meet on the Intervale Avenue subway station,
and I knew him as an actor. I didn't have to direct him in
certain parts of the film. All I had to say was "yes" or "no"
because he understood it totally. Like I know that there are
a lot of people who have feelings about *Fiddler on the Roof,*
who some of them are crazy about it and some of them who
know the background, so much a part of them, you know,
don't like it. And they don't like it primarily because—not for
good reasons—if it creates a theatrical truth, what the hell's
the difference? But because to them it becomes a kind of holy
ceremony and they feel [Zero] Mostel is wrong, he's doing a
vaudeville act, you know, all kinds of things. [Danny Stein's
father, Joseph Stein, wrote the book for the 1964 musical
Fiddler on the Roof, based on stories by Sholom Aleichem,
in which Mostel played Tevye. Joseph Stein also wrote the
screenplay for the 1971 film version.]
Q: The new movie that came out, *The Cincinnati Kid,* has
been called a bad *Hustler,* but I think that *Lilith* was called…
one critic called it a poor *David and Lisa.* I don't think that it
is compared often …
ROSSEN: What kind of critic was it?
Q: It was a critic for a film magazine.
ROSSEN: A man or woman?
Q: I don't remember. I think it was a man.
ROSSEN: The only thing I could tell you—I don't think
whoever it is knows what they're talking about. First of all,
I never saw *David and Lisa,* very deliberately. I didn't want

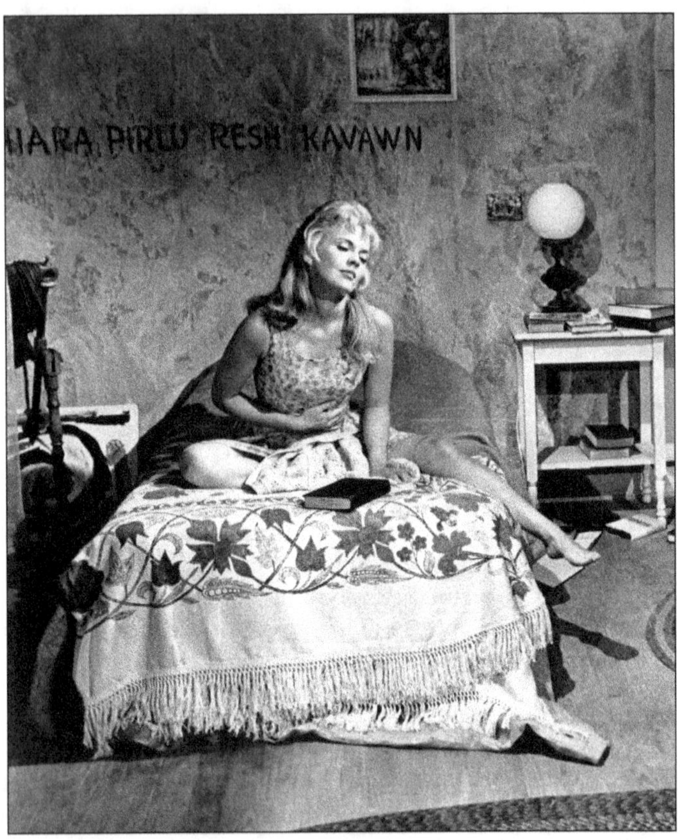

Jean Seberg as a delusional but seductive mental patient who
becomes catatonic in Rossen's 1964 film *Lilith*, based on
J. R. Salamanca's 1961 novel. Disdained in the U.S., *Lilith* was
praised by French critics and has grown in stature over the years.
(Columbia Pictures)

anything to be like it. See? And secondly, the theme...
I knew enough about it, and the theme of *David and Lisa*
is completely antithetical to the theme of *Lilith*. Like *David
and Lisa*, it seems to me, is a very—I understand it's very
well-made and all that, but it's a very small story and has no
implications outside of its immediate story, of any size. *Lilith*
I thought had a tremendous amount of implications. I don't
think... I think the critics were shocked by *Lilith*.

Q: Why?

ROSSEN: Shocked because I made it, for reason number one.

Q: Why?

ROSSEN: Because you never expected me to make that kind of picture. They'd associated me with everything else—

Q: With the tough type of *The Hustler?*

ROSSEN: That's right, and I think I knocked them right out on their ass, because critics like to stay, once they set you up in their mind—they may have created the image, they don't want you to destroy that image for them, because they're very comfortable and it's safe and sane for them to—how shall I put it—for you to stay in that image. They don't have to start saying, now why did he make this picture? What made him change? Why did he do it? This makes them work, and critics don't work.

Q: But actually it was a change more in style than in content.

ROSSEN: Yeah, in style. *[To Mrs. Rossen]* Danny was telling me something about Berkeley, he was out there, he saw *Lilith,* which we're talking about now. He said when the line came on about reality, you know, that psycho, and the kid said, "What's so wonderful about reality?" all those... they were graduate students, weren't they?

Q: Mostly graduate students.

ROSSEN: They all got up and applauded. They all applauded.

Q: I went to see it in San Francisco and in Wisconsin and nothing happened, but when I went to see it just two weeks ago they applauded that line.—What I was saying was that although the style was different in *Lilith* the content wasn't really, and that's what I think the critics missed. My question is, why do you think that they missed this? They didn't really examine the social aspects of *Lilith* at all.

ROSSEN: They didn't all miss it. There were critics who liked it very much. I got a copy of a French paper, *Combat.* Liked it very much and understood the picture. The first review, wasn't it *Good Housekeeping* or something? It was a fantastic reviewer. I really feel that critics don't like for you— not only me, I'm not talking personally—they don't like you to go out of the image they have created for you. I don't think they got all the.... for instance, I don't think a lot of the critics got *The Hustler,* the American critics. I think the European critics did. I don't think the American critics… I don't think Archer Winsten [of the New York *Post]* still knows what that picture's about.

Q: Do you think the American critics now are poor?

ROSSEN: Yeah. Very poor. Again, I think everybody's playing a game—they're wearing masks. They've created a certain style for themselves, they live up to the style. I think they are doing things for each other. It's like the in-group in literature, you know, they're writing to please each other. And I don't think they do any real work; it's too easy—they're established. It's the establishment.

Q: But was *Lilith* a financial success?

ROSSEN: No.

Q: It wasn't—and you would attribute this primarily…

ROSSEN: No, no, no. I had this settled—I think *Lilith* released today would do better financially than when released two or three years ago, whenever it was released.

Q: Why do you say that?

ROSSEN: Because I think that advances in films go very quickly. In other words, I think audiences catch on more. Two or three films behind you on any kind of a subject, you are better off, you see, if you've got a good film. For instance I think in *Alexander,* if *Alexander* had been released three years after it was released, still being the same picture, it would do a better business than it did then because you would already have had a kind of an audience being in tune to historical films, which they weren't at that time.

Q: Do you think part of that problem was that the audiences and the critics were tuned in to films like *David and Lisa* …

ROSSEN: Yes.

Q: … and that this film came right on its heels, so that they—

ROSSEN: Oh sure. I also think it was… I didn't see *David and Lisa* so I don't know—

Q: The same subject—

ROSSEN: Same subject, but I think *Lilith* is probably a more complex picture.

Q: I think that it's much, much better.

ROSSEN: Well, I found they could accept *David and Lisa.*

Q: But they were looking for the same thing in *Lilith.*

ROSSEN: They were, yes, well, maybe it didn't come off.

I thought it came off. There is one thing that I think I missed. I shot it but I cut it out. See, I think there was too far a separation, in terms of an audience, from the world that she had left to the world that she had gotten into, you see.

Q: Yes.

ROSSEN: Now, I had a couple of scenes in it, for instance, I had an elderly couple come to pick up their daughter or to visit their daughter on a Sunday. And her comments were so shrewd, and so sharp, you know… and the hurried kiss when they'd go, you know that? Here and there, almost unobtrusively, to show the outside world. And I had a great handicap working. I didn't know it but it finally almost killed me, of this sickness. I just made a terrible mistake in casting.

Q: Beatty?

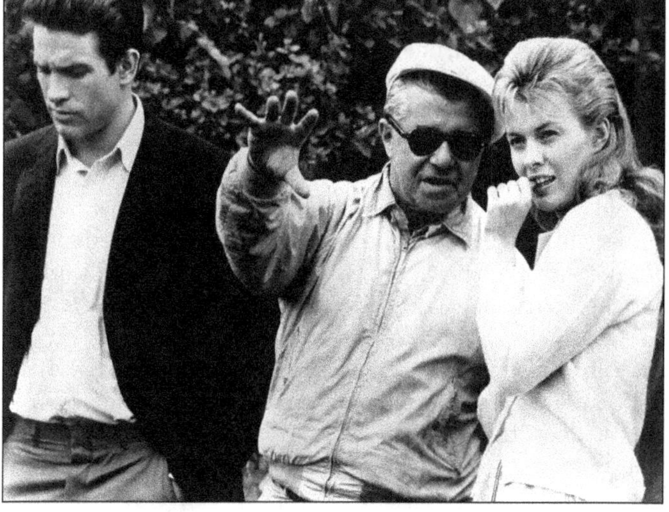

Warren Beatty clashed with Rossen (center) during the making of the director's last film, *Lilith*. Beatty plays a disturbed military veteran who becomes an occupational therapist at a mental institution, falls in love with the psychotic Lilith (Seberg) and checks himself in as a patient at the end. (Columbia Pictures)

ROSSEN: Yeah, he was just horrible, just horrible. Whatever chance you had of communication, there was only one chance you really had, a really big chance of communication that you had, and that was to make the audience become Beatty. A young guy who wants to do something good, who has all kinds of decent instincts, walks in there, totally healthy, totally well, and as he gets into this world, he too begins to have doubts, and he too on the basis of his own experience begins to get entangled. See, he never gave you the feeling of entanglement because right from the beginning, he belonged in that institution. He was psychotic.

Q: Yes, but part of that—now I understood this in the film— but part of what drew me away were the slight innuendos that he was already sick from the beginning.

ROSSEN: That's his own.

Q: Yes, but it was in the script too…

ROSSEN: I don't care.

Q: … with his mother.

ROSSEN: Oh, yeah, but that was in—yes, that was in the book too. But again, even with that—I took an awful lot of it out— but even with that, granted that, the point is if you had gotten the feeling that, well, this guy was an American boy who had gone through a war experience, came back, didn't want to take the old crappy jobs they had around, but was a guy who really meant what he said when he said, "I want to do something for people"—but you never believed him for a moment. There was nothing I could do, and I had terrible fights with him, and you know, a lot of the stuff I had was all through him. But you see, it was bad casting and there was nothing you could do about it, because he's so sick that he brings his sickness in any role that he does. In other words, the picture, instead of going in that direction, always goes like within his nexus. The picture becomes something else, and if he's got a leading role, you can't lick it. Because he don't believe it. He wouldn't want to help anyone. The man himself!

Q: I don't know, but in spite of that I saw it as the story of a "normal guy."

ROSSEN: You saw it because—you are bringing things to it. Look at it from an audience point of view… you take an average audience. They wanted to go with this picture. For instance, in New York this picture did very well. It really did very well, but they couldn't go with it outside because they couldn't find a means of identification. Now I played her [Jean Seberg] for a Midwestern, you know, drugstore owner's daughter, which is her own life. She was good… reality to her meant—what did it mean? Nothing. She was right. You had a feeling of conviction. But I have no feeling for him. And, no, I don't want to, you know…

Q: Yes.

ROSSEN: I like the picture. I think what it had to say is an important comment to make in today's society. I think it hasn't even been touched yet. This whole question of inner life…. I think there's only one man that I know of in films that really and truly understands how to do it. And comes close, and that's Bergman. I think Fellini's a fake, totally and completely, a depraved—not depraved, that's the wrong word—an Italian vaudevillian. I think to even compare Fellini and Bergman… I am perfectly willing to compare De Sica, not that they do the same things, but in terms of real honest intent. Or some of the younger Italians…

Q: I've heard you compared with De Sica.

ROSSEN: Yeah. Yeah. No, but I've been trying to say that Fellini to me… I saw this last picture *[Juliet of the Spirits]*, and I was sick, and I went in the afternoon, that's the only time I can see a picture—I walked out after an hour. I was insulted. I really was insulted. I was insulted at the choice of material, I was insulted at the fact that he gave me these experiences, traumatic experiences, which would make or not make her life… he did the same thing in *8½*!

Q: Yes.

ROSSEN: Big traumatic experience, a guy wants to screw a crazy witch, who hasn't wanted to screw a crazy witch? Used to live in the streets, what the hell is her name—"Crazy Mary" we used to call her. She'd come around singing about "hanging the Kaiser," you know, and the big thing was, the young kids, they didn't care who they got back in the back alley, they'd throw her on a bed… Big traumatic thing, and this guy passes it off as—even in *Dolce Vita* when you think of those sequences with the intellectuals, and the guy who kills the girl, the young daughter, wasn't it ?

Q: Yes.

ROSSEN: And the whole business about—I mean this guy's a fool, he's an idiot. I don't want to see his pictures.

Q: I liked some of his early ones. *La Strada.*

ROSSEN: *Strada*… I will tell you what I liked even more, I liked *Vitelloni.* I liked *Vitelloni. Vitelloni* seemed realer. But yes, he's a good man but he has no… I'm not making brains a prerequisite, I'm making intent the prerequisite. Brains, what the hell, I know a lot of brainy guys can't make a picture around the corner. See? But I think—but Bergman does things that are trying to really get into twentieth century… the whole approach to that part of life which is subjective and yet has to be objective because we have no other defense.

Q: What do you think of the films of Antonioni and the films of Sidney Lumet, the American director?

ROSSEN: Antonioni, I like a few. I think he begins to imitate himself. I liked *L'Avventura* very much; I liked parts of *La Notte,* especially the last part of it. I can't say I think very much of the rest of his films. Lumet I think lacks a thing that will stop him from—he'll always do good pictures, he'll never do a great one. He lacks spontaneity. Everything's too laid out. The television really got him over the years.

Q: Yes.

ROSSEN: Absolutely lacks it. It's too well-planned. He likes the taking advantage. That's why he likes to work in studios. See, anybody who likes to work in studios likes to work in them because you cannot improvise, it's very hard to improvise except within a given scene. You go on a location, or on a real set, and everything around you leads you into another idea. You can go down looking for that and find *that.* And you gotta have the guts and the spontaneous quality of getting that right away.

Q: I understand you shot a lot of *All the King's Men* spontaneously, that you took people, real people, and that you shot in actual hotel rooms.

ROSSEN: Oh yes, I only had one set in the whole picture, that's all.

Q: Really?

ROSSEN: One set.

Q: That I didn't know.

ROSSEN: The set in the governor's mansion, that's the only set, I shot...

Q: What about the judge's house?

ROSSEN: Older house in Stockton, California. I shot the impeachment scene with Stockton lawyers and judges in the courtroom.

Q: And the crowd scenes were all just...

ROSSEN: All.

Q: No extras—

ROSSEN: I gave 'em a phony camera too. I didn't even know what was going to happen. I had no Hollywood extras because I was over three hundred miles.

Q: You did the same thing in *The Brave Bulls*, didn't you?

ROSSEN: Totally. Totally. *The Brave Bulls* was all shot on location. I think again there were maybe one or two sets in the picture. I discovered the idea of "skills" in the first picture I did, of not using actors when the predominant quality in what they're doing is a skill. I did a picture called *Johnny O'Clock*.

Q: Your first one.

ROSSEN: And the guys who were backing the picture were gamblers, you know, gamblers, gunmen. And when it came down to shooting the game room scenes, it was very funny. They insisted on bringing their own equipment in, their mother-of-pearl chips and the whole business. Their own dealers. And, as they put it, it's gotta be effective because they were well-known, well-known in Havana, New York, you know. So I said "fine," bring the guys in, they'll show the actors what to do. And I got in there and I watched these guys—they were amazing. Nobody could riffle a deck or could make a call or could watch a customer like these guys. So I then said, what am I fooling around with actors for? And I stayed with that group in that picture.

Well, then when it came to *Body and Soul*, I knew a lot about fighting, I knew a lot of guys down in Los Angeles hanging around gyms, there were Seffarina, Garcia and that whole crowd. And [cinematographer] Jimmie [James Wong] Howe, Jimmie, you know he used to be [a bantamweight professional boxer]. And he knew a lot of these guys, he knew a lot about fighting, so we decided the whole mishmash,

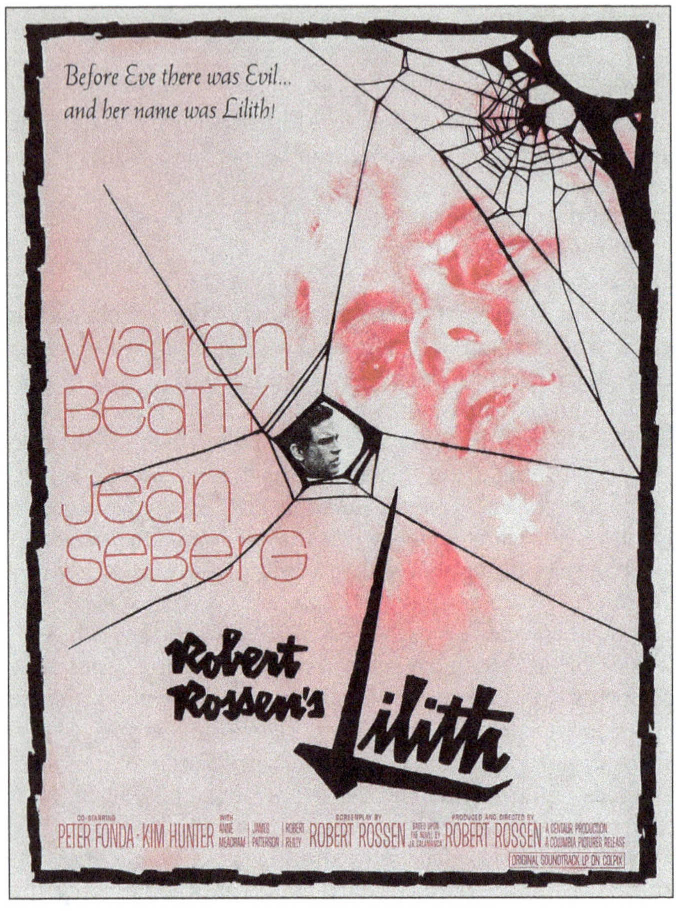

Original poster for *Lilith*. (Columbia Pictures)

you know, there'd be absolutely no actors in those scenes. And that's the way we shot it. And for years in Hollywood they used to be saying, "How do you get newsreel photography; how do you get it?" Well, we came up with an answer that was so simple it was really… you shoot it like a newsreel man. You use the same lights. This was early stuff; today it's taken for granted. You never use any lights, you don't have any fillers, you use the ring light. You have six Eyemo cameramen and you put newspaper names on their hats, so they shoot right into each other's lenses. You get every conceivable angle you want, which you see in the newsreels, and you get that grainy, wonderful quality. Now today—everybody does it. That was a big revolution.

Q: You were the first to use Eyemos [a small camera widely used by cameramen documenting World War II]?

ROSSEN: No, I was the first to use Eyemos without care of sight lines. People used Eyemos—*Open City* used Eyemos. I know, I talked to De Sica [*sic:* even though *Open City* was directed by Roberto Rossellini—Ed.] and some of those guys. They were shooting out of cellars. The Germans were right there, some of them. But we were the first to shoot Eyemos right into the other guy's lens. We had a good reason to. And we did the same thing in *The Bulls.* Christ, we had the goddam bullring covered with them.

Q: You had a lot of pressure with *The Bulls* from censorship…

ROSSEN: In Mexico. Oh, you mean here?

Q: And with Prevention of Cruelty to—

ROSSEN: Yeah, that's more pressure than anyone. They are tougher than any censorship group I know.

Q: And that's why you used telescopic lenses?

ROSSEN: Well, part of that. But you see, you can kill a man, they don't care. You fool around with an animal, boy…. I remember I used a trick there. We went down to—Mexico, every Saturday they have the newsreels of the preceding Sunday, and everything is shot. So I found a couple of real good, big bullfights, you know, important, in the newsreels, and found the suits they were wearing and used them as doubles, so that when the shot came for the bull to gore the man, it was a real shot, and I had a cut from it because it was taken in a newsreel. And I cut it right into the picture.

Q: You cut it into the action then.

ROSSEN: Sure, and I dressed my actor to suit the guy who was being gored, instead of the other way around.

Q: Had that ever been done before?

ROSSEN: I don't know. I don't think so. They still talk about that picture in Mexico. I'm going to have to—make it another time because I've been at it an hour…

Q: Oh, sure.

ROSSEN: And I'm getting a little woozy.

ARTHUR LENNIG, past president of the Wisconsin Film Society, is an assistant professor of art at the State University of New York at Albany. Since editing the Film Society's first two books, *Film Notes* and *Classics of the Film*, he has published two volumes of a study of the silent cinema, *The Silent Voice*, 1966, and *The Silent Voice: A Sequel*, 1967. He is completing a book on D. W. Griffith and is planning to shoot a feature film in the near future.

WILLIAM DONNELLY is a teaching assistant and PhD candidate in English at the University of Wisconsin. A past president of the Wisconsin Film Society, he also contributed to *Film Notes* and *Classics of the Film*.

ROBERT DALE, past president of the Wisconsin Film Society, is an associate professor of French at the University of Washington, and also coordinates the university film series. His doctoral dissertation was on the esthetics of Mérimée, and he has taught at Madison and at Aix. He contributed to *Classics of the Film* and is writing a book on René Clair. Audio Film Center distributes his film *Pandora's Bottle*.

JOSEPH McBRIDE is president of the Wisconsin Film Society. He has directed several short films and is currently working on a feature-length script.

HOWARD KOCH has written plays, radio scripts, and many film scripts, including those for *The Sea Hawk*, *Sergeant York*, *Casablanca*, *Mission to Moscow*, *The War Lover*, *Loss of Innocence* and *The Fox*. He is at work on a play and a film which he is writing and producing.

ANDREW SARRIS is film critic for *The Village Voice* and associate editor of *Film Culture*. He has a weekly radio program on WBAT-FM, is a member of the Program Committee of the New York Film Festival at Lincoln Center and is vice-chairman of the National Society of Film Critics. His book *The Films of Josef von Sternberg* was published by the Museum of Modern Art, 1966, and he edited *Interviews with Film Directors*, published by Bobbs-Merrill, 1967 [Sarris's *The American Cinema: Directors and Directions 1929-1968* was published by Dutton in 1968]. He has taught film courses of New York University and The School of Visual Arts.

JON ZWICKEY, poet and filmmaker, is "a University of Wisconsin dropout whose youthful sell-out thesis was on *Opium and the Films of Jean Cocteau*." He made *Bororo*, a film about pataphysical experience, and will soon publish *Invisible Poison*, a full-length study of Cocteau.

MICHAEL WILMINGTON, a senior at the University of Wisconsin, has written film criticism for *The Daily Cardinal* and acted in more than thirty plays on and around the campus. His roles have included Nick in *Who's Afraid of Virginia Woolf?*, The Ragpicker in *The Madwoman of Chaillot*, Leslie in *The Hostage*, Engstrand in *Ghosts*, Chance Wayne in *Sweet Bird of Youth*, John in the nude version of *Peter Pan* and Jerry in *The Zoo Story*.

RICHARD THOMPSON studied English and ran the Documentary Film Group at the University of Chicago. In the two years following that he has worked in 16mm film distribution; he is currently with Brandon Films. He writes hardboiled detective stories and will soon teach a film course in the Art Department of Prairie State College. "Predictably," he is currently involved in several book-length projects, none of them definite.

F. A. MACKLIN is an assistant professor of English at the University of Dayton. He is the editor of *Film Heritage*.

GERALD PEARY is a teaching assistant and PhD candidate in speech at the University of Wisconsin. He directs and acts in children's and student plays.

DANIEL STEIN, a senior in English at the University of Wisconsin, played a part in Carl Reiner's film *Enter Laughing*.

Acknowledgments [1968 Edition]

Michael Wilmington's essay "*Long Day's Journey Into Night*" appeared as "Sidney Lumet's Journey Into Light" in *The Daily Cardinal*, Madison, February 17, 1968; "For *The Birds*" appeared in earlier form as "Hitchcock's *The Birds* Revisited" in *The War Baby Review*, published by the *Cardinal*, May 1968; and "The Jewison Question" appeared as "Lover Come Back—'67 Style" in *The War Baby Review*, April 1968.

"*Citizen Kane*" by Joseph McBride appeared in *Film Heritage*, Fall 1968.

Parts of "Notes on the Production of *Casablanca*" by Howard Koch appeared as "*Casablanca*" in *Bard*, the alumni magazine of Bard College, May 1967. Koch's original treatment and other material for his article are in the collection of the State Historical Society of Wisconsin [now the Wisconsin Historical Society]. All material is printed by permission of Mr. Koch.

"The High Forties Revisited" appeared in *Film Culture*, Spring 1962, and is reprinted by permission of Andrew Sarris.

Richard Thompson's "Hawks at Seventy" appeared in *December*, Winter 1966, and "*7 Women*" appeared as "John Ford's *Seven Women*" in *FOCUS!*, May 1967. Both are reprinted by permission of Mr. Thompson.

"Robert Flaherty" appeared in *The Silent Voice: A Sequel* by Arthur Lennig, Troy, N.Y., 1967, and is reprinted by permission of Mr. Lennig.

"A Random Sampling of Directors" by William Donnelly appeared as "A Random Sample" in *Quixote*, Madison, May 1966.

"Robert Rossen's Last Interview" by Daniel Stein appeared in edited form as "An Interview with Robert Rossen" in *Arts in Society*, Winter 1966/67. The transcript from the tape of the interview is printed by permission of Mr. Stein.

Sticking Place Books (stickingplacebooks.com) is a New York-based publisher specializing in cinema, offering interview books, memoirs, critical and historical studies, screenplays, and essay collections. Our titles include:

Lessons with Kiarostami, edited by Paul Cronin

In the Shadow of Trees: The Collected Poetry of Abbas Kiarostami

Still Film Crazy (After All These Years) by Patrick McGilligan

It's Only a Movie by Bruce Joel Rubin

Three Visionary Screenplays by Bruce Joel Rubin

Playing Among the Stars: Conversations with Damien Chazelle by Nathan Réra

The Magic Eye: The Cinema of Stanley Kubrick by Neil Hornick

A Shared Cinema: Conversations with Michael Ciment by N. T. Bihn

The Naughty Bits: What the Censors Wouldn't Let You See in Hollywood's Most Famous Movies by Nat Segaloff

Mexico: The Aztec Account of the Conquest by Werner Herzog

Werner Herzog/Rogue Filmmaker by David LaRocca

De Palma on De Palma: Conversations with Samuel Blumenfeld and Laurent Vachaud

Publication as Autobiography: Occasional and Forsaken Texts— and Endangered Cinema Species by Scott MacDonald

Filmmakers Thinking by Adrian Martin

Secret Cinema: The Rise and Fall of the Blue Movie by John Baxter

Casualties of War: An Investigation by Nathan Réra

Hollywood on the Tiber by Hank Kaufman and Gene Lerner

What Made Cinema? Essays on Visual Culture and Early Film by Ian Christie

Travels in the Cities of Cinema: Conversations with Jonathan Rosenbaum by Ehsan Khoshbakht

Camera Movements that Confound Us by Jonathan Rosenbaum

Upon Open Sky by Guillermo Arriaga

Ambrose Chapel by Brian De Palma

Russian Poland by David Mamet

The Archival Impermanence Project by Ross Lipman

These Fragments I Have Shored Against My Ruin by Caveh Zahedi

Cinema Now and Then: Conversations with James Naremore by Craig S. Simpson